STUDY GUIDE

to accompany

MICROECONOMICS
DAVID N. HYMAN

Prepared by

DONALD P. MAXWELL
Central State University

1989

IRWIN

Homewood, IL 60430
Boston, MA 02116

Articles on pages 51, 69, 97, 126, 226, 240, 282, 294, 309, 324, 359, 373, 386, and 396 are reprinted by permission of the *Wall Street Journal* © Dow Jones & Company, Inc., 1988.

Contents

TO THE STUDENT

This <u>Study Guide</u> to accompany Hyman, <u>Economics</u> is designed as a set of interactive modules covering the key concepts developed in the textbook chapters and appendices. These modules will help you understand and apply the concepts you need to know. The <u>Study Guide</u> is based on my experiences teaching university economics for over a decade.

Each chapter of the <u>Study Guide</u> begins with **Chapter Challenges**, which give you the important learning objectives of the corresponding textbook chapter. This is followed by **In Brief: Chapter Summary**, which asks you to complete the summary, and in doing so review key concepts. The **Vocabulary Review** that follows is a fill-in exercise that will reinforce your understanding of the key terms in David Hyman's <u>Economics</u> glossary. Next comes a set of problems and exercises, **Skills Review**, selected to reinforce the main learning objectives of the chapter. These questions are presented in the same order as the concepts appear in the textbook. Each block of questions in the Skills Review section is subtitled according to the learning concept to which it applies, so that you can concentrate on areas that require extra study. These problems and exercises involve graphing, filling in tables, completing sentences, matching, listing, and discussion. For most chapters, advanced questions are included. These offer additional challenges and the opportunity to apply more advanced analysis, such as algebraic analysis, to certain problems.

After the Skills Review, a minitest of 15 to 20 multiple choice questions, like those you will encounter on exams, is included in the **Self-Test for Mastery**. These questions will give you feedback to determine how well you have mastered the important concepts of the chapter. The self-test is followed by 3 to 5 discussion questions that ask you to apply the concepts of the chapter to issues and problems. Following this **Discussion** section, 20 chapters of the <u>Study Guide</u> include a **Pop Quiz**. This exercise asks you to read a recent <u>Wall Street Journal</u> news article and answer one or two discussion questions. At the end of each chapter or appendix is an answer key. **Chapter Answers** include answers to all sections of the Study Guide, including discussion questions, so that you can check your progress.

In using this <u>Study Guide</u>, I suggest you first read the textbook chapter, paying particular attention to the introductory statement of learning objectives for the chapter and the concept checks that appear throughout the chapter. Next, complete the fill-in summary section of the <u>Study Guide</u>. Go back to the textbook and read and study the section for any parts of the summary that you answered incorrectly. Answer the vocabulary exercise next, after you review the glossary terms in the margins of the text chapter.

The problems and exercises in the Skills Review correspond closely to the examples used by David Hyman in the textbook. Try to answer the questions in the Skills Review and go back to the text for additional study if you have difficulty understanding how to answer a question. You can use the answer key for help, but you will get the most benefit by first studying the text and then working the problems in the <u>Study Guide</u>, rather than by going directly to the answer key.

After completing the Skills Review, take the self-test of multiple choice questions and compare your answers to those in the answer key to see where you need to spend additional study time. Review the concepts in the text and <u>Study Guide</u> that you have not yet mastered. Now try to answer the discussion questions from the Discussion and Pop Quiz sections. Read the answers to the discussion questions in the answer section. If there are discussion questions that you do not understand, go back to the corresponding sections of the text and <u>Study Guide</u> for additional study.

ACKNOWLEDGMENTS

I would like to thank the editors and staff at Times Mirror/Mosby and Irwin for suggesting this project and providing advice and support throughout the preparation of the manuscript. In particular, I would like to thank Jean Babrick, Developmental editor for Supplements, and Denise Clinton, Sponsoring Editor, for their encouragement and assistance. I would like to thank David Hyman for making this possible. I also want to thank the copy editors, Elisabeth Heitzeberg and Sandy Gilfillan for their work on the manuscript. Finally, thanks to Kathy Lumpkin, Production Editor, and her staff for bringing the Study Guide to you.

The Study Guide was reviewed by an expert in the design of of educational supplements and by several experienced university economics instructors for general content, appropriateness, and accuracy. Special thanks go to the technical reviewers of the manuscript, Kathy Gillespie of St. Louis University and Ben Childers of the University of Missouri, Columbia. Additional and very sincere thanks go to **Irwin Feller**, Penn State University, **James Kahn**, State University of New York, Binghamton, **William Witter**, University of North Texas, and **Richard Spivack** of Bryant College for reviewing the entire manuscript and providing valuable feedback and suggestions.

Don Maxwell
Central State University

1

Economics: What It's All About

CHAPTER CHALLENGES

After studying your text, attending class, and completing this chapter, you should be able to:

1. Describe the mechanism of the economy and the discipline of economics.
2. Understand the concepts of scarcity and opportunity costs.
3. Discuss major branches of economic inquiry: microeconomics, macroeconomics, positive analysis, and normative analysis.

IN BRIEF: CHAPTER SUMMARY

Fill in the blanks to summarize chapter content.

Economics is a study concerned with the use society makes of its
(1)_____ (scarce, abundant) resources in attempting to satisfy the
(2)_____ (normal, unlimited) desires of its members. The economy
represents the mechanism or structure that organizes scarce resources for the
purpose of producing the goods and services desired by society.
(3)_____ (Inflation, Scarcity) is the fundamental problem facing all
economies. It is also the reason decisions or choices involve
(4)_____ (opportunity costs, production costs).

The real cost or opportunity cost of any choice is the value of the sacrifice
required in making that decision. That sacrifice represents the foregone
opportunity to pursue the (5)_____ (next best, any) decision. A
fundamental problem confronting an economy is how to best meet the desires of
individuals in a world of scarcity. Economies do this by addressing several
basic questions: (a) What will be produced? (b) How will goods and services be
produced? (c) To whom will goods and services be distributed? An economy's
answers to the first two questions reveal the (6)_____ (fairness,
efficiency) with which resources are used to satisfy the desires of society.
The third question requires that society make value judgments regarding the
distribution of income.

The two major branches of economic analysis are macroeconomics and
microeconomics. (7)_____ (Macroeconomics, Microeconomics) is concerned
with the economic behavior of individual decision-making units in the economy.
(8)_____ (Macroeconomics, Microeconomics) is concerned with the
effects of the aggregate economic behavior of all individuals, firms, and
institutions. Inflation and unemployment are two topics that are studied in
(9)_____ (macroeconomics, microeconomics), whereas the determination of
prices and an analysis of markets are subjects dealt with in
(10)_____ (macroeconomics, microeconomics).

Positive economic analysis seeks to determine (11)_____ ("what ought to be", "what is"). (12)_____ (Positive, Normative) economic analysis emphasizes the "should" or "ought to" approach. Positive analysis tries to uncover cause-and-effect relationships that are subject to empirical observation and verification. In contrast, normative analysis depends upon the analyst's (13)_____ (value judgment, mathematical skills). Disagreements arise among practitioners in any discipline. With positive analysis, it is possible to resolve disagreements empirically. With normative analysis, disagreements stem from different value systems and must be resolved in ways other than looking at the "facts."

VOCABULARY REVIEW

Write the key term from the list below next to its definition.

Key Terms

Economy	Macroeconomics
Economics	Unemployment rate
Scarcity	Inflation
Opportunity cost	Positive analysis
Microeconomics	Normative analysis

Definitions

1. _____: the cost of choosing to use resources for one purpose measured by the sacrifice of the next best alternative for using those resources.

2. _____: economic analysis concerned with the individual choices made by participants in the economy--also called price theory.

3. _____: the rate of upward movement in the price level for an aggregate of goods and services.

4. _____: seeks to forecast the impact of changes in economic policies or conditions on observable items, such as production, sales, prices, and personal incomes, and then tries to determine who gains and who loses as a result of the changes.

5. _____: the mechanism through which the use of labor, land, structures, vehicles, equipment, and natural resources is organized to satisfy the desires of those who live in a society.

6. _____: the imbalance between the desires of society and the means with which those desires are satisfied.

7. _____: evaluates the desirability of alternative outcomes according to underlying value judgments about what is good or bad.

8. _____: a study of society's use of scarce resources in the satisfaction of the unlimited desires of its members.

9. _____: economic analysis that considers the overall

performance of the economy with respect to total national production, consumption, average prices, and employment levels.

10. _____: measures the ratio of the number of people classified as unemployed to the total labor force.

SKILLS REVIEW

Concept: **Describe the mechanism of the economy**

1. List the three basic questions that all economies must answer:

   a. _____
   b. _____
   c. _____

Concept: **Opportunity cost**

2. Identify the likely opportunity costs associated with the following decisions.

   Hint: Think in terms of what would likely be sacrificed in pursuing a decision. In other words, what would have been the next best use of your time, money, or resources?

   a. You decide to attend a university full time.
   b. Your decision to purchase a new home results in a larger portion of your income committed to mortgage payments.
   c. You are having such a good time in the Caribbean, that you decide to extend your vacation by taking an additional week of vacation at no pay.
   d. As a manager, you decide to commit some of the corporation's resources to a plant expansion project.

3. Advanced Problem. Suppose that you are a farmer capable of producing corn or soybeans. Over the years you have maintained records regarding your total production of both crops. Assume that you have made full and efficient use of your resources throughout this period. Furthermore, assume that the only reason corn relative to soy production has changed is because of your desire to grow the combination of crops that produce the highest net farm income. Referring to your production data below, determine the opportunity cost of producing an additional bushel of soybeans. If the current price of a bushel of corn is $7, what is the dollar value of that opportunity cost?

Production Data
(000s of bushels)

	Soy	Corn
1981	100	20
1982	50	40
1983	25	50
1984	0	60
1985	75	30
1986	150	0
1987	125	10

a. Opportunity cost measured in bushels of corn: _____ bushels

b. Opportunity cost measured in dollars: $ _____

Concept: Positive and normative analysis

4. In the blanks provided, indicate whether the following statements involve positive (P) or normative (N) analysis:

    a. ____ Fred ought to get his act together.
    b. ____ My professor arrives for class late every morning.
    c. ____ The drought in the Midwest is increasing corn prices.
    d. ____ Government is too obtrusive and therefore its power should be reduced.
    e. ____ Lower state income tax rates are always preferable to higher rates.
    f. ____ Poverty is a serious problem in the United States.

5. Monitor your own statements as you interact with friends, family members, or fellow students and try to determine if your statements are based upon fact or observation or value judgments. For one day, carry a sheet of paper divided into two columns--label one column "fact" and the other "value judgment." Record your interactions with others and think about whether positive or normative statements are being made.

SELF-TEST FOR MASTERY

Select the best answer.

1. Which of the following best describes the study of economics?

    a. A study concerned with how to make money
    b. A fuzzy combination of Wall Street and insurance
    c. A study of how society uses its goods and services in determining the proper distribution of income
    d. A study of how society uses its scarce economic resources in satisfying the unlimited desires of society

2. The mechanism through which resources are organized in order to satisfy the desires of society is known as:

    a. A corporation.
    b. Government.
    c. An economy.
    d. A factory.

3. Scarcity means that:

    a. Resources are in finite supply.
    b. Poverty takes its toll on those with limited means.
    c. Choices are unnecessary.
    d. An imbalance exists between desires and the means by which those desires are satisfied.

4. The real cost of a choice or decision is its opportunity cost. Which of the following best defines opportunity cost?

    a. The actual dollar outlay required to produce a good or service
    b. The value of the forgone next best alternative
    c. The value to the resources required to implement the decision

d. The value of the loss that occurs when a speculative investment does not meet profit expectations

5. If a state government had a limited amount of tax and other revenue but decided to substantially increase the amount of appropriations to public education, appropriations to other functions such as corrections, health, and welfare would diminish. What concept is represented by this statement?

   a. Opportunity costs
   b. Normative analysis
   c. Efficiency
   d. None of the above

6. Microeconomics is a branch of economics that:

   a. Studies the impact of inflation on the unemployment rate.
   b. Studies the behavior of individual decision-making units in the economy.
   c. Studies the effects and consequences of the aggregate behavior of all decision-making units.
   d. Is only concerned with the determination of income.

7. Macroeconomics is a branch of economics that:

   a. Studies the effects and consequences of the aggregate behavior of all decision-making units in the economy.
   b. Is only concerned with the determination of individual market prices.
   c. Studies the behavior of individual decision-making units in the economy.
   d. Studies neither inflation nor unemployment.

8. Topics such as business cycles, unemployment, and inflation are studied in _____, whereas the determination of prices and the study of individual markets are studied in _____.

   a. Positive analysis/normative analysis
   b. Normative analysis/positive analysis
   c. Microeconomics/macroeconomics
   d. Macroeconomics/microeconomics

9. The rate of unemployment is defined as:

   a. The number of job seekers.
   b. The number of individuals who have been laid off or are unemployed but seeking work.
   c. The number of job seekers as a percentage of total employment.
   d. The number of individuals who have been laid off or are unemployed but seeking work expressed as a percentage of the labor force.

10. With respect to inflation, which of the following is true?

    a. A one-time price increase of bananas constitutes inflation.
    b. Inflation represents a widespread and continuing increase in prices.
    c. Inflation represents the main or fundamental problem faced by all economies.
    d. Inflation is studied in microeconomics.

11. Which of the following involves value judgments?

    a. Normative analysis
    b. Positive analysis

c.   The search for a superconducting material operable at room
     temperature
d.   The decision to install lifeline (discount) electric utility rates
     for the elderly
e.   A and d

12. _____ makes "ought to" or "should" statements, whereas
    _____ makes statements based upon observable events and
    therefore can be subjected to empirical verification.

    a. Positive analysis/normative analysis
    b. Normative analysis/positive analysis
    c. Macroeconomics/microeconomics
    d. Microeconomics/macroeconomics

THINK IT THROUGH

1.   Define economics, including its branches, microeconomics and
macroeconomics. What are some topics typically addressed by each of these
branches?

2.   Explain why scarcity and opportunity costs are related. Give an example
from your personal or business experiences of the opportunity cost of a
decision.

3.   As you will discover later in the text, under certain assumptions it can
be shown theoretically that a perfectly competitive economy will produce a
distribution of income where labor receives an income based upon its productive
contribution to the enterprise. This is consistent with the protestant ethic
which states that hard work and reward should go hand in hand. This statement
involves both positive and normative analysis. Discuss.

CHAPTER ANSWERS

In Brief: Chapter Summary

1. Scarce   2. Unlimited   3. Scarcity   4. Opportunity cost   5. Next best
6. Efficiency   7. Microeconomics   8. Macroeconomics   9. Macroeconomics   10.
Microeconomics   11. "What is"   12. Normative   13. Value judgments

Vocabulary Review

1. Opportunity costs 2. Microeconomics   3. Inflation   4. Positive analysis
5. Economy   6. Scarcity   7. Normative analysis   8. Economics   9.
Macroeconomics   10. Unemployment rate

Skills Review

1.   a.   What will be produced?
     b.   How will goods and services be produced?
     c.   To whom will goods and services be distributed?

2.   a.   If you attend a university full time, there are a number of potential
          sacrifices all of which have value. The most obvious sacrifice is
          the potential income you could have earned had you been employed full

time. You may have less time to spend with your family and friends, as well as less leisure time. Direct outlays on tuition, room, and board could have been invested or saved.

b. As recently as the early 1970s it was not uncommon for homeowners to allocate only 15% of their incomes to mortgage payments. Today it is more common for families to spend as much as 25% to 35% of their incomes for housing. If you commit a much larger share of your income to housing, given scarcity (or a limited income), you must cut your spending elsewhere. The reduction in the value of goods and services consumed as a result of purchasing a more expensive home represents the opportunity cost of your decision.

c. If you choose to take a week of vacation without pay, you obviously sacrifice the income you would have earned otherwise. That extra week, as a result, is much more costly to you than the previous week of vacation.

d. If corporate funds are to be used for a specific project, they cannot be used for alternative investment projects. Depending on the needs of the firm, the funds could be invested in financial assets generating an interest income. The funds could be used for other investment projects yielding income. Businesses interested in achieving the highest level of profit will usually allocate funds to the projects yielding the highest return because to do otherwise would mean that the firm would be sacrificing opportunities to earn profit.

3. a. Two fifths of a bushel of corn. Historical production data reveal that for every 10,000-bushel increase in corn production, there is a 25,000-bushel decrease in soy output. Because the farmer is fully using his or her resources and employing these resources efficiently, the only way soy production can be increased is by withdrawing resources from corn production and employing those resources in soy production. Consequently, for every bushel increase in corn production, there is a 2.5-bushel decrease in soy production. In other words, for every additional bushel of soy produced, corn production must be reduced by two fifths of a bushel.

b. Two fifths of a bushel times $7 per bushel = $2.80. The opportunity cost of producing a bushel of soy measured in dollars represents the dollar value of that sacrificed output of corn.

4. a. N   b. P   c. P   d. N   e. N   f. N

Self-Test for Mastery

1. d   2. c   3. d   4. b   5. a   6. b   7. a   8. d   9. d   10. b   11. e
12. b

Think it Through

1. Economics is a study of how society uses its scarce resources to satisfy the unlimited wants of its members. Macroeconomics is a study of the effects of the aggregate economic behavior of all decision-making units in the economy, whereas microeconomics is concerned with an analysis of the decision making of individual firms, households, or other decision-making units. Business cycles, inflation, and unemployment are topics covered in macroeconomics. Microeconomics, also known as price theory, analyzes among other things individual markets and the determination of prices.

2.   If there were no scarcity, the opportunity costs of decisions requiring the use of resources would be zero. There would be such a thing as a "free lunch." If resources were available everywhere and in unlimited supply, the farmer in the above example could at any time produce more soy or corn without having to sacrifice the output of the other.

3.   The first statement regarding a competitive economy's ability to reward labor on the basis of labor's productive contribution is deduced from economic theory, which itself is a collection of postulates based upon empirically verifiable observations. In this sense, this statement involves positive analysis. The second statement declares that this method of income distribution is "good." But this is based upon a value system consistent with the protestant ethic, which is only one of many possible value systems. It is therefore a normative statement.

Basic Tools for Analyzing Economic Relationships

IN BRIEF: APPENDIX SUMMARY

Fill in the blanks to summarize appendix content.

Describing data graphically requires a number of considerations. Does the variable take on positive values only or does it also take on negative values? What is the unit of measurement? For what purpose are the data to be plotted? If you want to present a cause-and-effect relationship between two variables, a plot of the variables on a (1)_____ (set of axes, bar graph) would be appropriate. If you are interested in the cause-and-effect relationship of a third variable, a (2)_____ (bar graph, set of axes) cannot be used. If you are only interested in presenting the fluctuation in a variable over time, a plot on a set of axes is usually all that is required, although a bar graph can be employed.

Because most economic variables take on positive values, a set of axes having an origin in the extreme (3)_____ (northeast, southwest) corner is required. As you read vertically upward or horizontally rightward from the origin, units of measurement become increasingly positive. Each axis is defined in terms of a unit of measurement. Units of measurement can be discrete or continuous. A (4)_____ (discrete, continuous) variable is expressed in units that are indivisible. A (5)_____ (discrete, continuous) variable is divisible into fractions of a whole.

A plot of a specific set of values or (6)_____ (coordinates, intersections) of two variables on a set of axes produces a curve when the points are connected by a line. The curve can reveal important information regarding the association among the two variables plotted. If the variable on the vertical axis increases when the variable plotted on the horizontal axis increases, there is a (7)_____ (positive, negative) relationship between the two variables. If the variable on the vertical axis decreases when the variable plotted on the horizontal axis increases, the relationship is a (8)_____ (positive, negative) one. If there is no change in the variable plotted on the vertical axis when the variable on the horizontal axis changes, there is no relationship between the variables.

The (9)_____ (intersection, slope) of a curve describes the rate of change in the variable on the vertical axis given a change in the variable on the horizontal axis. A curve describing a positive relationship between variables has a (10)_____ (positive, negative) slope. A curve describing a negative relationship has a (11)_____ (positive, negative) slope, and a curve indicating no relationship between the two variables has a slope of zero. On a bowl-shaped or inverted bowl-shaped curve, a slope of zero represents the point at which the curve (or the value of the variable plotted on the vertical axis) reaches a maximum or minimum value. Two curves that just touch each other but do not intersect have (12)_____ (unequal, equal) slopes at that point of tangency. If two curves (13)_____ (intersect, are tangent), the two slopes at that point can both be positive or negative or one can be positive and the other negative, but they cannot be equal to each other as is the case with (14)_____ (an intersection, a tangency).

VOCABULARY REVIEW

Write the key term from the list below next to its definition.

Key Terms

Origin	Coordinate
Curve	Positive relationship
Slope	Negative relationship
Bar graph	Discrete variable
Intersection	Continuous variable
Tangency	Time series data

Definitions

1. _____: Measures the rate at which the variable on the vertical axis rises or falls as the variable on the horizontal axis increases.

2. _____: Data that show fluctuations in a variable over time.

3. _____: The point on a set of axes at which both variables, X and Y, take on a value of zero.

4. _____: A graph that shows that value of Y as the height of a bar for each corresponding value of X.

5. _____: The point at which two curves cross on a set of axes.

6. _____: Variable Y increases whenever variable X decreases and vice versa.

7. _____: Variable Y increases whenever variable X increases and vice versa.

8. _____: A variable that can realistically and meaningfully take on minute fractions of a variable.

9. _____: A point at which two curves just touch but do not intersect.

10. _____: A pair of numbers that corresponds to a pair of values for variables X and Y when plotted on a set of axes.

11. _____: A variable that cannot vary by fractions of units.

12. _____: A straight or curved line drawn to connect points plotted on a set of axes.

SKILLS REVIEW

1. a. Using the production data from question 3 in the Skills Review
        section in Chapter 1, construct the following bar charts:

	Soybeans (000s of bushels)	Production Data Corn (000s of bushels)
1981	100	20
1982	50	40
1983	25	50
1984	0	60
1985	75	30
1986	150	0
1987	125	10

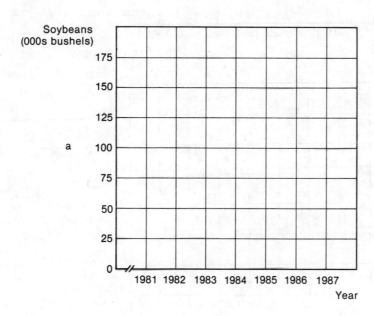

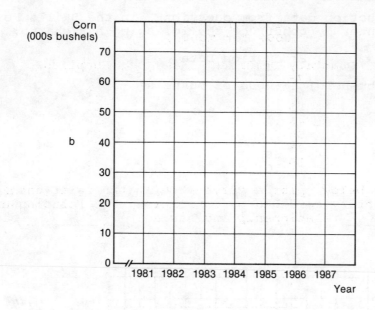

Corn
(000s bushels)

70
60
50
b 40
30
20
10
0

1981 1982 1983 1984 1985 1986 1987

Year

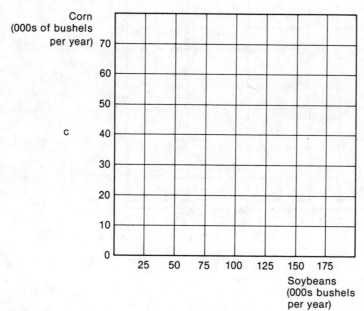

Corn
(000s of bushels
per year)

70
60
50
c 40
30
20
10
0

25 50 75 100 125 150 175

Soybeans
(000s bushels
per year)

b.   Which of the above bar charts depict time series data and which
     depict a functional relationship representing the concept of
     opportunity costs?

     1.   Figure A _____
     2.   Figure B _____
     3.   Figure C _____

12

2. The following data represent quantities of tennis rackets demanded by consumers and supplied by producers at various prices:

Tennis Rackets
(000s per month)

Price per Racket	Quantity Demanded	Quantity Supplied
$10	75	15
20	65	20
30	55	25
40	45	30
50	35	35
60	25	40
70	15	45

a. In the figure below, plot a curve showing the relationship between price and quantity demanded by consumers. The relationship is a _____ relationship and has a _____ slope.

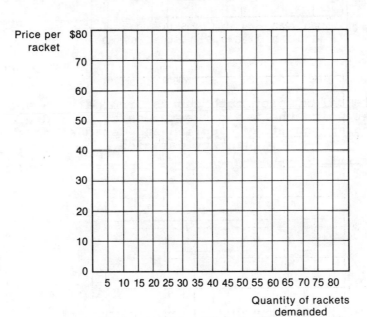

b. In the figure below, plot a curve showing the relationship between price and quantity supplied by producers. The relationship is a _____ relationship and has a _____ slope.

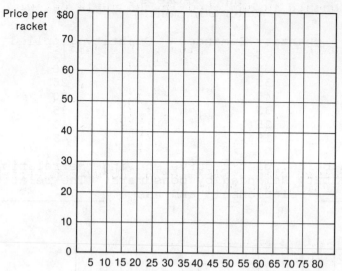

Price per $80
racket
   70
   60
   50
   40
   30
   20
   10
    0
      5 10 15 20 25 30 35 40 45 50 55 60 65 70 75 80
                              Quantity of rackets
                              supplied
                              (000s per month)

c. In the figure below, plot both curves from parts a and b above. The coordinate at which the two curves cross is called a/an _____.
At what price and quantity supplied and demanded do the two curves cross? Price_____, quantity demanded_____, quantity supplied_____.

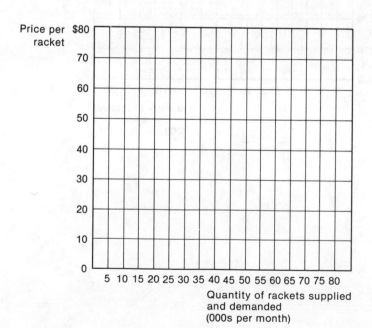

Price per $80
racket
   70
   60
   50
   40
   30
   20
   10
    0
      5 10 15 20 25 30 35 40 45 50 55 60 65 70 75 80
                          Quantity of rackets supplied
                          and demanded
                          (000s per month)

14

3. Suppose that you are a manager for a producer of business forms and you have noticed that over time your sales of business forms appear to increase as the rate of growth in the nation's output or GNP increases. That observed relationship is depicted in the table below:

	Rate of Growth in GNP (%)	Sales of Business Forms
Year 1	3.0	15,000
2	3.5	17,000
3	2.0	11,000
4	5.5	25,000
5	6.0	27,000

a. In the figure below, plot a time series curve describing the behavior of the rate of growth in GNP.

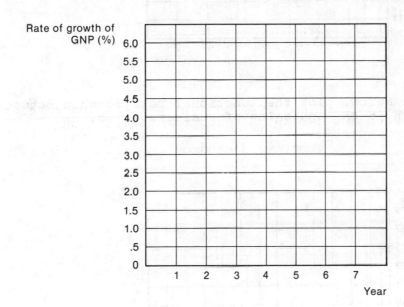

b. In the figure below, plot a time series curve describing the behavior of business forms sales.

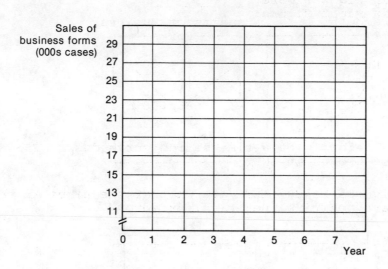

c. In the figure below, plot the functional relationship between the rate of growth in GNP and sales of business forms.

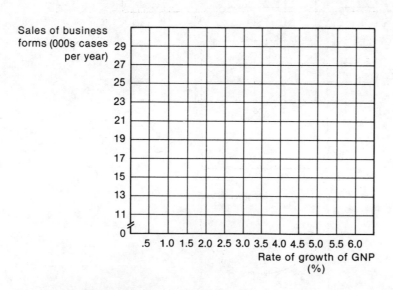

d. <u>Advanced Question.</u> If the rate of growth in GNP is expected to be 4.5% in year 6, what would you predict to happen to business form sales?

4. a. For the figures below, indicate whether a tangency exists or an intersection occurs at:

    Point A in left figure: _____
    Point B in right figure: _____

b. For the figures below, indicate whether the curves at the point of
    tangency or intersection have a positive or negative slope.

        Curve 1 in left figure: _____
        Curve 2 in left figure: _____
        Curve 1 in right figure: _____
        Curve 2 in right figure: _____

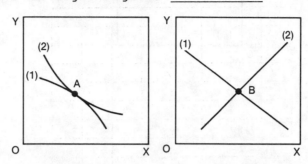

5. Referring to the figures below, indicate whether the slope at the
    designated points are positive, negative, or zero.

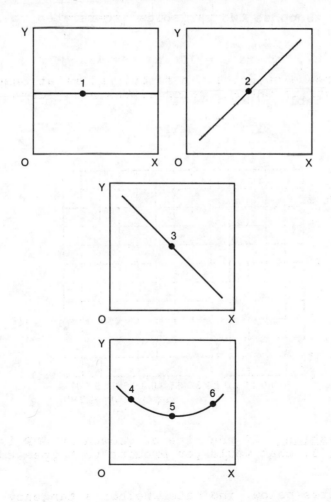

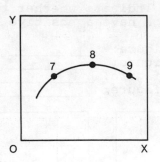

1. _____
2. _____
3. _____
4. _____
5. _____
6. _____
7. _____
8. _____
9. _____

6. __Advanced Problem__. Suppose two variables are related to each other by the following equation:

$$Y = a + bX, \quad \text{where } a = 10 \text{ and } b = 1/2$$

a. Complete the table. (Use the Y1 column for the case where a = 10.)

X	Y1	Y2
100		
200		
300		
400		
500		
600		
700		
800		

b. Plot the relationship between X and Y1 in the figure below.
    (1) The slope =_____.
    (2) The intercept (value of Y1 at X = 0) =_____.

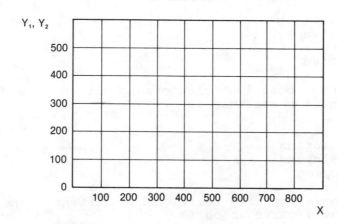

c. Assume that the constant term a in the above equation increases from
    10 to 60. Complete column Y2 above and plot the new relationship in
    the figure in part b. The curve has shifted _____. The
    slope =_____ and the intercept = _____.

SELF-TEST FOR MASTERY

Select the best answer.

1. Which of the following does not indicate a functional relationship between
    variables X and Y?

    a. As X increases, Y increases
    b. As X decreases, Y increases
    c. As X increases, Y remains unchanged
    d. As X decreases, Y decreases

2. When a value for X is paired with a value for Y on a set of axes, this
    combination of values is known as:

    a. A tangency.
    b. An intersection.
    c. A coordinate.
    d. The origin, if at least one value is zero.

3. A curve represents a set of coordinates that are connected by a line.
    Which of the following statements is true?

    a. A curve by definition cannot be a straight line.
    b. A curve must have either a positive or negative slope.
    c. A line of zero slope is not a function and therefore is not a curve.

19

d. A curve may be a straight or a curved line. If it is a curved line, it is possible to have a positive, negative, or zero slope at different points on that curve.

4. If _Y_ increases as _X_ is increased, there is a _____ relationship between _X_ and _Y_. If _Y_ decreases as _X_ is increased, the functional relationship is said to be a _____ one.

   a. Adverse, positive
   b. Negative, positive
   c. Obtuse, negative
   d. Positive, negative

5. A function exhibiting a positive relationship between _X_ and _Y_ has a _____ slope and a curve that is _____.

   a. Positive, upsloping
   b. Negative, downsloping
   c. Positive, downsloping
   d. Negative, upsloping

6. A function exhibiting a negative relationship between _X_ and _Y_ has a _____ slope and a curve which is _____.

   a. Positive, upsloping
   b. Negative, downsloping
   c. Positive, downsloping
   d. Negative, upsloping

7. Which of the following defines the origin?

   a. The origin is the beginning of a set of time series data.
   b. The origin is the coordinate on a set of axes where the value of variables _X_ and _Y_ are both zero.
   c. The origin is the coordinate on a set of axes where the values of variables _X_ and _Y_ represent the initial values of the data plotted.
   d. The origin is that point on the northeast corner of a set of positive axes.

8. The slope can be defined as the:

   a. Change in _Y_/change in _X_.
   b. Rate of change in _Y_ over time.
   c. Rate of change in _X_ over time.
   d. None of the above.

9. A _____ variable is indivisible into fractions of a unit, whereas a _____ variable is divisible into fractions of a whole.

   a. Continuous, discrete
   b. Discrete, continuous
   c. Positive, negative
   d. Time series, constant

10. Which of the following variables have discrete units of measurement?

   a. Automobiles
   b. Gasoline
   c. Coffee beans
   d. The nation's money supply

11. Of the following variables, which one is a continuous variable?

    a.   Computer
    b.   House
    c.   Basketball
    d.   Natural gas

12. When two curves just touch each other, they have _____ slopes.

    a.   Equal
    b.   Unequal
    c.   Positive and negative
    d.   Only zero

13. The point at which two curves just touch each other is called:

    a.   A tangency.
    b.   The origin.
    c.   A data point.
    d.   An intersection.

14. The point at which two curve cross is called:

    a.   A tangency.
    b.   The origin.
    c.   A data point.
    d.   An intersection.

15. The values of X and Y at an intersection:

    a.   Will be the same on both curves.
    b.   Will be the same on both curves for the X variable only.
    c.   Will not be the same on both curves.
    d.   Depend upon the placement of the origin.

THINK IT THROUGH

1. Referring to the data below, plot the price and quantity demanded data on the axes below. On the same set of axes, plot the price and quantity supplied data and interpret the meaning of the intersection. Suppose a third variable changes, such as the introduction of VCRs, and as a result the quantity of movie tickets demanded at each price level declines by 20,000 tickets per week. What happens to the curve representing the demand data? What happens to the intersection?

Price per Ticket	Quantity Demanded	Quantity Supplied
	(000s per week)	
$2	80	20
3	70	30
4	60	40
5	50	50
6	40	60
7	30	70

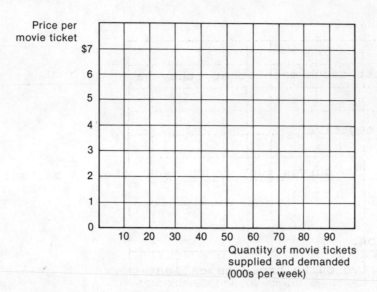

Price per movie ticket

Quantity of movie tickets supplied and demanded (000s per week)

2. The following data represent the relationship between interest rates and building permits issued for new residential construction in a local housing market. Plot the relationship on the axes below and determine if a positive or negative relationship exits. Because of a regional recession, assume that local incomes decline and outmigration of people reduce the demand for new housing and thus reduce building permits issued by 100 permits per month at each mortgage rate. Plot the new relationship on the same set of axes and compare the position and slope of the new curve to the one that you previously plotted.

Mortgage Rate %	Permits Issued (000s per month)
8.5	1050
9.0	1000
9.5	950
10.0	900
10.5	850
11.0	800
11.5	750

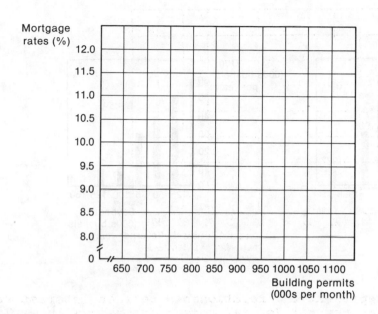

Mortgage rates (%)

Building permits (000s per month)

ANSWERS TO CHAPTER APPENDIX

In Brief: Appendix Summary

1. A set of axes or a bar graph 2. Bar graph 3. Southwest 4. Discrete 5. Continuous 6. Coordinates 7. Positive 8. Negative 9. Slope 10. Positive 11. Negative 12. Equal 13. Intersect 14. Tangency

Vocabulary Review

1. Slope 2. Time series data 3. Origin 4. Bar graph 5. Intersection 6. Negative relationship 7. Positive relationship 8. Continuous variable 9. Tangency 10. Coordinate 11. Discrete variable 12. Curve

Skills Review

1.   a.

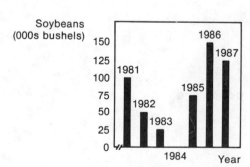

Soybeans (000s bushels)

Year

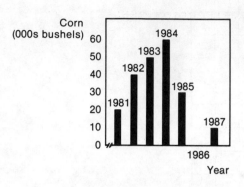

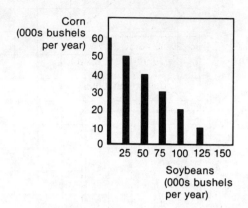

b. (1) Time series
    (2) Time series
    (3) Functional relationship

2.

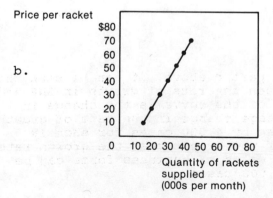

a.

Negative, negative

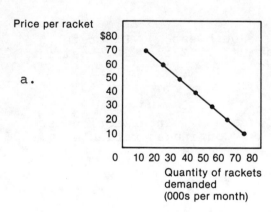

b.

Positive, positive

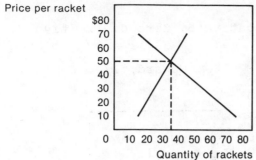

Price per racket

c. Intersection, $50, 35, 35

Quantity of rackets supplied and demanded (000s per month)

3.

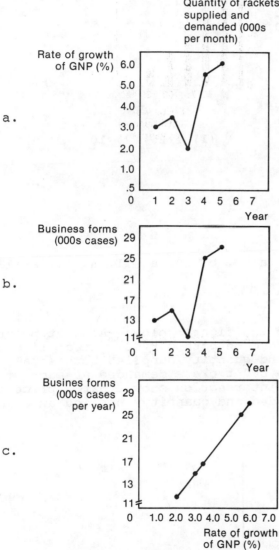

a. Rate of growth of GNP (%)

Year

b. Business forms (000s cases)

Year

c. Busines forms (000s cases per year)

Rate of growth of GNP (%)

d.   From the functional relationship in part c above, it can be seen that a positive relationship exists between the rate of growth in GNP and sales of business forms. The slope of the curve is the change in business form sales for each percentage change in the rate of growth of GNP. Business form sales increase by 4,000 cases for each 1% increase in the GNP growth rate. If you expect that the growth rate of GNP will be 4.5% in year 6, then sales of business forms can be predicted to fall from 27,000 to 21,000 cases.

4.   a.   Tangency, intersection
     b.   Negative, negative, positive, positive

5. 1. Zero 2. Positive 3. Negative 4. Negative 5. Zero 6. Positive 7.
    Positive 8. Zero 9. Negative

6. a. Y1   c. Y2   Upward, 1/2. 60
        60   110
        110   160
        160   210
        210   260
        260   310
        310   360
        360   410
        410   460

    b.
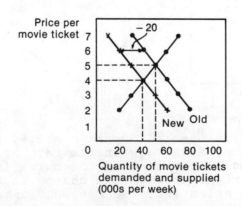
                                        (1) 1/2 (2) 10

Self-Test for Mastery

1. c 2. c 3. d 4. a 5. a 6. b 7. b 8. a 9. b 10. a 11. d 12. a 13. a
14. d 15. a

Think It Through

1. The two curves intersect at point A in the figure below. At that point,
the values for price and quantity are the same on both curves. At a price per
movie ticket of $5, the quantity demanded and quantity supplied both equal
50,000 tickets per week. A reduction of 20,000 tickets demanded at each price
shifts the demand curve leftward. The new intersection shows that a price of
$4 is now required to equate quantity demanded and quantity supplied at a level
of 40,000 tickets per week.

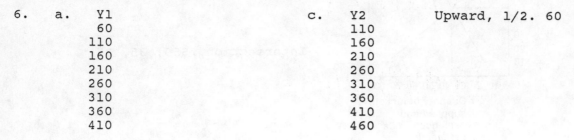

2. The relationship between mortgage rates and new building permits issued is
a negative one. If building permits issued decline at each mortgage rate by
100 permits per month, the new curve lies to the left of the old curve but has
the same slope.

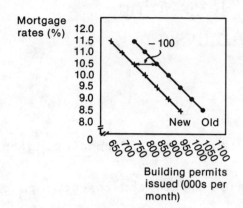

Mortgage rates (%)

12.0
11.5
11.0
10.5
10.0
9.5
9.0
8.5
8.0

−100

New   Old

0

650
700
750
800
850
900
950
1000
1050
1100

Building permits
issued (000s per
month)

2

The Economic Way of Reasoning: Models and Marginal Analysis

CHAPTER CHALLENGES

After studying your text, attending class, and completing this chapter, you should be able to:

1. Understand the purpose of theory and the concept of an economic model and its uses.
2. Develop the notion of rational behavior and a general method of analyzing the way individuals make decisions, which is called marginal analysis.

IN BRIEF: CHAPTER SUMMARY

Fill in the blanks to summarize chapter content.

Economic analysis helps us understand the world around us. It helps us understand the functioning of the various sectors in the economy and the choices made by individual decision-making units. (1)_____ (Assumptions, Economic theories) simplify reality so that the underlying cause-and-effect relationships among variables can be understood. (2)_____ (Economic variables, Data) are quantities or dollar amounts that have more than one value. Theories are necessary in order to better understand the complexities of reality.

(3)_____(A bar graph, An economic model) is a simplified way of expressing a theory. It can be expressed verbally, graphically, in tables, or mathematically. Assumptions underlie a theory because theories are (4)_____(depictions of, abstractions from) reality, and it is necessary to establish the environment and motivation of people for which the theory holds. Economic models can be used to develop hypotheses. (5)_____ (An assumption, A hypothesis) is a statement of relationship between two variables that can be tested by empirical verification. Deductive reasoning is used when taking a general body of knowledge or theory and using implications of the theory to construct hypotheses. Hypotheses that have been subjected to repeated empirical verification and have withstood the test of time become (6)_____ (hypotheses, economic principles or laws). A good model is one that can generate accurate predictions. But even a model that does not predict perfectly can still be useful in helping us understand the causal relationships among variables and the consequence of the assumptions underlying the model. The causal relationships that we want to understand are difficult to isolate unless we make the assumption of (7)_____(ceteris paribus, the invisible hand). Otherwise, we cannot be sure that we have identified the exact relationship between the two variables of interest.

Economic analysis makes the assumption of rationality. Rationality means that most people behave as if they are comparing the additional gains or benefits from a choice or decision to the sacrifices or opportunity costs associated with that decision. The opportunity cost of a decision is known as its marginal (8)_____(benefit, cost). If the marginal benefits of a decision exceed the marginal costs, the individual's net gain or benefit (9)_____(increases, decreases). If the marginal cost of a decision exceeds the marginal benefits, the decision would not be undertaken because the individual would experience a net (10)_____(loss, gain). If a choice or decision is pursued to the point where marginal benefits and marginal costs are equal, the individual achieves the (11)_____(maximum, minimum) net gain.

VOCABULARY REVIEW

Write the key term from the list below next to its definition.

Key Terms

Marginal analysis	Ceteris paribus
Theory	Behavioral assumptions
Variable	Rational behavior
Economic model	Marginal benefit
Hypothesis	Marginal cost

Definitions

1. _____: a quantity or dollar amount that can have more than one value.

2. _____: "other things being equal"--used to acknowledge that other influences aside from the one whose effect is being analyzed must be controlled for in testing a hypothesis.

3. _____: establishes the motivation of persons for the purpose of understanding cause-and-effect relationships among economic variables.

4. _____: a decision-making technique involving a systematic comparison of benefits and costs of actions.

5. _____: the additional benefit obtained when one extra unit of an item is obtained.

6. _____: the sacrifice made to obtain an additional unit of an item.

7. _____: an abstraction or simplification of actual relationships; establishes cause-and-effect relationships.

8. _____: statement of a relationship between two or more variables.

9. _____: seeking to gain by choosing to undertake actions for which the extra benefit exceeds the associated extra cost.

10. _____: a simplified way of expressing economic behavior or how some sector of the economy functions.

SKILLS REVIEW

Concept: Economic models and uses

1. Develop a hypothesis regarding the level of family spending on goods and
    services and the level of family income. Describe that hypothesized
    relationship by setting up two columns of data reflecting the variables in
    your hypothesis. Is the hypothesized relationship a positive or negative
    relationship? Suppose that you gathered actual data on your variables and
    for some families your hypothesized relationship did not hold. Of what
    use is the ceteris paribus assumption in trying to isolate the
    relationship between family spending and income?

        Family Spending on Goods   Family Income ($)
             and Services ($)

2. Suppose that you want to investigate the relationship between prices of
    restaurant meals and the quantity of meals demanded by local area
    households. Economic theory implies that there is a negative relationship
    between price and quantity demanded but that income, tastes, preferences,
    and other variables also influence quantity demanded. Clearly state your
    hypothesis and its underlying assumptions.

Concept: Marginal analysis

3. During the presidential campaign, Republican George Bush recommended that
    his party's platform include a proposal for child care payments of up to
    $1,000 to low-income working families and a tax credit for other families
    with children under age 4 in which at least one parent works. Assume that
    you are a single parent with young children. Using marginal analysis,
    assess the impact of such a program on your decision to work or to work
    additional hours.

4. Assume that the price you are willing to pay for an additional unit of a
    good measures the marginal benefit received. How could you measure the
    marginal cost of the decision to consume that extra unit?

5. A rational decision maker comparing the extra gains and losses of a
    decision will _____ net gains if the decision or choice is
    pursued to the point where _____ equals _____. Explain the
    logic of this statement.

6. Advanced Question. You are an administrator of the Environmental
    Protection Agency concerned with allocating cleanup funds from the
    agency's Superfund for the removal of toxic wastes. The following data
    represent the marginal benefits and costs associated with removing units
    of pollution from a polluted river. Your task is to decide if there is a
    net gain to society from cleaning the river and what level of pollution
    reduction would maximize that net gain.

Units of Pollution Reduction	Marginal Benefits	Marginal Costs
	(millions of dollars)	
0	$ 0	$ 0
1	10	2
2	8	4
3	6	6
4	4	8
5	2	10

30

a. Is there a net gain to society from cleaning the river? Discuss.

b. Nets gains are maximized at a level of pollution reduction of _____, where marginal benefits and marginal costs are _____.

SELF-TEST FOR MASTERY

1. The decision-making technique involving a systematic comparison of the benefits and costs of actions is known as:

    a. Deductive reasoning.
    b. Total gains analysis.
    c. Marginal analysis.
    d. Ceteris paribus.

2. A/An _____ is a simplification of reality seeking to uncover the underlying cause-and-effect relationships among economic _____.

    a. Assumptions/variables
    b. Economic theory/assumptions
    c. Hypothesis/theories
    d. Economic theory/variables

3. Which of the following is true regarding economic variables?

    a. Economic variables have more than one value.
    b. Economic variables are quantities or dollar amounts.
    c. Economic variables are necessary to economic theories and models.
    d. All of the above.

4. A/An _____ is a simplified way of expressing an economic theory.

    a. Economic model
    b. Assumption
    c. Abstraction
    d. Economic principle

5. Which of the following assumptions is necessary in order to isolate the relationship between two variables?

    a. "All things allowed to vary"
    b. "All things held constant"
    c. "Ceteris paribus"
    d. B and c

6. If gasoline prices rise, the quantity of gasoline demanded will fall. This statement is a/an:

    a. Assumption.
    b. Theory.
    c. Abstraction.
    d. Hypothesis.

7. Economic hypotheses that have been subjected to repeated empirical investigation over time and have not been rejected, become:

    a. Economic policy
    b. Assumptions

31

c. Economic principles or laws
d. None of the above

8. If household purchases of automobiles are determined by both the level of household income and the interest rate and you want to isolate the relationship between interest rates and auto sales, you must assume:

a. That the interest rate remains unchanged.
b. That auto sales remain unchanged.
c. That household income remains unchanged.
d. None of the above because you would want to know both the effect of interest rates and income on auto sales.

9. Which of the following best defines rational behavior?

a. Seeking to gain by choosing to undertake actions for which the marginal benefits exceed the associated marginal costs
b. A comparison of the total gains and losses from a decision
c. Decisions that avoid habit or impulse purchases
d. Improving net gain by pursuing decisions in which the marginal costs of a decision exceed the marginal benefits

10. _____ can be defined as the extra benefit received from undertaking some action.

a. Total benefit
b. Total gain
c. Marginal benefit
d. Total net gain

11. _____ can be defined as the extra cost associated with some action.

a. Total cost
b. Marginal cost
c. Total loss
d. Total net loss

12. The total net gain from a decision or action reaches a _____ when a decision or action is pursued to the point where _____ equals _____.

a. Maximum,total cost,total benefit
b. Minimum, marginal benefit,marginal cost
c. Minimum, total benefit, marginal benefit
d. Maximum, marginal benefit, marginal cost

13. The sacrifice made to obtain an additional unit of an item is known as:

a. Opportunity cost.
b. The maximum tradeoff.
c. Marginal cost.
d. A and c.
e. B and c.

THINK IT THROUGH

1. Define the concepts of economic theory and economic models. Discuss the importance of assumptions underlying models and theories.

2. Pollution is harmful to society, and the reduction of pollution levels increase society's total benefits. But if a 50% reduction in the pollution level resulted in an equality between the marginal benefits and marginal costs associated with pollution reduction, society would be better off if pollution were not eliminated completely. Reconcile the two statements.

3. A rational person would never engage in habit or impulse buying. Discuss.

4. A hypothesis requires the use of the ceteris paribus assumption. Why? Give an example.

5. A theory must depict reality. Do you agree? Explain.

CHAPTER ANSWERS

In Brief: Chapter Summary

1. Economic theories 2. Economic variables 3. Economic model 4. Abstractions from 5. Hypothesis 6. Economic principles or laws 7. Ceteris paribus 8. cost 9. Increase 10. Loss 11. Maximum

Vocabulary Review

1. Variable 2. Ceteris paribus 3. Behavioral assumptions 4. Marginal analysis 5. Marginal benefit 6. Marginal cost 7. Theory 8. Hypothesis 9. Rational behavior 10. Economic model

Skills Review

1. _Hypothesis_: Other things held constant, family spending on goods and services is expected to be positively related to family income.

   If upon gathering data on family spending and income it is found that the relationship between spending and income is not positive, that does not mean that your hypothesis is invalid. To determine the validity of your hypothesis, you must isolate the relationship you are interested in from all other variables that might influence family spending. If you do not, you cannot be sure that an increase in family spending is the result of increases in income or some third variable.

2. Hypothesis: Other things being the same, the price of restaurant meals and the quantity of restaurant meals demanded are expected to be inversely (negatively) related.

   The ceteris paribus assumption is necessary to control for other factors that influence quantity demanded, such as income and tastes and preferences. For instance, prices could be falling but incomes could fall as well. A family might dine out less often even at lower prices if their income has fallen.

3. As a working parent and particularly a single working parent, one of the major costs associated with work is child care. If you worked full time

at the minimum wage of $3.35 per hour and paid $450 per month for child care for two children, you would have $86 dollars left over to support you and your family. There is little incentive to work full time for a month just to bring home $86. But suppose that as a result of new legislation, $100 of that monthly child care bill is paid for by the government. You are now left with $186 per month. This amount, although insufficient to meet the minimum needs of a family of three, is nevertheless still very important. If you were deterred from working before the new law, publicly subsidized child care payments increase the net gain to you from work and might induce you to seek employment. If you are already working, these payments might induce you to work additional hours because now the net gains from work are higher.

The marginal benefits from working an additional hour include among other things the value of goods and services that can be purchased with the income earned from that hour of work. The marginal cost of work involves the sacrifices incurred in order to work. These sacrifices include the loss of leisure time, the loss of time spent with family and friends, and the resources spent on such things as child care and transportation that could have otherwise been spent on goods and services.

Child care subsidies can be viewed as reducing the marginal cost of an hour of work or as increasing the marginal benefits realized from work. A reduction in day care costs increases the amount of the hourly wage available for non-day care expenditures. In this sense, the marginal benefit of an hour of work increases. Regardless of how the problem is viewed, total net gains from work increase. This will likely increase employment among single parents.

4. The marginal cost of a decision to consume a unit of a good is the sacrificed next-preferred goods that could have been consumed. The dollar value of this forgone consumption is a measure of marginal cost.

5. Maximize, marginal costs, marginal benefits

   If marginal benefits exceed marginal costs from some action, a person can add more to his or her total benefits than total costs by undertaking the action. In other words, net benefit or gain increases. As long as marginal benefits exceed marginal costs, total net gains can be increased by pursuing an activity. When an activity has been pursued to the point where marginal benefits and costs are equal, no further increases to net benefits can be realized because the addition to total benefits would just be offset by the addition to total costs of the action.

6. a. Yes, because marginal benefits from pollution reduction up to a point exceed the sacrifice incurred in reducing pollution.

   b. 3, equal at $6 million. At this point, society's total benefits and costs equal $24 million and $12 million, respectively. Society's net gain is therefore $12 million. No other level of pollution reduction will result in as large of a net gain.

Self-Test for Mastery

1. c 2. d 3. d 4. a 5. d 6. d 7. c 8. c 9. a 10. c 11. b 12. d 13. d

Think it Through

1. Economic theory is a simplification of reality seeking to establish and explain important cause-and-effect relationships in the economy. An economic

model is a simplified way of expressing a theory. A model can be presented verbally, in tables, in graphs, or mathematically. Assumptions are necessary for both theories and models because they outline the environment or motivation of people for which the theory and model hold.

2. If pollution reduction were undertaken to the point where marginal benefit and marginal cost were equal and that happened to be at a 50% level of pollution reduction, then no further net gains to society could be realized by additional reductions in pollution. In fact, if additional pollution reduction beyond the 50% level resulted in marginal costs exceeding marginal benefits, society would experience a net loss and be worse off than when there was more pollution.

3. In fact it might be quite rational for a person to engage in habit or impulse buying if that person experiences psychic loss, dissatisfaction, or stress associated with certain actions or choices. A person may buy the first used car he or she sees but may be doing so in part because of a distaste for bargaining and haggling. A person may shop only locally because of an aversion to driving in traffic.

4. A hypothesis is a statement of relationship between two economic variables. To be certain that you have isolated the cause-and-effect relationship between the two variables, it is necessary to hold the effect of other influencing variables constant. Otherwise, you cannot be sure that the relationship you have hypothesized is valid or instead results from some third variable that you have not considered.

5. A good theory yields accurate predictions, but even a theory that predicts inaccurately is of value in establishing cause-and-effect relationships and determining the significance of assumptions.

3

Production Possibilities and Opportunity Cost

CHAPTER CHALLENGES

After studying your text, attending class, and completing this chapter, you should be able to:

1. Show how limited available technology and scarce resources imply limited production possibilities over a period.
2. Demonstrate that the use of productive capacity to make more of any one good or service available involves sacrificing the opportunity to make more of other items available.
3. Discuss the basic determinants of a nation's production possibilities and how these can expand over time.
4. Understand the concept of productive efficiency and discuss its significance.
5. Demonstrate that when you use income over a period to buy more of one item, you sacrifice the opportunity to buy more of some other item over the period.

IN BRIEF: CHAPTER SUMMARY

Fill in the blanks to summarize chapter content.

(1)_____(Economy, Production) is the process of using economic resources or inputs in order to produce output. Economic resources consist of labor, (2)_____(capital, money), natural resources, and entrepreneurship. The quantity and productivity of economic resources and the extent and efficiency with which they are employed determine the output potential of a nation during a given period of time. Constraints in the availability or use of resources represent the (3)_____ (opportunity costs, scarcity) confronting nations. (4)_____(Technology, A larger labor force) allows us to delay the sacrifices implied by scarce resources by increasing the productivity of resources. Improvements in resource productivity mean that a nation can produce more output with a given endowment of resources.

A (5)_____(marginal benefit, production possibilities) curve is a convenient tool for showing the implications of scarce resources. Assuming (a) a given quantity and productivity of resources, as well as a given state of the art with respect to technology and (b) full and efficient employment of resources, it can be shown that a nation can produce more of one class of goods only by (6)_____(sacrificing, increasing) the production of other goods. That sacrifice is a nation's (7)_____ (dollar outlay, opportunity cost) of producing more of a given good. As a nation produces more of a good, the opportunity cost (8)_____(rises, falls) because resources that are increasingly (9)_____(less, more) productive must be transferred from the production of other goods. This implies that a given increase in the production of one good will require ever (10)_____(smaller, larger) reductions in output of other goods. The law of increasing costs exists because resources (11)_____(are, are not) equally adaptable to all employments.

A point on the production possibilities curve represents a combination of the two classes of goods in question where output is at a maximum. A point inside the curve implies either (12)_____(unemployed, fully employed) resources or (13)_____(efficiently, inefficiently) employed resources. A point outside the curve represents a combination of goods that is (14)_____(attainable, unattainable) in the short run. But with an increase over time in the quantity and productivity of resources, together with improvements in technology, a point outside the curve is attainable in the long run.

Maximum production is attainable in the short run when resources are employed fully and efficiently. Productive efficiency means that a nation (15)_____(can, cannot) reallocate resources among the production of goods and services and achieve a gain in the output of one good only by causing a reduction in the output of another. Specialization and the division of labor are critical for the attainment of maximum productive efficiency.

The process of economic growth can be shown as (16)_____(inward, outward) shifts over time in the production possibilities curve. A nation can generally produce more of all goods over time as long as it experiences resource growth and an improvement in the quality of resources and technology. A nation's growth is influenced by its willingness to forgo some (17)_____(future, current) production of consumable output so that resources can be used for the production of (18)_____(consumable outputs, capital). Production of capital today increases the production possibilities in the future not only by increasing the quantity of capital but also by increasing the productivity of other resources.

The problem of scarcity confronting nations also confronts the individual. An individual has a limited amount of income per time period with which to consume and save. Given the prices of goods and services, that limited income can purchase, at a maximum, those combinations of goods and services which require the full expenditure of income. A curve representing these various combinations of goods and services is known as a (19)_____(budget line, production possibilities curve). An increase in income over time allows the individual to consume more of all goods. This is shown by an (20)_____ (inward, outward) shift of the budget line. Holding income constant but allowing prices to fall likewise (21)_____(increases, decreases) the quantities that can be purchased. This too shifts the budget line (22)_____(inward, outward). Rising prices or inflation will shift the budget line (23)_____ (inward, outward) if income remains constant. Finally, given a limited income and constant prices, the only way an individual can consume more of one good is by reducing consumption of other goods. The opportunity cost of consuming more of one good is the (24)_____(increase, reduction) in consumption of quantities of other goods.

VOCABULARY REVIEW

Write the key term from the list below next to its definition.

Key Terms

Economic resources
Labor
Capital
Natural resources
Entrepreneurship
Technology

Production possibilities curve
Law of increasing costs
Productive efficiency
Division of labor
Economic growth
Budget line

Definitions

1. _____: the inputs used in the process of production.

2. _____: the specialization of workers in particular tasks that are part of a larger undertaking to accomplish a given objective.

3. _____: shows an individual's opportunities to purchase two goods if he or she spends an entire month's income on these two goods at their current prices.

4. _____: the equipment, tools, structures, machinery, vehicles, materials, and skills created to help produce goods and services.

5. _____: shows the maximum possible output of one good that can be produced with available resources given the output of the alternative good over a period.

6. _____: the talent to develop products and processes and to organize production of goods and services.

7. _____: the expansion in production possibilities that results from increased availability and increased productivity of economic resources.

8. _____: the knowledge of how to produce goods and services.

9. _____: the physical and mental efforts of human beings in the production of goods and services.

10. _____: attained when the maximum possible output of any one good is produced given the output of the other goods. At this point it is not possible to reallocate economic resources to increase the output of any single good or service without decreasing the output of some other good or service.

11. _____: acreage and the physical terrain to locate structures, ports, and other facilities; also, natural resources that are used in crude form in production.

12. _____: the opportunity costs of extra production of any one good in an economy will increase as more and more specialized resources best suited for the production of other goods are reallocated away from their best use.

SKILLS REVIEW

Concept: Scarce resources and limited production possibilities

1. List four economic resources:

    a. _____
    b. _____
    c. _____
    d. _____

2. Which of the following uses of resources will likely increase labor
    productivity? (+, Increase; 0, No change.)

    a. _____ Expenditures on capital
    b. _____ Expenditures on more fashionable clothes
    c. _____ Expenditures on health care
    d. _____ Expenditures on education and training
    e. _____ Expenditures on military goods

Concept: Production possibilities and opportunity cost

3. The data in the table below represent the production possibilities for a
    nation producing two classes of goods.

Production Possibilities	Consumer Goods	Capital Goods
	(millions of units)	
A	0	90
B	20	80
C	40	65
D	60	47
E	80	26
F	100	0

    a. On the axes below, plot a production possibilities curve from the
        data in the table above.

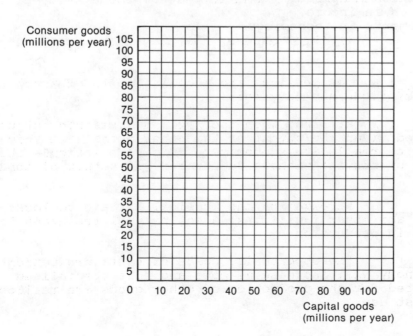

39

b.   What is the meaning of a point <u>on</u> the production possibilities curve?
c.   What is the opportunity cost associated with an increase in the
     production of consumer goods by 20 million units?
          (1) From point B to C? _____ units of capital
          (2) From point C to D? _____ units of capital
          (3) From point D to E? _____ units of capital
          (4) From point E to F? _____ units of capital
d.   Do opportunity costs rise or fall as additional units of consumer
     goods are produced? Explain.

4.   Referring to the figure below:

     a.   Interpret the meaning of point A.
     b.   Interpret the meaning of point B.

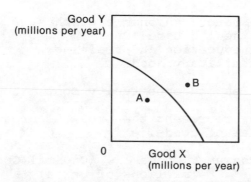

Concept: Determinants of a nation's production possibilities

5.   Indicate whether the following events would cause the production
     possibilities curve to shift outward (O) or would leave it unchanged (U):

     a.   _____   Increased production of houses at full employment
     b.   _____   Increases in the quantity of resources
     c.   _____   Improvements in the quality and productivity of economic
                   resources
     d.   _____   A reduction in prices
     e.   _____   Increases in income
     f.   _____   Improvements in technology

40

6. a. On the axes below, draw a production possibilities curve for a
        nation. Now assume that economic growth is taking place. Draw a new
        production possibilities curve on the same axes reflecting this
        growth.

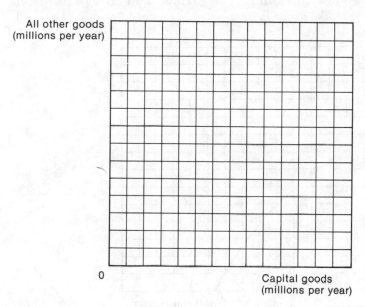

All other goods
(millions per year)

0   Capital goods
                     (millions per year)

   b. On the axes below, draw a production possibilities curve for a
       nation. Assume as above that the nation is experiencing growth, but
       also assume that the economy is investing more heavily in capital and
       technology than the economy shown above in part a. Draw a new
       production possibilities curve reflecting this.

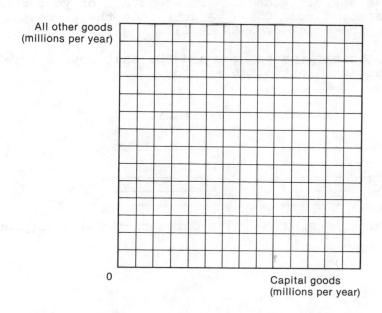

All other goods
(millions per year)

0   Capital goods
                     (millions per year)

7. a. If a nation used resources for capital or technological improvements
        for a specific industry, such as the aircraft industry, what are the
        implications regarding future levels of production not only in the
        aircraft industry but for other industries as well?
    b. Show the shift in a nation's production possibilities curve that
        results from the use of resources discussed above.

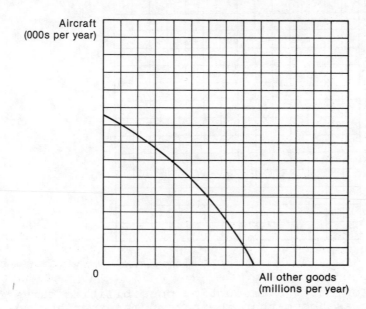

Concept: Limited income and opportunity cost

8. Suppose that as a university student you receive $50 per month from your
    parents to be used as spending money. You spend all of your money each
    month on beer or compact discs (CDs). Assume that the price per six-pack
    of beer is $2.50 and the price of a CD is $10.

    a. Determine six combinations of beer and CDs that cost a total of $50.
        List the combinations in the table below.

Combination	Beer (six packs)	CDs (units)
A	_____	_____
B	_____	_____
C	_____	_____
D	_____	_____
E	_____	_____

    b. Plot these combinations below. The curve that you have plotted is
        called a _____.

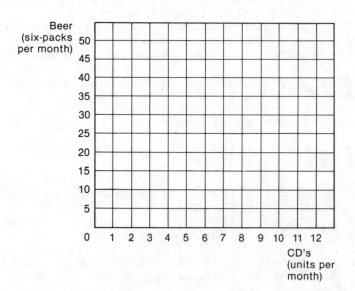

Beer
(six-packs
per month)

CD's
(units per
month)

c. On the figure in part b, show what would happen to the curve if:
    (1) your parents began to send $100 per month
    (2) your total funds are still $50, but the price of beer
        increases to $5 and the price of CDs decreases to $5.

9. Advanced Question

    a. Derive the equation for the budget line in Question 8, part b.
    b. In question 8, part c1 alters the equation for the budget line in
        what way? Part c2 alters the equation in what way?

SELF-TEST FOR MASTERY

Select the best answer.

1. Which of the following can be defined as the process of using economic
    resources to produce outputs?

    a. Economics
    b. Production
    c. Economy
    d. Technology

2. Economic resources consist of:

    a. Money, credit, and capital
    b. Labor, capital, and money
    c. Labor, capital, natural resources, and money
    d. Labor, capital, natural resources, and entrepreneurship

3. Which of the following best defines capital?

    a. Money
    b. Plant and tools

43

c.   Investment funds available for speculative financial outlays
d.   Goods or skills that are produced in order to produce goods and services

4.   Scarcity exists in the short run because:

a.   At a given point in time technological growth increases at a constant rate.
b.   At a given point in time the quantity and quality of resources and the state of technology are fixed.
c.   Resources are usually employed inefficiently.
d.   The world's resources are in finite supply.

5.   A nation must sacrifice the output of some goods in order to produce other goods during a given period of time if:

a.   There is less than full employment of resources.
b.   Resources are inefficiently employed.
c.   There is both full and efficient use of economic resources.
d.   A nation relies on capital goods production.

6.   If a nation is currently operating at a point on its production possibilities curve, in order to increase production of one good, the production of other goods must be:

a.   Held constant.
b.   Increased.
c.   Decreased.
d.   None of the above.

7.   If a nation is currently operating at a point inside its production possibilities curve, it:

a.   Has full employment.
b.   Has unemployed and/or inefficiently employed resources.
c.   Is operating at full potential.
d.   Must reduce the output of one good in order to produce more of another good.

8.   The law of increasing costs states that:

a.   Opportunity costs rise as more of a good is produced.
b.   Opportunity costs fall as more of a good is produced.
c.   Rising resource prices are inevitable because of scarcity.
d.   Economic growth is always associated with inflation.

9.   The law of increasing costs is the result of the fact that:

a.   Resources can be easily adapted to the production of any good.
b.   Scarcity reduces supply and increases costs.
c.   Resources are not equally adaptable to all employments.
d.   People reach a point of satiation at which they no longer purchase goods.

10. Economic growth is the process whereby the production possibilities curve shifts:

a.   Inward
b.   Outward
c.   Either inward or outward
d.   Outward, then inward

11. Points outside of the production possibilities curve are _____ in
    the _____.

    a. Attainable/short run
    b. Unattainable/short run
    c. Attainable/long run
    d. Unattainable/long run
    e. B and c

12. Production efficiency is achieved:

    a. If resources are reallocated among the production of goods and
        services and the output of one good can be increased without
        decreasing the output of other goods.
    b. If there is no waste in the production process.
    c. If resources are reallocated among the production of goods and
        services and the output of one good can be increased only by reducing
        the output of other goods.
    d. At a point within the production possibilities curve.

13. If nation A commits a larger share of its resources to capital and
    technological improvements than nation B, then over time _____ will
    realize _____ outward shifts in its production possibilities curve.

    a. Nation B/larger
    b. Nation A/smaller
    c. Nations A and B/the same
    d. Nation B/smaller

14. An individual's ability to consume goods and services depends upon:

    a. Income only.
    b. The rate of inflation.
    c. The individual's income and the prices of the goods and services
        consumed.
    d. Tastes.

15. A/An _____ is a curve indicating an individual's ability to consume
    various combinations of two goods or services over a period of time.

    a. Production possibilities curve
    b. Income curve
    c. Price line
    d. Budget line

16. The budget line shifts _____ when there is a/an _____ in income.

    a. Inward/increase
    b. Outward/decrease
    c. Inward/decrease
    d. Outward/decrease or increase

17. An individual's ability to increase the consumption of goods and services
    is _____ when the price of one or both goods _____.

    a. Increased/decrease
    b. Decreased/decrease
    c. Increased/increase
    d. Unchanged/increase unless income decreases

18. The sacrifice or opportunity cost associated with an individual's consumption of an additional good :

   a. Is the reduction in other goods consumed when the individual does not spend all of his or her income.
   b. Is the increase in other goods consumed when unused income is spent.
   c. Is the reduction in other goods consumed when an individual has no additional income.
   d. None of the above

THINK IT THROUGH

1. Explain why a nation's endowment of economic resources necessitates choices between current and future uses of resources.

2. Explain under what conditions a nation incurs an opportunity cost as it produces more of a good. How does the law of increasing cost fit into your discussion?

3. How do technology and capital expenditures improve the quality or productivity of "other" economic resources?

4. Assume that the United States contributes disproportionately more resources to the defense of Western Europe than do the other NATO allies, and as a consequence these other countries can invest a larger share of their resources in capital and other goods and services. Use production possibility curves to show both the short- and long-run consequences regarding the economies of the United States and Western Europe.

POP QUIZ   Read the news brief at the end of this chapter and answer the questions below.

1. Explain the nature of the short-run opportunity cost associated with the housing boom of the 1970s.

2. What are some of the long-run consequences of the housing boom? In other words, short-run choices affect long-run choices. Explain.

CHAPTER ANSWERS

In Brief: Chapter Summary

1. Production 2. Capital 3. Scarcity 4. Technology 5. Production possibilities curve 6. Sacrificing 7. Opportunity cost 8. Rises 9. Less 10. Larger 11. Are not 12. Unemployed 13. Inefficiently 14. Unattainable 15. Can 16. Outward 17. Current 18. Capital 19. Budget line 20. Outward 21. Increases 22. Outward 23. Inward 24. Reduction

Vocabulary Review

1. Economic resources 2. Division of labor 3. Budget line 4. Capital 5. Production possibilities curve 6. Entrepreneurship 7. Economic growth 8.

Technology 9. Labor 10. Productive efficiency 11. Natural resources 12. Law
of increasing costs

Skills Review

1. a.   Labor b. Capital c. Natural resources d. Entrepreneurship

2. a.   + b. 0 c. + d. + e. 0

3. a.

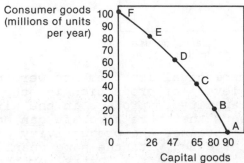

   b.   A point on the production possibilities curve represents a maximum
         level of production over a period of time for consumer and capital
         goods. At this level of production, resources are fully and
         efficiently employed.
   c.   (1) 15   (2) 18   (3) 21   (4) 26
   d.   Rise. Opportunity costs rise because in order to produce more and
         more consumer goods, increasing quantities of resources have to be
         reallocated from the capital goods industry to the consumer goods
         industry, and these resources are increasingly less adaptable to
         consumer goods production.

4. a.   A point inside the curve represents a level of production involving
         unemployed resources or inefficient production or both.
   b.   A point outside the curve is unattainable in the short run because of
         resource constraints. In the long run, however, it is possible to
         reach point B if the productivity and quantity of resources increase.

5. a.   U b. O c. O d. U e. U f. O

6. a.

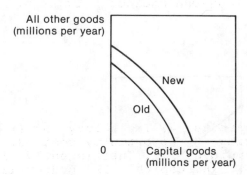

b.

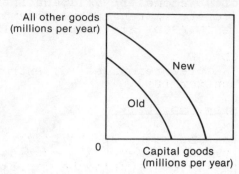

7. a. Even if capital or technological improvements were made only in the aircraft industry, the levels of production in other industries would likely increase. The capacity to produce in the aircraft industry has increased, which means that more aircraft <u>can</u> be produced than before. Since capital increases the productivity of other resources, more aircraft could be produced with the same quantity of resources previously employed in the aircraft industry, or the same number of aircraft could be produced as before but now with fewer resources. These resources, therefore,could be used elsewhere in producing other goods and services.

b.

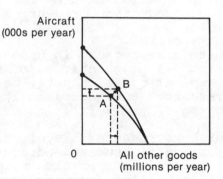

8. a.

Combination	Beer	CDs
A	20	0
B	16	1
C	12	2
D	8	3
E	4	4
F	0	5

b. Budget line

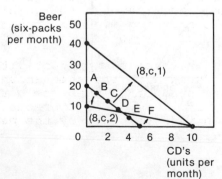

c. (1) (on figure above)
   (2) (on figure above)

9.   a.   Assume that the student's income (I) is spent in its entirety on beer (B) and compact discs (CDs). Furthermore, assume the price of beer (PB) and the price of a CD (PCD) are $2.50 and $10, respectively.

$$I = (PB)(B) + (PCD)(CD)$$

Solve the above equation for (B).

$$B = I/PB - (PCD/PB)(CD)$$

Notice that the vertical intercept of the budget line is the level of income divided by the price of beer. Also notice that the slope of the budget line is negative and equals the ratio of prices of the two goods.

b.   (1)   An increase in income will increase the intercept term or constant term in the above equation. The budget line will shift upward.

(2)   A decrease in the price of CDs and an increase in the price of beer will make the slope less negative and will decrease the intercept term. The budget line becomes flatter, with the vertical intercept decreasing.

Self-Test for Mastery

1. b 2. d 3. d 4. b 5. c 6. c 7. b 8. a 9. c 10. b 11. e 12. c 13. d 14. c 15. d 16. c 17. a 18. c

Think it Through

1.   A nation's endowment of resources, whether plentiful or limited, is a constraint to future growth. With full and efficient use of resources, a nation can produce only so much over a given period of time. Using resources today for capital means giving up the consumption of other goods today. But capital increases the future capacity to produce and also increases the productivity of economic resources. Because of this, a nation that forgoes consumption today and invests in capital will be able to consume more tomorrow.

2.   A nation incurs a sacrifice or opportunity cost associated with the use of resources when (a) there is full employment of resources and (b) efficient production of output. If this were not the case, a nation could produce more of one good without necessarily reducing the consumption of other goods by either employing its resources more fully or by more efficiently producing its output.
     At full employment and efficient production, a nation incurs rising opportunity costs if it produces more and more of a given good because of the law of increasing costs. Because resources are not completely adaptable to all uses, they must be withdrawn in increasing amounts from other industries in order to produce given quantities of the good.

3.   Both capital and technology increase the productivity of the production process. More output can be produced with the same amount of resources. A farmer with a tractor is far more productive than one with a digging stick. This is the story of American agriculture. The enormous productivity increases in the U.S. farm sector have been made possible by the mechanization of agriculture.

4.   The United States not only sacrifices output of consumer goods and
services in the short run but also sacrifices a higher rate of future economic
growth and living standards.

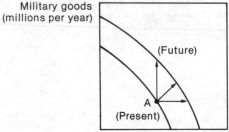

United States

Military goods
(millions per year)

(Future)

A
(Present)

0   Capital and other goods
(millions per year)

Western Europe, in contrast, is able to consume both more capital and
other goods in the short run and because of greater capital investments will
realize a faster rate of GNP growth in the future.

Western Europe

Military goods
(millions per year)

(Future)

A
(Present)

0   Capital and other goods
(millions per year)

Pop Quiz

1.   The housing market boomed in the 1970s because of distortions caused by
high marginal tax rates and inflation. It was not uncommon for a homeowner in
the 1970s to face a negative real rate of mortgage interest. Even though
family size and real median family income were falling and energy costs were
rising significantly, these distortions were significant enough relative to
these demographic and economic factors to result in not only a large increase
in the quantity of housing, but also an increase in the average size per home.
A sizable portion of the nation's savings went into housing rather than into
business capital investment. Inflation had the effect of reducing the private
after-tax return on business investment. In the short run, the additional
housing was acquired at the expense of less business investment.

2.   The short-run choice of more housing and less business investment implies
long-run consequences. A nation that underinvests in productive capital will
experience a slower rate of economic growth and lower living standards in the
future. Edwin Mills estimated the socially-optimal combination of investment
funds and concluded that the housing stock is 25% too large and other forms of
capital stock need to be increased by 12%. If the economy operated with the
socially-optimal composition of investment, Mills estimates that GNP would be
$3.606 trillion in 1983 rather than $3.278 trillion--a difference of $4,410 per
family. Thus, long-run living standards were sacrificed for short-run
consumption of additional housing.

50

More Costly Housing No Cause for Alarm

By Dwight R. Lee

Home ownership is the American dream, and a vibrant housing industry is associated with a healthy economy. Yet concern has been expressed recently that this dream is increasingly out of reach for many young Americans. A study cited in Housing Affairs Letter in March finds the homeownership rate among households in the 25-29 age bracket fell 17% between 1980 and 1987, and "finds [the] less affluent paying an increasing percentage of income for a dwindling supply of affordable housing." Yesterday, Michael Dukakis, campaigning at a housing redevelopment project in Cincinnati, spoke of "the problem of home ownership for young families."

But is less affordable housing a problem that warrants concern? Before concluding that it is, consider that homeownership was more affordable in the 1970s for reasons that were harmful to the economy then and for which we are still paying a price today. There are reasons for applauding the fact that homeownership has become a more costly dream and that the housing industry is not as robust as it was in the '70s.

Record in Housing Starts

The 1970s saw both a record number of housing starts and a steady increase in the size of houses. This occurred despite the fact that after-tax real income actually declined for the family of median income during the '70s and average family size was decreasing.

On the basis of sound economic decision-making, fewer new houses would have been constructed and those that were constructed would have been smaller. But economic circumstances in the 1970s were not conducive to sound decision-making. The housing boom can be explained by two factors that spelled gloom for the overall performance of the economy: high marginal tax rates and inflation.

Both distort economic decisions and by doing so make the economy less productive. High marginal tax rates reduce the private cost of consumption while at the same time reducing the private return on productive activities. Inflation, in addition to creating noise in the crucial allocative signals of changing relative prices, discourages commitments to long-term investments by increasing the uncertainty in future price levels. During the '70s, while reducing overall economic performance, high marginal tax rates in combination with inflation gave an artificial boost to the housing industry.

Consider being faced with a 40% marginal income-tax rate (common in the '70s), an inflation rate of 10% (exceeded at times during that decade), and a new mortgage. The interest rate on the mortgage will be about 14% (a 4% real rate plus 10% to account for inflation), and the after-tax interest rate will be 60% of that, or 8.4%. But since inflation is decreasing the value of money by 10% a year, the real after-tax interest rate is not 8.4%, but negative 1.6%. This negative interest rate serves as a tremendous subsidy to the purchase of a new house. And it is a subsidy that increases with both the inflation rate and the marginal tax rate.

During the '70s, this subsidy not only increased artificially the number of houses demanded, it also had a perverse effect on the size of houses. By any realistic standard, the size of newly constructed houses should have decreased. The average family size declined from 3.24 people in 1970 to 2.76 in 1980. The cost of home heating and cooling skyrocketed with the price of energy. And median family income, after adjusting for inflation and taxes, was $436 less in 1980 than in 1970. Nonetheless, during the 1970s the size of the average new house increased to 1,760 square feet from 1,510 square feet. Rather than expanding the nation's productive capital, Americans were putting their savings into larger houses for smaller families to be heated and cooled by increasingly costly energy.

These 1970 distortions in the housing industry are of more than just historical interest. The 1970s may be history, but we are still paying dearly for the distortions just described.

The housing industry attracts a significant percentage of the nation's saving in direct competition with other capital goods such as new plants and equipment. And while inflation and high marginal tax rates were increasing the private after-tax return on housing investment in the 1970s, they were decreasing the private after-tax return on business capital investment.

Since business capital is carried on the books at its historical cost, depreciation expense always understates the real replacement cost of capital during inflation, and therefore taxable profits are overstated. Also, the capital gains tax is assessed against increases in the nominal value of capital stock, which is always greater than increases in the real value during inflation. Again, taxable profits are overstated and investment in business capital is discouraged. So the success of the housing industry in the 1970s came at the expense of the type of investment that would have increased the productivity of the economy and meant higher incomes in the 1980s.

In a study published earlier this year, economist Edwin S. Mills estimated that if investment funds had been allocated between housing and other forms of capital investment in the proportion that maximized their combined social return, then the housing stock would have been approximately 25% smaller, and other forms of capital stock about 12% larger, than was the case in 1983. Mr. Mills also estimated that had we benefited from such an investment mix, gross national product would have been $3.606 trillion in 1983 (in 1983 dollars) instead of the $3.278 trillion actually achieved. This is a difference of about $4,410 for each family in the U.S.

It should be pointed out that Mr. Mills's study considers the effect of the distortion in investment not only over the 1970s, but also over several previous decades. But because of the high inflation rates and high marginal tax rates during the 1970s, a significant proportion of the distortion—and its adverse consequences for our current GNP—occurred in the 1970s.

Fortunately for the future productivity of the economy and for our incomes, the inflation rate was down to a little less than 5% in 1987 and marginal tax rates have been reduced significantly by the 1986 tax reform. A bias in favor of housing still exists because mortgage-interest payments remain fully deductible against taxable income. But this bias is now far less than it was in the 1970s.

Misplaced Concern

While good for the economy, lower inflation and reduced marginal tax rates have indeed increased the private cost of homeownership. This higher cost affects all home buyers, but since marginal tax rates declined more at higher income levels than at lower income levels, the increased cost is greater for higher-income families. According to a study published earlier this year by economist Theodore Crone, tax reform (assuming a 5% inflation rate and a 10.4% mortgage-interest rate) has increased the first-year cost of homeownership by 6.9% for a family with a $20,000 annual income and by 23.1% for a family with a $40,000 annual income.

It is more difficult for all young families to purchase their first home now than it was in the '70s. And when they are able to buy a home, it is more likely to be a smaller home than their counterparts were buying a decade ago. Considered in isolation this may appear to be cause for concern. But such concern is seen to be misplaced when the changes in economy that explain the higher cost of homeownership are considered. Indeed, young families are better off today than they were 10 years ago for the same reason it is more costly for them to buy that first home.

Mr. Lee is Ramsey professor of economics at the University of Georgia and a visiting professor at the Center for the Study of American Business at Washington University in St. Louis.

4

Market Transactions: Basic Supply and Demand Analysis

CHAPTER CHALLENGES

After studying your text, attending class, and completing this chapter, you should be able to:

1. Discuss the purposes and functions of markets.
2. Explain how a demand curve illustrates the law of demand and distinguish between a change in demand and a change in quantity demanded.
3. Show how a supply curve illustrates the law of supply and distinguish between a change in supply and a change in quantity supplied.
4. Describe the conditions required for market equilibrium and locate the equilibrium point on a supply and demand diagram.
5. Explain the consequences of shortages and surpluses in markets and how prices adjust in a free and unregulated competitive market to eliminate shortages or surpluses.
6. Show how changes in supply and demand affect market equilibrium.

IN BRIEF: CHAPTER SUMMARY

Fill in the blanks to summarize chapter content.

Understanding the concept of a market and the role it plays in the allocation of resources and the distribution of output is critical to an understanding of how economies function. (1)_____ (Markets, Trade publications) communicate information to buyers and sellers alike. The forces of supply and demand, which are basic to every market, interact to produce a (2)_____ (market quantity, market price) that acts as a vehicle for communicating the wants of buyers to sellers. (3)_____(Cost-benefit analysis, Supply and demand analysis) is a method of isolating the forces of supply and demand so that the factors determining market prices can be understood. This allows us to better understand the communication and rationing functions of the price system.

Demand constitutes amounts of goods and services that buyers are willing and able to buy at a given price during a given period. A (4)_____(demand schedule, demand curve) is a table of data showing the relationship between the prices of a good and the associated quantities demanded, holding all other influencing factors unchanged. A (5)_____ (demand curve, demand schedule) is a plot of the price-quantity demanded coordinates. The demand schedule and its demand curve show that price and quantity demanded are negatively related. This relationship is known as the law of (6)_____(increasing returns, demand). When there is a change in price, quantity demanded changes. This is called a (7)_____(change in demand, change in quantity demanded). A change in demand determinants other than the price of the good will shift the demand curve. A shift in the demand curve means that, at a given price, quantity demanded will either increase or decrease. This is called a (8)_____(change in demand, change in quantity demanded). Changes in demand are caused by changes in (a) income, (b) wealth, (c) the prices of related goods, (d) price expectations, (e) tastes, and (f) the number of buyers in the market.

Supply represents the quantities that sellers are willing and able to produce and make available to the market at a given price during a given period. A (9)_____(supply schedule, supply curve) is a table of data showing the relationship between the prices of a good and the associated quantities supplied by sellers, all other influences on supply remaining the same. A (10)_____(supply curve, supply schedule) is a plot of the price-quantity supplied coordinates. The relationship between price and quantity supplied is a positive one and is called the law of (11)_____ (monetary incentives, supply). A (12)_____(change in quantity supplied,change in supply) is caused by a price change. This is shown by a movement along a given supply curve. A (13)_____(change in quantity supplied, change in supply) is the result of influences other than price, such as (a) the price of inputs, (b) prices of other goods, (c) technology, (d) price expectations, and (e) the number of sellers in a market. These nonprice influences shift the supply curve.

The forces of supply and demand interact to produce a market (14)_____ (outcome, equilibrium), or state of balance, where the quantities demanded by buyers are just equal to the quantities supplied by sellers. In a state of equilibrium, buyers and sellers have no incentive to alter levels of consumption or production. It is the market (15)_____(price, quantity) that equates the quantities supplied and demanded.

A price above a market equilibrium price results in a (16)_____(shortage, surplus) because the quantity supplied at this price exceeds the quantity demanded. A price below the equilibrium price causes a (17)_____(shortage, surplus) because the quantity demanded exceeds the quantity supplied. In a competitive market, a seller tries to get rid of surpluses by (18)_____(increasing inventories, cutting prices). Falling prices will reduce surpluses. When the price falls enough to equal the market equilibrium price, the (19)_____ (shortage, surplus) is eliminated completely.

Shortages require some form of rationing. Sellers ration the limited supply of goods among competing buyers by (20)_____(increasing, decreasing) prices. But price increases reduce the quantities demanded and increase the quantities supplied, which in turn reduce the shortage. Shortages are completely eliminated when the price has risen (21)_____(above, equal to) the market equilibrium price. Market prices remain unchanged in a competitive market unless the underlying forces of supply or demand change. A change in demand, a change in supply, or a change in both supply and demand (22)_____ (can, cannot) alter the market equilibrium price and quantity.

VOCABULARY REVIEW

Write the key term from the list below next to its definition.

Key Terms

Market	Market equilibrium
Change in quantity	Quantity supplied
demanded	Demand
Supply and demand	Supply
analysis	Law of supply

Quantity demanded
Demand schedule
Law of demand
Complements
Demand curve
Surplus
Change in relative
    price
Change in demand

Supply schedule
Supply curve
Change in quantity
    supplied
Substitutes
Change in supply
Shortage
Equilibrium

Definitions

1. _____: an increase or decrease in the price of a good relative to an average of the prices of all goods.

2. _____: a graph that shows how quantity demanded varies with the price of a good.

3. _____: a table that shows how the quantity supplied of a good is related to the price.

4. _____: the quantity of a good sellers are willing and able to make available in the market over a given period at a certain price, other things being equal.

5. _____: a relationship between the price of an item and the quantity supplied by sellers.

6. _____: other things being equal, the higher the price of a good, the greater the quantity of that good sellers are willing and able to make available over a given period.

7. _____: an arrangement through which buyers and sellers meet or communicate for the purpose of trading goods or services.

8. _____: explains how prices are established in markets through competition among many buyers and sellers, and how those prices affect the quantities traded.

9. _____: attained when the price of a good adjusts so that the quantity buyers are willing and able to buy at that price is just equal to the quantity sellers are willing and able to supply.

10. _____: exists if the quantity demanded exceeds the quantity supplied of a good over a period of time.

11. _____: prevails when economic forces balance so that economic variables neither increase nor decrease.

12. _____: exists if the quantity supplied exceeds the quantity demanded of a good over a period of time.

13. _____: a change in the relationship between the price of a good and the quantity supplied in response to a supply determinant other than the price of the good.

14. _____: a change in the amount of a good buyers are willing and able to buy in response to a change in the price of the good.

15. _____: a change in the relationship between the price of a good and the quantity demanded caused by a change in a demand determinant other than the price of the good.

16. _____: goods whose use together enhances the satisfaction a consumer obtains from each.

17. _____: goods that serve a purpose similar to that of a given good.

18. _____: a graph that shows how the quantity supplied varies with the price of a good.

19. _____: other things being equal, the lower the price of a good, the greater the quantity of that good buyers are willing and able to purchase over a given period.

20. _____: a change in the amount of a good sellers are willing to sell in response to a change in the price of the good.

21. _____: a relationship between the price of an item and the quantity demanded.

22. _____: a table that shows how the quantity demanded of a good would vary with price, given all other demand determinants.

23. _____: the amount of an item the buyers are willing and able to purchase over a period at a certain price, given all other influences on their decision to buy.

SKILLS REVIEW

Concept: Demand, law of demand, changes in demand and quantity demanded

1. The following is a demand schedule for corn:

Price per Bushel	Quantity Demanded (000s bushels per week)	
	(a)	(b)
$4.00	850	_____
3.75	900	_____
3.50	950	_____
3.25	1,000	_____
3.00	1,050	_____
2.75	1,100	_____
2.50	1,150	_____

a. Plot the demand curve on the diagram below.

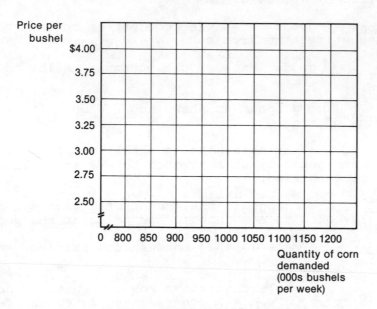

Price per bushel

b. What kind of relationship exists between the price per bushel of corn and the quantity of corn demanded?
c. Assume that the prices of other vegetables are falling relative to the price of corn. Will this cause the demand curve to shift? Why?
d. Assume that the quantity of corn demanded decreases by 50,000 bushels at every price level. Show the impact of this by completing column b above.
e. Show the impact from part d on the demand curve that you plotted in part a.

2. List six nonprice determinants of demand:

    a. _____
    b. _____
    c. _____
    d. _____
    e. _____
    f. _____

3. Indicate for each of the following if a demand curve for automobiles will shift to the right (R), left (L), or remain unchanged (U):

    a. _____ Auto prices fall
    b. _____ Price of gasoline triples
    c. _____ Incomes decrease
    d. _____ Stock market gains increase wealth
    e. _____ Public transit fares fall to zero
    f. _____ Auto price increase expected

Concept: Supply, law of supply, changes in supply and quantity supplied

4.   The following is a supply schedule for corn:

Price per Bushel	Quantity Supplied (000s of bushels per week)	
	(a)	(b)
$4.00	1600	
3.75	1400	_____
3.50	1200	_____
3.25	1000	_____
3.00	800	_____
2.75	600	_____
2.50	400	_____

   a.   Plot the supply curve on the diagram below.

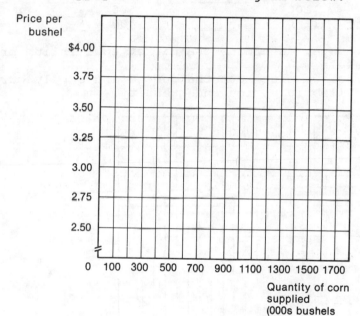

Price per bushel

$4.00
3.75
3.50
3.25
3.00
2.75
2.50

0 100 300 500 700 900 1100 1300 1500 1700

Quantity of corn
supplied
(000s bushels
per week)

   b.   Is there a positive or negative relationship between the price of
        corn and the quantity of corn supplied? Explain.
   c.   Suppose a serious drought reduces corn output at each price by
        100,000 bushels. Show the impact in column b above by completing the
        table.
   d.   Plot the new supply curve from column b on the diagram from part a.

5.   List five nonprice determinants of supply:

   a.   _____
   b.   _____
   c.   _____
   d.   _____
   e.   _____

6.   Which of the following will cause the supply curve for hamburgers to shift
     to the right (R), left (L), or remain unchanged (U)?

   a.   _____ Increase in the price of hamburger meat
   b.   _____ Increase in the price of hamburgers

c. _____ Increase in the price of chicken nuggets
d. _____ Introduction of new cost-saving technology
in the hamburger industry

Concept: Market equilibrium price and quantity; shortages and surpluses

7. The table below contains the price, quantity supplied, and quantity demanded data from column a of questions 1 and 4.

Price per Bushel	Quantity Demanded		Quantity Supplied	
	(000s of bushels per year)			
	(a)	(b)	(c)	(d)
$4.00	850		1600	
3.75	900	_____	1400	_____
3.50	950	_____	1200	_____
3.25	1000	_____	1000	_____
3.00	1050	_____	800	_____
2.75	1100	_____	600	_____
2.50	1150	_____	400	_____

a. From the table above, determine the market equilibrium price and quantity in bushels.
b. On the diagram below, plot both the demand and supply curves. Identify the equilibrium price and quantity.

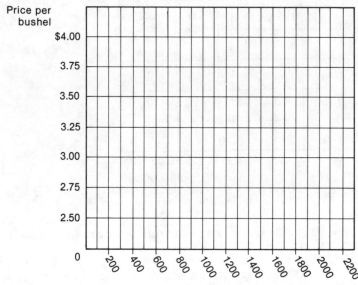

Quantity of corn demanded and supplied
(000s of bushels per week)

c. At a price of $3.75, a _____ exists in the amount of _____ because quantity demanded is _____ than quantity supplied.
d. At a price of $2.75, a _____ exists in the amount of _____ because quantity demanded is _____ than quantity supplied.
e. What is meant by the statement that competitive markets are self-equilibrating?

Concept: Changes in supply and demand and market equilibrium

8.   Referring to the supply and demand schedules in question 7 above:

   a.   Suppose that an increase in income causes the demand for corn to increase by 250,000 bushels at each price. Show the change in question 7, column b. Plot the new demand curve on the diagram in question 7.

   b.   The market equilibrium price has _____ from $_____ to $_____. Market equilibrium output has _____ from _____ bushels to _____ bushels.

   c.   Suppose that because of excellent weather, corn production increases at every price by 500,000 bushels. Show the change by completing column d from question 7. Plot the new supply curve on the diagram in question 7.

   d.   Comparing the original equilibrium--demand curve a and supply curve c--to the new equilibrium with supply curve d, market equilibrium price has _____ from $_____ to $_____. Market quantity has _____ from _____ bushels to _____ bushels.

   e.   Comparing the original equilibrium--demand curve a and supply curve c--to a new equilibrium with demand curve b and supply curve d, market equilibrium price has _____ from $_____ to $_____ and market quantity has _____ from _____ to _____ bushels.

9.   Indicate below if the market price and quantity of concert tickets increases (+), decreases (-), or is indeterminate (0):

		Price	Quantity
a.	Stock market losses reduce wealth	_____	_____
b.	Income increases	_____	_____
c.	Season ticket prices are expected to rise	_____	_____
d.	Musicians union wins large pay increase	_____	_____
e.	Price of movie tickets falls	_____	_____
f.	Population migrating to an area increases	_____	_____

10.   Advanced Question. Let the following equations represent demand and supply curves for some good:

   Demand curve: $Qd = a - bP$
   Supply curve: $Qs = c + dP$

              where   a, b, c, and d are positive constants
                         Qd = quantity demanded
                         Qs = quantity supplied
                         P = price

   a.   Solve the above equations for the market equilibrium price.
   b.   Solve for the equilibrium quantity.
   c.   Interpret the equations for price and quantity. What causes price or quantity to rise or fall?

SELF-TEST FOR MASTERY

Select the best answer.

1.   In a free and unregulated competitive economy:

   a.   Wants are communicated to producers by the purchase orders of
        wholesalers.
   b.   Wants of buyers are communicated to sellers through the determination
        of prices in markets.
   c.   Sellers use market survey instruments to determine what and how much
        to produce.
   d.   Markets play an insignificant role.

2.   The quantities of goods that buyers are willing and able to purchase at a
     specific price over a period of time, other influences held unchanged, is
     a definition for:

   a.   Quantity demanded.
   b.   Supply.
   c.   Total sales.
   d.   Demand.

3.   The demand _____ is a table of price and quantity demanded data in
     which the ceteris paribus assumption is employed. The _____ is a
     plot of that data.

   a.   Table/scatter diagram
   b.   Schedule/marginal cost curve
   c.   Curve/schedule
   d.   Schedule/demand curve

4.   The law of demand states that, other things being the same:

   a.   Price and income are positively related.
   b.   Income and sales are positively related.
   c.   Price and quantity demanded are positively related.
   d.   Price and quantity demanded are inversely related.

5.   Which of the following will not cause a change in demand?

   a.   Change in income
   b.   Change in the price of the good in question
   c.   Change in the prices of related goods, such as complements or
        substitutes
   d.   Expectation of higher prices

6.   If two goods are substitutes and the price of one good increases, the
     demand for the other good will:

   a.   Not change.
   b.   Increase.
   c.   Not be related.
   d.   Decrease.

7.   If two goods are complementary goods and the price of one good increases,
     the demand for the other will:

   a.   Not change.
   b.   Increase.

c.   Not be related.
d.   Decrease.

8.   If a good is a normal good, an increase in income will:

a.   Increase supply.
b.   Decrease demand.
c.   Increase demand.
d.   Decrease supply.

9.   The quantities of a good that sellers are willing and able to produce and make available to the market at a specific price over a given period, other things being constant, is a definition of:

a.   Demand.
b.   Equilibrium.
c.   Demand curve.
d.   Supply.

10. The law of supply states that, other influences being unchanged:

a.   Price and quantity demanded are inversely related.
b.   Price and quantity supplied are inversely related.
c.   Income and quantity supplied are unrelated.
d.   Price and quantity supplied are positively related.

11. A change in quantity supplied can be caused by a change in

a.   Price.
b.   Income.
c.   Technology.
d.   Price of inputs.

12. A shift in a supply curve is known as a:

a.   Supply shift.
b.   Change in quantity supplied.
c.   Rotation.
d.   Change in supply.

13. Which of the following will not cause a leftward shift in the supply curve?

a.   Decrease in input prices
b.   Increase in the prices of other goods that could be produced with the same resources and technology
c.   Expectation of lower product prices
d.   Decrease in the number of sellers

14. Market equilibrium occurs when:

a.   The forces of supply and demand oppose each other.
b.   The forces of price and quantity oppose each other.
c.   A market price just equates quantity demanded and quantity supplied.
d.   A market quantity just equates quantity supplied and quantity demanded.

15. A price above the market equilibrium price results in:

a.   A shortage.
b.   Inflation.

c.   Excess demand.
d.   A surplus.

16. A price below the market equilibrium price results in:

a.   A shortage.
b.   Inflation.
c.   Insufficient demand.
d.   A surplus.

17. An increase in the demand for a good will _____ price and _____ quantity.

a.   Decrease/decrease
b.   Increase/decrease
c.   Increase/increase
d.   Decrease/increase

18. A decrease in supply of a good will _____ price and _____ quantity.

a.   Decrease/decrease
b.   Increase/decrease
c.   Increase/increase
d.   Decrease/increase

19. An increase in both demand and supply will _____ price and _____ quantity.

a.   Decrease/ decrease
b.   Have an indeterminate effect on/increase
c.   Increase/increase
d.   Increase/have an indeterminate effect on

20. If the price of movie tickets increases significantly, then the price of VCRs will probably _____ and the market quantity of VCRs will _____.

a.   Increase/decrease
b.   Increase/increase
c.   Decrease/decrease
d.   Decrease/increase

THINK IT THROUGH

1.   A market economy is a type of economy that relies on the market to .... (Complete the statement as thoroughly as you can.)

2.   Use supply and demand analysis to assess the impact of the drought that occurred in the farm belt in the Spring and Summer of 1988.
     a.   Discuss the impact of the drought on the market for corn.
     b.   Discuss the probable impact on feedlots that use corn as feed.

3.   If a market is currently in equilibrium and an increase in demand occurs, what happens to the market price? Explain.

4.   If the price of golf course greens fees increases nationally, using supply and demand analysis, discuss the impact on the market for golf balls.

62

5.   Suppose that you operate a dry cleaning firm in a small city and you and the other dry cleaners are earning handsome profits. Because of the profit potential, a national dry cleaning firm enters the area and opens several new dry cleaners. Assess the impact on the market for dry cleaning in this city.

POP QUIZ   Read the news brief at the end of this chapter and answer the question below.

Identify the forces affecting the supply and demand for gasoline and explain the probable impact on market price and quantity.

CHAPTER ANSWERS

In Brief: Chapter Summary

1. Markets 2. Market price 3. Supply and demand analysis 4. Demand schedule 5. Demand curve 6. Demand 7. Change in quantity demanded 8. Change in demand 9. Supply schedule 10. Supply curve 11. Supply 12. Change in quantity supplied 13. Change in supply 14. Equilibrium 15. Price 16. Surplus 17. Shortage 18. Cutting prices 19. Surplus 20. Increasing 21. Equal to 22. Can

Vocabulary Review

1. Change in relative price 2. Demand curve 3. Supply schedule 4. Supply 5. Quantity supplied 6. Demand schedule 7. Market 8. Supply and demand analysis 9. Market equilibrium 10. Shortage 11. Equilibrium 12. Surplus 13. Change in supply 14. Change in quantity demanded 15. Change in demand 16. Complements 17. Substitutes 18. Supply curve 19. Law of demand 20. Change in quantity supplied 21. Quantity demanded 22. Demand schedule 23. Demand

Skills Review

1.   a.

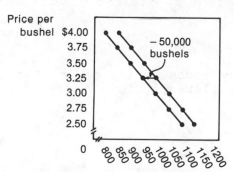

Price per bushel

Quantity of corn demanded (000s bushels per week)

   b.   Negative or inverse
   c.   If other vegetables are considered substitutes for corn, the demand for corn falls and the demand curve shifts leftward as the prices of other vegetables are falling.

d. e. The demand curve shifts leftward as
   (b)   shown in the diagram above in part
   800   a.
   850
   900
   950
  1000
  1050
  1100

2.   a. Income b. Wealth c. Prices of substitutes and complements d. Price
     expectations e. Tastes f. Number of buyers

3.   a. U b. L c. L d. R e. L f. R

4.   a.

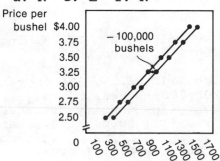

     Price per
     bushel $4.00
            3.75
            3.50
            3.25
            3.00
            2.75
            2.50

          0 100 300 500 700 900 1100 1300 1500 1700
                 Quantity of corn supplied
                 (000s bushels per week)

     b.   Positive, higher prices increase the willingness and ability of
          suppliers to increase production.
     c.   d. The supply curve shifts leftward as
          (b)   shown in the diagram above in part
          1500   a.
          1300
          1100
           900
           700
           500
           300

5.   a. Prices of other goods b. Prices of inputs c. Technology d. Price
     expectations e. Number of sellers

6.   a. L b. U c. L d. R

7.   a. $3.25, 1,000,000

     b.

     Price per
     bushel $4.00
            3.75
            3.50
            3.25
            3.00
            2.75
            2.50

          0 200 400 600 800 1000 1200 1400 1600 1800 2000 2200
                 Quantity of corn
                 demanded and supplied
                 (000s of bushels

64

c. Surplus, 500,000 bushels, less
d. Shortage, 500,000 bushels, greater
e. Competitive markets are self-equilibrating because market forces will eliminate shortages and surpluses. Shortages are eliminated as market prices rise and surpluses are eliminated as suppliers lower prices to sell excess inventory.

8. a. (b)
      1100
      1150
      1200
      1250
      1300
      1350
      1400

   b. Increased, $3.25, $3.50, increased, 1,000,000, 1,200,000

   c. (d)
      2100
      1900
      1700
      1500
      1300
      1100
       900

   d. Decreased, $3.25, $2.75, increased, 1,000,000, 1,100,000

   e. Decreased, $3.25, $3, increased, 1,000,000, 1,300,000

9.

	Price	Quantity
a.	-	-
b.	+	+
c.	+	+
d.	+	-
e.	-	-
f.	+	+

10. Market equilibrium requires that Qd = Qs. Setting the supply and demand curves equal to each other:

$$a - bP = c + dP$$

and solving for P, the market equilibrium price, gives:

a. $P = (a - c)/(d + b)$

Substituting this expression for P into either the demand or supply equation and solving for Q, the market equilibrium quantity, yields:

b. $Q = (ad + bc)/(d + b)$

c. Q is positive and P must be positive. P is positive if the intercept of the demand curve a exceeds the intercept of the supply curve c. This always is expected to be the case. Changes in the nonprice determinants of supply and demand influence the supply and demand equations by changing the value of the intercept terms, a or c. For instance, an increase in income would increase a assuming the good is a normal good. If it is an inferior good, the increase in income will reduce a. As can be seen from the equations above, an increase in a will increase P and Q. A decrease in a will decrease P and Q. An increase in c caused by a nonprice determinant of supply causes P to decrease and Q to increase.

Self-Test for Mastery

1. b 2. d 3. d 4. d 5. b 6. b 7. d 8. c 9. d 10. d 11. a 12. d 13. a 14. c 15. d 16. a 17. c 18. b 19. b 20. b

Think it Through

1.   A market economy is a type of economy that relies on the market to allocate resources and distribute output. The impersonal interaction of the forces of supply and demand communicate the wishes of consumers to sellers via the market price. Changes in demand alter the price, and it is the change in price that causes a supplier to respond by altering production. As producers alter levels of production, they alter their levels of employment of resources. Thus markets determine what is to be produced and in what quantities. Resources flow to markets experiencing increases in quantity and away from markets experiencing decreases in production. Output is distributed based upon a buyer's ability to pay. Other things being constant, rising market prices reduce the ability to pay, whereas decreases in market prices increase the ability to pay.

2.   a. As is shown in the diagram below, the drought reduces the supply of corn increasing the price per bushel of corn and reducing the market quantity of corn.

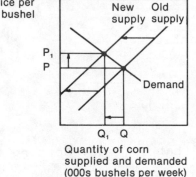

Price per bushel

Quantity of corn
supplied and demanded
(000s bushels per week)

     b.   If corn is an input to feedlot operations and the price of corn is increasing, the supply of feedlot services will decrease, causing the price of those services to increase and the quantity of feedlot services to fall.

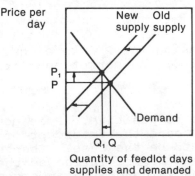

Price per day

Quantity of feedlot days
supplies and demanded

3.   If demand increases, then at the current market price there is a shortage because quantity demanded exceeds quantity supplied. In order to ration the limited number of goods or services among many buyers, the price of the good or service is increased. Increases in price reduce quantity demanded but increase quantity supplied. This in turn reduces the shortage. As long as a shortage exists, the rationing function of prices implies that prices will continue to rise. Prices will no longer increase when the shortage is eliminated. The shortage no longer exists at the new market equilibrium.

4.   Greens fees and golf balls are complementary goods. If the price of greens fees increases, the demand for golf balls will decrease. As can be seen in the figure below, a decrease in the demand for golf balls reduces the market price and quantity.

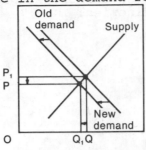

Price per package

Old demand

Supply

P_1
P

New demand

O Q_1Q

Quantity of golf balls supplied and demanded (millions of packages)

5.   If several new dry cleaners open for business, the local market supply of dry cleaning services will increase. This causes a decrease in the price of dry cleaning services, but an increase in total market quantity.

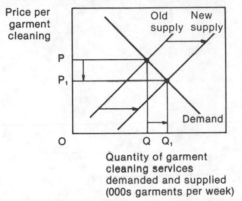

Price per garment cleaning

Old supply   New supply

P

P_1

Demand

O Q Q_1

Quantity of garment cleaning services demanded and supplied (000s garments per week)

Pop Quiz

Gasoline prices have remained "firm" in spite of a $4 decline in the price of crude oil. In the long run, the price of crude oil is an important determinant of gasoline prices, but in the short run other forces affecting the supply of and demand for gasoline may be changing and thus offsetting the effect of lower crude prices on gasoline prices. On the demand side of the gasoline market, demand is expected to increase 2% in 1988 in part because many states raised speed limits, resulting in increased fuel consumption. Further, a decline in the international value of the dollar made foreign vacations more expensive relative to domestic vacations. The American Automobile Association projected that 10 million more automobile vacations would be taken in 1988 than in 1987.

On the supply side of the gasoline market, the summer drought reduced shipments of gasoline on the Mississippi River by 50,000 barrels per day. Gasoline barges required several more days between river terminals than normal. Coastal refineries had to purchase and bring in fresh water because river levels were not high enough to prevent the intrusion of salt water. Several refineries experienced breakdowns. Refineries were able to produce only 294 million gallons daily at capacity and quantity demanded was 319 million gallons per day. The number of refineries has fallen by about one-third from 213 in the early 1980s. Finally, the yield of gasoline per barrel of crude has fallen because of the government's ban on the use of lead additives.

In short, demand is strong and expected to grow, but supply is constrained-- there are bottlenecks in delivery and refineries are operating at capacity. These forces would normally result in an increase in market price and in time market quantity, but the decline in crude prices and the 11% increase in the stocks of crude oil have been an offsetting factor. Also, the industry is becoming less competitive; 80% of all gasoline used in the U.S. is produced by just 15 refineries. Major oil companies have been eliminating the independent retail segment of the market and have increasingly marketed and sold at retail the gasoline output of their refineries.

Array of Forces Bolstering The Pump Price of Gasoline

By Allanna Sullivan
Staff Reporter of The Wall Street Journal

For years, the cost of a road trip to, say, Yellowstone National Park has been largely determined by the councils of OPEC. But not this summer.

Long-term changes in the gasoline business—as well as some special, short-term factors—have drastically altered the dynamics of pricing in the more than $150 billion-a-year gasoline market. "Things aren't crystal clear anymore," says Thomas Burns, manager of economics at Chevron Corp. "The underlying reasons for price moves are more obscure."

The effect, however, is clear enough: Retail gasoline prices have remained firm, despite depressed prices for crude oil. In the long run, of course, the price of crude will continue to control whether gasoline prices rise or fall. But this summer, at least, "the gasoline market is marching to its own drummer," says Trilby Lundberg, whose Lundberg Letter tracks retail gasoline prices across the country.

Gasoline prices currently average around $1 a gallon nationwide, up about one cent from a year ago, even though the spot-market price of crude has dropped more than $4 a barrel in the same period, to $15.45 as of Friday. What's more, U.S. gasoline inventories have fallen sharply in recent weeks, to almost 10% below last year's levels, while stocks of crude oil are nearly 11% higher than they were a year ago. (Last week's explosion of a huge North Sea oil platform could help to shrink those inventories somewhat by eliminating for a time 300,000 barrels a day of production from the glutted crude market.)

The Role of Big Oil

One reason for the resilience of gasoline prices, some independent marketers say, is that the major oil companies' grip on the market is growing tighter in many areas. The majors can exclude costly middlemen by refining and selling their own products, in addition to producing the crude from which they're made. With their lower costs and deeper pockets, the major companies have been gobbling up larger chunks of re-

gional markets at a time when independent station owners and marketers are abandoning their businesses because of slim profit margins.

Steven Riggins, whose family runs 16 gas stations in New Jersey, says half of the independent gasoline wholesalers in his market have dropped out in just the past year. As a result, he notes, he's stuck with buying more often from major companies, and pricing is less competitive. "There's definitely not the pick anymore," he says.

Demand, which averaged 7.2 million barrels a day in 1987 and is expected to jump a hefty 2% this year, is also bolstering gasoline prices. Even as the price creeps up, gasoline remains a bargain in the minds of most U.S. motorists. Only five years ago, regular unleaded in such areas as New York City cost $1.24 a gallon, compared with a top price there of $1.07 a gallon today. And with many states abolishing the 55-mile-an-hour speed limit, autos are soaking up more fuel.

Moreover, the declining value of the U.S. dollar is promoting more domestic vacations while attracting tourists from overseas. The American Automobile Association expects Americans to take 10 million more driving vacations this year than the 243 million taken last year. Through May, the Automobile Club of New York had fielded nearly 120 million requests for highway-travel information, up 7% from a year ago. "Our branches have never been so crowded," says a club spokesman.

The supply side, too, is keeping gasoline prices strong. On a regional basis, a number of special factors are tipping the balance against the consumer. For one thing, the delivery each day of at least 50,000 barrels of gasoline along the Mississippi River has been slowed because of drought conditions in that area. The tugboat Amoco Missouri River, for instance, is spending 15 days rather than the usual five to push its gasoline barges between two terminals.

Another drought-related problem: Low river levels are permitting saltwater to reach farther north in Louisiana. This has forced some coastal refineries to use

barges, at great expense, to bring in the fresh water needed for their operations.

Meanwhile, a spate of breakdowns and maintenance stoppages has caused at least five major refineries to cut back on gasoline production in recent weeks. The explosion in May of Shell Oil Co.'s huge Norco, La., refinery alone took 130,000 barrels of gasoline a day off the market. "The Shell explosion sure hasn't helped," says Ted Eck, chief economist for Amoco Corp.

Indeed, even while operating nearly flat out last month, U.S. refineries were able to supply only about 294 million gallons of gasoline daily—against demand of 319 million gallons a day. The shortfall was filled from inventories and through imports from Venezuela, Brazil and Canada.

Fewer Refineries

A broader factor in the production squeeze is that the number of refineries in the U.S. has dwindled by almost a third, to 213, since the abolition earlier this decade of oil price controls, which virtually assured refiners of a profit. Of the survivors, no more than 15 provide 80% of the gasoline used by U.S. motorists, says Vic Rasheed, executive director of Service Station Dealers of America, a Washington-based trade group.

As refining capacity has shrunk, so, too, has the yield of gasoline from a barrel of crude, thanks to a government ban on using lead additives to boost octane. This problem is likely to become only more acute as motorists clamor for greater quantities of high-octane premium gasoline to fuel increasingly popular high-performance automobiles.

"The industry is producing (gasoline) at close to sustainable capacity already," says Rodger W. Murtaugh, vice president of operations, planning and transportation for Amoco. He calls current gasoline supplies "tight but manageable."

Mr. Burns, the Chevron economist, says similarly that, after years of glut, gasoline supplies are in "fairly good balance." But this, he adds, means "any accumulation of small things can tip that balance."

5

Using Supply and Demand Analysis

CHAPTER CHALLENGES

After studying your text, attending class, and completing this chapter, you should be able to:

1. Demonstrate how market equilibrium prices deal with the problem of scarcity by rationing goods and services and explain why prices would be zero for nonscarce goods.
2. Explain how supply and demand conditions affect the price and sales potential for new products.
3. Show how wages and interest are determined in competitive markets.
4. Use supply and demand analysis to show how government control of prices in competitive markets can result in shortages or surpluses.
5. Discuss nonprice rationing systems and show how these alternatives work when the rationing function of prices in markets is impaired.

IN BRIEF: CHAPTER SUMMARY

Fill in the blanks to summarize chapter content.

Supply and demand analysis is a useful tool for analyzing personal, business, and social problems and issues. It shows the importance of prices in the allocation of resources. Prices help us deal with the problem of scarcity in both the allocation of resources and the distribution of output. Do prices have a role when scarcity does not exist? Goods in abundant supply such as air are called (1)_____ (essential commodities, nonscarce goods) because there is no positive price for which quantity demanded exceeds quantity supplied. If a positive price is not possible, markets do not develop. Markets develop only when positive prices are possible.

But even at positive prices, a market may not develop if the minimum price required by sellers exceeds the maximum price that buyers are willing and able to pay for the first unit of output. A market for new products can only develop when demand and supply have reached a point where the (2)_____(maximum, minimum) price buyers are willing and able to pay for the first unit of output exceeds the (3)_____(maximum, minimum) price sellers are willing to take for that unit.

In addition to the markets for goods and services, supply and demand analysis can be used to assess changes in competitive labor and credit markets. The price per unit of labor is called the (4)_____(labor cost, wage). When the supply of labor equals the demand, there is a market wage and quantity of labor employed. Everyone who wants to work at that wage is employed. If the demand for the product produced by that labor increases, the demand for labor by employers will likewise increase. This causes the wage to (5)_____(rise, fall) and the quantity of labor employed to (6)_____(decrease, increase). In a recession, as the demand for goods and services falls, the demand for labor declines, causing both wages and employment to also (7)_____(rise, fall).

Changes in the demand and supply of loanable funds determine interest rate movements. In an economic expansion, individuals, businesses, and government as a group borrow more. Interest rates (8)_____(rise, fall) as the demand for loanable funds increases. If the supply of loanable funds increases, say as a result of an increase in savings by both businesses and individuals, interest rates will (9)_____(rise, fall) and (10)_____(more, less) credit will be extended by lenders.

Prices are not always allowed to perform the rationing function. Society will often sanction government price controls as an attempt to aid certain interest groups, such as farmers, unskilled workers, and low-income renters and borrowers. (11)_____ (Price ceilings, Price floors) are government-mandated prices that are set below market equilibrium prices. A price below the market price causes (12)_____(surpluses, shortages). Rent controls, while helping those fortunate enough to pay controlled rents, cause (13)_____(surpluses, shortages) of low-income housing and reduce the incentive of landlords to maintain properties. Usury laws that prevent interest rates from rising to their market levels, while benefiting those people able to obtain the regulated credit, will cause a (14)_____ (surplus, shortage) of loanable funds. The least credit worthy (and also the lowest income) members of society will have difficulty finding credit. Price ceilings will cause (15)_____ (surpluses, shortages) only when the regulated price is (16)_____(below, above) the market price. If market interest rates were to fall, for example, below the usury ceiling, there would be no (17)_____(shortage, surplus) of loanable funds.

When shortages develop there must be a way to allocate the limited goods and services among the buyers. A market system relies on prices to do this. But with price ceilings, prices are not allowed to perform that function. Waiting in line, eligibility criteria, and ration stamps are three methods of nonprice rationing. All three are less efficient than prices in responding to shortages. There will still be those people willing and able to pay prices above the controlled price. In response to this potential market, illegal or (18)_____ (new markets, black markets) develop.

(19)_____(Price ceilings, Price floors) are controlled prices that are set above the market price. Prices above market equilibrium prices cause (20)_____(surpluses, shortages). Whereas prices fall to eliminate the surplus, other means have to be used to deal with surpluses, such as with agricultural price-support programs. Farmers either have to be rewarded to reduce plantings or the surpluses have to be purchased, stored, and distributed by government. Resources that could have been used elsewhere in the economy are being used to eliminate or deal with surpluses that would have been efficiently eliminated by a functioning price system. Although farmers as a special interest group benefit, consumers lose in that they pay (21)_____(lower, higher) prices, and the allocation of resources in the economy is (22)_____(less, more) efficient.

Minimum wage laws set minimum wages at a level above the market wage in most labor markets. The intent of such legislation is to increase the income of the poorest members of society, those individuals who also happen to have the lowest skill levels. But as was the case with agricultural price supports, (23)_____(surpluses, shortages) develop. The unemployment rate among the unskilled is (24)_____(lower, higher). The minimum wage benefits those lucky enough to find employment at that wage, but causes (25)_____(more, less) unemployment in that segment of society that can least afford to be unemployed.

Price controls distort the economy. They benefit some at the expense of others and prohibit a competitive economy from efficiently rationing resources. If the motives underlying price controls are socially desirable, society would gain if methods other than price controls could be employed to make certain interest groups better off without impairing the functioning of a competitive economy.

VOCABULARY REVIEW

Write the key term from the list below next to its definition.

Key Terms

Nonscarce good   Price ceiling
Wages   Nonprice rationing
Credit   Black market
Interest   Price floor

Definitions

1. _____: a good for which the quantity demanded does not exceed the quantity supplied at a zero price.

2. _____: establishes a maximum price that can legally be charged for a good or service.

3. _____: the price paid for labor services.

4. _____: the price for the use of funds, expressed as a percentage per dollar of funds borrowed.

5. _____: a minimum price established by law.

6. _____: a market in which sellers sell goods to buyers for more than the legal prices.

7. _____: the use of loanable funds supplied by lenders to borrowers, who agree to pay back the funds borrowed, according to an agreed-upon schedule.

8. _____: a device that distributes available goods and services on a basis other than willingness to pay.

SKILLS REVIEW

Concept: The determination of wages and interest rates in competitive markets

1. You are a manager of a business and you are trying to decide if you should borrow funds for plant expansion today at the current interest rate of 12%. The morning newspaper reports that the Federal Reserve System has announced that within the next month it will begin to expand the funds that banks have on hand to extend credit.

a. Show the impact on the supply of loanable funds curve in the diagram below.

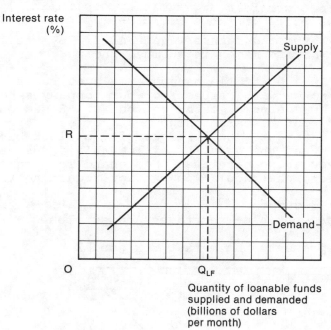

Interest rate (%)

R

O   Q_LF

Quantity of loanable funds
supplied and demanded
(billions of dollars
per month)

b. How will your analysis of future interest rates influence your decision to borrow today?

2. You are a college sophomore trying to decide if you should major in mechanical engineering. Employability and income prospects are important considerations in your choice. As shown in the diagram below, the market for engineers is currently producing high entry market wages.

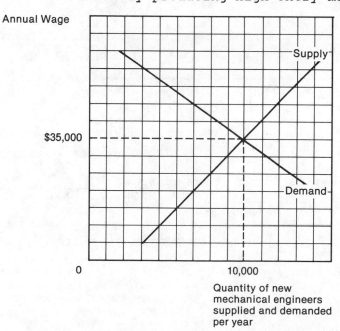

Annual Wage

$35,000

0   10,000

Quantity of new
mechanical engineers
supplied and demanded
per year

a. If you and thousands of other college students are induced by the high entry wages to become majors in engineering, in time the supply

73

of engineers will _____. Show the future supply curve on the diagram above.

b. Entry wages in the future would _____, and the total employment of engineers would _____.

c. How might these expected future wages and employment levels influence your decision today to major in engineering?

3. <u>Advanced Question</u>. As a portfolio manager you must react to anticipated changes in interest rates with respect to your company's holding of financial assets such as stocks, cash, and bonds. Based on the current interest rate of 10%, our research shows that for each one percentage point change in the interest rate, the quantity of loanable funds supplied changes by $2 billion and the quantity of loanable funds demanded changes by $3 billion. If you anticipate that the demand for loanable funds will increase by $5 billion, what would you predict regarding the future rate of interest?

Concept: Government price controls--shortages and surpluses

4. The diagram below represents the market for good X.

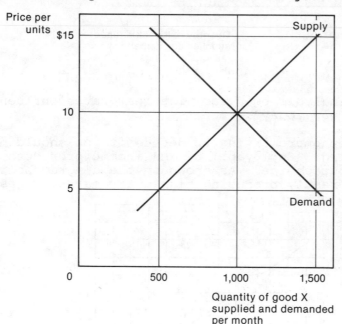

a. The market price is $_____, and the market quantity equals _____ units of X.

b. If a price ceiling is established at $5, a _____ would exist in the amount of _____ units. Show on the diagram above the impact of this price ceiling.

c. If a price floor is set at $15, a _____ would exist in the amount of _____ units. Show this on the graph above.

5.   Given the market for unskilled labor in the diagram below:

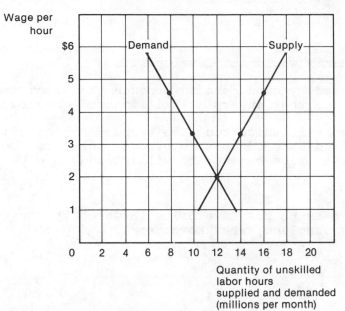

Wage per hour

Quantity of unskilled
labor hours
supplied and demanded
(millions per month)

a.   The market wage and level of employment equals $_____ and
     _____ hours, respectively.
b.   A minimum wage is now established at $3.35 per hour.
     (1)   Show on the graph above.
     (2)   Wages _____ from $_____ to $_____ and
           employment _____ from _____ hours to
           _____ hours.
c.   What would happen if the minimum wage increased from $3.35 to $4.70
     per hour?
     (1)   Show on the above graph.
     (2)   Wages _____ from $_____ to $_____ and
           employment _____ from _____ hours to
           _____ hours.

Concept: **Nonprice rationing systems**

6.   List three forms of nonprice rationing:

     a.   _____
     b.   _____
     c.   _____

Select the best answer.

1. Markets for new products would not develop if:

   a. The price required by producers to produce the first unit of output exceeded the price that buyers are willing and able to pay for that first unit.
   b. Profits exceeded that which could be earned on financial assets.
   c. The price required by producers to produce the first unit of output was less than the price buyers are willing and able to pay for the first unit.
   d. None of the above

2. Goods for which there is no positive price in which the quantity demanded exceeds the quantity supplied, are known as:

   a. Scarce goods.
   b. Normal goods.
   c. Inferior goods.
   d. Nonscarce goods.

3. An important function of prices in competitive markets is:

   a. The rationing function.
   b. To ensure that producers make profits.
   c. To eliminate any unemployment.
   d. To communicate to buyers the wishes of sellers.

4. In a competitive labor market, wages are determined:

   a. By buyers.
   b. By unions.
   c. By sellers.
   d. By the forces of supply and demand.

5. An increase in the demand for labor by businesses _____ wages and _____ employment.

   a. Increases/decreases
   b. Decreases/decreases
   c. Increases/increases
   d. Decreases/increases

6. If because of a recession the demand for loanable funds decreases, what would happen to market interest rates and the quantity of credit extended?

   a. Interest rates would increase and the quantity of credit would decrease.
   b. Interest rates would decrease and the quantity of credit would not change.
   c. Interest rates would not change but the quantity of credit would fall.
   d. Both interest rates and the quantity of credit would decline.

7. Usury laws that prevent interest rates from rising to market levels are called:

   a. Monetary regulations.

b.   Price ceilings.
c.   Price floors.
d.   Rationing methods.

8.   Rents controls:

a.   Are price ceilings.
b.   Cause shortages of low-income housing.
c.   Result in the deterioration of low-income housing through the lack of maintenance.
d.   All of the above.

9.   The minimum wage law is an example of:

a.   An employment enhancement strategy.
b.   A price ceiling.
c.   A price floor.
d.   A well-designed policy intended to reduce teenage unemployment.

10. Price ceilings cause:

a.   No change in market quantities.
b.   Shortages.
c.   Quantity supplied to increase.
d.   Surpluses.

11. Price floors cause:

a.   No change in market quantities.
b.   Shortages.
c.   Quantity demanded to increase.
d.   Surpluses.

12. Agricultural price supports:

a.   Benefit farmers.
b.   Harm consumers.
c.   Require the use of scarce resources to deal with surpluses.
d.   All of the above

13. If in some labor markets the market wage for unskilled labor exceeds the minimum wage:

a.   Unemployment would result.
b.   Wages would rise.
c.   The minimum wage law would not have an adverse impact on unemployment.
d.   Wages would fall.

14. Which of the following cannot be considered true regarding price controls?

a.   Some people within special interest groups gain.
b.   Some people within the targeted special interest groups may actually lose.
c.   Resources are more efficiently used in the economy.
d.   Resources are less efficiently used in the economy.

15. Which of the following is not a nonprice form of rationing?

a.   Grouped staging
b.   Waiting in line

c.   Ration stamps
d.   Eligibility criteria

16. Price ceilings create an environment conducive to the development of:

a.   New products.
b.   Black markets.
c.   Higher employment.
d.   A saving ethic.

THINK IT THROUGH

1.   Discuss the importance of the price system in a market-based economy.

2.   Discuss how interest rates are determined in a competitive market for loanable funds. Identify the gainers and losers from usury laws. Under what conditions would the usury laws be ineffective? If it is socially desirable to make credit available at below-market interest rates, what are other ways to benefit the targeted interest group without resulting in as much economic inefficiency as usury laws.

3.   In 1988 Democrats in Congress began a push to increase the minimum wage from its present level of $3.35 per hour to around $5 per hour. Identify the likely gainers and losers. If it is socially desirable to increase the incomes of the unskilled beyond the levels that would prevail in a competitive labor market, what are other ways of doing this so that unskilled workers can be better off without causing as much inefficiency as would be the case with price controls?

4.   In the early 1970s, President Nixon installed a series of wage and price controls. Prices were temporarily frozen on all goods and services. The supply of and demand for gasoline put upward pressure on gasoline prices, but these prices were temporarily controlled. In effect, the price freeze acted as a price ceiling. What do you think occurred in the gasoline market? Explain.

CHAPTER ANSWERS

In Brief: Chapter Summary

1. Nonscarce goods 2. Maximum 3. Minimum 4. Wage 5. Rise 6. Increase 7. Fall 8. Rise 9. Fall 10. More 11. Price ceilings 12. Shortages 13. Shortages 14. Shortage 15. Shortages 16. Below 17. Shortage 18. Black markets 19. Price floors 20. Surpluses 21. Higher 22. Less 23. Surpluses 24. Higher 25. More

Vocabulary Review

1. Nonscarce good 2. Price ceiling 3. Wages 4. Interest 5. Price floor 6. Black market 7. Credit 8. Nonprice rationing

Skills Review

1. a.

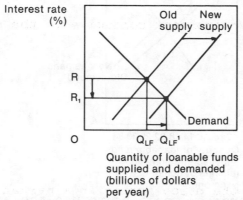

Interest rate (%)

Old supply   New supply

R
R₁

Demand

O   Q_LF Q_LF'

Quantity of loanable funds
supplied and demanded
(billions of dollars
per year)

   b. If you expect interest rates to fall, then other things being equal,
       you could lower borrowing costs by delaying borrowing until interest
       rates have fallen.

2. a. Increase

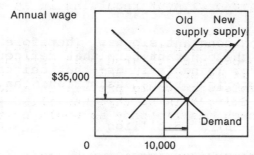

Annual wage

Old supply   New supply

$35,000

Demand

0   10,000

Quantity of mechanical engineers
supplied and demanded
per year

   b. Decease, increase
   c. You might be deterred from becoming an engineering major in
       anticipation of lower market wages that might prevail at the time you
       graduate and enter the labor force. This, of course, assumes that
       nothing else is expected to influence wages in the future and that
       you are placing a very high priority on entry level wages relative to
       other benefits received from an occupation or course of study.

3. This question can be solved graphically or algebraically with just the
    information given. Assume that the demand and supply curves for loanable
    funds are linear. This means that the slopes of both curves are constant.
    Assume also that no other influences are shifting the supply or demand
    curves other than the increase in demand of $5 billion. We are told that
    the current interest rate is 10%. This is the rate at which the supply
    and demand curves intersect. Increasing or decreasing the interest rate
    by one percentage point increases or decreases the quantity of loanable
    funds supplied by $2 billion and decreases or increases the quantity of
    loanable funds demanded by $3 billion. As can be seen in the figure
    below, this produces supply and demand curves that intersect at a market
    interest rate of 10%. Shifting the demand curve rightward by $5 billion
    increases the market interest rate to 11%.

79

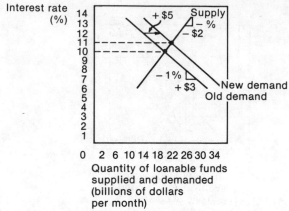

Interest rate (%)

Quantity of loanable funds
supplied and demanded
(billions of dollars
per month)

Another way to solve the problem would be to use the equilibrium price equation derived in question 10 from Chapter 5. Except in this case let's call the price the interest rate.

Let R = (a - c)/(d + b), where R = the interest rate

A change in R = 1/(d + b) x the change in (a - c)

Recall that we are assuming constant slopes. Therefore d and b remain unchanged. The a term is the constant term that reflects noninterest rate influences on the demand for loanable funds--that shifts the demand curve. Since we are making the <u>ceteris paribus</u> assumption, the c term is held constant.

A change in R = 1/(2 + 3) x $5 billion
                     = 1%

Interest rates are expected to rise from 10% to 11%

4.   a. $10, 1000
      b.   Shortage, 1000

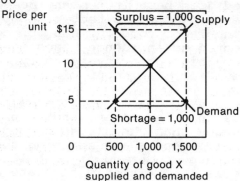

Quantity of good X
supplied and demanded
per month

      c.   Surplus, 1000

5. a. $2, 12 million
    b.   (1)   Wage per hour

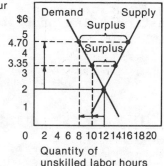

Quantity of
unskilled labor hours
supplied and demanded
(millions per month)

         (2)   Increase, $2, $3.35, decreases, 12 million, 10 million
    c.   (1)   Answer on the above diagram
         (2)   Increase, $3.35, $4.70, decreases, 10 million, 8 million

6. a.   Waiting in line
    b.   Ration stamps
    c.   Eligibility criteria

Self-Test for Mastery

1. a 2. d 3. a 4. d 5. c 6. d 7. b 8. d 9. c 10. b 11. d 12. d 13.
c 14. c 15. a 16. b

Think it Through

1.   Your answer needs to emphasize the rationing function of prices. Price
changes will in time eliminate shortages or surpluses. The price system
allocates resources efficiently. Prices represent the vehicle by which the
wishes of buyers are communicated to sellers. In short, prices coordinate the
purchase plans of buyers with the production plans of sellers.

2.   In a competitive market for loanable funds, the forces of supply and
demand determine the market rate of interest and the market quantity of credit.
Usury laws benefit those lucky enough to obtain loans at the controlled rate
(those people with higher incomes and credit ratings), but impose costs on
those who must go without credit (those people with lower incomes and poorer
credit ratings). One alternative to regulated interest rates might be
subsidies to low-income borrowers or those with poor credit ratings to be used
to defer the cost of borrowing at the market rate of interest. Lenders could
be encouraged to make loans to these people if lenders were protected from loan
defaults by some form of government guarantee. This alternative would still
require the use of scarce resources that would not have been required in a
market involving no intervention. But at least the price system can perform
its rationing function.

3.   An increase in the minimum wage will increase the incomes of those able to
find employment at that wage. But the level of unemployment will increase
among those least able to afford the loss of a job--the poor and unskilled.
Incomes and employability can be increased a number of ways without having to
resort to price controls. Job training programs that increase the productivity
of the unskilled will increase their prospects for employment and better wages.
Income transfers (such as Aid to Families with Dependent Children) can be used
to supplement the incomes of the poor and unskilled. Again, these alternatives
require the use of scarce resources but at least do not prevent the price
system from functioning.

4.   Severe gasoline shortages developed at the frozen price. Because prices could not perform their rationing function, people waited endlessly in line at service stations all across the nation. The problem continued to be serious until the price controls were removed.

6

The Price System: How It Functions and When It Fails

CHAPTER CHALLENGES

After studying your text, attending class, and completing this chapter, you should be able to:

1. Examine the framework of a pure market economy and show how the circular flow of income and expenditure in a capitalistic economy keeps it functioning.
2. Provide an overview of the price system as a mechanism for coordinating decisions and allocating resources to influence what is to be produced, how it is produced, and how output is distributed.
3. Point out the defects of a pure market system by showing how the price system doesn't attain all possible gains from resource use and how it sometimes results in low living standards for large numbers of people.
4. Briefly outline the functioning of the modern mixed economy.

IN BRIEF: CHAPTER SUMMARY

Fill in the blanks to summarize chapter content.

(1)_____ (Capitalism, Socialism) is an economic system characterized by private ownership, freedom of choice and enterprise, and a limited economic role for government. A capitalistic economy relies on the (2)_____ (benevolence of sellers, price system) to answer the "what, how, and to whom" questions basic to all economies. (3)_____ (Profit, Money) is the guiding force in capitalistic systems. It is what induces sellers to acquire resources to produce goods that are profitable to produce and to withdraw resources from other uses that are less profitable or involve no profit. (4)_____ (Economic chivalry, Economic rivalry) is also an essential characteristic in which there are large numbers of both buyers and sellers in markets and in which economic power is dispersed among many sellers and buyers such that no one seller or buyer dominates market outcomes.

For a market system to operate efficiently, it must not only produce output efficiently, but buyers and sellers must also be allowed to engage in mutually gainful trades or transactions. An economy attains the state of (5)_____ (allocative efficiency, production efficiency) when it is producing the maximum output for a given quantity of resources and buyers and sellers have engaged in mutually beneficial trades to the point where no further mutual gains can be achieved.

Transactions in a (6)_____ (money, barter) economy do not involve the exchange of money for goods, but the exchange of goods for goods. It is an inefficient form of exchange because of the high transaction costs involved in finding "producers-consumers" with which to trade. Barter requires a (7)_____ (single coincidence of wants, double coincidence of wants). Money greatly facilitates the exchange process because it allows individuals to specialize in the production of a single good, to convert any surplus into money by selling it in the market, and to spend the money on goods and services produced by other sellers. With money, a double coincidence of wants (8)_____(is, is not) required.

A (9)_____(supply and demand diagram, circular flow diagram) is a useful way of identifying the major sectors in a pure market economy and the relationships among those sectors. Businesses purchase resources from households in order to produce the output of goods and services consumed by households. Households derive their income from the sale of resources to the business sector. It is in this market for resources that supply and demand conditions determine the market prices that businesses must pay for resources and therefore the market wages, rents, and interest plus profits received by households. A household's income is the result of the quantities of resources sold in the resource market and the market prices at which those resources sell.

Households use their income, in part, to purchase the output of business. Household expenditures become the firm's sale revenue. The revenue from sales is used by businesses to purchase the resources necessary to produce output. In the markets for goods and services, supply and demand determine prices, which in turn influence the quantities of goods and services demanded and supplied.

In a pure market economy, the price system answers the three basic questions: What is produced? How are goods produced? To whom are goods distributed? Goods are produced if they are profitable to produce. Resources are used first to produce the most (10)_____(profitable, desirable) goods and services. Profitability depends, in part, upon the prices prevailing in both product and resource markets. Because of economic rivalry, successful producers are those that are able to earn enough income over time to continue in business. Sellers who introduce new technology can realize lower costs and, as a result, higher profits. But increased production resulting from higher profits increases market supply and reduces prices. This requires other sellers to adopt the new technology just to maintain profits. The (11)_____(newest, least costly) methods of production are adopted and quickly disseminated among other sellers. The market distributes goods based upon a buyer's willingness and ability to pay. Ability to pay is determined by household income and the prices of goods and services purchased.

Markets often fail to achieve allocative efficiency. Private firms will not produce some goods that benefit society because prices cannot be used to exclude those unwilling to pay. These goods are known as (12)_____(private goods, public goods). Markets may overproduce or underproduce if market prices do not reflect all benefits and costs associated with the production or consumption of output. (13)_____(Negative, Positive) externalities occur when costs accrue to parties other than sellers and buyers. Sellers in this case make decisions based upon marginal costs that do not reflect these external or "third-party" costs. Their costs are lower than if all costs were considered and that induces them to produce (14)_____(less, more) than they would otherwise. In contrast, the production or consumption of goods may confer benefits on third parties, implying that market demand curves do not reflect all benefits associated with goods, but just those benefits received by the buyer of the good.
(15)_____(Negative, Positive) externalities result in too (16)_____(much, little) output in that persons other than direct consumers benefit from the good. Sellers respond only to the effective demands registered by buyers, not third parties.

Externalities occur because property rights do not exist or because the property rights are not enforced. Property rights are not enforced when the

transaction costs involved in enforcing these rights are very
(17)_____(high, low). Some of the environment, such as air and navigable
waterways, involve common ownership and are often polluted because no one
individual has a property right or the capacity to enforce the right.

Other problems of a market system involve the absence of competition in markets
and the ability of sellers to control market outcomes to the disbenefit of
society. A market system can produce a skewed distribution of income in which
a small percentage of families receive a much larger percentage of income and
own an even larger percentage of the nation's wealth. A market system does not
guarantee the absence of unemployment or poverty. Because of market
shortcomings, modern economies rely on (18)_____(significant, limited)
government intervention in the economy to improve upon the allocation of
resources or to correct other market problems. These modern market economies
are known as (19)_____(mixed economies, pure market economies) because
decisions regarding resource use are made by both the private and public
sectors of the economy.

VOCABULARY REVIEW

Write the key term from the list below next to its definition.

Key Terms

Capitalism	Market failure
Mixed economy	Public goods
Price system	Externalities
Allocative efficiency	Property rights
Barter	Transaction costs
Money	

Definitions

1. _____: costs incurred in enforcing property rights to
traded goods, locating trading partners, and actually carrying out the
transaction.

2. _____: goods consumed equally by everyone whether they
pay or not.

3. _____: what sellers usually accept as payment for goods
and services.

4. _____: attained when all possible mutual gains from
exchange can be enjoyed.

5. _____: a mechanism by which resource use in an economy
is guided by prices.

6. _____: privileges to use or own goods, services, and
economic resources.

7. _____: characterized by private ownership of economic
resources and freedom of enterprise in which owners of factories and other
capital hire workers to produce goods and services.

8. _____: the process of exchanging goods and services.

85

9. _____: occurs when the price system fails to allocate resources so as to achieve allocative efficiency.

10. _____: costs or benefits of market transactions that are not reflected in the prices buyers and sellers use to make their decisions.

11. _____: an economy in which governments as well as business firms provide goods and services.

SKILLS REVIEW

Concept: Framework of a pure market economy; circular flow of income and expenditure

1. List six characteristics of a pure market economy:

    a. _____
    b. _____
    c. _____
    d. _____
    e. _____
    f. _____

2. In the diagram below, match the flow or box with one of the following:

    a. _____   1. Market for goods and services
    b. _____   2. Resource market
    c. _____   3. Rents, interest, wages, and profits
    d. _____   4. Economic resources
    e. _____   5. Goods and services
    f. _____   6. Expenditures on goods and services

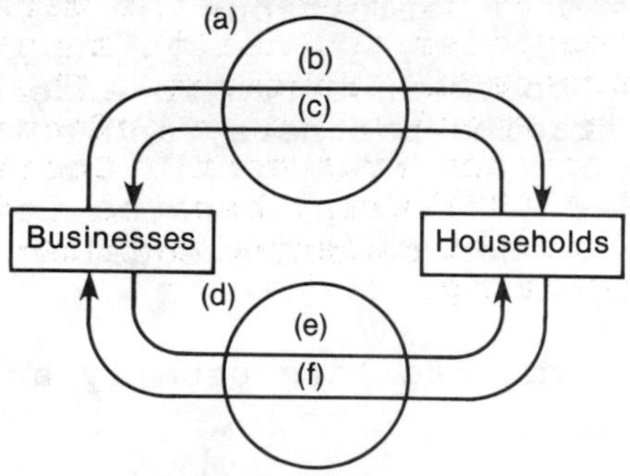

Concept: Defects of a pure market economy

3. List four failings of a market economy:

    a. _____
    b. _____
    c. _____
    d. _____

4. The diagram below represents the market for electricity. Electric power companies are burning bituminous coal and emitting sulfur into the atmosphere, creating acid rain that destroys forests and kills lakes.

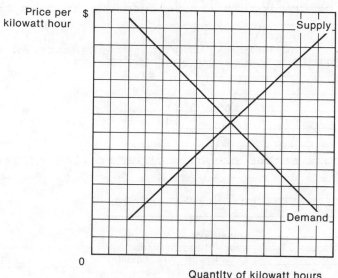

Price per kilowatt hour

Quantity of kilowatt hours supplied and demanded (millions of hours per month)

a. This is an example of a good involving _____ externalities.

b. On the diagram, show what would happen if these electric power companies were required to install scrubbers to remove sulfur from their emissions?

c. Market price of electricity _____ and market quantity _____.

d. Why is government required to correct the market failure?

5. Suppose the following diagram represents the market for AIDS therapy. Private pharmaceutical companies and health suppliers are in a race to discover and market a successful treatment. The demand for AIDS therapy reflects only the private demand of those infected with the virus and willing and able to pay for the treatment. Society as a whole, however, benefits from successful AIDS therapy because individuals who would have otherwise been infected are not infected because of the treatment that persons with AIDS are receiving.

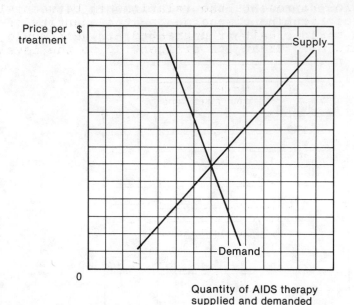

Price per $
treatment

Supply

Demand

0

Quantity of AIDS therapy
supplied and demanded
(000s treatments per month)

a. This is an example of a good involving _____ externalities.

b. Presently, there are too _____ resources allocated to AIDS therapy.

c. If government subsidizes AIDS research and the development of successful treatments, show on the diagram the likely impact on the market for AIDS therapy.

d. Market price of AIDS treatment _____ and market quantity _____.

e. Why must government be involved?

6. Advanced Question. The Sleaze E Chemical Company is presently dumping untreated effluent into a river. Downstream residents and other users of the river suffer from pollution. You are a policy maker in charge of determining the socially desirable level of pollution for the river and the appropriate effluent tax or charge per gallon of untreated effluent to impose on Sleaze E. You want to impose a tax high enough to induce Sleaze E to treat its discharge up to the point at which the proper level of pollution is reached.

Sleaze E Treated Discharge (000s gallons)	Units of Pollution Reduction	Marginal Benefits	Marginal Costs
0	0	$0	$0
10	1	10	2
20	2	8	4
30	3	6	6
40	4	4	8
50	5	2	10

a. Using the marginal benefits and marginal costs columns, determine the units of pollution reduction that maximize the net gain to society. Assume that the marginal benefit and cost data include external costs and benefits. How many gallons of discharge will Sleaze E have to treat in order to reach that level of pollution reduction?

88

b. The diagram below represents the relationship between Sleaze E's marginal cost of treating discharge and the quantity of discharge treated. What tax per unit of untreated effluent would be sufficient to induce Sleaze E to treat its effluent up to the level desired by society?

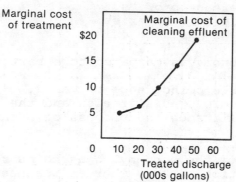

SELF-TEST FOR MASTERY

Select the best answer.

1. Which of the following is not true of a pure market system?

    a. Private ownership
    b. Freedom of enterprise and choice
    c. Significant economic role of government
    d. Presence of economic rivalry

2. A pure market economy relies on which of the following to answer the three basic questions: (1) What is produced? (2) How are goods produced? (3) To whom are goods distributed?

    a. Barter
    b. Money
    c. Property rights
    d. Price system

3. The catalyst or driving force in a market system that induces sellers to acquire resources to produce products is:

    a. Money.
    b. Profit.
    c. Price.
    d. Benevolence.

4. Economic rivalry means:

    a. That there are large numbers of consumers, but not sellers in markets.
    b. That the survival of the fittest criterion of business behavior is operative in the economy.
    c. There are large numbers of buyers and sellers in markets such that no one buyer or seller dominates market outcomes.
    d. That competitive firms produce profitable goods.

5. When an economy is operating at a point on its production possibilities curve and buyers and sellers have engaged in trade to the point where no further mutual gains from trade are possible:

    a. Production efficiency is said to exist.
    b. All firms are earning excess profits.
    c. Allocative efficiency is said to exist.
    d. Distributive efficiency is said to exist.

6. The advantage of a money economy as compared to a barter economy is :

    a. The avoidance of a double coincidence of wants.
    b. That money allows economic specialization and the division of labor.
    c. That money greatly facilitates the process of exchange.
    d. All of the above

7. In a circular flow diagram of the economy, households represent the _____ side of the resource market, whereas business represents the _____ of the market for goods and services.

    a. Demand/demand
    b. Supply/supply
    c. Demand/supply
    d. Supply/demand

8. In a circular flow diagram of the economy, households provide _____ and receive _____, which when _____ become the _____ of businesses.

    a. Goods/money/saved/capital
    b. Money/bonds/employed/capital
    c. Economic resources/money income/expended/sales revenue
    d. Money income/employment/used/property

9. Economic rivalry in a pure market economy ensures that:

    a. Only the healthiest firms use the most advanced technology.
    b. New cost-saving technology is rapidly disseminated among sellers in the economy.
    c. Firms will adopt the least-cost combination of resources.
    d. B and c
    e. A and c

10. Goods are distributed in a pure market economy:

    a. By government.
    b. By both the private and public sectors.
    c. On the basis of the buyer's willingness and ability to pay for goods and services.
    d. To those with the highest wages.

11. Private businesses will not allocate resources to the production of goods when prices cannot be used to exclude those unwilling to pay. These goods are known as:

    a. Inferior goods.
    b. Public goods.
    c. Loss goods.
    d. External goods.

12. Goods that when consumed or produced impose costs on third parties involve:

   a. Public external effects.
   b. Positive externalities.
   c. Marginal costs.
   d. Negative externalities.

13. Goods that when consumed or produced confer benefits on third parties involve:

   a. Public external effects.
   b. Positive externalities.
   c. Marginal benefits.
   d. Negative externalities.

14. Goods involving positive externalities result in :

   a. An efficient allocation of resources.
   b. Productive efficiency, but not allocative efficiency.
   c. An overallocation of resources to the production of the good.
   d. An underallocation of resources to the production of the good.

15. Externalities exist because:

   a. Businesses are often operated by uncaring individuals.
   b. Businesses do not investigate production problems as thoroughly as they should.
   c. Property rights are completely assigned and enforced.
   d. Property rights either do not exist, are not enforced, or are too costly to enforce.

16. High transaction costs associated with the assignment and enforcement of property rights increase the likelihood that:

   a. Externalities will not exist.
   b. Government will not intervene in the economy.
   c. Externalities will exist.
   d. Allocative efficiency will be achieved.

17. Actual market economies give rise to all but one of the following:

   a. A skewed distribution of income
   b. Poverty among plenty
   c. Full employment
   d. Less than competitive markets

18. In a market economy subject to market failures, society's well-being can be improved:

   a. By no government intervention.
   b. By government intervention that corrects resource misallocation and modifies other market outcomes consistent with the desires of society.
   c. By the price system.
   d. If decisions regarding public goods production are left to the private sector.

19. Modern market economies that rely on both the private and public sectors of the economy to answer the three basic questions are known as:

    a. Modern market economies.
    b. Pure market systems.
    c. Pure capitalistic economies.
    d. Mixed economies.

THINK IT THROUGH

1. Distinguish between concepts of productive efficiency and allocative efficiency.

2. During inflationary periods of the 1970s, a number of barter services were established as a means of eliminating inflation. These barter arrangements made use of computers to register the goods and services that the users were willing to supply and the goods that would be acceptable in exchange. Would such a barter system be as efficient as one with money? Explain.

3. A basic function of government in a pure market economy is to facilitate the functioning of the economy, but not to modify market outcomes. Discuss.

4. For a pure market economy, explain why producers employ the least costly techniques of production. If the price of labor rises relative to the price of capital and other inputs, how would this affect a competitive seller's combination of resources employed in production?

5. Education in the United States is provided by both the private and public sectors. Why?

POP QUIZ   Read the news brief at the end of this chapter and answer the
                question below.

In addition to the sources of market failure discussed in the text, markets may also fail to allocate resources efficiently if they do not operate competitively. Briefly describe the credit-card industry and indicate how resource allocation might be affected.

CHAPTER ANSWERS

In Brief: Chapter Summary

1. Capitalism 2. Price system 3. Profit 4. Economic rivalry 5. Allocative efficiency 6. Barter 7. Double coincidence of wants 8. Is not 9. Circular flow diagram 10. Profitable 11. Least costly 12. Public goods 13. Negative 14. More 15. Positive 16. Little 17. High 18. Significant 19. Mixed economies

Vocabulary Review

1. Transaction costs   2. Public goods   3. Money   4. Allocative efficiency   5. Price system   6. Property rights   7. Capitalism   8. Barter 9. Market failure 10. Externalities   11. Mixed economy

Skills Review

1. a. Private ownership
   b. Freedom of choice and enterprise
   c. Limited economic role for government
   d. Reliance on the price system to allocate resources
   e. Profit motive
   f. Economic rivalry

2. a. 2 b. 3 c. 4 d. 1 e. 5 f. 6

3. a. Externalities
   b. Lack of competition in markets
   c. Skewed distribution of income
   d. Doesn't eliminate poverty or unemployment

4. a. Negative
   b. If power companies are required to bear the cost of cleaning their emissions, the market supply curve would shift leftward.

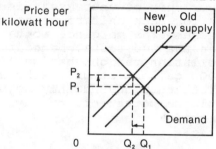

   c. Increases, decreases
   d. Individual property rights do not exist to the atmosphere and to most lakes and a good portion of timber lands. Where property rights do exist in the ownership of forests and lakes, it is far too costly for any one property owner to identify the source of pollution and to seek remedy in court. Therefore government must intervene and enforce the collective property rights of society to commonly owned resources. Government can also reduce the transaction costs of enforcing property rights for individual property owners. In both cases, government improves resource allocation.

5. a. Positive
   b. Few
   c. Government subsidies increase the net gain to those conducting AIDS research and developing therapies. In time there will be a rightward shift in the supply curve.

93

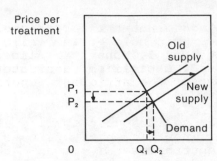

Price per treatment

Old supply

New supply

Demand

P_1
P_2

0   Q_1 Q_2

Quantity of AIDS therapy
supplied and demanded
(000s treatments per month)

d.   Decreases, increases

e.   A market system relies on pricing to allocate resources. Market prices do not reflect the external benefits accruing to third parties. Markets will underproduce goods involving positive externalities. Governments can produce net gains for society by engaging in activities that reallocate more resources to the production of goods with positive externalities.

6.   a.   Marginal benefits and costs become equal at three units of pollution reduction. This is the level of pollution that maximizes society's net gain. Sleaze E will have to treat 30,000 gallons of discharge for this level of pollution reduction to be realized.

b. $10. A tax of $10 per unit of untreated discharge will result in a net gain to Sleaze E for each unit of treated discharge up to 30,000 gallons. This is because the marginal cost of treating a gallon of effluent is less than the additional benefit associated with not having to pay the pollution tax on that gallon. This holds true up to the level of 30,000 gallons at which the marginal cost of treatment is $10. Treatment beyond this level would not take place because Sleaze E would be better off by paying the tax than treating the discharge.

Self-Test for Mastery

1. c 2. d 3. b 4. c 5. c 6. d 7. b 8. c 9. d 10. c 11. b 12. d 13. b 14. d 15. d 16. c 17. c 18. b 19. d

Think It Through

1. Production efficiency occurs when an economy is operating on its production possibilities curve. Here, resources are efficiently and fully employed. But allocative efficiency is not achieved if any trades can occur between buyers and sellers such that some people can be made better off without making anyone worse off. Allocative efficiency is reached only when trades and exchanges have taken place to the point at which the gains to some parties can only come at the expense of others.

2. Barter systems, whether or not they are operated by computers, must develop "prices" or exchange ratios for the goods involved. This requires scarce resources. A double coincidence of wants is required, which reduces the efficiency of exchange. A middleman must be paid to provide a service that is naturally provided as part of the functioning of a market economy using money.

3. In a pure market system, there are no failures. There are no externalities, markets provide employment for everyone willing and able to work at prevailing wages, all markets involve economic rivalry, and incomes are based strictly on the resources that households supply to the market and the prices at which they sell. In short, it is assumed that allocative efficiency

is achieved by the market without government interference. Government, nevertheless, performs a vital economic role by assigning property rights and enforcing those rights via a system of laws, courts, and police protection. Government also provides money and the basic infrastructure of roads, water supply, sewerage, etc., necessary for the efficient functioning of a market system.

4.   Economic rivalry implies that sellers must operate at least cost. If they did not, in time they would incur insufficient profits to remain in business. Firms that stay in business in a pure market system are those that are able to use the least costly combination of inputs and technology in order to at least generate a minimally sufficient level of profit. If the price of labor rises relative to the cost of other inputs, a least cost producer will substitute the relatively less costly resources for labor. By making capital more productive relative to labor, technology reduces the cost of capital relative to labor in the production of output. This is what happened in American agriculture. Technology made farm labor more expensive relative to capital, inducing farmers to mechanize.

5.   Education is a good involving positive externalities. A market system produces too little education from society's point of view. Government can increase the net gain to society by providing more education than that provided by a market system alone. But this does not necessarily mean the we have to have the current public-private system in order to achieve this outcome. Education could be entirely publicly provided or it could be provided entirely by a private sector encouraged to produce more with subsidies. Alternatively, students could be given education vouchers that supplement their own funds for education. These funds could be spent entirely in the private sector or even in the current public-private system.

Pop Quiz

Jeff Bailey poses an important question regarding the social consequences of the current structure of the credit-card industry: "A plastic OPEC?" Although 3000 financial institutions are issuing Visa and MasterCard, the ten largest credit-card issuers now have a 50% share of the market, up from about one-third in 1980. While other rates of interest have fallen markedly in the 1980s, credit-card rates have remained in the 17.5% to 20% range. These dominant credit-card issuers are oligopolists and have avoided a rate war by refusing to lower rates. Instead, they compete by spending huge sums in advertising on television and through direct mailings, whereas most of the other more price competitive issuers have inadequate resources to compete through advertising. Critics argue that there is not "prominent disclosure" of interest rates and fees and that issuers should be required to prominently display this information. Other critics contend that if the industry does not engage in price competition, rate caps should be employed, limiting the interest income earned by the large issuers.

Dominant credit-card companies are able to prevent interest rates from reflecting changes in the supply of and demand for consumer credit. If rates do not change to equate supply and demand, then there is a misallocation of resources in that there is either a shortage or surplus of consumer credit. If rates are prevented from falling given a decline in demand, less credit is demanded than would be the case if interest rates fell to restore equilibrium in the market. If consumers are being persuaded through mailings or other advertising to make choices with incomplete or misleading information, then consumer choices will result in a combination of goods and services consumed that is inferior to the combination chosen when consumers have access to full and complete information. Also, Jeff Bailey notes that for the dominant card issuers, the credit-card business is "hugely" profitable--three times as profitable as banking in general in terms of pretax profits as a percent of outstanding loans. These excess profits are received at the expense of possibly ill-informed consumers. This constitutes a redistribution of income from credit-card holders to issuers.

Major Credit-Card Issuers Tighten Grip On Market Despite High Interest Charges

YOUR
MONEY
MATTERS

By Jeff Bailey
Staff Reporter of The Wall Street Journal

A plastic OPEC?

Some banking industry critics contend that something close to that is emerging in the credit-card business. They are worried that a small number of card issuers are increasingly dominating the business and keeping card interest rates high.

"The business is really an oligopoly," says Rep. Charles E. Schumer, a New York Democrat who backs legislation that would force bank-card issuers to disclose their interest rates and fees rates more prominently. "There isn't true (price) competition," he says.

What bothers Mr. Schumer and other critics is that, since 1980, the 10 largest Visa and MasterCard issuers have expanded their combined share of the hugely profitable business to about half of the market from one third. And despite all the talk about credit-card wars, they have managed to do so without a rate battle.

Indeed, instead of falling sharply along with other interest rates, as many people expected, credit-card rates have edged down only slightly during the 1980s. A look at the top 10 card issuers shows current rates bunched in a range of 17.5% to 20%.

Rates Set Independently

The two bank card associations, Visa International and MasterCard International, along with the banks, see nothing wrong with that. They say interest rates are set independently and certainly aren't ever discussed among issuers. "We would never talk to anybody about pricing," says Ira Rimmerman, who heads Citicorp's card business.

That apparently includes consumers, too. Most promotions aimed at getting consumers to take new cards are distinguished by features other than the basic price of using the card, such as the size of the credit limit, the color of the card, free travel insurance and extra frequent flier miles. The issuers who do promote their cards based on a low interest rate repre-

sent only a tiny segment of the market.

With a lack of competition on pricing, the dominant issuers have little incentive to lower their rates. In fact, "the industry's resolve to *not* lower rates has stiffened," says a banker who runs one of the 10 biggest card operations.

That resolve was in question a year and a half ago when American Express Co. introduced its Optima bank card at 13.5%. Rate wars were predicted. But Optima has since won little of the market and earlier this month raised its rate to 14.25%.

In the meantime, borrowing by plastic is actually getting more expensive because

> **I**SSUERS that do promote their credit cards based on a low interest rate represent only a tiny segment of the market.

provisions of the 1986 tax law are rapidly phasing out deductions for credit-card interest payments. They'll be gone completely by 1991. Borrowing nevertheless has continued to grow.

Consumers are at least partly to blame for the fact that out of some 3,000 financial institutions issuing Visa and MasterCards, a handful dominate the business. For one thing, few people shop for cards. Instead, they are more likely to respond to direct-mail solicitations, the vast majority of which come from the major credit-card companies.

Generally, as few as 1% of consumers respond to a mailing. But some big issuers are able to back up mailings with heavy advertising and thus increase response rates. Citicorp, which aims to add three million new accounts this year, says its television advertising campaign—"Not just MasterCard. Citibank MasterCard"—has helped response rates to its mailings, though it won't say by how much.

Those consumers who seek out banks that charge lower rates find that they often require a better credit history and won't offer the big credit limits that larger issuers will. Despite its 10.92% rate and a periodic listing in this newspaper and other

publications, Arkansas Federal Savings in Little Rock has attracted less than $3 million in credit-card loans. But Arkansas Federal is among those with more stringent credit requirements and lower credit limits.

Card issuers have found, too, that many consumers disregard interest rates because they never intend to borrow money by plastic, but then do. "Most people believe they will pay the balance every month," says Philip J. Purcell, who oversees Sears, Roebuck & Co.'s Discover bank-card business. Only about half do, according to Visa.

Pretax Profits

It's clear why the large credit-card issuers want to increase their share of the business. Combined Visa and MasterCard loans total nearly $100 billion. And the profits on that business are huge. Citicorp's pretax profit on its $16 billion in credit-card loans appears to run at about $800 million a year, a figure that Citicorp's Mr. Rimmerman doesn't dispute. Bank-America Corp., with about $6 billion in loans, makes more than $300 million before taxes. And First Chicago Corp., with about $4.5 billion in loans, makes more than $200 million before taxes.

For the larger issuers, the credit-card business brings in revenue generally totaling 21% of their loans outstanding. This includes interest payments and annual fees from cardholders and merchants. After subtracting the cost of funds, loan losses and operating costs—including processing, labor and marketing—the pretax profit is roughly 5% of the loans outstanding. That figure is roughly three times the level of a healthy bank's overall profit margin.

But some public officials would like to see the government trim card issuers' earnings. Rep. Schumer says that if the prominent disclosure of interest rates and fees on credit cards doesn't lead to more price competition, he would favor a national cap on credit-card rates.

Jerry Cosentino, Illinois state treasurer, isn't waiting. He wants a rate cap now and last year pulled state funds out of First Chicago to protest its 19.8% rate on credit cards. "They're gouging the consumer every day. There is so much greed in those top 10 issuers," he says. "It's like a conspiracy."

7

Elasticity of Supply and Demand

CHAPTER CHALLENGES

After studying your text, attending class, completing this chapter, you should be able to:

1. Explain the purpose and concept of price elasticity of demand.
2. Show how price elasticity of demand can be calculated for points on a given demand curve and discuss some uses of elasticity.
3. Explain how to use other elasticity measures, including the income elasticity of demand, the cross-elasticity of demand, and the price elasticity of supply.
4. Show how the price elasticities of demand and supply are relevant for explaining the impact of taxes on market prices of goods and services.

IN BRIEF: CHAPTER SUMMARY

Fill in the blanks to summarize chapter content.

The laws of supply and demand indicate the direction in which quantity supplied or demanded changes in response to a price change but they do not reveal the sensitivity of sellers or buyers to given price changes. The concept of elasticity is employed to gauge the sensitivity of buyers and sellers to price changes. Specifically, the (1)_____(income, price) elasticity of demand is a number measuring the sensitivity of buyers to a 1% change in price. If the percentage change in quantity demanded is (2)_____(greater, smaller) than the percentage change in price, demand is said to be elastic, and the price elasticity of demand coefficient is (3)_____(greater, smaller) than 1 (ignoring the minus sign). If the percentage change in quantity demanded is (4)_____(greater, smaller) than the percentage change in price, demand is said to be inelastic, and the price elasticity of demand coefficient is (5)_____ (more, less) than 1 (ignoring the minus sign)but greater than 0. A coefficient equal to (6)_____(1, 0) means that demand is unit elastic. Unit elasticity means that a given percentage change in price will result in (7)_____(a greater, the same) percentage change in quantity demanded.

The price elasticity of demand is determined by taking the percentage change in (8)_____(price, quantity demanded) divided by the percentage change in (9)_____ (price, quantity demanded). The elasticity coefficient or number is influenced by (a) the availability of substitutes, (b) time, and (c) the percentage of income spent on a good. Demand becomes (10)_____(more, less) elastic with increases in the availability of substitute goods, time, and increases in the proportion of income spent on the good. Decreases in the availability of substitutes, time, or the percentage of income expended on a good cause demand to become (11)_____(more, less) elastic.

The price elasticity of demand is not the slope of the demand curve. For a linear demand curve with a constant slope, the price elasticity of demand changes from being (12)_____ (inelastic, elastic) in the upper portion of the demand curve to being (13)_____(inelastic, elastic) in the lower segment of the curve. Exceptions to this would be the cases of perfectly elastic and perfectly inelastic demand curves. A vertical demand curve is perfectly inelastic and has a price elasticity coefficient of (14)_____(1, 0). A horizontal demand curve is perfectly elastic and has a price elasticity coefficient of (15)_____(0, infinity).

A useful application of the price elasticity of demand is an analysis of the behavior of total revenue or expenditures given percentage price changes. If demand is elastic over the range of a price decrease, total revenues and expenditures will (16)_____(fall, rise). This is because the increase in quantity demanded more than offsets the decline in price. If demand is inelastic over the range of a price increase, total revenue and expenditures also (17)_____(fall, rise). In this case, the price increase more than dominates the decline in quantity demanded. Therefore price and total revenue or expenditures are positively related when demand is inelastic and are negatively related when demand is elastic. When the price elasticity of demand is unit elastic, a change in price (18)_____(increases, has no impact on) revenue or expenditures.

Other elasticity concepts include the income elasticity of demand, the cross-elasticity of demand, and the price elasticity of supply. The income elasticity of demand measures the sensitivity of consumer purchases to changes in income. If the income elasticity coefficient is (19)_____ (greater, smaller) than 0, the good in question is a normal good. If the coefficient is (20)_____(greater, smaller) than 0, the good is an inferior good. The cross-elasticity of demand is a way to identify goods as being substitutes, complements, or unrelated. If the cross-elasticity is (21)_____ (negative, positive), the two goods in question are substitutes. The percentage quantity demanded of one good increases when the price of the other good increases by a given percentage. Two goods are complements when the cross-elasticity coefficient is (22)_____(negative, positive). In this case, the percentage quantity demanded of one good decreases when the price of the other good increases by a given percentage. Two goods are unrelated when the cross-elasticity is (23)_____(1, 0).

The price elasticity of supply measures the sensitivity of sellers to percentage price changes. If the percentage change in quantity supplied is greater than the percentage change in price, supply is (24)_____ (elastic, inelastic), with an elasticity coefficient greater than 1. If the percentage change in quantity supplied is less than the percentage change in price, supply is (25)_____(elastic, inelastic), with an elasticity coefficient greater than 0 but less than 1. A coefficient of 0 represents unit supply elasticity, where quantity supplied does not change given a change in price. Supply is (26)_____(more, less) elastic when (a) the additional costs of producing a unit of output rise slowly with increases in output and (b) sufficient time is allowed for the firm or industry to respond to price changes. As with demand, supply can also be perfectly inelastic or perfectly elastic. A vertical supply curve, one that is perfectly (27)_____ (elastic, inelastic), has a supply elasticity coefficient of 0. A horizontal supply curve is perfectly (28)_____(elastic, inelastic) with a coefficient of infinity.

Price elasticities of supply and demand can be used in determining the portion of a tax levied on producers that is shifted to buyers. A tax per unit of output levied on sellers will shift the supply curve (29)_____ (downward, upward) by the amount of that tax per unit. Prices rise, but if they rise less than the tax, some of the tax is borne by sellers and the remainder is borne by consumers. A firm would be successful in passing or shifting all of the tax to consumers when the demand curve is perfectly (30)_____ (inelastic,

elastic) or when the supply curve is perfectly (31)_____(inelastic, elastic). In the opposite case, where the demand curve is (32)_____(horizontal, vertical) and the supply curve is (33)_____(horizontal, vertical), the entire tax would be borne by sellers. With conventionally sloped demand and supply curves, both sellers and buyers bear a portion of the tax.

VOCABULARY REVIEW

Write the key term from the list below next to its definition.

Key Terms

Price elasticity of demand
Elastic demand
Inelastic demand
Total revenue
Unit elastic demand
Total expenditure
Income elasticity of demand

Normal goods
Inelastic supply
Inferior goods
Price elasticity of supply
Elastic supply
Unit elastic supply
Tax shifting
Cross-elasticity of supply

Definitions

1. _____: goods that have positive income elasticity of demand.

2. _____: prevails if the price elasticity of demand for a good is a number that exceeds 1, ignoring the minus sign.

3. _____: occurs when a tax levied on sellers of a good causes the market price of the good to increase.

4. _____: a number representing the percentage change in quantity demanded of a good resulting from each 1% change in the price of a good.

5. _____: a number used to measure the sensitivity of consumer purchases of one good to each 1% change in the prices of related goods.

6. _____: prevails when the price elasticity of supply is equal to or greater than 0 but less than 1.

7. _____: the dollars sellers of a product take in; the amount sold over a period multiplied by the price (PQ).

8. _____: prevails if the price elasticity of demand for a good exactly equals 1 when the minus sign is ignored.

9. _____: goods that have negative income elasticity of demand.

10. _____: a number used to measure the sensitivity of

changes in quantity supplied to each 1% change in the price of a good, other things being equal.

11. _____: prevails if the price elasticity of demand for a good is equal to or greater than 0, but less then 1, ignoring the minus sign.

12. _____: prevails when the price elasticity of supply is greater than 1.

13. _____: over any given period, the number of units of a product purchased multiplied by the price of the product (PQ); equals the total revenue of sellers.

14. _____: a number that measures the sensitivity of consumer purchases to each 1% change in income.

15. _____: prevails when elasticity of supply just equals 1.

SKILLS REVIEW

Concept: Price elasticity of demand; measurement, uses, determinants

1.   Referring to the diagram below:

   a.   Calculate the price elasticity of demand over the demand curve segment a-b. _____   Demand is _____.
   b.   Calculate the price elasticity of demand over segment e-f. _____   Demand is _____.
   c.   Calculate the price elasticity of demand over segment c-d. _____   Demand is _____.
   d.   Total revenue (P X Q) at point   a = _____
                                        b = _____
                                        c = _____
                                        d = _____
                                        e = _____
                                        f = _____
   e.   A decline in price from $6 to $5 _____ total revenue by $_____.
   f.   A decline in price from $2 to $1 _____ total revenue by $_____.
   g.   A decline in price from $4 to $3 _____ total revenue by $_____.

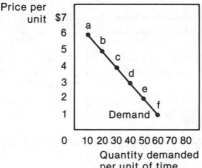

101

2. Will the following make the elasticity of demand more elastic or less
    elastic?

    a. _____ Decrease in the percentage of income spent on a good
    b. _____ Import tariffs reduce the availability of substitute goods
    c. _____ More time to respond to price changes
    d. _____ Increase in the availability of substitutes

3. Given your knowledge of the determinants of the price elasticity of
    demand, which of the following goods are likely to have elastic demands
    and which are likely to be inelastic?

    a. _____ Diamonds
    b. _____ Hamburgers
    c. _____ Toothpaste
    d. _____ Automobiles
    e. _____ Gasoline
    f. _____ Cigarettes
    g. _____ Movies

Concept: Other concepts of elasticity; measurement, uses, determinants

4. Suppose you observe that as incomes increase by 10%, the quantity of some
    good purchased:

    a. Increases by 20%. Determine the income elasticity of demand. The
        good in question is a/an_____ good.
    b. Decreases by 5%. Determine the income elasticity of demand. The
        good is a _____ good.

5. Determine the cross-elasticity of demand if a 5% decrease in the price of
    good X:

    a. Increases the quantity of good Y purchased by 15% _____. Good Y is a
        _____ to good X.
    b. Decreases the quantity of good Y purchased by 5% _____. Good Y is
        _____ to good X.
    c. Does not change the quantity of good Y purchased _____.
        Good Y is _____ to good X.

6. Referring to the diagram below:

    a. Calculate the elasticity of supply over the supply curve segment a-b.
        _____ Supply is _____.
    b. Calculate the elasticity of supply over segment e-f. _____ Supply is
        _____.
    c. List two determinants of the elasticity of supply:
        (1)_____
        (2)_____

Price per unit
Quantity supplied per unit of time

102

Concept: Price elasticity of demand and supply; impact of taxes on prices

7.   Referring to the diagram below:

   a.   Show the impact on the supply curve for cigarettes of a tax of $1 per
        pack.
   b.   Market price _____ from $_____ to $_____ .
   c.   Consumers pay _____ cents of the tax and sellers pay the other
        _____ cents.
   d.   Assume that cigarette smoking is such an addiction that the demand
        for cigarettes is perfectly inelastic.
        (1)   Show a perfectly inelastic demand curve on the diagram.
        (2)   How much of the tax is paid by consumers? _____ cents   By
              sellers? _____ cents

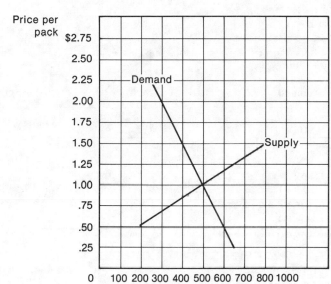

Quantity of cigarette packs
supplied and demanded
(millions of packs
per year)

8. For which of the following diagrams is a per unit tax completely borne by:
    a. Consumers?_____
    b. Sellers?_____

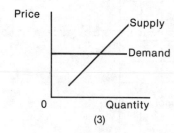

(1)

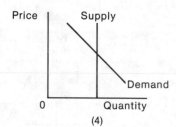

(2)

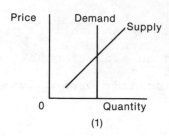

(3)

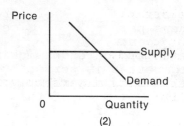

(4)

9. <u>Advanced Question</u>. The market demand and supply equations from Chapter 4, question 10, are as follows:

$$Qd = a - bP$$
$$Qs = c + dP$$

    where a, b, c, and d are positive constants
    Qd = quantity demanded
    Qs = quantity supplied
    P = price

Suppose that in the absence of per unit taxes on output, Qs is a positive function of P. If a tax, T, is levied on sellers, Qs becomes a function of the after-tax price rather than the before-tax price, P.

    a. Modify the supply equation to incorporate a per unit tax, T.
    b. Derive an expression for the market equilibrium price.
    c. How can that expression be used to determine the portion of a tax, T, that is shifted to buyers?

SELF-TEST FOR MASTERY

Select the best answer.

1. The price elasticity of demand is measured by:

    a. Dividing the percentage change in quantity demanded into the percentage change in income.
    b. Dividing the percentage change in quantity demanded into the percentage change in supply.

c. Dividing the percentage change in price into the percentage change in quantity demanded.
d. Dividing price into quantity demanded.

2. If the price elasticity of demand is greater than 1, it is said to be:

   a. Unit elastic.
   b. Elastic.
   c. Inelastic.
   d. A normal good.

3. If the price elasticity of demand is greater than 0, but less than 1, it is said to be:

   a. Unit elastic.
   b. Elastic.
   c. Inelastic.
   d. A normal good.

4. A _____ elastic demand curve is one where the price elasticity coefficient is infinity.

   a. Unit
   b. Less
   c. Completely
   d. Perfectly

5. A demand curve for insulin is likely to be:

   a. Perfectly inelastic.
   b. Perfectly elastic.
   c. Somewhat elastic.
   d. Moderately inelastic.

6. Moving from the upper range of a linear demand curve southeast to the lower portions is associated with a price elasticity of demand that becomes increasingly:

   a. Elastic.
   b. Inelastic.
   c. Large.
   d. Difficult to estimate.

7. Which of the following is a determinant of the price elasticity of demand?

   a. Time
   b. The percentage of income spent on the good
   c. The availability of substitutes
   d. All of the above

8. Other things being equal, an increase in the availability of substitutes:

   a. Has no impact on the price elasticity of demand.
   b. Decreases the price elasticity of demand.
   c. Increases the price elasticity of demand.
   d. None of the above

9. If demand is elastic and the price falls, total revenue will:

   a. Not change.
   b. Increase.

    c.   Decrease.
    d.   Increase if the supply elasticity is not 0.

10. If demand is inelastic and the price falls, total revenue will:

    a.   Not change.
    b.   Increase.
    c.   Decrease.
    d.   Increase if the supply elasticity is not 0.

11. A good having a positive income elasticity of demand is called a:

    a.   Positive good.
    b.   Public good.
    c.   Inferior good.
    d.   Normal good.

12. A good having a negative income elasticity of demand is called a:

    a.   Positive good.
    b.   Public good.
    c.   Inferior good.
    d.   Normal good.

13. Two goods that are substitutes in consumption have a _____ cross-elasticity of demand.

    a.   Positive
    b.   Elastic
    c.   Inelastic
    d.   Negative

14. Two goods that are complements in consumption have a _____ cross-elasticity of demand.

    a.   Positive
    b.   Elastic
    c.   Inelastic
    d.   Negative

15. Which of the following is not a determinant of the price elasticity of supply?

    a.   Availability of substitutes
    b.   Time
    c.   The marginal cost associated with producing additional units of output
    d.   Percentage of income spent on a good
    e.   A and d

16. A perfectly elastic supply curve is:

    a.   Positively sloped.
    b.   Vertical.
    c.   Negatively sloped.
    d.   Horizontal.

17. If the supply of some good is unit elastic and the price of the good increases by 10%:

    a.   Quantity supplied increases by more than 10%.

b.   Quantity demanded decreases by at least 10%.
c.   Quantity supplied increases by 10%.
d.   Quantity supplied does not change.

18. If a per unit tax is levied on sellers and the demand for the good is perfectly elastic, sellers:

a.   Will pass all of the tax to consumers in the form of higher prices.
b.   Will not be able to shift the tax.
c.   Will share the burden of the tax equally with buyers.
d.   None of the above

19. If a per unit tax is levied on sellers and the demand for the good is perfectly inelastic, sellers:

a.   Will pass all of the tax to consumers in the form of higher prices.
b.   Will not be able to shift the tax.
c.   Will share the burden of the tax equally with buyers.
d.   Will pay most of the tax.

20. If a per unit tax is levied on sellers and the supply and demand curves are conventionally sloped, sellers:

a.   Will pass all of the tax to consumers in the form of higher prices.
b.   Will not be able to shift the tax.
c.   Will share the burden of the tax equally with buyers.
d.   Will share the burden of the tax with buyers.

THINK IT THROUGH

1.   You have been asked by a physician to determine if his fees should be increased. He wants to generate additional revenues. Based upon what you know about the determinants of the price elasticity of demand, determine first if the demand for physicians services is elastic or inelastic and then determine what fee change will increase the physician's revenues.

2.   The demand for unskilled labor is generally regarded as elastic. Why? An increase in the minimum wage will increase wages for those employed, but will reduce the total wages paid to unskilled labor as a whole. Why?

3.   How could knowledge of the price, cross-price, and income elasticities of demand for various goods be useful in helping a discount store manager predict the probable consequences of price changes?

4.   Sumptuary taxes are taxes intended to discourage the consumption of goods considered harmful to individuals. A tax per quart of whiskey is such a tax. Based upon what you know about determinants of the price elasticity of demand, is a per unit tax on whiskey likely to curb consumption?

CHAPTER ANSWERS

In Brief: Chapter Summary

1. Price 2. Greater 3. Greater 4. Smaller 5. Less 6. 1 7. The same 8. Quantity demanded 9. Price 10. More 11. Less 12. Elastic 13. Inelastic

14. 0 15. Infinity 16. Rise 17. Rise 18. Has no impact on 19. Greater 20. Smaller 21. Positive 22. Negative 23. 0 24. Elastic 25. Inelastic 26. More 27. Inelastic 28. Elastic 29. Upward 30. Inelastic 31. Elastic 32. Horizontal 33. Vertical

Vocabulary Review

1. Normal goods 2. Elastic demand 3. Tax shifting 4. Price elasticity of demand 5. Cross-elasticity of demand 6. Inelastic supply 7. Total revenue 8. Unit elastic demand 9. Inferior goods 10. Price elasticity of supply 11. Inelastic demand 12. Elastic supply 13. Total expenditure 14. Income elasticity of demand 15. Unit elastic supply

Skills Review

1. a. 3.67, elastic
    b. 0.27, inelastic
    c. 1, unit elastic
    d. (a) $60, (b) $100, (c) $120, (d) $120, (e) $100, (f) $60
    e. Increase, $40
    f. Decrease, $40
    g. Changes, $0

2. a. More
    b. Less
    c. More
    d. More

3. a. Elastic   4. a. +2, normal
    b. Elastic   b. -1/2, inferior
    c. Inelastic
    d. Inelastic   5. a. -3, complement
    e. Inelastic   b. +1, substitute
    f. Inelastic   c. 0, unrelated
    g. Elastic

6. a. 1, unit elastic
    b. 1, unit elastic
    c. (1) Additional cost of producing a unit of output as more output is
           produced
       (2) Time

7. a.

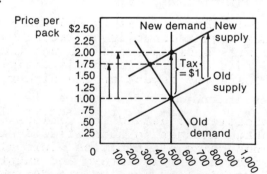

Quantity of cigarette packs
supplied and demanded
(millions of packs per year)

    b. Increase, $1, $1.75
    c. 75, 25
    d. (1) Shown on diagram above
       (2) 100, 0

8. a. Figures (1) and (2)
    b. Figures (3) and (4)

9. a. Let Qs = c + d (P - T)
    b. Equilibrium requires setting Qd = Qs. Therefore:

$$a - bP = a + d (P - T)$$

Solving for P gives:

$$P = (a - c + dT)/(b + d)$$

    c. Let the change in P = [d/(b + d)] x change in T

If d/(b + d) is greater than 0 but less than 1, both sellers and
buyers share the tax burden. If d/(b + d) equals 0, the tax is borne
by sellers. If d/(b + d) equals 1, the tax is borne by buyers. When
d/(b + d) is 0, d = 0 or b equals infinity. d = 0 when supply is
perfectly inelastic. b = infinity when demand is perfectly elastic.
d/(b + d) is 1 when b = 0 or when d = infinity. b = 0 when demand is
perfectly inelastic and d = infinity when supply is perfectly
elastic. Conventionally sloped supply and demand curves yield a
value for d/(b + d) greater than 0 but less than 1.

Self-Test for Mastery

1. c 2. b 3. c 4. d 5. a 6. b 7. d 8. c 9. b 10. c 11. d 12. c 13.
a 14. d 15. e 16. d 17. c 18. b 19. a 20. d

Think it Through

1.   People perceive physician services as having no close substitutes.
Because care usually cannot be delayed, the demand for physician services is
regarded as inelastic. If the physician wants to increase revenues from his
practice, he should increase his fees.

2.   Unskilled labor is considered to have an elastic demand, in part because
many types of labor can be substituted for unskilled labor, but unskilled
workers are not substitutes for those requiring special skills, education, or
training. Also, there is typically a ready pool of unskilled labor that can be
employed with minimal training cost to the firm.

     If the demand for unskilled labor is elastic and the minimum wage
increases, total wages (minimum wage x quantity of labor hours employed) paid
to unskilled labor as a group will decrease, even though those employed at the
minimum wage are better off. This occurs because the unemployment caused by
the minimum wage more than offsets the impact of the higher wage on the total
wages paid to labor.

3.   Knowledge of price elasticities of demand for various goods would allow
the manager to predict percentage changes in quantities demanded for given
percentage price changes. Cross-price elasticities would allow predictions
regarding the quantities demanded of complementary and substitute goods.
Income elasticities of demand would allow predictions for those goods that are
normal or inferior. This would be useful, for instance, in areas experiencing
a significant influx of higher income households. All of this assumes that the
national or regional data used to estimate these coefficients are applicable to
a local economy. In other words, the relationships that hold for the economy
as a whole are assumed to pertain to the local economy as well.

4.   For whiskey consumers, there are probably few close substitutes for whiskey. The demand for whiskey is probably inelastic. A sumptuary tax would primarily increase the price of whiskey, having only a modest negative impact on the quantity of whiskey demanded.

8

Consumer Choice and the Theory of Demand

CHAPTER CHALLENGES

After studying your text, attending class, and completing this chapter, you should be able to:

1. Explain the difference between total and marginal utility and show how the way marginal utility varies with purchases can reflect a person's preferences.
2. Describe the conditions for consumer equilibrium as expressed by the equimarginal principle for purchases.
3. Show how total and marginal benefits relate to total and marginal utility.
4. Demonstrate that buying any particular good up to the point at which its marginal benefit equals its price maximizes the total net benefit of giving up money to purchase the good.
5. Analyze the impact of changes in prices and incomes on consumer choices.
6. Derive a demand curve for a good for an individual consumer from data on marginal benefit and show how marginal benefit, and therefore demand, shifts when income changes.
7. Derive a market demand curve from the demand curves of individual buyers.

IN BRIEF: CHAPTER SUMMARY

Fill in the blanks to summarize chapter content.

An understanding of the demand side of the market requires an understanding of consumer choice. Marginal analysis is used to explain the choices made by consumers. Consumers seek to maximize their net gain from consumption. The consumption of goods increases a consumer's total satisfaction or (1)_____ (marginal, total) utility. But the additional satisfaction realized from the consumption of each additional unit of a good decreases. The law of diminishing (2)_____ (returns, marginal utility) states that marginal utility falls as more of a good is consumed over a period. Consumers will try to allocate their income such that they consume goods up to the point where the marginal utility per dollar expended on a good (3)_____ (equals, is greater than) the marginal utility per dollar spent on each and every other good. This is known as the equimarginal principle. Consuming according to the equimarginal principle will maximize a consumer's utility.

To a consumer, total and marginal utility is valued by the (4)_____ (minimum, maximum) sum of money that the consumer is willing and able to give up to have the total quantity or additional unit, respectively. Because of (5)_____ (declining, increasing) marginal utility, the maximum sum that consumers are willing and able to give up to obtain an additional unit of a good (6)_____ (increases, declines) as more of the good is consumed. This is known as the law of declining marginal benefit. As long as buyers consume goods for which marginal benefits (7)_____ (are less than, exceed) the price of the good, their net benefits increase. Net benefit is maximized when consumption is carried to the point where marginal benefit (8)_____ (is still greater than, equals) the price. On units of goods consumed up to the point where marginal benefits equal price, the consumer realizes a surplus. Consumer surplus is the total benefit received in excess of the (9)_____(dollar expenditure, marginal benefit) necessary to obtain the goods.

Consumers will not necessarily prefer to purchase an additional unit of a good having a high marginal benefit over one yielding less additional satisfaction if the price of the former good is high. Nor will a consumer purchase any units of a good when the price (10)_____(exceeds, is greater than) the marginal benefit received. This is because the value of the goods and services that the consumer will have to give up are worth more than the marginal benefits received from consuming the good. Consumers will prefer those goods for which marginal benefits exceed the price by the greatest margin.

Income affects a consumer's ability to pay. Total and marginal benefits are the maximum sum of dollars that buyers are willing and able to give up to obtain some total or additional quantity of a good. An increase in income therefore increases the consumer's ability to give up dollars for benefits. For (11)_____(inferior goods, normal goods), an increase in income causes the marginal benefit curve to shift upward. At any quantity, the maximum additional dollars that a buyer is willing and able to give up for an additional unit of output increases. For (12)_____(inferior goods, normal goods), an increase in income shifts the marginal benefit curve downward. The maximum additional dollars that a buyer is willing and able to give up for an additional unit of output decreases.

(13)_____(Market, Individual) demand curves can be derived from the individual's marginal benefit curve. A price-quantity demanded coordinate on a demand curve represents a point of consumption at which a utility-maximizing consumer has equated price and marginal benefit. If the price falls, the buyer's marginal benefit temporarily exceeds price. The consumer can increase net benefits by increasing consumption to the point where price and marginal benefit are once again equal. Thus lower prices are associated with higher quantities demanded. This assumes that income, tastes, and other influences are held unchanged.

Price changes have two effects: the income effect and the substitution effect. A decrease in price, for instance, increases the purchasing power of a given income and increases the consumer's ability to consume more of all normal goods, including the one for which prices have decreased. This is known as the (14)_____(substitution, income) effect. A decrease in price relative to the prices of other goods will induce the buyer to substitute the relatively less costly good for more expensive goods. With the income effect neutralized, the (15)_____(substitution, income) effect means that price and quantity demanded are always inversely related. For normal goods, the income effect (16)_____(complements, offsets to some extent) the substitution effect in that both effects work to increase quantities consumed as the price decreases. For inferior goods, the income effect (17)_____ (complements, to some extent offsets) the substitution effect of a price change. For a special variety of goods called Giffen goods, the income effect (18)_____(more than offsets, does not offset) the substitution effect, causing prices to be positively related to quantity demanded!

The market demand curve is a horizontal summation or aggregation of the demand curves of individual buyers in the market. The market demand is downsloping and shifts when individual demand curves shift.

VOCABULARY REVIEW

Write the key term from the list below next to its definition.

Key Terms

Preferences   Net benefit
Utility   Marginal benefit
Total utility   Paradox of value
Marginal utility   Income effect
Law of diminishing   Substitution effect
  marginal utility   Total benefit
Consumer equilibrium   Market demand curve
Equimarginal principle   Consumer surplus

Definitions

1. _____: the change in consumption of a good only as a result of the variation in the purchasing power of money income caused by a price change.

2. _____: the change in consumption of a good only as a result of a change in its price relative to the prices of other goods.

3. _____: shows the relationship between the price of a product and the total quantity demanded by all consumers willing and able to purchase the product at each price, other things being equal.

4. _____: states that the marginal utility of any item tends to decline as more is consumed over any given period.

5. _____: the maximum sum of money a consumer is willing and able to give up to obtain another unit of a good.

6. _____: the difference between the total benefit of a given quantity purchased by a consumer and the expenditure necessary to purchase that quantity.

7. _____: people are willing to give up zero or very small amounts of money to obtain certain items that provide them great total benefit.

8. _____: total satisfaction enjoyed from consuming any given quantity of a good.

9. _____: the maximum sum of money a consumer would give up to obtain a certain quantity of a good.

10. _____: the total benefit of the quantity of a good purchased less the dollar sacrifice necessary to purchase that quantity.

11. _____: the extra satisfaction received over a given period by consuming one extra unit of a good.

12. _____: the satisfaction consumers receive from items they acquire, activities they engage in, or services they use.

13. _____: states that to maximize utility, a consumer must equalize the marginal utility per dollar spent on each good.

14. _____ :   individual likes and dislikes.

15. _____ :   attained when a consumer purchases goods over a period until the marginal utility per dollar is the same for all goods consumed.

SKILLS REVIEW

Concept: Total and marginal utility

1. The table below contains quantity and total utility data for consumption of good X.

Units of Good X	Total Utility	Marginal Utility
1	50	_____
2	90	_____
3	120	_____
4	140	_____
5	150	_____
6	150	_____
7	140	_____

a. Complete the marginal utility column above.
b. Plot the total and marginal utility data on the diagrams below.

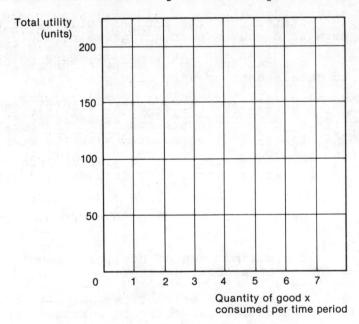

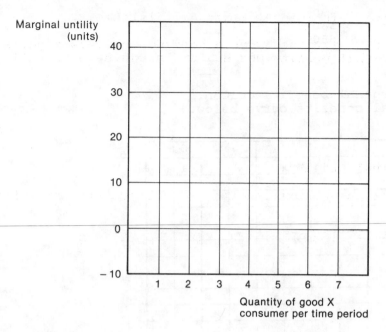

Marginal untility (units)

Quantity of good X
consumer per time period

c.   Marginal utility is the _____ of the total utility curve. When
     total utility reaches a maximum, marginal utility equals _____.

Concept: Equimarginal principle

2.   Assume that an individual has an income of $150 per week to be spent on
     either ballpark tickets or sweaters. The price of each ballpark admission
     is $5 and the price of a sweater is $25. The individual is assumed to
     spend all income each week. Given the total utility data below:

     a.   Complete the marginal utility (MU) columns.
     b.   Complete the marginal utility per dollar (MU/P) columns.
     c.   Determine the individual's utility-maximizing combination of ballpark
          tickets and sweaters. _____ tickets and _____ sweaters
     d.   Determine the total utility (TU) associated with the combination of
          goods consumed from part c. _____ units of utility

	Ballpark Tickets				Sweaters		
Units	TU	MU	MU/P	Units	TU	MU	MU/P
1	60	___	___	1	400	___	___
2	115	___	___	2	750	___	___
3	165	___	___	3	1050	___	___
4	210	___	___	4	1300	___	___
5	250	___	___	5	1500	___	___
6	285	___	___	6	1650	___	___
7	315	___	___				

Concept: Total and marginal benefits; the impact of price and income

3.   The following represent total and marginal benefit data for a consumer:

Units of Good X	Total Benefits ($)	Marginal Benefits ($)
1	$250	___
2	380	___

3	490	___
4	580	___
5	650	___
6	700	___
7	730	___

a. Complete the marginal benefits column.
b. Plot the marginal benefits curve below.

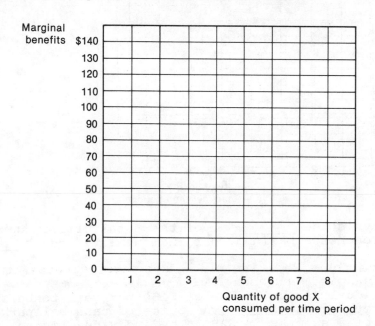

Quantity of good X
consumed per time period

c. If price equals $90 per unit, how many units of good X would be
    consumed?_____units. At this level of consumption, total benefits
    equal $_____, consumer surplus equals $_____.
d. If price equals $50 per unit, how many units of good X would be
    consumed?_____units. At this level of consumption, total benefits
    equal $_____, consumer surplus equals $_____.
e. If price equals $200, how many units of the good would be
    consumed?_____ units Why?

f.   Plot the price-quantity demanded coordinates from parts c and d above
     in the diagram below. This curve is called a/an _____ .

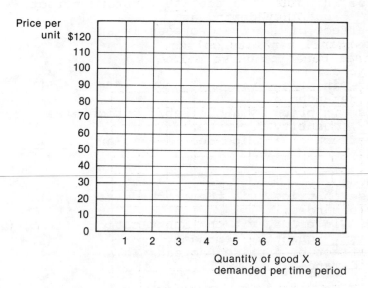

4.   The following diagram represents the price and marginal benefits curve
     associated with a consumer's purchases of a good.

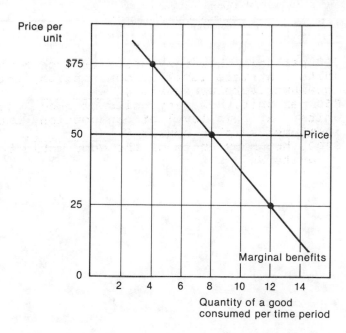

     a.   In the diagram, show the impact of an increase in income if the good
          is a normal good. Quantity consumed _____ .
     b.   In the diagram, show the impact of an increase in income if the good
          is an inferior good. Quantity consumed _____ .

117

5. a. For normal goods:
        (1) A decrease in price, via the income effect, will _____
             quantity demanded.
        (2) A decrease in price, via the substitution effect, will
             _____ quantity demanded.
        (3) The net effect of a price decrease is an _____ in quantity
             demanded.

    b. For inferior goods:
        (1) A decrease in price, via the income effect, will _____
             quantity demanded.
        (2) A decrease in price, via the substitution effect, will
             _____ quantity demanded.
        (3) The net effect of a price decrease is an _____ in quantity
             demanded.

    c. For Giffen goods,
        (1) A decrease in price, via the income effect, will _____
             quantity demanded.
        (2) A decrease in price, via the substitution effect, will
             _____ quantity demanded.
        (3) The net effect of a price decrease is an _____ in
             quantity demanded.

Concept: **Market demand curve**

6. Derive the market demand curve in diagram d below from the individual
    demand curves shown in figures a, b, and c.

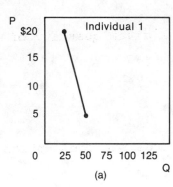

(a)

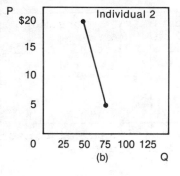

(b)

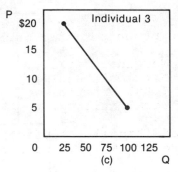

(c)

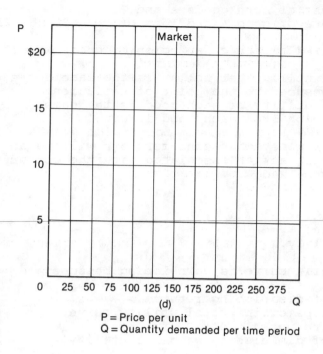

(d)

P = Price per unit
Q = Quantity demanded per time period

SELF-TEST FOR MASTERY

Select the best answer.

1. The total satisfaction received by a consumer from a given quantity of consumption per time period is known as:

    a. Marginal utility.
    b. Marginal benefit.
    c. Total benefit.
    d. Total utility.

2. The additional satisfaction received by a consumer from the consumption of an additional unit of a good is known as:

    a. Marginal utility.
    b. Marginal benefit.
    c. Total benefit.
    d. Total utility.

3. Which of the following defines the law of diminishing marginal utility?

    a. Total utility rises at an increasing rate as additional units of a good are consumed
    b. Marginal utility rises at an increasing rate as additional units of a good are consumed.
    c. Marginal utility falls as more of a good is consumed over a period.
    d. Total utility falls as more of a good is consumed over a period.

4. If the marginal utility per dollar (MU/P) of good A exceeded the MU/P of good B, a consumer could increase utility by:

    a. Not altering the combination of goods A and B consumed.
    b. Consuming more of good B and less of good A.

119

c.   Consuming less of both goods A and B.
d.   Consuming more of good A and less of good B.

5.   Utility is maximized in the consumption of goods when:

a.   The marginal utility per dollar is the same for each good.
b.   Goods are consumed to the point of satiation.
c.   The marginal utility of each good is the same.
d.   The satisfaction from each good is equal.

6.   The maximum sum of money that consumers are willing and able to pay for the additional satisfaction associated with the consumption of an extra unit of output is called:

a.   Income.
b.   Total benefit.
c.   Marginal benefit.
d.   Marginal utility.

7.   The marginal benefit curve is downsloping because:

a.   Of the law of diminishing returns.
b.   It is the slope of the total utility curve.
c.   Most goods are normal goods.
d.   Of the law of diminishing marginal utility.

8.   A consumer can maximize net benefits by consuming a good to the point where marginal benefit:

a.   Equals the price.
b.   Equals marginal utility.
c.   Equals total benefit.
d.   Is equal for all goods.

9.   If goods A and B are associated with marginal benefits of $5 and $10, respectively, for the first unit consumed, a consumer would _____ if the price of good A equaled $6 and the price of good B equaled $12.50.

a.   Purchase both goods A and B
b.   Not purchase either good
c.   Prefer A to B
d.   Prefer B to A

10. Which of the following terms represents total benefits received in excess of the dollar expenditure necessary to obtain goods?

a.   Consumer excess
b.   Net gain
c.   Consumer surplus
d.   B or c

11. If the excess of marginal benefits over the product price for good A exceeds that of good B, a consumer:

a.   Is indifferent regarding the purchase of goods A and B.
b.   Would prefer A to B.
c.   Would not prefer either good.
d.   Would prefer B to A.

12. An increase in income shifts the marginal benefit curve _____, resulting in an increase in consumption if the good in question is a _____ good.

    a. Upward, inferior
    b. Downward, normal
    c. Upward, normal
    d. Upward, Giffen

13. The income effect reinforces the substitution effect for:

    a. Normal goods.
    b. Inferior goods.
    c. Giffen goods.
    d. Public goods.

14. The income effect to some extent offsets the substitution effect for:

    a. Normal goods.
    b. Inferior goods.
    c. Public goods.
    d. All goods and services.

15. The income effect more than offsets the substitution effect for:

    a. Normal goods.
    b. Inferior goods.
    c. Public goods.
    d. Giffen goods.

16. A market demand curve:

    a. Is a horizontal summation of individual demand curves.
    b. Is downsloping.
    c. Is the culmination of utility-maximizing choices by consumers.
    d. All of the above.

THINK IT THROUGH

1. You go to a restaurant, look at the menu, and find that the price of a cheese omelette is $3.50 and the price of a short stack of pancakes is $2. Your marginal benefits associated with the next order of an omelette or pancakes are $5 and $2.75, respectively. Which do you prefer? Why?

2. Explain the logic underlying the equimarginal principle.

3. You complain because your spouse always purchases the more expensive good when confronted with a choice. Assume that price and product quality are not always positively related. Is your spouse a utility maximizer? Discuss.

4. Why are people often willing and able to spend large sums on goods with limited usefulness like gold money clips when these same people are willing to spend little if any money for essential goods like air or water?

Read the news brief at the end of this chapter and answer the
question below.

Explain, using supply and demand analysis, why condominium prices are rising
everywhere but the Midwest.

CHAPTER ANSWERS

In Brief: Chapter Summary

1. Total 2. Marginal utility 3. Equals 4. Maximum 5. Declining 6. Declines
7. Exceed 8. Equals 9. Dollar expenditure 10. Exceeds 11. Normal goods 12.
Inferior good 13. Individual 14. Income 15. Substitution 16. Complements
17. To some extent offsets 18. More than offsets

Vocabulary Review

1. Income effect 2. Substitution effect 3. Market demand curve 4. Law of
diminishing marginal utility 5. Marginal benefit 6. Consumer surplus 7.
Paradox of value 8. Total utility 9. Total benefit 10. Net benefit 11.
Marginal utility 12. Utility 13. Equimarginal principle 14. Preference 15.
Consumer equilibrium

Skills Review

1. a.

Units	MU
1	50
2	40
3	30
4	20
5	10
6	0
7	-10

b.

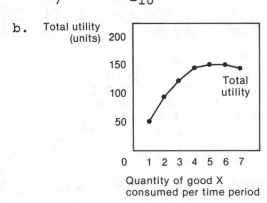
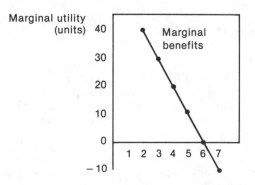

c.   Slope, zero

2. a.   and b.

	Tickets			Sweaters		
Units	MU	MU/P	Units	MU	MU/P
1	60	12	1	400	16
2	55	11	2	350	14
3	50	10	3	300	12

4	45	9		4	250	10
5	40	8		5	200	8
6	35	7		6	150	6
7	30	6				

    c.   5, 5
    d.   1750

3.   a.

Units	MB ($)
1	
2	130
3	110
4	90
5	70
6	50
7	30

    b.

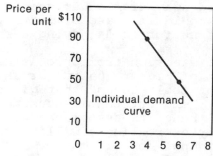

    c.   4, $580, $220
    d.   6, $700, $400
    e.   None. Price exceeds marginal benefits for the first unit consumed.
    f.   Individual demand curve

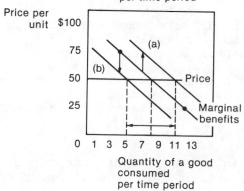

4.   a.   Increases

     b.   Decreases

5.   a.   (1) Increase   (2) Increase   (3) Increase
      b.   (1) Decrease   (2) Increase   (3) Increase
      c.   (1) Decrease   (2) Increase   (3) Decrease

6.

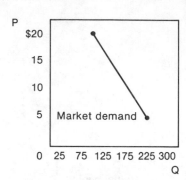

Self-Test for Mastery

1. d 2. a 3. c 4. d 5. a 6. d 7. d 8. a 9. b 10. d 11. b 12. c 13. a 14. b 15. d 16. d

Think it Through

1.   For both goods, marginal benefits exceed price. But for an omelette, the difference between the marginal benefit and price is greater than it is for pancakes. The net gain to you is greater if you purchase an omelette rather than pancakes. You prefer, therefore, an omelette to pancakes.

2.   A consumer maximizes utility when the marginal utility per dollar for each good consumed is the same. If the MU/P for some good exceeded that for other goods, dollars could be reallocated away from other goods and spent on the good with the higher MU/P. A consumer could increase utility by reallocating a given income. The reverse holds true for goods having a smaller MU/P.

3.   Your spouse probably gets satisfaction from purchasing more expensive goods. It might be the perception of higher quality or an attempt to keep up with the Joneses or the need to not feel "cheap" that gives your spouse "tastes" for higher priced goods. Remember that a consumer's preferences depend on both prices and marginal benefits associated with goods. For higher priced goods, your spouse is simply expressing a willingness and ability to pay a higher maximum sum--a higher marginal benefit curve. But for the higher priced good to be chosen, the excess of marginal benefits over the price must be larger than for lower priced goods, or it would be irrational to purchase the more expensive good.

4.   Plentiful goods such as air or water command either no market price or a very minimal price. The additional benefit of a gallon of water is very small. The price you are willing to pay is likewise very small even though the total benefit associated with water consumption is quite large. Because of their scarcity, the additional benefit of a gold clip is high. Some people are willing to pay high prices for gold money clips even though the total benefits received from the clips are very small relative to the consumption of water.

Pop Quiz

Single-family homes and condominiums are substitutes in consumption. If two goods are substitutes, an increase in the price of one good causes the demand

124

for the other good to increase. In all regions of the country except the Midwest, the median prices of single-family homes have been increasing. Prices have increased 10.5% in the South, 5.8% in the West, and 2% in the Northeast. As the price of single-family homes increases, the demand for condominiums increases. As the demand for condominiums rises relative to the supply of condominiums, condominium prices rise and market quantity increases.

Prices for Condominiums Are on the Rebound

CONDOMINIUM prices declined in the early 1980s because of overbuilding: too many condos, not enough buyers. Now the glut is drying up—and prices are on the rise.

In the Northeast, South and West, prices for condos have increased on average about 18% over the five quarters through March 31, according to the National Association of Realtors.

The reason for the reversal: In many markets, the rising costs of single-family homes have sent buyers searching for less expensive alternatives, and condos have been the answer. As a result, their prices have jumped.

During the first quarter of 1988, this was especially true in the South, where median prices soared 10.5%, to $65,300 from $59,-100. In the West, prices rose 5.8%, to $105,100 from $99,300. And in the Northeast, where more than half of all condos are now sold, prices rose 2%, to $111,100 from $108,900.

The only region where prices are continuing to decline is the Midwest, where they dipped to $57,600 from $58,700. That's because the region still has a healthy supply of affordable single-family homes.

Indifference Curve Analysis

IN BRIEF: APPENDIX SUMMARY

Fill in the blanks to summarize appendix content.

(1)_____(Marginal, Indifference curve analysis) is a technique for analyzing the choices that consumers make between alternatives. The indifference curve and budget constraint are the essential elements of the analysis. Applied to goods, an indifference curve shows the various combinations of two goods that can be consumed while maintaining (2)_____(the same level, different levels) of utility. The curve is negatively sloped because in order to keep utility unchanged, the consumer must give up some consumption of a good in order to increase the consumption of another good. The slope of the indifference curve becomes less negative as more of the good on the horizontal axis is consumed. The slope is called the (3)_____(marginal utility, marginal rate of substitution). It indicates the quantity of one good that a consumer is willing to give up to have a unit of another good, while maintaining the level of utility. The marginal rate of substitution of x for y (MRSxy) (4)_____ (decreases, increases) as more of good X is consumed. This is known as the diminishing marginal rate of substitution. The consumer is willing to give up large quantities of Y in order to have the first few units of good X. As more and more units of X are consumed, the consumer is willing to sacrifice smaller and smaller quantities of good Y. Marginal utility and marginal benefits fall as additional units of X are consumed. But reducing the consumption of Y increases the marginal utility and benefit of Y. At the margin, units of X become increasingly less valuable in terms of the sacrifice of good Y. Indifference curves (5)_____(closer to, further from) the origin are associated with higher levels of utility.

   (6)_____(The budget constraint, Income) determines the consumer's ability to maximize satisfaction from the consumption of goods X and Y. The budget constraint is determined by the income per period available to the consumer and the relative prices of the two goods consumed. The slope of the budget line is negative and is the ratio of the price of good X to the price of good Y. Changes in (7)_____(income, prices) shift the budget line, whereas changes in (8)_____(income, prices) alter the slope.

   Consumer equilibrium occurs when the market value of good Y that you are willing to give up just equals what the market requires you to pay for a unit of good X. This occurs where the budget line (9)_____(intersects, is just tangent to) the highest indifference curve. Here the marginal rate of substitution equals the ratio of the price of good X to the price of good Y. The consumer spends all income and allocates it in a way that maximizes utility. It can be shown that the MRSxy also equals the ratio of the marginal utility of good X to the marginal utility of good Y. MUx/MUy also equals the price ratio. The point of tangency between the indifference curve and budget constraint is equivalent to the equimarginal principle when the slope of the indifference curve is interpreted as the ratio of these marginal utilities.

An increase in income shifts the budget constraint curve (10)_____ (outward, inward) parallel to the old budget line such that a new point of tangency is reached on a higher indifference curve. For instance, if goods are normal, an income increase will cause the consumption of both goods to (11)_____(fall, rise). A decrease in the price of X will cause the budget line to become less steep. The consumption of X increases, and the consumer attains a higher level of utility. A demand curve for good X can be derived by changing the price of good X, all other things being equal, and determining the consumer's utility-maximizing quantity demanded. Plotting these price-quantity demanded coordinates yields the consumer's individual demand curve.

VOCABULARY REVIEW

Write the key term from the list below next to its definition.

Key Terms

Indifference curve analysis   Consumer equilibrium
Market basket   Budget constraint
Indifference curve   Indifference map
Marginal rate of   Diminishing marginal
    substitution   rate of substitution

Definitions

1. _____: the marginal rate of substitution of good X for Y will tend to decline as more X is substituted for Y along any consumer's indifference curve.

2. _____: represents the combination of goods purchased that maximizes utility subject to the budget constraint.

3. _____: a technique for explaining how choices between two alternatives are made.

4. _____: as defined by a consumer's income and its purchasing power; indicates that income must equal expenditure.

5. _____: a graph of various market baskets that provide a consumer with equal utility.

6. _____: the quantity of one good a consumer would give up to obtain one more unit of another good while being made neither better off nor worse off by the trade.

7. _____: a combination of goods and services.

8. _____: a way of describing consumer preferences.

SKILLS REVIEW

1.   In the diagram below, draw a budget constraint where the consumer has income of $100 per week and the prices of goods X and Y are both $5.

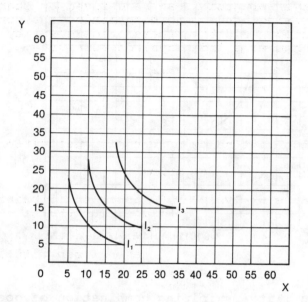

a.   The consumer's utility-maximizing combination of goods X and Y are _____ units of good X and _____ units of good Y.

b.   Show on the diagram above the effect of an increase in income to $150 per week. The consumption of good X _____ to _____ units and the consumption of good Y _____ to _____ units. The goods must be _____ goods.

c.   Holding income at $150 per week, show the impact of a price reduction of good X to $2.50. The consumption of good X _____ to _____ units; the consumption of good Y _____ to _____ units.

2. Referring to the diagram below, let income equal $120 and assume that the prices of X and Y equal $10.

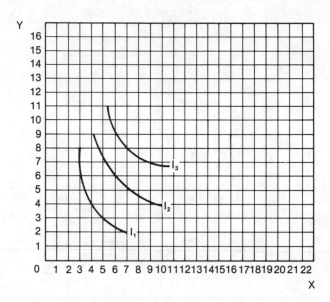

a. Determine the utility-maximizing combination of goods X and Y.
_____ units of X, _____ units of Y

b. Let the price of X fall to $6. The utility-maximizing quantity of X consumed is _____ units. Of Y consumed the utility-maximizing quantity is _____ units.

c. Let the price of X rise from $10 to $20. The utility-maximizing combination of X and Y is _____ units of X and _____ units of Y.

d. Construct this consumer's individual demand curve in the diagram below for good X from the information in parts b and c above.

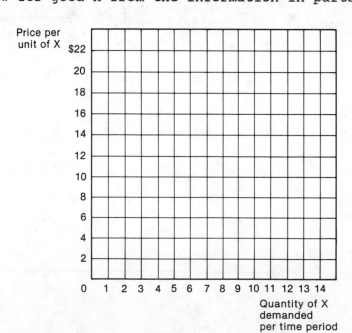

SELF-TEST FOR MASTERY

Select the best answer.

1. Which of the following are true regarding an indifference curve?

    a. The slope is negative.
    b. The MRSxy increases as more of good X is consumed.
    c. The MRSxy decreases as more of good X is consumed.
    d. Indifference curves farther from the origin imply a higher level of utility.
    e. A, c, and d.

2. The budget constraint:

    a. Has a positive slope.
    b. Must be curvilinear if the prices of the two goods are held unchanged.
    c. Has a slope equal to -(Px/Py).
    d. None of the above.

3. Increases in income shift the budget constraint:

    a. Inward.
    b. Outward.
    c. To a different slope.
    d. Such that it no longer limits consumer purchases.

4. A change in price of either good X or Y will:

    a. Shift the indifference curve.
    b. Shift the budget constraint.
    c. Rotate the indifference curve.
    d. Rotate the budget constraint about one of its two intercepts.

5. Consumer equilibrium occurs when:

    a. The budget constraint and the indifference curve intersect.
    b. Two indifference curves intersect.
    c. The highest indifference curve on the indifference curve map is attained.
    d. The budget constraint is just tangent to the highest indifference curve.

6. In an indifference curve system, an increase in the price of good X will _____ the budget constraint toward the origin and _____ the quantity of good X consumed.

    a. Rotate, decrease
    b. Rotate, increase
    c. Shift, decrease
    d. Shift, increase

7. In an indifference curve system, an increase in income will _____
    the budget constraint away from the origin, and the quantity of good X
    consumed will _____ if good X is a normal good.

    a. Rotate, decrease
    b. Rotate, increase
    c. Shift, decrease
    d. Shift, increase

8. Which one of the following is true regarding consumer equilibrium?

    a. MRSxy = MUx = MUy
    b. MRSxy = (MUx/MUy) = (Px/Py)
    c. (Px/Py) + MRSxy = (MUx/MUy)
    d. None of the above

THINK IT THROUGH

1. Every point on a consumer's individual demand curve represents a utility-
maximizing decision. Discuss.

2. Explain how market demand curves can be derived from individual demand
curves.

APPENDIX ANSWERS

In Brief: Appendix Summary

1. Indifference curve analysis 2. The same level 3. Marginal rate of
substitution 4. Decreases 5. Further from 6. Budget constraint 7. Income
8. Prices 9. Is just tangent to 10. Outward   11. Rise

Vocabulary Review

1. Diminishing marginal rate of substitution 2. Consumer equilibrium 3.
Indifference curve analysis 4. Budget constraint 5. Indifference curve 6.
Marginal rate of substitution 7. Market basket 8. Indifference map

Skills Review

1.

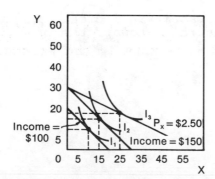

    a. 10, 10
    b. Increases, 15, increases, 15, normal
    c. Increases, 25, increases, 17 1/2

132

2.

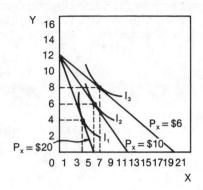

a. 6, 6
b. 7, 8
c. 4, 4

d.

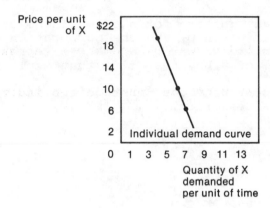

Self-Test for Mastery

1. c 2. c 3. b 4. d 5. d 6. b 7. d 8. b

Think it Through

1.   A coordinate on the consumer's individual demand curve represents a utility-maximizing response to a given price of the good relative to other product prices, other things being equal. This is true of other coordinates on the demand curve. Each point on the demand curve represents a state of consumer equilibrium.

2.   Market demand curves represent the utility-maximizing responses of all consumers to relative prices. It can be derived by horizontally summing the individual demand curves of all consumers in the market.

9

The Business Firm: A Prologue to the Theory of Market Supply

CHAPTER CHALLENGES

After studying your text, attending class, and completing this chapter, you should be able to:

1. Explain how various aspects of production and distribution are integrated within a single firm.
2. Outline the advantages of alternative forms of business organization (the sole proprietorship, the partnership, and the corporation) and discuss the functions of business firms.
3. Describe a simplified model of a business firm that explains market supply.
4. Show how the concept of opportunity cost must be applied to accurately measure the profit of a business firm.

IN BRIEF: CHAPTER SUMMARY

Fill in the blanks to summarize chapter content.

Business firms, each of which is under one management, are engaged in earning profits for the owners by producing items for sale in markets. They operate one or more plants producing one or more products and in some cases are vertically integrated. Vertical integration means that all stages of operation, including the acquisition of raw materials, the processing of resources to produce output, and the distribution and marketing of goods are handled by (1)_____ (several firms, a single firm). A (2)_____ (conglomerate, corporation) is a firm that produces many kinds of goods and services. Firms selling (3)_____(different, similar) products are in the same industry.

A firm can be structured as a sole proprietorship, a partnership, or a corporation. A (4)_____(partnership, corporation) is a legal person. It has some distinct advantages over other business enterprises. Corporations can issue both stocks and bonds and the owners of the corporation (the stockholders) have (5)_____(limited, unlimited) liability. Both of these characteristics greatly (6)_____ (reduce, increase) the amount of funds that can be attracted for expansion and growth. Stockholders can easily sell their rights in the firm. Individuals can reduce the risk associated with owning firms by diversifying their holdings. This increases the total amount of funds available for stock ownership. Another factor that induces individuals to provide more funds to the corporation is (7)_____(limited, unlimited) liability. This too reduces the risk of ownership in that a stockholder's liability relates to the amount of stock held. Other business enterprises are at (8)_____ (an advantage, a disadvantage) compared to corporations in that they have unlimited liability and cannot issue stocks and bonds.

In corporations, ownership and management (9)_____(are, are not) separated. If management pursues goals that are inconsistent with the owners' goals, profits decrease because managers use corporate resources to attain managerial goals that would have otherwise been used to further the goals of the owners. Also, owners must use resources to monitor management to ensure that the owners' goals are met. Another disadvantage of corporations is that they are not only subject to a corporate income tax, but the (10)_____ (retained earnings, dividends) paid to stockholders are subject to individual income taxes as well. Thus the income of the corporation is taxed twice. This (11)_____(is, is not) the case for other business enterprises.

The functions of business firms include the production of goods and services, the assignment of tasks to either employees or to outside firms for various stages of production, and a determination of the appropriate division of labor within the firm. Managers assist in these functions by helping to decide what and how much to produce and whether certain operations should be handled internally or contracted out. Operations are likely to be (12)_____ (contracted out, kept within the firm) if a reliable flow of materials and services is considered important and there is a possibility that outside suppliers might prove unreliable. A firm might want to control a strategic input and thus put other firms in the industry at a disadvantage. Or a firm might put a premium on internal communication or the ability to easily adapt to new technology. All of these things would probably induce a firm to vertically integrate--to handle all production stages within the firm. Managers also have to assign labor-specific tasks or responsibilities so that the firm can operate at least cost. Managers reward efficient employees with a compensation system designed to maintain and enhance labor productivity.

In studying the behavior of firms, it is necessary to abstract from the complexities of the modern economy and make some assumptions regarding the structure or goals of firms so that the basic features of firm behavior can be understood. It is assumed that there (13)_____(is, is no) separation between ownership and management. Firms are assumed to be (14)_____ (multiproduct, single product), having owner-operators who make decisions regarding resource use and production that maximize (15)_____(revenues, profits).

Profit is defined as total revenue less total costs in which total costs include (16)_____(in addition to, only) the accounting costs, (17)_____(but not the,the) cost of owner-supplied resources. (18)_____ (Total, Accounting) costs are the explicit outlays by the firm for resources bought in resource markets. Owner-supplied inputs are not purchased by the firm but entail opportunity costs. These (19)_____ (explicit, implicit) costs must be imputed or estimated. They are estimated by determining the opportunity cost of the owner-supplied inputs. Revenues in excess of accounting and implicit costs are called (20)_____(economic, normal) profit. (21)_____(Economic, Normal) profit is treated as a cost (the implicit costs associated with owner-supplied resources). It is a return to the owner-operator just equal to the opportunity cost of self-owned resources.

VOCABULARY REVIEW

Write the key term from the list below next to its definition.

Key Terms

Business firm
Plant
Vertical integration
Conglomerate
Industry
Sole proprietorship
Partnership
Corporation
Dividend
Retained earnings
Limited liability

Manager
Personnel management
Multiproduct firm
Single-product firm
Profit
Economic cost
Implicit cost
Accounting cost
Normal profit
Economic profit

Definitions

1. _____: that portion of a firm's costs that is not included in accounting costs. A measure of the implicit cost of owner-supplied resources in a firm over a given period.

2. _____: profit in excess of the normal profit; the difference between total revenue and the opportunity cost of all inputs used by a firm over a given period.

3. _____: the portion of a corporation's profit paid to its stockholders.

4. _____: the portion of corporate profits not paid out as dividends.

5. _____: the monetary value of all inputs used in a particular activity or enterprise over a given period.

6. _____: the cost of nonpurchased inputs to which a cash value must be imputed because the inputs are not purchased in a market transaction.

7. _____: a group of firms selling a similar product in a market.

8. _____: a business that is legally established under state laws that grant it an identity separate from its owners.

9. _____: an organization under one management set up for the purpose of earning profits for its owners by making one or more items available for sale in markets.

10. _____: a business owned by one person.

11. _____: a physical structure in which a firm's owners or employees conduct business.

12. _____: a business owned by two or more persons, each of whom receives a portion of any profits.

13. _____: a firm that owns plants used in various stages of its production.

14. _____: measures the explicit costs of operating a business, those which result from purchases of input services.

15. _____: a firm's operating plants that produce many different kinds of goods and services.

16. _____: a person who coordinates decisions within the firm.

17. _____: a firm that produces only one type of item for sale.

18. _____: a firm that produces several different items for sale.

19. _____: a legal provision that protects the owners of a corporation (its stockholders) by putting a ceiling equal to the purchase price of their stock on their liability for debts of the corporation.

20. _____: the difference between the revenues a firm takes in over any given period and the costs incurred in operating the firm over the same period.

21. _____: the process by which managers monitor worker performance and provide rewards for workers who perform efficiently.

SKILLS REVIEW

Concept: Alternative forms of business organization

1.   Which of the following characteristics are associated with corporations (C), sole proprietorships (PR), and/or partnerships (PT)?

    a.   _____   Limited liability
    b.   _____   Unlimited liability
    c.   _____   Separation of ownership and management
    d.   _____   Presence of owner-operators
    e.   _____   Ability to issue stock and bonds
    f.   _____   Can pay dividends
    g.   _____   Income is subject to personal income
                       taxes only
    h.   _____   Income is subject to taxation twice
    i.   _____   Is a legal person

Concept: Functions of business

2.   List three functions of business firms:

    a.   _____
    b.   _____
    c.   _____

3. List three ways in which managers assist business firms in the fulfillment
    of their functions:

    a. _____
    b. _____
    c. _____

4. You manage a U.S.-based corporation, the XYZ Aluminum Company, and you are
    trying to decide whether to mine your own raw input, bauxite, internally
    or to purchase it from outside firms. Assume that bauxite is found only
    in Africa and must be processed into aluminum ingots before shipment to
    fabrication plants in the United States. For each of the scenarios below,
    are you _more_ or _less_ inclined to contract out? Explain.

    a. _____ War develops, closing sea lanes.
    b. _____ Civil wars are no longer occurring in African
                  nations, raising the possibility of long-term
                  peace and political stability.
    c. _____ There are no substitutes for bauxite in the
                  production of aluminum.
    d. _____ XYZ is battling with four other companies
                  for a larger share of the aluminum market.
    e. _____ XYZ finds that closer managerial
                  communication among the various stages of
                  production enhances the firm's efficiency.
    f. _____ XYZ patents a process that reduces the
                  cost of mining bauxite.
    g. _____ Because the world supply of bauxite and
                  aluminum ingots is produced by firms
                  specializing in the production of these inputs,
                  they produce a large volume, realizing
                  efficiencies associated with large-scale
                  production and specialization.

Concept: Cost and profit measures

5. Given the data in the table below for Fred's Bar and Grill, determine
    Fred's:

    a. Accounting cost_____
    b. Explicit cost   _____
    c. Implicit cost   _____
    d. Normal profit   _____
    e. Total cost   _____
    f. Economic profit_____

Fred's Bar and Grill
(annual data)

Wages	$25,000
Depreciation	15,000
Interest paid	7,000
Other expenditures for inputs	17,000
Imputed cost of owner-supplied labor	20,000
Imputed cost of owner-supplied plant	6,000
Imputed interest associated with owner-supplied resources	2,000
Total revenue	108,000

6. Discuss the implications if Fred's Bar and Grill earned $85,000 of revenue instead of $108,000.

SELF-TEST FOR MASTERY

Select the best answer.

1. A business firm that engages in several stages of production from the acquisition of resources to the distribution of output is known as a:

    a. Conglomerate.
    b. Single-product firm.
    c. Multiproduct firm.
    d. Vertically integrated firm.

2. A business firm that sells output in many different industries is known as a:

    a. Conglomerate.
    b. Single-product firm.
    c. Multiproduct firm.
    d. Vertically integrated firm.
    e. A and c.

3. Which of the following best describes an industry?

    a. A collection of markets
    b. A group of firms
    c. A group of firms selling similar products
    d. A collection of markets for unrelated goods

4. Unlimited liability is a characteristic of:

    a. Corporations.
    b. Sole proprietorships.
    c. Partnerships.
    d. B and c.

5. The ability to issue stock and bonds is a characteristic of:

   a. Corporations.
   b. Sole proprietorships.
   c. Partnerships.
   d. B and c.

6. The separation of ownership and management is a characteristic of:

   a. Corporations.
   b. Sole proprietorships.
   c. Partnerships.
   d. B and c.

7. Which of the following is a legal person?

   a. Corporation
   b. Sole proprietorship
   c. Partnership
   d. None of the above

8. The main advantage of a corporation over other forms of business enterprise is that:

   a. Other forms of business enterprise have their incomes taxed twice.
   b. Other forms of business enterprise have limited liability.
   c. Corporations have unlimited liability.
   d. Corporations can raise larger sums of money for expansion and growth.

9. That portion of corporate income which is not paid as dividends or used to meet the corporation's tax liability is called:

   a. Depreciation.
   b. Retained earnings.
   c. Normal profit.
   d. Implicit cost.

10. A business firm is less likely to contract out for production or services if:

    a. Communication within the firm between various production stages is relatively unimportant.
    b. Controlling a strategic input is unimportant to the firm.
    c. Adapting to changing technology is considered unimportant.
    d. There is a possibility that outside suppliers might prove unreliable.

11. A business firm is more likely to contract out when:

    a. Communication within the firm between various stages of production is important.
    b. Controlling a strategic input is considered important.
    c. Adapting to changing technology is important.
    d. Outside suppliers are reliable.
    e. All of the above

12. Abstracting from the complexities of the modern economy to better understand the essential features of business firm behavior, several simplifying assumptions are made. Which of the following is not one of these?

    a. Ownership and management are not separated.
    b. The firm is a single-product firm.
    c. The goal of the firm is to maximize profits.
    d. The firm is vertically integrated.

13. The total actual payments made by a firm to acquire inputs are known as:

    a. Accounting costs.
    b. Normal profit.
    c. Implicit costs.
    d. Marginal costs.

14. Accounting costs are also called:

    a. Explicit costs.
    b. Total costs.
    c. Total normal costs.
    d. Imputed costs.

15. The cost of nonpurchased owner-supplied resources is known as:

    a. Implicit costs.
    b. Explicit costs.
    c. Accounting costs.
    d. Total costs.

16. Implicit costs are measured by the:

    a. Accounting costs less the imputed costs.
    b. Imputed costs plus the explicit costs.
    c. Total revenues less total costs.
    d. Opportunity cost of owner-supplied resources.

17. Total costs are the sum of:

    a. Accounting costs and explicit costs.
    b. Accounting costs and the opportunity costs of owner-supplied resources.
    c. Imputed costs and the opportunity costs of owner-supplied resources.
    d. Accounting costs and implicit costs.
    e. B and d.

18. A return to the owner just equal to the opportunity costs of the owner's self-owned resources provided to the firm is called:

    a. Total revenue.
    b. Imputed revenue.
    c. Normal profit.
    d. Economic profit.

19. Economic profit is defined as:

   a. A return to the owner just equal to the opportunity costs of the
       owner's self-owned resources provided to the firm.
   b. Total revenue less accounting costs.
   c. Total revenue less the sum of accounting costs and implicit costs.
   d. Normal profit plus imputed revenues.

THINK IT THROUGH

1. Of the three forms of business enterprise, why are sole proprietorships
and partnerships so numerous and corporations so large?

2. The microcomputer industry is populated by many more firms operating at a
single stage of production than by vertically integrated firms. Explain why.

3. Why is it necessary to consider implicit costs in decisions?

4. You are considering owning and operating a day care center. You determine
that the annual cost to hire labor is $35,000. You plan to use one of your
rental houses for the location of the center. You estimate that $25,000 of
capital equipment is required. Because you have only $5,000 in cash, you
expect to borrow $20,000. The interest cost on the loan would be $2,000 per
year. Other miscellaneous inputs are expected to cost $15,000 annually. You
would consider it a success if you just break even the first year--if your
revenues just cover your costs. You estimate that you can do this if revenues
for the first year are $52,000. Discuss.

CHAPTER ANSWERS

In Brief: Chapter Summary

1. Single firm 2. Conglomerate 3. Similar 4. Corporation 5. Limited 6.
Increases 7. Limited 8. Disadvantage 9. Are 10. Dividends 11. Is not 12.
Kept within the firm 13. Is 14. Single product 15. Profits 16. In addition
to 17. The 18. Accounting 19. Implicit 20. Economic 21. Normal

Vocabulary Review

1. Normal profit 2. Economic profit 3. Dividend 4. Retained earnings 5.
Economic cost 6. Implicit cost 7. Industry 8. Corporation 9. Business firm
10. Sole proprietorship 11. Plant 12. Partnership 13. Vertical integration
14. Accounting cost 15. Conglomerate 16. Manager 17. Single-product firm
18. Multiproduct firm 19. Limited liability 20. Profit 21. Personnel
management

Skills Review

1.   a. C b. PR, PT c. C d. PR, PT e. C f. C g. PR, PT h. C i. C

2.   a.   Production of goods and services
     b.   Assignment of tasks to employees of the firm or to outside firms
     c.   Determination of the appropriate division of labor and specialization
          of resources

3. a. Helps decide what and how much to produce
    b. Helps decide whether or not to contract out for production or services
    c. Assigns labor-specialized tasks, monitors their efforts, and rewards them accordingly

4. a. Less. If you rely on African suppliers to ship ingots to the United States, there is likely to be an interruption in supply. Whereas if you develop the resource yourself, you might be able to stockpile ingots or build fabrication plants in Africa in anticipation of impending events.

    b. More. The likelihood of interruptions in the availability of ingots is lessened.
    c. Less. If you must have ingots to produce aluminum and if survival is considered important, it might be wise to develop the capability to mine and process bauxite.
    d. Less. One way to lessen competition is to gain control over an input strategic to all competitors.
    e. Less. If least-cost production is important and it is found that for XYZ internal communication is critical to achieving that goal, it might make sense to vertically integrate.
    f. Less. If XYZ can mine and process bauxite at less cost than outside suppliers because of this new technology, it can reduce costs by vertically integrating. It could even compete as a seller in the bauxite market.
    g. More. Outside suppliers specializing in the production of aluminum ingots can deliver the ingots to you less expensively and more reliably than if you were vertically integrated.

5. a. $64,000
    b. $64.000
    c. $28,000
    d. $28,000
    e. $92,000
    f. $16,000

6. Fred would incur an economic loss of $7,000. Total revenues are less than total costs by $7,000. The opportunity cost of Fred's self-owned resources used in the firm are $28,000, but only $21,000 of this is earned in the current employment of these resources. Fred would in time probably consider employing his self-owned resources elsewhere.

Self-Test for Mastery

1. d 2. e 3. c 4. d 5. a 6. a 7. a 8. d 9. b 10. d 11. d 12. d 13. a 14. a 15. a 16. d 17. e 18. c 19. c

Think it Through

1. Sole proprietorships and partnerships involve limited resources and maximum freedom and are easy to establish. There are simply many more firms that have modest resource requirements than there are firms that require very large sums of money. The largest firms are corporations because of their ability to attract funds for expansion and growth.

2. The microcomputer industry has chip makers, producers of microprocessors, assemblers of cards or boards, component manufacturers such as producers of disk drives and modems, final assemblers, sales distributors, etc. In this case, technology is changing very fast and involves many small upstart companies. Because of the number of firms, the supply of inputs is reliable

and available at competitive market prices. To stay abreast of the technology and to purchase inputs at minimum prices, many companies rely on a large network of outside suppliers.

3.   It is necessary to consider implicit costs in a decision because if you did not, you would not be considering the total costs of some action or alternative. You would likely make a decision that would not result in the best use of your resources. You would be sacrificing more productive uses of your resources.

4.   In this case, you are not considering total costs , but rather accounting costs. If you indeed realize revenues of $52,000, you are covering accounting costs but not providing any revenues toward your implicit costs of owner-supplied resources. You have sacrificed the opportunity to have used your own resources in their next-best employment. To break even, your revenues must be high enough to cover both accounting and implicit costs.

10
Production and Cost

After studying your text, attending class, and completing this chapter, you should be able to:

1. Analyze productive relationships and show how the law of diminishing marginal returns implies a certain pattern of variation in output in the short run when the use of some inputs cannot be varied.
2. Explain the distinction between variable cost and fixed cost and describe the pattern of variation in total cost and other cost concepts as a single-product firm varies production.
3. Explain the relationship between cost and productivity of inputs.
4. Explain how long-run cost curves can be derived
5. Show how marginal cost is affected by changes in input prices.

IN BRIEF: CHAPTER SUMMARY

Fill in the blanks to summarize chapter content.

To understand the supply side of product markets, it is necessary to first examine productivity and costs associated with producing output. Inputs are used in the production process to produce output. Some inputs are in fixed quantities over a period, whereas other inputs can be varied. (1)_____ (Fixed, Variable) inputs can be varied over the short run. Some resources are fixed in the short run. These resources are known as (2)_____ (fixed, variable) inputs. In the (3)_____(long run, short run), all inputs are variable.

In the short run, if a variable input such as labor is increased to produce output, while other resources such as plant and equipment are held constant, then in time the extra output resulting from each additional unit of the variable input will decline. This is known as the law of diminishing marginal (4)_____(utility, returns). The total product curve will in time increase at a (5)_____(decreasing, increasing) rate as additional units of the variable input are employed. The slope of the total product curve (change in total output/change in a unit of variable input) is known as the (6)_____ (total, marginal) product of a variable input. Marginal product begins to (7)_____(decline, increase) at the point at which diminishing marginal returns set in. Average product, or output per unit of the variable input, (8)_____(falls, rises) as long as marginal product is greater than average product and (9)_____(declines, increases) when marginal product is less than average product. Diminishing marginal returns occur when a variable input is continually added to a fixed quantity of other inputs. This is because continued employment of the variable input will eventually strain and surpass a plant's capacity to productively utilize the variable input.

Short-run costs can be derived from the short-run productivity relationships. (10)_____(Fixed, Variable) costs are the costs of the variable inputs. These costs (11)_____ (do not vary, vary) with the level of output. They are determined by the quantity of variable inputs, valued at their market prices, required to produce output. (12)_____(Fixed, Variable) costs are the costs associated with fixed inputs. They (13)_____(do, do not) vary with levels of output. Total costs are the sum of variable costs and fixed costs. Other short-run cost concepts include (14)_____(average total, total) cost, which is the sum of average fixed cost and average variable cost. (15)_____(Total, Average) fixed cost is total fixed costs divided by total output. (16)_____(Marginal, Average variable) cost is total variable costs divided by total output. Finally, (17)_____(marginal, average variable) cost is the cost associated with production of one additional unit of output.

The behavior of short-run costs and the shape of the short-run cost curves are related to the behavior of the short-run productivity relationships. Although total product initially increases at an increasing rate, total variable costs and total costs increase at a/an (18)_____(decreasing, increasing) rate. But when diminishing marginal returns set in, total product increases at a/an (19)_____(decreasing, increasing) rate and both the total and variable cost curves increase at a/an (20)_____(decreasing, increasing) rate. When the average productivity of the variable input is increasing, a unit of output can be produced with increasingly smaller quantities of the variable input. The average variable cost and average total cost therefore (21)_____ (decrease, increase). When average product declines, the average variable and average total cost (22)_____(decrease, increase). When the marginal product of a variable input is rising, an additional unit of output can be produced with smaller quantities of the variable input. The marginal cost of producing that additional unit of output (23)_____ (decreases, increases). When marginal product declines, marginal cost (24)_____(decreases, increases). Thus short-run costs depend upon the quantity and productivity of the resources employed and the market prices at which they sell.

In the long run, (25)_____(only variable inputs, all inputs) are variable. Costs are not only influenced by the rate at which plants are utilized, but also by the size and number of plants operated. If the manager's objective is to find the combination of inputs that minimizes costs, the (26)_____ (largest, least cost) plant size must be utilized and it must be operated at minimum average cost. Long-run minimum average costs are attained at the minimum point on the average cost curve of the most efficient size plant. Declining long-run average costs are known as (27)_____ (diseconomies, economies) of scale, whereas increasing long-run average costs are called (28)_____(diseconomies, economies) of scale. Constant returns to scale mean that a number of plant sizes have the same minimum average total cost.

VOCABULARY REVIEW

Write the key term from the list below next to its definition.

Key Terms

Production	Fixed costs
Inputs	Variable costs
Production function	Total cost
Short run	Average cost
Variable input	Average variable cost

Fixed input
Law of diminishing
  marginal returns
Total product curve
Point of diminishing
  returns
Total product of a
  variable input
Long run
Marginal product
Marginal cost

Average fixed cost
Long-run cost
Average product
Economies of scale
  (increasing returns to
  scale)
Diseconomies of scale
  (decreasing returns to
  scale)
Constant returns to
  scale

Definitions

1. _____: costs that do not vary as a firm varies its output; also called overhead costs.

2. _____: costs that change with output; the costs of variable inputs.

3. _____: the total output produced over a given period divided by the number of units of that input used.

4. _____: corresponds to the level of usage of the variable input at which its marginal product begins to decline.

5. _____: the sum of the value of all inputs used to produce goods over any given period; the sum of fixed costs and variable costs.

6. _____: the process of using the services of labor and capital together with other inputs, such as land, materials, and fuels, to make goods and services available.

7. _____: states that the extra production obtained from increases in a variable input will eventually decline as more of the variable input is used with the fixed inputs.

8. _____: the increase in output from one more unit of an input when the quantity of all the inputs is unchanged.

9. _____: a period of production long enough that producers have adequate time to vary all the inputs used to produce a good.

10. _____: fixed costs divided by the number of units of output produced over a given period.

11. _____: the extra cost of producing one more unit of output.

12. _____: the labor, capital, land, natural resources, and entrepreneurship that are combined to produce products and services.

13. _____: total cost divided by the number of units of output produced over a given period; also called unit cost.

14. _____: describes how output varies in the short run as more of any one input is used with fixed amounts of other inputs under current technology.

15. _____: variable cost divided by the number of units of output produced over a given period.

16. _____: describes the relationship between any combination of input services and the maximum attainable output from that combination.

17. _____: the amount of output produced over any given period when that input is used along with other fixed inputs.

18. _____: a period of production during which some inputs cannot be varied.

19. _____: an input whose quantity can be changed.

20. _____: an input whose quantity cannot be changed.

21. _____: the minimum cost of producing any given output when all inputs are variable.

22. _____: reductions in unit costs resulting from increased size of operations; also called economies of mass production.

23. _____: increases in average costs of operation resulting from problems in managing large-scale enterprises.

24. _____: prevail when economies of scale no longer exist and when average costs do not increase as a result of diseconomies of scale in the long run.

SKILLS REVIEW

Concept: **Productive relationships in the short run**

1. The following represents daily production data for a small manufacturer of cup holders.

Units of Labor	Total Product	Marginal Product	Average Product
		(number of cup holders)	
0	0		
1	50		
2	130	_____	_____
3	230	_____	_____
4	320	_____	_____
5	400	_____	_____
6	465	_____	_____
7	525	_____	_____
8	575	_____	_____

a. Complete the marginal and average product columns in the table above.

b.   Plot the total product (TP), marginal product (MP), and average
     product (AP) curves in the diagram below.

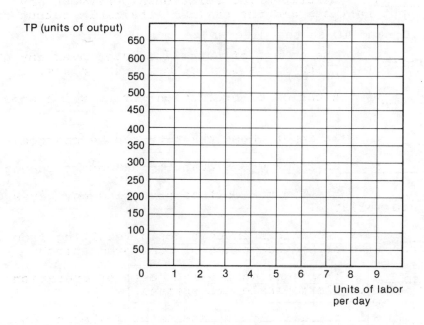

TP (units of output)

Units of labor
per day

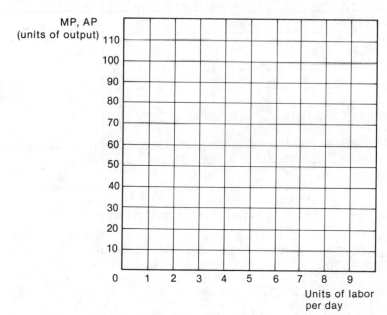

MP, AP
(units of output)

Units of labor
per day

c.   When MP exceeds AP, AP is _____. When MP is less than AP, AP
     is _____.

d.   When TP is rising at an increasing rate, MP is _____. When TP
     is rising at a decreasing rate, MP is _____.

Concept: Costs in the short run

2. Using the production data above and assuming that total fixed costs (TFC)
    equal $50 and the price per unit of labor is $20:

    a. Complete the table below.
    b. Plot TFC, TVC, and TC in the diagram below.

Units of Output	Labor (units)	TFC $	TVC $	TC $
0	0			
50	1	_____	_____	_____
130	2	_____	_____	_____
230	3	_____	_____	_____
320	4	_____	_____	_____
400	5	_____	_____	_____
465	6	_____	_____	_____
525	7	_____	_____	_____
575	8	_____	_____	_____

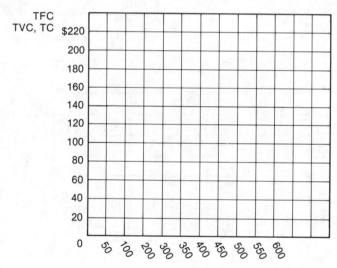

TFC
TVC, TC

Output
(units per day)

c. When TP is rising at an increasing rate, TVC and TC are rising at a
    _____ rate. When TP is rising at a decreasing rate, TVC and
    TC are rising at an _____ rate.

3. Given the cost and output data in question 2,

    a. Complete the table below (round to two decimal places).
    b. Plot the average fixed cost (AFC), average variable cost (AVC),
        average total cost (ATC), and marginal cost (MC) in the diagram
        below.

Units of Output	AFC $	AVC $	ATC $	MC $
0				
50				
130	___	___	___	___
230	___	___	___	___

150

```
320    ___  ___  ___  ___
400    ___  ___  ___  ___
465    ___  ___  ___  ___
525    ___  ___  ___  ___
575    ___  ___  ___  ___
```

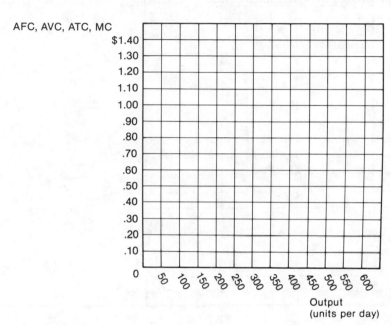

AFC, AVC, ATC, MC

Output
(units per day)

c.   When MP is rising, MC is _____ and both TVC and TC are rising
     at a/an _____ rate. When MP is falling, MC is
     _____ and both TVC and TC are rising at a/an _____
     rate.
d.   When AP is rising, AVC is _____. When AP is falling, AVC
     is _____.
e.   When MC is below AVC, AVC is _____. When MC is above AVC,
     AVC is _____. When MC is below ATC, ATC is _____. When
     MC is above ATC, ATC is _____.

4.   If total fixed costs are $80 and marginal costs are given below:

a.   Complete the table below (round to two decimal places).
b.   Plot TFC, TVC, TC, AVC, ATC, and MC on the diagrams below.

Units of Output	MC $	TVC $	TFC $	TC $	AFC $	AVC $	ATC $
0							
1	75	___	___	___		___	___
2	65	___	___	___	___	___	___
3	55	___	___	___	___	___	___
4	65	___	___	___	___	___	___
5	75	___	___	___	___	___	___
6	85	___	___	___	___	___	___
7	95	___	___	___	___	___	___

151

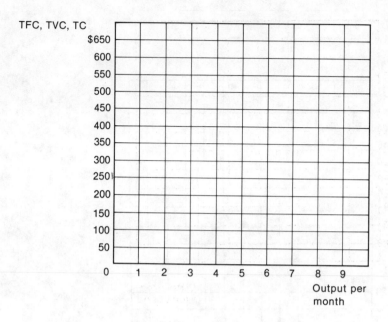

TFC, TVC, TC

Output per month

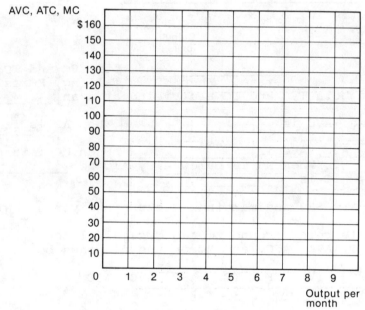

AVC, ATC, MC

Output per month

5. <u>Advanced Question</u>. If TFC equals $100 and TVC increases by $30 for every one unit increase in output:

    a. Find equations for TFC, TVC, TC, AFC, AVC, ATC, and MC.
    b. Plot TFC, TVC, TC, AVC, ATC, and MC on the diagrams below for levels of output from one to five units.
    c. Does the MC curve ever intersect the ATC curve?

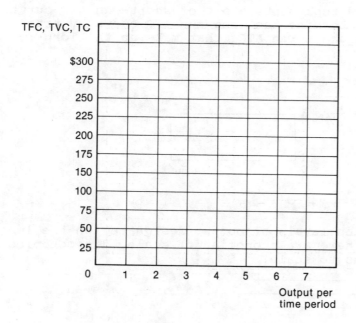

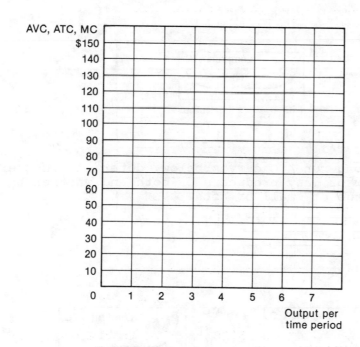

Concept: Costs in the long run

6.   a.   The figure below represents a set of short-run ATC curves for various
          plant sizes.   Determine the long-run ATC curve by tracing over those
          segments of the short-run ATCs that make up the long-run ATC.

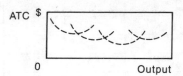

     b.   Determine for the levels of output designated on the long-run ATC
          below whether there are economies of scale, diseconomies of scale, or
          constant returns to scale.
              (1) _____
              (2) _____
              (3) _____

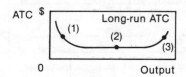

     c.   For the three long-run ATC curves below, determine whether there are
          likely to be few or many producers or both and whether they are
          likely to be large or small or both.
              (1) _____
              (2) _____
              (3) _____

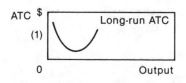

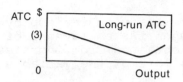

7. a.   Economies of scale exist because:
        1. _____
        2. _____
        3. _____
        4. _____

    b.   Diseconomies of scale exist because:
        1. _____
        2. _____

SELF-TEST FOR MASTERY

Select the best answer.

1. A period of time during which some inputs are variable and some are fixed is known as the:

    a.   Market period.
    b.   Short run.
    c.   Interim period.
    d.   Long run.

2. A period of time during which all inputs can be varied is known as the:

    a.   Market period.
    b.   Short run.
    c.   Interim period.
    d.   Long run.

3. A _____ input is one that varies with output in the short run.

    a.   Marginal
    b.   Economic
    c.   Fixed
    d.   Variable

4. A _____ input is one that does not vary with output in the short run.

    a.   Marginal
    b.   Economic
    c.   Fixed
    d.   Variable

5. The law of diminishing marginal returns states that:

    a. Total product begins to fall as a result of continued employment of a variable input.
    b. Marginal product increases when the employment of variable inputs increases and falls when the employment of variable inputs falls.
    c. The extra production obtained from increases in a variable input will eventually decline as more of the variable input is used with the fixed inputs.
    d.. The total production obtained from increases in a variable input will eventually decline as more of the variable input is used with the fixed inputs.

6. Marginal product is defined:

    a. As total product divided by total output.
    b. As total product divided by the change in total output.
    c. As the change in total product divided by total product.
    d. As the change in total product divided by the change in variable input.

7. Average product

    a. Increases when marginal product is greater than average product.
    b. Is defined as total product divided by the quantity of variable input employed.
    c. Reaches a peak when marginal product and average product are equal.
    d. All of the above.

8. _____ costs do not vary with the level of output.

    a. Accounting
    b. Explicit
    c. Variable
    d. Fixed

9. Total costs equal the sum of:

    a. Variable costs and fixed costs.
    b. Marginal costs and imputed costs.
    c. Average variable costs and marginal costs.
    d. Economic costs less implicit costs.

10. Average variable costs can best be defined as:

    a. Total variable costs times the average level of production.
    b. Total product divided by total variable costs.
    c. Average total costs less average fixed costs.
    d. None of the above.

11. Marginal cost is the:

    a. Change in production costs divided by output.
    b. Change in total variable cost divided by a change in total product.
    c. Change in total cost divided by a change in total product.
    d. B and c.

12. The marginal cost curve:

    a. Intersects the total variable cost and total cost curves from below
       at their minimum points.
    b. Falls when the point of diminishing marginal returns is reached.
    c. First rises and then declines.
    d. Increases when the average total cost curve lies above the average
       variable cost curve.

13. When the marginal product is rising, _____ is _____.

    a. Average total cost, rising
    b. Average variable cost, rising
    c. Marginal cost, rising
    d. Marginal cost, falling

14. When marginal product is falling, marginal costs are _____ and
    both the total cost and total variable cost curves are _____ at
    a/an _____ rate.

    a. Falling, falling, decreasing
    b. Falling, rising, increasing
    c. Rising, falling, decreasing
    d. Rising, rising, decreasing

15. The point of diminishing returns occurs when:

    a. The average product curve has reached a peak.
    b. The marginal cost curve has reached a trough.
    c. The total product curve has reached a peak.
    d. The marginal product curve has reached a trough.

16. Economies of scale mean that:

    a. Short-run average total cost decreases.
    b. Long-run average total cost decreases.
    c. Long-run total costs decrease.
    d. Long-run marginal costs exceed long-run average total costs.

17. The rising portion of the long-run average total cost curve is called:

    a. Diseconomies of scale.
    b. Economies of scale.
    c. Mass production economies.
    d. Constant returns to scale.

18. An industry with firms having long-run average total cost curves that
    initially decline sharply, flatten out over a range of output, and then
    begin to increase suggest that the industry is probably composed of firms:

    a. That are both large and small, producing at the minimum long-run
       average cost.
    b. That are large and few in number.
    c. That are numerous and very small.
    d. That must be large to realize economies of scale.

19. Which of the following is not considered a cause of economies of scale?

    a. Specialization and division of labor
    b. Inability to shift to new production methods as the firm becomes
       larger

c. Ability to purchase inputs in large quantity at quantity discounts
d. As output is increased, a proportionate increase in inputs is not required.

20. Which of the following has been suggested as a cause of diseconomies of scale?

a. Inability to purchase inputs at a discount
b. Ability to shift to new production methods as the firm becomes bigger
c. Impaired managerial communication
d. Government regulation

THINK IT THROUGH

1. A producer never produces at a level of output where marginal product is negative. Why?

2. Explain how changes in wages influence the average variable cost and marginal cost associated with the use of labor in producing output.

3. Why are fixed costs irrelevant to decisions in the short run involving marginal costs?

4. In many American industries a handful of very large capital-intensive firms dominate sales. Why?

5. Clearly explain why total variable costs rise at an increasing rate when the point of diminishing returns is reached.

CHAPTER ANSWERS

In Brief: Chapter Summary

1. Variable 2. Fixed 3. Long run 4. Returns 5. Decreasing 6. Marginal 7. Decline 8. Rises 9. Declines 10. Variable 11. Vary 12. Fixed 13. Do not 14. Average total 15. Average 16. Average variable 17. Marginal 18. Decreasing 19. Decreasing 20. Increasing 21. Decrease 22. Increase 23. Decrease 24. Increases 25. All inputs 26. Least cost 27. Economies 28. Diseconomies

Vocabulary Review

1. Fixed cost 2. Variable cost 3. Average product 4. Point of diminishing returns 5. Total cost 6. Production 7. Law of diminishing marginal returns 8. Marginal product 9. Long run 10. Average fixed cost 11. Marginal cost 12. Imports 13. Average cost 14. Production function 15. Average variable cost 16. Total product curve 17. Total product of a variable input 18. Short run 19. Variable input 20. Fixed input 21. Long run cost 22. Economies of scale 23. Diseconomies of scale 24. Constant returns to scale

Skills Review

1. a.
MP	AP
50	50
80	65
100	76.67
90	80
80	80
65	77.50
60	75
50	71.88

b.

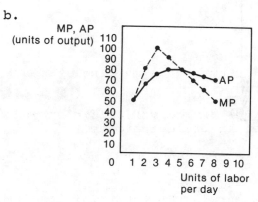
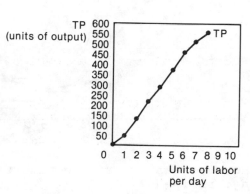

c.   Rising, falling
d.   Increasing, falling

2. a.
TFC	TVC	TC
50	0	50
50	20	70
50	40	90
50	60	110
50	80	130
50	100	150
50	120	170
50	140	190
50	160	210

b.

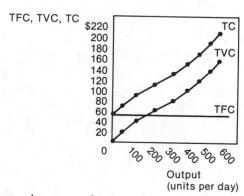

c.   Decreasing, increasing

159

3. a.

AFC	AVC	ATC	MC
1.00	.40	1.40	.40
.38	.31	.69	.25
.22	.26	.48	.20
.16	.25	.41	.22
.13	.25	.38	.25
.11	.26	.37	.31
.10	.27	.36	.33
.09	.28	.37	.40

b.

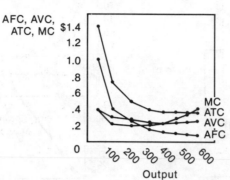

c. Falling, decreasing, rising, increasing
d. Falling, rising
e. Falling, rising, falling, rising

4. a.

TVC	TFC	TC	AFC	AVC	ATC
0	80	80			
75	80	155	80	75	155
140	80	220	40	70	110
195	80	275	26.67	65	91.67
260	80	340	20	65	85
335	80	415	16	67	83
420	80	500	13.33	70	83.33
515	80	595	11.43	73.57	85

b.

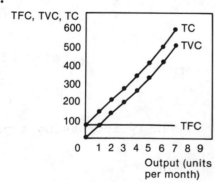 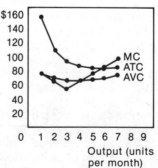

5. a. TFC = $100
        TVC = $30 TP
        TC = $100 + $30 TP
        AFC = $100/TP
        AVC = $30
        ATC = $100/TP + $30
        MC = $30

160

b.

TP	TFC	TVC	TC	ATC	AFC	AVC	MC
0	100	0	100				
1	100	30	130	130	100	30	30
2	100	60	160	80	50	30	30
3	100	90	190	63.33	33.33	30	30
4	100	120	220	55	25	30	30
5	100	150	250	50	20	30	30

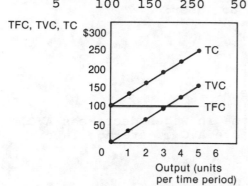

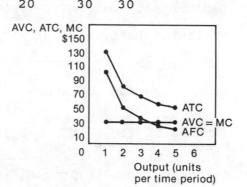

c. For MC and ATC to intersect, MC = ATC. Let:

$$MC = \$30 = \$100/TP + \$30 = ATC$$

As TP approaches infinity, $100/TP approaches zero. ATC approaches MC as TP approaches infinity, but never touches it.

6. a.

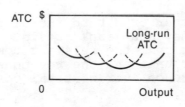

b. (1) Economies of scale
    (2) Constant returns to scale
    (3) Diseconomies of scale
c. (1) Many small firms
    (2) Both large and small firms
    (3) A few large firms

7. a. (1) Can increase output without proportionately increasing inputs
        (2) Quantity discounts
        (3) Specialization and division of labor
        (4) Ability of use new methods of production
    b. (1) Strained managerial communication
        (2) Shirking of labor and difficulty of monitoring performance

Self-Test for Mastery

1. b 2. d 3. d 4. c 5. c 6. d 7. d 8. d 9. a 10. d 11. d 12. a 13. d 14. d 15. b 16. b 17. a 18. a 19. b 20. c

Think it Through

1. A negative marginal product means that using more variable inputs reduces output! No manager would increase total costs in order to reduce output.

2. Average variable costs equal total variable costs divided by output. Total variable costs equal the quantity of variable inputs purchased times the respective input prices per unit. With regard to labor:

$$AVC = (Units\ of\ Labor \times wage)/TP$$

or

$$AVC = Wage/(TP/units\ of\ labor) = Wage/AP$$

An increase in wages increases AVC and a decrease in wages decreases AVC. Notice that an increase in wages will not increase AVC if average labor productivity increases more than wages.

Similarly, marginal cost can be expressed as:

$$MC = (Change\ in\ the\ units\ of\ labor \times wage)/change\ in\ TP$$

or

$$MC = Wage/(change\ in\ TP/change\ in\ the\ units\ of\ labor)$$

$$= Wage/MP$$

MC rises when wages increase and falls when wages decrease unless the marginal product of labor changes sufficiently to offset the impact of wages.

3. If a decision involves whether or not to increase output by a unit, fixed costs are unimportant in that they are "sunk" costs. If a goal of the firm is to maximize profits in the short run, the relevant comparison is between the marginal costs of producing that unit and the revenues received from the sale of that unit. Fixed costs influence average total costs but not marginal costs.

4. These industries comprise a few very large firms that have long-run average total cost curves that decline over a very large range of output. They must be large in order to realize economies of scale. This is because the least-cost combination of inputs requires a capital-intensive operation with large fixed costs in plant and equipment. It takes a large level of production to spread the overhead costs. Large-scale production runs take advantage of cost-saving technology. Purchasing inputs in mass quantity allows the firm to realize quantity discounts. And the larger the firm, the greater the extent to which the division of labor and the specialization of resources can be achieved.

5. When the point of diminishing returns is reached, production requires increasing quantities of a variable input in order to produce a given quantity of output. Therefore, the cost of the variable input must rise at an increasing rate for given increases in output.

Isoquant Analysis: Choosing the Method of Production

IN BRIEF: APPENDIX SUMMARY

Fill in the blanks to summarize appendix content.

Indifference curve analysis can be used to analyze the choice of production methods. The analysis assumes that firms have a goal to minimize the costs of producing a given output.

An (1)_____(isoquant, isocost line) represents various combinations of two inputs that can be used to produce a given level of output. It is (2)_____ (positively, negatively) sloped because the use of additional labor requires a/an (3)_____(reduction, increase) of capital in order to keep output unchanged. The slope is called the marginal rate of technical substitution (MRTS) of labor for capital. Because of the law of diminishing marginal (4)_____(returns, utility), the slope of the isoquant becomes (5)_____(less, more) negative as more labor is employed. This is because the MRTS of labor for capital equals the ratio of minus the change in capital to the change in labor. This ratio in turn equals the ratio of the marginal product of labor to the marginal product of capital. Therefore as more labor is used and less capital is employed along an isoquant, the marginal product of labor (6)_____ (decreases, increases), and the marginal product of capital (7)_____(decreases, increases), causing the isoquant slope to become (8)_____(less, more) steep. An isoquant map shows isoquants at various distances from the origin. Isoquants lying farther from the origin represent (9)_____(higher, lower) levels of output.

Total costs can be thought of as the quantity of inputs employed in producing a given output multiplied by their respective market resource prices. An (10)_____(isoquant, isocost line) can be derived by solving the total cost equation for capital in terms of labor. The slope of the isocost line is (11)_____ (positive, negative) and equals the ratio of the price of labor to the price of capital. Changes in the price of capital and the price of labor will (12)_____ (shift, alter the slope of) the isocost line. Changes in total cost (13)_____ (shift, alter the slope of) the isocost line--higher costs shift the line outward from the origin and vice versa.

Costs are minimized when an isoquant for a given level of output is just tangent to the isocost line (14)_____ (farthest, closest) to the origin. This occurs where the MRTS of labor for capital equals the ratio of the price of labor to the price of capital. The cost-minimizing combination of capital and labor used in producing a given output is influenced by the prices of labor and capital and technology that influences marginal products and the MRTS.

VOCABULARY REVIEW

Write the key term from the list below next to its definition.

Key Terms

Isoquant   Marginal rate of technical
Isocost line   substitution (MRTS) of labor for
Isoquant map   capital

Definitions

1. _____ :   a measure of the amount of capital each unit of
labor can replace without increasing or decreasing production.

2. _____ :   gives all combinations of labor and capital that
are of equal total cost.

3. _____ :   a curve showing all combinations of variable
inputs that can be used to produce a given quantity of output.

4. _____ :   shows the combinations of labor and capital that
can be used to produce several possible output levels.

SKILLS REVIEW

1. Given the isoquant map in the diagram below:

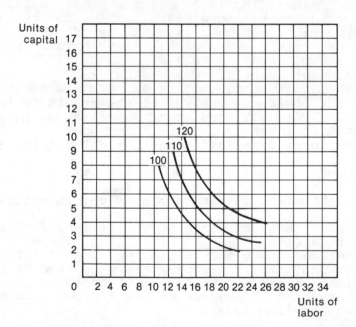

a. Derive the isocost line, assuming that the price per unit to labor is
$10, the price per unit of capital is $20, and total cost equals
$300. Plot the line on the diagram.

164

b. Find the cost-minimizing combination of labor and capital:
    (1) _____ units of labor
    (2) _____ units of capital
    (3) _____ level of output at this combination of inputs
c. Show the effect on the diagram of an increase in the price of labor
    to $15. The cost-minimizing combination of labor and capital changes
    to _____ units of labor and _____ units of capital.
d. Show the effect on the diagram of an increase in the price of capital
    to $30, assuming the price of labor is $10. The cost-minimizing
    combination of inputs changes to _____ units of labor and
    _____ units of capital.

SELF-TEST FOR MASTERY

Select the best answer.

1. An isoquant is :

    a. The level of production possible from a given stock of resources.
    b. A curve giving various combinations of two inputs that are equal in
        total cost.
    c. A curve showing all combinations of variable inputs that can be used
        to produce a given quantity of output.
    d. The producer's demand curve for labor and capital.

2. A _____ gives all combinations of labor and capital that can be used
    to produce several possible output levels.

    a. Isoquant
    b. Isocost
    c. Isoquant map
    d. Isocost map

3. The slope of an isoquant is negative and equal to:

    a. The ratio of the change in capital to the change in labor.
    b. The ratio of the marginal product of labor to the marginal product of
        capital.
    c. The marginal rate of technical substitution of labor for capital.
    d. B and c.
    e. All of the above.

4. Which of the following concepts best explains the curvature of an
    isoquant?

    a. Equimarginal principle
    b. Law of decreasing costs
    c. Law of diminishing marginal returns
    d. Law of diminishing marginal utility

5. The slope of an isocost line is:

    a. The ratio of the marginal products of labor and capital.
    b. The product price divided by the price of labor and capital.
    c. The change in capital divided by the change in labor.
    d. Negative and equal to the price per unit of labor divided by the
        price per unit of capital.

6. A/An _____ in the price of labor makes the isocost line _____ steep.

    a. Increase, more
    b. Decrease, more
    c. Increase, less
    d. Change, increasingly

7. A/An _____ in the price of capital makes the isocost line _____ steep.

    a. Increase, more
    b. Decrease, more
    c. Decrease, less
    d. Change, neither more nor less

8. The cost-minimizing combination of labor and capital can be found where

    a. The MRTS of labor for capital = the change in capital/change in labor.
    b. The MRTS of labor for capital = the ratio of input marginal products.
    c. The MRTS of labor for capital = the ratio of the price of capital to the price of labor.
    d. The MRTS of labor for capital = the ratio of the price of labor to the price of capital.

THINK IT THROUGH

1. Explain why the slope of the isoquant becomes increasingly less steep as more labor is used relative to capital.

2. What condition must be satisfied in order to find the cost-minimizing combination of labor and capital? Explain.

APPENDIX ANSWERS

In Brief: Appendix Summary

1. Isoquant 2. Negatively 3. Reduction 4. Returns 5. Less 6. Decreases 7. Increases 8. Less 9. Higher 10. Isocost line 11. Negative 12. Alter the slope of 13. Shift 14. Closest

Vocabulary Review

1. Marginal rate of technical substitution of labor for capital 2. Isocost line 3. Isoquant 4. Isoquant map

Skills Review

a.

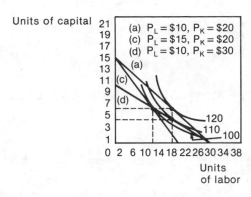

Units of capital

(a) $P_L = \$10$, $P_K = \$20$
(c) $P_L = \$15$, $P_K = \$20$
(d) $P_L = \$10$, $P_K = \$30$

Units of labor

b. (1) 18 (2) 6 (3) 120
c. 12, 6
d. 18, 4

Self-Test for Mastery

1. c 2. c 3. e 4. c 5. d 6. a 7. b 8. d

Think it Through

1. Output is constant along a given isoquant. An increase in labor times the marginal product of labor must equal the decrease in capital times the marginal product of capital in order to keep the production level unchanged. But as more labor is added and capital is reduced, the marginal product of labor decreases and the marginal product of capital increases. This is due to the law of diminishing marginal returns. Since the slope of the isoquant is the ratio of the marginal product of labor to the marginal product of capital, the slope becomes less negative as more labor is used.

2. To find the least-cost combination of labor and capital, the MRTS of labor for capital must equal the ratio of the price of labor to the price of capital. The rate at which it is technically feasible to substitute labor for capital is just equal to the rate at which labor can be exchanged for capital as determined by market prices and the total cost of production. The cost-minimizing condition can be alternatively expressed as follows:

(MP of labor/price of labor) = (MP of capital/price of capital)

Costs are minimized in producing a given output when the last dollar's worth of labor and capital yields the same marginal product.

11

The Profit-Maximizing Competitive Firm and Market Supply

CHAPTER CHALLENGES

After studying your text, attending class, and completing this chapter, you should be able to:

1. Explain the concept of perfect competition in markets.
2. Explain why the demand curve for a competitive firm is perfectly elastic at the market equilibrium price.
3. Explain how the total profit a competitive firm can earn over a given period varies with the output actually sold given the market price of the product.
4. Use marginal analysis to explain how the firm chooses its output so as to maximize profits.
5. Use graphs to show the actual profits a firm earns and to show how the market price of the product affects the profitability of the firm.
6. Explain under what conditions the firm will cease operations in the short run.
7. Show how a supply curve can be derived for a competitive firm that maximizes profit from selling a single product and how the market supply curve can be derived from the supply curves of individual firms in an industry.
8. Demonstrate how changes in input prices affect the supply curve in the short run.

IN BRIEF: CHAPTER SUMMARY

Fill in the blanks to summarize chapter content.

In order to construct a theory of supply, it is necessary to make simplifying assumptions. The goal of the firm is (1)_____ (profit maximization, market share). The firm produces a single product and operates in a perfectly competitive market. The assumptions underlying perfect competition are: (a) (2)_____(few, many) sellers, (b) (3)_____ (homogeneous, heterogeneous) goods, (c) (4)_____ (large, very small) market shares, (d) firms are (5)_____ (unconcerned, concerned) about the decisions of competing firms, (e) information is (6)_____(costly, freely available), and there is (f) freedom of (7)_____(entry and exit, enterprise). The firm is a price taker, producing the quantity of output that maximizes profit or minimizes losses in the short run.

The market demand curve for an industry is downward sloping, but the demand curve faced by a competitive firm is horizontal or perfectly (8)_____ (inelastic, elastic). The firm can sell any quantity it desires at the market price without influencing market supply and hence the equilibrium price. A firm maximizes profit in the short run by producing at that level of production where total revenue exceeds total cost by the (9)_____ (greatest, smallest) amount. At zero output, total costs (10)_____ (exceed, are less than) total revenues because of fixed costs and zero sales revenue. At high levels of output, total costs (11)_____ (are also less than, will also exceed) total revenue because of the law of diminishing marginal returns. In between are levels of production where total revenues exceed total costs, but there is only one level of output where economic profit is at a maximum. If market prices are low enough, there may be no levels of output where total revenues exceed total costs.

Marginal analysis can also be used to determine the profit-maximizing level of production in the short run. A producer will increase or decrease output if there is a net gain from doing so. If the additional benefits from altering production (12)_____(exceed, equal) the additional costs, then it would be rational to change the level of output to the point where the net gain from doing so is at a maximum. If the marginal revenue associated with the sale of an additional unit of output (13)_____(exceeds, is less than) the marginal cost of producing that unit, more is added to revenue than to costs and profit must (14)_____(decrease, increase)--marginal profit is positive. If marginal cost (15)_____(is less than, exceeds) marginal revenue, profit can be increased by reducing output. Cutting output by one unit reduces total costs more than total revenues and as a result (16)_____ (decreases, increases) profit. Where marginal revenue and marginal cost are equal, marginal profit is (17)_____ (zero, negative), meaning that a one-unit increase or decrease in output will have no effect on profit. At this level of output, either profits are maximized or losses are minimized. For a perfectly competitive firm, price and marginal revenue are equal because the slope of the total revenue curve, marginal revenue, is constant and equal to the market price. Therefore the rule for maximizing profit in the short run for a competitive firm is either (18)_____ (MR = MC or P = MC,MR = AC or P = MR).

A competitive firm will operate in the short run and produce output as long as the market price exceeds the minimum average (19)_____(variable, total) cost. If price exceeds average variable cost, a portion of the firm's (20)_____ (marginal, fixed) costs will be covered by revenue. Even though the firm is not earning sufficient normal profits to retain the services of the entrepreneur for very long, it can minimize losses by producing at a positive level of output and deferring some of the firm's overhead or fixed costs. If the market price is (21)_____(above, below) average variable cost, the loss-minimizing strategy would be to shut down in the short run and not produce any output. This is because the firm's loss would be limited to the payment of fixed costs. If the firm produced output, its losses would (22)_____ (exceed, be less than) its fixed costs.

At prices above the minimum average variable cost, the firm is induced to produce output. As prices rise it is profitable to increase production. For the firm, the supply curve is that segment of the firm's (23)_____ (average variable, marginal) cost curve that lies above the (24)_____ (average variable, marginal) cost curve. The market supply curve is an aggregation or summation of the supply curves of all the individual firms in that industry.

Factors that influence and shift the market supply curve are: (a) the number of firms, (b) the average productive capacity of firms, (c) the prices of (25)_____(fixed, variable) inputs, and (d) technology. An increase or decrease in the number of firms will shift the market supply curve to the right or left, respectively. A change in productive capacity will shift the marginal cost curve to either the right or the left. A decrease in variable input prices or an improvement in technology will shift the marginal cost curve (26)_____ (downward, upward) and vice versa. Because the market supply curve is an aggregation of individual firms' supply curves, shifts in their marginal cost curves shift the market supply curve and affect market equilibrium prices. While a change in the price of a variable input affects marginal cost and the market supply curve, a change in the price of a fixed input has no effect on marginal costs, market supply, or price, but does influence the producer's (27)_____(market share, profits).

VOCABULARY REVIEW

Write the key term from the list below next to its definition.

Key Terms

Perfectly competitive market   Marginal profit
Competitive firm   Shutdown point
Average revenue   Short-run supply curve
Marginal revenue   Market supply curve

Definitions

1. _____: one that sells its product in a perfectly competitive market in which it is a price taker.

2. _____: total revenue per unit of a good sold.

3. _____: the change in profit from selling an additional unit of a good, representing the difference between the marginal revenue from that unit and its marginal cost.

4. _____: the portion of a firm's marginal cost curve above the minimum point of its average variable cost curve.

5. _____: gives the sum of the quantities supplied by all firms producing a product at each possible price over a given period.

6. _____: exists when (1) there are many sellers in the market; (2) the products sold in the market are homogeneous; (3) each firm has a very small market share of total sales; (4) no seller regards competing firms as a threat to its market share; (5) information is freely available on prices; (6) there is freedom of entry and exit by sellers.

7. _____: the extra revenue obtained from selling an additional unit of a good.

8. _____: the point a firm reaches when price has fallen to a level below that which just allows the firm to cover its minimum possible average variable cost.

SKILLS REVIEW

Concept: Perfectly competitive market

1.   List six conditions necessary for the existence of a perfectly competitive
     market.

     a. _____
     b. _____
     c. _____
     d. _____
     e. _____
     f. _____

Concept: Perfectly elastic demand curve; economic profit and output

2.   If you operate a business in a perfectly competitive market and the
     current market equilibrium price is $12 per unit:

     a.   Show on the diagram below the demand curve you face.

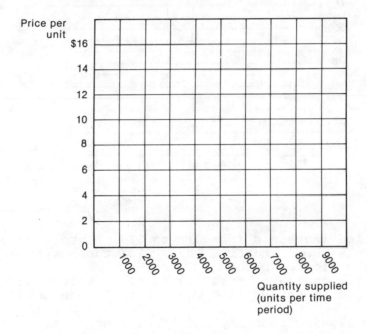

     b.   On the diagram above, show the effect of an increase in price from
          $12 to $15.
     c.   On the diagram above, show the effect of a decrease in price from $12
          to $10.

3. a. Find total revenue from the quantity and P1 columns in the table
        below and enter the results in the TR1 column. Plot the total
        revenue curve, TR1, in the diagram below the table.

Quantity	P1	P2	P3	TR1	TR2	TR3
0	$12	$___	$___	$_____	$_____	$_____
10	12	___	___	_____	_____	_____
20	12	___	___	_____	_____	_____
30	12	___	___	_____	_____	_____
40	12	___	___	_____	_____	_____
50	12	___	___	_____	_____	_____
60	12	___	___	_____	_____	_____

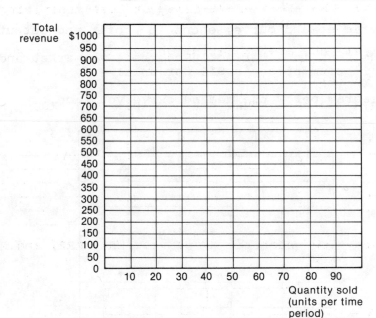

Total revenue
Quantity sold
(units per time period)

    b. Assume price increases from $12 to $15. Enter the price in column P2
        in the table above and find TR2. Plot the new total revenue curve,
        TR2, on the figure above.
    c. Assume price decreases from $12 to $10. Enter the price in column P3
        in the table above and find TR3. Plot TR3 on the diagram above.

4. Consider the following quantity and total cost data:

Quantity	Total Cost
0	$ 50
10	120
20	220
30	330
40	450
50	600
60	780

    a. Plot the total cost curve, TC, on the figure above in question 3.
    b. Referring to TC and TR1, at zero output, economic profit (or loss)
        equals $_____.

172

c. As output increases, what happens to profit (or loss)?

Quantity	Profit (Loss)
10	$_____
20	_____
30	_____
40	_____
50	_____
60	_____

d. At what level of output are profits at a maximum? _____ units
e. Referring to TC and TR3, what relationship exists between output and profit or loss? The profit-maximizing or loss-minimizing level of output is _____ units.

Concept: Marginal analysis and profit maximization

5. a. Complete the table.

Q	P1	TR1	MR1	P2	TR2	MR2	P3	TR3	MR3
0	$12	$___	$___	$15	$___	$___	$10	$___	$___
10	12	___	___	15	___	___	10	___	___
20	12	___	___	15	___	___	10	___	___
30	12	___	___	15	___	___	10	___	___
40	12	___	___	15	___	___	10	___	___
50	12	___	___	15	___	___	10	___	___
60	12	___	___	15	___	___	10	___	___

b. In the diagram below, plot the MR curves: MR1, MR2, and MR3.

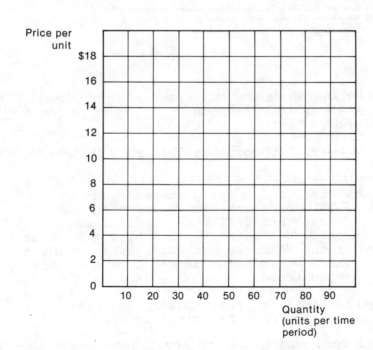

6. a. Complete the table.

Q	TC	TVC	MC	AVC	ATC
0	$ 50	$_____			
10	120	_____	$_____	$_____	$_____
20	220	_____	_____	_____	_____
30	330	_____	_____	_____	_____
40	450	_____	_____	_____	_____
50	600	_____	_____	_____	_____
60	780	_____	_____	_____	_____

b. Plot the MC, AVC, and ATC curves in the diagram below.

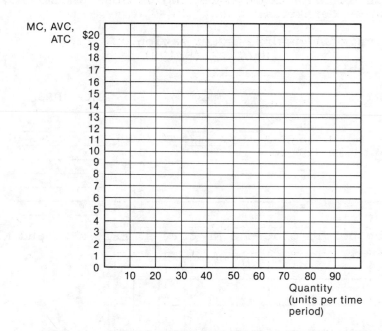

c. On the figure above, show the MR1 curve from question 5 (b) (P1 = MR1 = $12). Profit is maximized where _____ equals _____ at _____ units of output.

7. Advanced Question A perfectly competitive firm's MR and MC curves can be expressed as follows:

MR = P   where P and Q are price and quantity,
MC = a + bQ a is a constant term reflecting the
             forces that influence marginal cost
             other than quantity, and b is the slope
             of the MC curve reflecting the extent to
             which diminishing marginal returns are
             encountered.

a. Find an expression for the profit-maximizing quantity.
b. If price increases, the profit-maximizing quantity _____ and vice versa.
c. If marginal costs increase due to influences other than quantity--if a increases--the profit-maximizing output _____ and vice versa.
d. If new technology reduces the effect of diminishing returns such that the slope, b, of the MC curve decreases, the profit-maximizing output _____.

Concept: Shutdown point; a competitive firm's short-run supply curve

8.   a.   On the figure above, show the marginal revenue curve, MR2, from
            question 5 (P2 = MR2 = $15). The profit-maximizing output is
            _____ units, and profit equals $_____.
      b.   On the figure above, show the marginal revenue curve, MR3, from
            question 5 (P3 = MR3 = $10). The profit-maximizing (or loss-
            minimizing) output is _____ units, and profit (or loss) equals
            $_____. Will the firm shut down at this price? Why or why
            not?
      c.   If the market price falls to $7, will the firm shut down? Why or why
            not?

9.   a.   Complete the profit-maximizing quantity column in the table below
            using the results derived in questions 6 and 7.

            Price   Profit-Maximizing or Loss-Minimizing
                                        Quantity (units)
            $15   _____
             12   _____
             10   _____
              7   _____

      b.   In the figure below, plot the price and quantity supplied data from
            the completed table above.

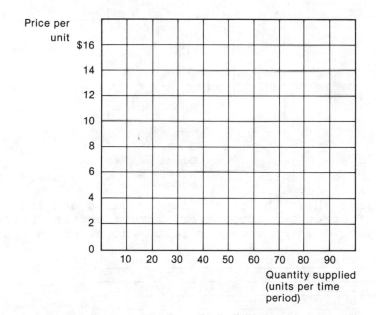

      c.   The curve that you have plotted above is called the firm's
            _____ and is that segment of the _____ curve lying above
            the _____ curve.

Concept: Market supply; determinants of market supply

10. Assume there are 100 firms comprising an industry with cost curves
     identical to that plotted in question 6.

     a. Complete the table below.

Price	Profit Maximizing (Loss-Minimizing) Quantity from Question 9	Quantity Supplied in the Market
$15	_____	_____
12	_____	_____
10	_____	_____
7	_____	_____

     b. Plot the market supply curve from the data above.

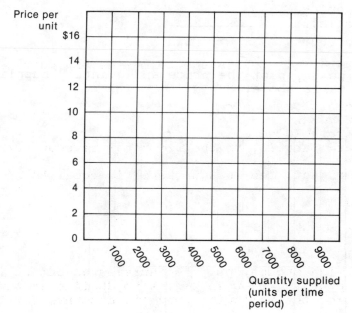

11. List four factors that shift the market supply curve and indicate for each
     one, whether the effect of an increase or improvement in the factor shifts
     the supply curve up or down or right or left, whichever is appropriate.

     a. _____
     b. _____
     c. _____
     d. _____

SELF-TEST FOR MASTERY

Select the best answer.

1. Which of the following is a characteristic of perfectly competitive
    markets?

    a. Many sellers
    b. Very small market shares of firms
    c. Information on prices is freely available
    d. Freedom of entry and exit
    e. All of the above

2. The demand curve faced by a perfectly competitive firm:

    a. Is perfectly inelastic.
    b. Is horizontal.
    c. Is downward sloping.
    d. Is perfectly elastic.
    e. B and d

3. An increase in market price shifts the firm's demand curve _____ and
    rotates its total revenue curve _____.

    a. Downward, counterclockwise
    b. Upward, clockwise
    c. Upward, counterclockwise
    d. Downward, upward parallel to the old total revenue curve

4. At a zero level of output, the loss incurred is equal to

    a. Variable costs.
    b. Fixed costs.
    c. Marginal costs.
    d. Price.

5. If market price is high enough, profits increase as output increases up to
    a maximum level of profits and then begins to decline as output continues
    to increase. Which of the following concepts accounts for this
    relationship?

    a. The law of supply
    b. The law of marginal profit
    c. The law of diminishing marginal returns
    d. Marginal analysis
    e. None of the above

6. For the case of perfect competition, which of the following is true?

    a. Price always equals average revenue.
    b. Profit maximization occurs at the level of output where MR = MC.
    c. Profit maximization occurs at the level of output where P = MC.
    d. A and c.
    e. All of the above.

7. When price exceeds marginal cost, a profit-maximizing producer will:

    a. Increase production.
    b. Decrease production.
    c. Lower price and increase production.
    d. Leave the level of output unchanged.

8. When price is less than marginal cost, a profit-maximizing producer will:

    a. Increase production.
    b. Decrease production.
    c. Raise the price and decrease output.
    d. Leave the level of output unchanged.

9. If at the level of output where MR = MC the market price is less than a competitive firm's ATC but is greater than its AVC:

    a. The firm would continue to operate indefinitely.
    b. The firm would shut down.
    c. The firm would continue to operate in the short run.
    d. The firm would increase output to increase sales and profit.

10. If at the level of output where MR = MC the market price is less than the competitive firm's AVC:

    a. The total fixed-cost loss exceeds the operating loss and the firm will shut down.
    b. The variable-cost loss is less than the fixed-cost loss and the firm will continue to operate in the short run.
    c. The firm can minimize losses by producing where MR = MC.
    d. The firm can minimize losses by raising prices.
    e. The firm will raise prices and increase production.

11. A firm's short-run supply curve is:

    a. The segment of the variable cost curve below the total cost curve.
    b. The marginal cost curve.
    c. The market supply curve.
    d. The section of the marginal cost curve below the average total cost curve.
    e. The segment of the marginal cost curve above the minimum point of the average variable cost curve.

12. Which of the following does not influence the firm's short-run supply curve?

    a. The number of firms
    b. The productivity of the firm
    c. The prices of variable inputs
    d. Improvements in technology

13. The market supply curve is a horizontal summation of:

    a. Industry output.
    b. The marginal cost curves of all the firms selling in the market.
    c. The total cost curves of all the firms selling in the market.
    d. Prices times quantity demanded for all the firms selling in the market.
    e. The short-run supply curves of all the firms selling in the market.

14. An increase in the number of firms in an industry:

    a. Shifts the market supply curve upward at each level of output.
    b. Shifts the market supply curve downward at each level of output.
    c. Shifts the marginal cost curve upward.
    d. Shifts the market supply curve rightward at each price.
    e. Shifts the market supply curve leftward at each price.

15. An increase in wages will:

    a. Shift the market supply curve upward at each price.
    b. Shift marginal cost curves downward at each level of output and shift
        the market supply curve leftward.
    c. Shift the total cost curve upward, shifting the market supply curve
        to the right.
    d. Shift marginal cost curves upward at each level of output and shift
        the market supply curve leftward.

16. A decrease in the price of a variable input will shift the market supply
    curve _____ and cause the equilibrium price to _____.

    a. Rightward, fall
    b. Leftward, fall
    c. Rightward, rise
    d. Leftward, rise
    e. The supply curve will not shift, and the market price will not
        change.

17. An increase in insurance premiums (a fixed input) will shift the market
    supply curve _____ and cause the equilibrium price to
    _____.

    a. Rightward, fall
    b. Leftward, fall
    c. Rightward, rise
    d. Leftward, rise
    e. The supply curve will not shift, and the market price will not
        change.

THINK IT THROUGH

1. Why is the market for wheat considered to be a competitive market?

2. This is a free country. You can raise or lower the price of a good or
service if you wish. Why then do we say that the competitive firm is a price
"taker" rather than a price "maker"?

3. Discuss the rationale underlying the MR = MC rule for profit maximization.
If it is a rule for the maximization of profits, then how can it also be a rule
for the minimization of losses?

4. You are a manager in a firm within a competitive industry that is heavily
reliant upon electricity as a source of power to propel the assembly line. An
embargo of oil from the Middle East causes increases in the price of oil and
its substitutes such as natural gas and coal. Coal-fired electric power plants
will experience an upward shift in their marginal cost curves, resulting in an
increase in the price of electricity. What are the implications for your
industry and your firm?

CHAPTER ANSWERS

In Brief: Chapter Summary

1. Profit maximization 2. Many 3. Homogeneous 4. Very small 5. Unconcerned
6. Freely available 7. Entry and exit 8. Elastic 9. Greatest 10. Exceed
11. Are also less than 12. Exceed 13. Exceeds 14. Increase 15. Exceeds 16.
Increases 17. Zero 18. MR = MC or P = MC 19. Variable 20. Fixed 21. Below
22. Exceed 23. Marginal 24. Average variable 25. Variable 26. Downward 27.
Profits

Vocabulary Review

1. Competitive firm 2. Average revenue 3. Marginal profit 4. Short-run
supply curve 5. Market supply curve 6. Perfectly competitive market 7.
Marginal revenue 8. Shutdown point

Skills Review

1.   a. Many sellers b. Homogeneous goods c. Firms with very small market
     share d. Firms unconcerned about rivals e. Information on prices is
     freely available f. Freedom of entry and exit

2.

3.

	P2	P3	TR1	TR2	TR3
	$15	$10	$ 0	$ 0	$ 0
	15	10	120	150	100
	15	10	240	300	200
	15	10	360	450	300
	15	10	480	600	400
	15	10	600	750	500
	15	10	720	900	600

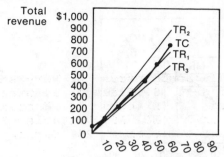

Total revenue

Quantity sold (units per time period)

4. a. TC plotted on figure above.
    b. -$50
    c. Profit (Loss)
        $ 0
        20
        30
        30
        0
        (60)
    d. 40
    e. There is a loss at every output, but the loss is minimized at an output of 20 units.

5. a.

TR1	MR1	TR2	MR2	TR3	MR3
$ 0	$12	$ 0	$15	$ 0	$10
120	12	150	15	100	10
240	12	300	15	200	10
360	12	450	15	300	10
480	12	600	15	400	10
600	12	750	15	500	10
720	12	900	15	600	10

    b.

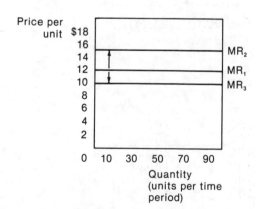

Price per unit

Quantity (units per time period)

6. a.

TVC	MC	AVC	ATC
$ 0	$	$	$
70	7	7	12
170	10	8.50	11
280	11	9.33	11
400	12	10	11.25
550	15	11	12
730	18	12.10	13

b.

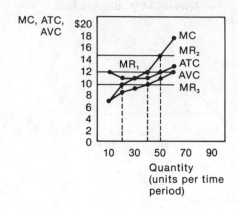

MC, ATC, AVC $20 ... MC ... MR₂ ... ATC ... AVC ... MR₃

Quantity
(units per time
period)

c. MR, MC, 40

7. a. Set marginal revenue equal to marginal cost and solve for the profit-maximizing quantity.

$$MR = MC$$
$$P = a + bQ$$

$$Q = (P - a)/b$$

b. Increases   c. Falls   d. Increases

8. a. 50, 150
    b. 20, -20 ; No, because the operating loss is less than the fixed-cost loss.
    c. At $7, the firm is indifferent because the operating loss is equal to the fixed-cost loss. Any price below this, however, will force the firm to shut down because the operating loss will exceed the fixed-cost loss.

9. a. Profit-Maximizing (Loss-Minimizing)
        Quantity (units)

            50
            40
            20
            10

    b.

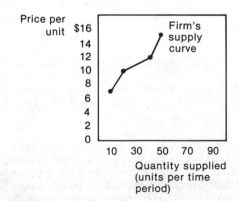

Price per unit $16 ... Firm's supply curve

Quantity supplied
(units per time
period)

    c. Short-run supply curve, MC, minimum point of the average variable cost curve

10. a.

Quantity Supplied (Firm)	Quantity Supplied (Market)
50	5,000
40	4,000
20	2,000
10	1,000

b.

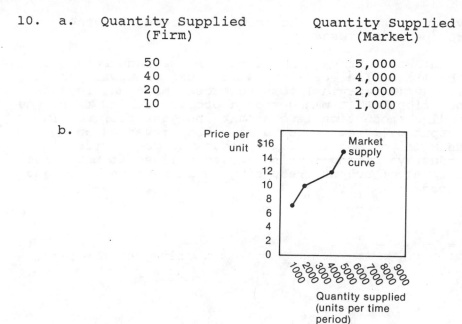

11. a. Number of firms, right b. Technology, down c. Prices of variable inputs, up d. Average productive capacity, right

Self-Test for Mastery

1. e 2. e 3. c 4. b 5. c 6. e 7. a 8. b 9. c 10. a 11. e 12. a 13. e 14. d 15. d 16. a 17. e

Think it Through

1.   There are a number of characteristics similar to those required for perfectly competitive markets. There are many producers, so no one farmer can change production enough to affect market prices. Wheat farmers are price takers and have very small market shares. Wheat is not strictly homogeneous in terms of quality, but the wheat produced by one farmer is a very close substitute if not a perfect substitute for the wheat produced by other farmers. Wheat farmers can sell all they produce at the market price and are therefore unconcerned with decisions of rival farmers. Information regarding wheat prices is freely available in that prices are published daily in most newspapers and announced on many television stations. There are certainly freedom of entry and exit, but the financial investment required to enter the wheat-farming industry as a competitive producer would probably be sizable and thus to some extent would impede entry.

2.   Because there are many firms with very small market shares producing goods that are perfect substitutes for each other, any one firm choosing to raise price above the market price would experience a loss of most if not all sales. Consumers would simply go elsewhere and buy the identical product at the lower market price.

3.   If marginal revenue exceeds marginal cost, an increase in output by a unit will increase revenues more than costs and will either increase profits or reduce losses, depending on whether or not the market price exceeds average total cost. If marginal revenue is less than marginal cost, a one-unit decrease in output will increase profits or reduce losses. If marginal revenue equals marginal cost, a one-unit change in output will change revenues and costs by the same amount, leaving the profit or loss unchanged. At this point profits are at a maximum or losses are at a minimum again, depending on whether

or not the price exceeds average total cost. It should be noted that the losses being referred to are operating losses.

4.   Because electricity is an important variable input to the manufacture of your good, an increase in the price of electricity will cause an upward shift in your marginal cost curve, causing marginal cost to exceed marginal revenue at your current rate of production. As a manager of a profit-seeking firm, you have to make decisions regarding production levels that increase profit. In this case, a reduction in output will reduce costs more than revenues and result in a higher profit than if you continued to produce at your current level of output. For the industry, rising marginal costs will shift the market supply curve upward at each level of output, resulting in an eventual increase in the market price of the good.

12

Long-Run Supply in Competitive Markets

CHAPTER CHALLENGES

After studying your text, attending class, and completing this chapter, you should be able to:

1. Explain the concept of long-run competitive equilibrium in a market and analyze the characteristics of the equilibrium for product prices.
2. Show how profits and losses act a signals that cause shifts in market supply in the long run.
3. Derive long-run supply curves for products sold in perfectly competitive markets and show how long-run supply differs from short-run supply.
4. Analyze the long-run impact of taxes and subsidies on prices and quantities traded in perfectly competitive markets.
5. Evaluate outcomes in markets in the long run using normative criteria.

IN BRIEF: CHAPTER SUMMARY

Fill in the blanks to summarize chapter content.

Firms in a competitive industry are in long-run equilibrium when there is neither entry to nor exit from the industry and when firms within the industry are neither expanding nor contracting. In long-run competitive equilibrium, economic profits are (1)_____(zero, positive), but the opportunity costs of the owner's self-owned resources (2)_____(are not, are) being covered. The existence of short-run economic profits in a competitive industry induces firms to (3)_____(enter, exit) the industry. Entry of new firms (4)_____ (decreases, increases) market supply and (5)_____ (increases, reduces) market prices and economic profits in the long run. Prices (6)_____(fall, rise) until entry stops. This occurs at a market price equal to minimum (7)_____(average variable, average total) cost in the long run. Here economic profits equal zero although normal profits are being earned. Consumers are paying a price equal to the minimum possible average cost of production.

Assuming competitive long-run equilibrium initially, the impact of an increase in market demand for a good (8)_____ (decreases, increases) the market price, causing existing firms to experience economic (9)_____ (profits, losses) and the incentive to (10)_____(decrease, increase) production. Firms (11)_____(decrease, increase) output because marginal revenue has risen relative to marginal cost. But short-run profits induce firms to (12)_____ (exit, enter) the market, causing the market supply curve to shift (13)_____ (leftward, rightward). As market supply (14)_____ (rises, falls) relative to market demand, the equilibrium price (15)_____(rises, falls) until the economic profits are eliminated-- where price equals both short- and long-run marginal cost and minimum average cost. If the expansion of the industry does not affect input prices, the price will return to its former level. The long-run market supply curve is

(16)_____ (horizontal, upward sloping) for the above case of constant costs. If industry expansion is significant enough to cause the market prices of inputs to rise, the marginal and average cost curves will shift upward. Thus prices will not have to fall as much in the long run to restore market equilibrium. For the case of increasing costs, the long-run market supply curve is (17)_____(horizontal, upward sloping).

An improvement in technology increases the productivity of inputs and reduces both marginal and average costs. As average costs (18)_____(fall, rise) relative to the market price, firms realize economic (19)_____(losses, profits). Also, as marginal costs fall relative to marginal revenue, firms have an incentive to (20)_____(contract, expand) production. The economic profits result in new firms entering the industry and cause an increase in market supply. As supply rises relative to demand, prices fall, but in this case prices will fall (21)_____(below, to) their initial level because the long-run minimum average cost has (22)_____(declined, increased) due to the technological improvement and prices must equal this minimum to establish the new equilibrium.

For the case of constant costs, an increase in a tax per unit of output will shift the long-run average cost curve upward by the amount of the tax. If firms were in long-run equilibrium prior to the tax, the tax would impose losses on the firms, causing some of them to (23)_____(enter, exit) the industry. Market supply would (24)_____(rise, fall) and price would (25)_____(rise, fall) eventually to equal the higher average costs. Prices would therefore increase by the upward shift in the average cost curve or by the increase in the tax since average costs and taxes increase by the same amount. For the case of increasing costs, market prices would increase by (26)_____ (less, greater) than the tax per unit because the industry decline would reduce input prices and keep average costs from increasing as much as in the constant-costs case.

A competitive market in long-run equilibrium achieves allocative efficiency when the marginal benefit associated with the use of resources (27)_____(equals, is greater than) the marginal cost of those resources. The value consumers place on an additional unit of a good consumed is just equal to the producer's opportunity cost of the resources employed to produce that unit. Net gains to both consumers and producers are maximized. A point on the market demand curve represents marginal benefit--the (28)_____ (minimum, maximum) price that the consumer is willing and able to pay for an additional unit of a good rather than go without. The market supply curve, being a summation of individual firm marginal cost curves, represents the marginal cost of producing an additional unit of output. Market equilibrium occurs where the demand and supply curves intersect or, in terms of benefits and costs, where the marginal benefit and marginal cost curves intersect. A perfectly competitive market results in a level of output where marginal benefit and marginal cost are (29)_____(unequal, equal) and net gains to producers and consumers are at a maximum. Consumers are maximizing utility and producers are maximizing profit, although in the long run only normal profits are earned and consumers pay a price equal to the lowest possible average cost of production.

VOCABULARY REVIEW

Write the key term from the list below next to its definition.

Key Terms

    Long-run competitive equilibrium
    Constant-costs industry
    Long-run industry supply curve
    Increasing-costs industry

Definitions

1. _____: one for which the prices of at least some of the inputs used increase as a direct result of the expansion of the industry.

2. _____: a relationship between price and quantity supplied for points where the industry is in long-run equilibrium.

3. _____: exists in an industry when there is no tendency for firms to enter or leave the industry or to expand or contract the scale of their operations.

4. _____: one for which input prices are unaffected by the quantity produced or the number of firms in the industry.

SKILLS REVIEW

Concept: **Long-run equilibrium for a firm and market; role of profits and losses**

1.   a.   On the diagram below, draw the competitive firm's demand curve and label the curve d1.

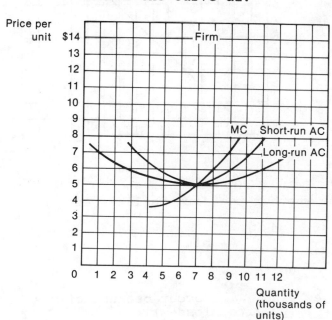
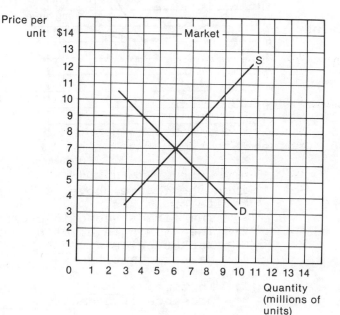

b. Given the figure above, determine whether the firm is realizing economic profits or losses.
    (1) The firm's short-run economic profits (losses) = $_____
    (2) The firm's level of output = _____ units
    (3) Market price = $_____
    (4) Market quantity = _____ units

c. (1) In time, _____ (entry, exit) will occur because of the presence of economic _____ (profits, losses).
    (2) Show graphically in the figure above the long-run adjustment of both the market and the firm assuming the firm operates in a constant-costs industry.
    (3) As a result of _____ (entry, exit), economic _____ (profits, losses) will _____ (rise, fall). (Entry, Exiting) will continue until market price _____ (rises, falls) sufficiently to eliminate economic _____ (profits, losses).

d. In the long run, price equals both short- and long-run _____ and _____. Consumers pay a price equal to the minimum _____. Producers earn _____ economic profits but continue to earn _____ profits. Referring to the figure above, in long-run equilibrium the firm's economic profit (or loss) equals $_____ and its level of production is _____ units. Market price and quantity are $_____ and _____ units, respectively.

2. a. On the diagram below, draw the firm's demand curve and label it d2.

Price per unit — Firm — $15 ... MC, Short-run AC, Long-run AC — Quantity (thousands of units)

Price per unit — Market — $15 ... S, D — Quantity (millions of units)

b. Given the figure above, determine whether the firm realizes economic profits or losses.
    (1) The firm's economic profit (or loss) = $_____
    (2) The firm's level of output = _____ units
    (3) Market price = $_____
    (4) Market quantity = _____ units

c. (1) In time, _____ (entry, exiting) will occur because of the presence of economic _____ (profits, losses).

(2) Show graphically in the figure above the long-run adjustment of both the market and the firm assuming the firm operates in a constant-costs industry.

(3) As a result of _____ (entry, exiting), economic _____ (profits, losses) will _____ (rise, fall). _____ (Entry, Exiting) will continue until market price _____ (rises, falls) sufficiently to eliminate economic _____ (profits, losses).

d. In long-run equilibrium, price equals both short-and long-run _____ and _____. Consumers pay a price equal to the minimum _____. Producers earn _____ economic profits but continue to earn _____ profits. Referring to the figure above, in long-run equilibrium the firm realizes economic _____ (profits, losses) of $_____ and produces _____ units of output. Market price and quantity equal $_____ and _____ units, respectively.

Concept: Long-run market supply curves

3. a. Given the figure below representing a competitive firm and market in long-run equilibrium, show the short-run impact of an increase in market demand of 20 million units at every price.

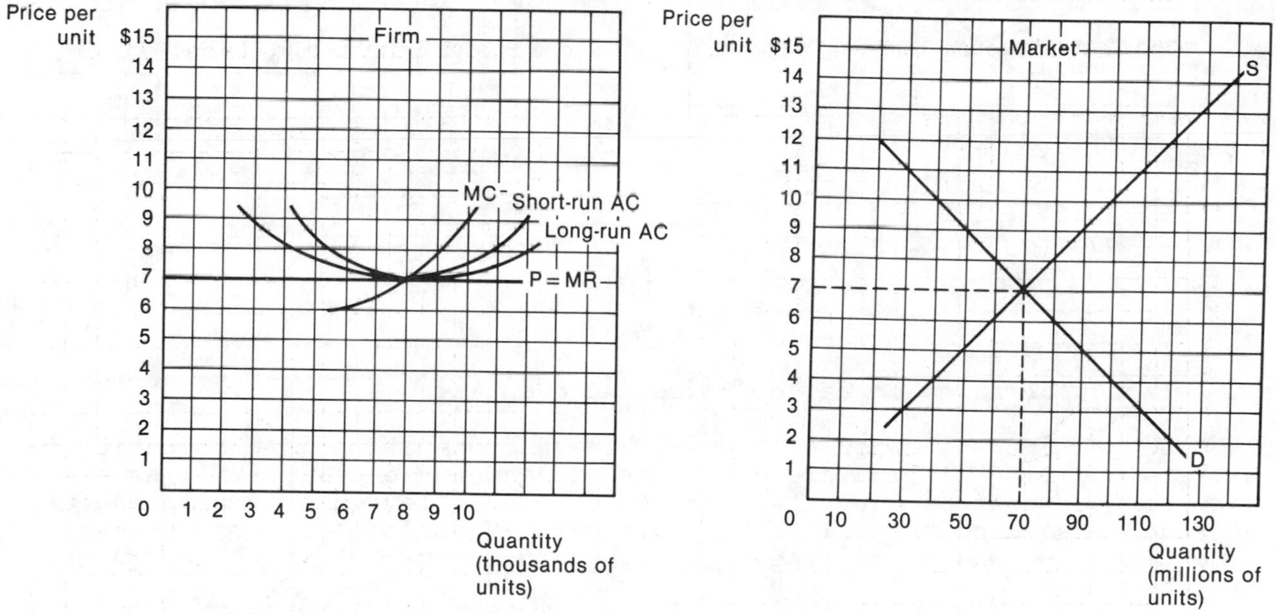

Market price _____ to $_____, and market quantity _____ to _____ units.

b. Assuming the case of constant costs, on the figure above show the adjustments that move the firm and the market to long-run equilibrium.

c. Show the long-run supply curve in the figure above. The long-run supply curve has a _____ slope.

189

4. For the case of an increasing-costs industry, show graphically on the figure below:

    a. The short-run effect of an increase in market demand of 40 million units at every price.
    b. The impact of industry expansion on the firm's costs (assume that the marginal and average cost curves shift upward by $1 at each level of output).
    c. The adjustment of the firm and market to long-run equilibrium.
    d. The long-run market supply curve. The long-run market supply curve has a _____ slope.

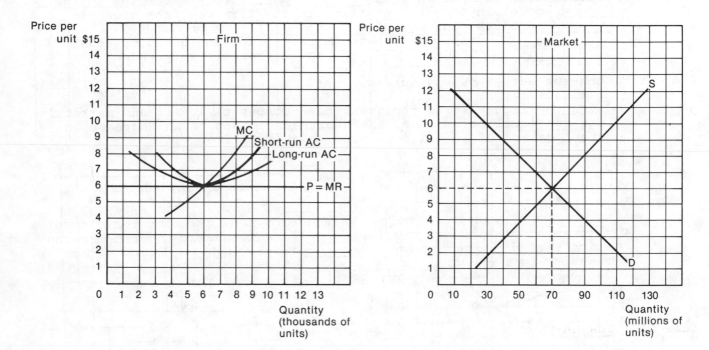

Concept: Impact of taxes on market price and quantity

5. Suppose you are the owner of a small vineyard operating in a competitive market in California and are currently in long-run equilibrium. An excise tax (tax per unit of output) of $1 per bottle is levied on your production of wine. Assuming that all other California wineries are subject to the same tax, what would you expect to happen to the market price and quantity of wine?

a. Using the figure below, show the short-run impact of the tax.

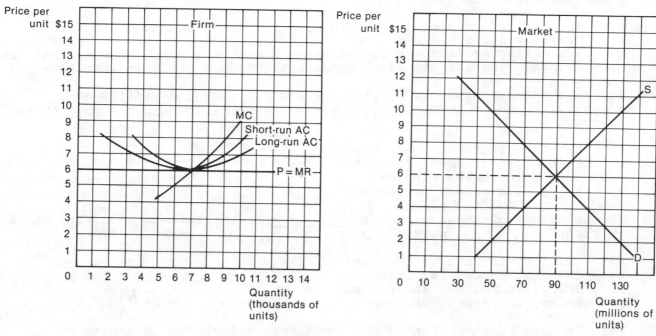

b. In the short run, you and other producers of wine will experience
    _____ (losses, profits). In the long run, assuming the case of a
    constant-costs industry, firms _____ (enter, exit), causing market
    price to _____ by $_____ to $_____ and market
    quantity to _____ to _____ units. Prices _____ (rise,
    fall) by what percentage of the $1 excise tax? _____%

SELF-TEST FOR MASTERY

Select the best answer.

1. Long-run competitive equilibrium occurs when:

    a. Firms are neither entering nor exiting the industry.
    b. Firms within the industry are neither expanding nor contracting.
    c. Economic profits are zero.
    d. The opportunity costs of the owner's self-owned resources are just
        being covered.
    e. All of the above.

2. In long-run competitive equilibrium, price equals not only _____,
    but also _____.

    a. Average variable costs, marginal cost
    b. Marginal cost, minimum possible average cost
    c. Marginal cost, total benefit
    d. The lowest price available to the consumer, total revenues to the
        firm.

3. Which of the following is correct regarding profits in long-run competitive equilibrium?

   a. Normal profits are zero.
   b. Normal profits are zero, but economic profits are being covered.
   c. Accounting profits are zero.
   d. Economic profits are zero, but normal profits are being covered.

4. The existence of economic profits induces _____ from/into an industry, which in turn _____ market supply and _____ market price.

   a. Exiting, increases, increases
   b. Exiting, decreases, increases
   c. Entry, increases, increases
   d. Entry, increases, decreases

5. The existence of losses induces _____ from/into an industry, which in turn _____ market supply and _____ market price.

   a. Exiting, increases, increases
   b. Exiting, decreases, increases
   c. Entry, increases, increases
   d. Entry, increases, decreases

6. For the case of a constant-costs industry, an increase in demand will:

   a. Result in a higher price in the short run and a lower price in the long run as compared to the current market price.
   b. Increase the firm's profits in the long run.
   c. Result in a higher price in the short run and the same price in the long run as compared to the current market price.
   d. Cause short-run profits but long-run losses.
   e. C and d.

7. The long-run market supply curve for a constant-costs industry is:

   a. Vertical.
   b. Upward sloping.
   c. Downward sloping.
   d. Horizontal.

8. For the case of an increasing-costs industry, an increase in demand will:

   a. Result in a higher price in the short run, but in the long run price will fall to a level above the original market price.
   b. Result in short-run profits but long-run losses.
   c. Increase profits in the long run.
   d. Cause an expansion of the industry that will increase input prices and shift the firm's average cost curve downward.

9. The long-run market supply curve for an increasing-costs industry is:

   a. Vertical.
   b. Upward sloping.
   c. Downward sloping.
   d. Horizontal.

10. An improvement in technology in an industry:

    a. Shifts the marginal cost curve upward and causes production and profit to rise.
    b. Shifts the average cost curve upward due to increased labor productivity.
    c. Results in short-run economic profits and a decline in price below the initial market price in the long run.
    d. Produces an upward sloping market supply curve.

11. For the case of a constant-costs industry, a per-unit tax levied on a good:

    a. Shifts the competitive firm's average cost curve down by less than the amount of the tax and increases the market price.
    b. Increases supply and causes the price to fall.
    c. Shifts the competitive firm's average and marginal cost curves upward by the amount of the tax per unit and in the long run results in an increase in the market price that is equal to the unit tax.
    d. None of the above.

12. For the case of an increasing-costs industry, a per-unit tax:

    a. Results in an increase in the long-run market price equal to the tax per unit.
    b. Results in an increase in the short-run market price equal to the tax per unit.
    c. Results in an increase in the long-run market price less than the tax per unit.
    d. Results in an increase in the long-run market price greater than the tax per unit.

13. Net gain is maximized where:

    a. Price equals marginal revenue.
    b. Marginal cost equals marginal benefit.
    c. The average variable cost is low.
    d. Economic profits are high.

14. A market demand curve can be thought of as a marginal benefit curve because:

    a. The price reflects the opportunity costs of scarce resources.
    b. Quantities consumed yield benefits.
    c. The price represents a measure of the additional benefit received from consuming one unit of a good--the price on a demand curve represents the maximum price that the consumer is willing and able to pay rather than go without.
    d. Price times marginal benefit equals total net gain.

15. Allocative efficiency occurs where:

    a. Marginal benefits equal marginal costs.
    b. Net benefits are maximized from the allocation of resources.
    c. The maximum price that consumers are willing and able to pay for an additional unit of a good just equals the price required by firms to produce that unit.
    d. All of the above.

16. Competitive markets can maximize the net gain to both buyers and producers because:

    a.   Marginal benefits exceed the supply of the good.
    b.   The market demand curve reflects marginal benefits and the market supply curve reflects marginal costs, and in equilibrium, supply equals demand; hence marginal benefits equal marginal costs.
    c.   They are efficient and do not waste resources.
    d.   Optimal exchange takes place to the point where total benefits equal total costs.

THINK IT THROUGH

1. Oil prices are determined by the world supply of and demand for oil. In the early 1970s, the member nations of OPEC reduced production of the world's available supply of oil. Although the oil industry is not perfectly competitive, the forces of supply and demand determine prices. Using your knowledge of the short- and long-run adjustments in markets, what would you predict to happen to oil prices in the short run and the long run as a result of OPEC's restriction of output?

2. Discuss the impact of technological improvement on the competitive firm, the competitive market, and the long-run market supply curve.

3. How do perfectly competitive markets maximize the net gains to producers and consumers?

CHAPTER ANSWERS

In Brief: Chapter Summary

1. Zero 2. Are 3. Enter 4. Increases 5. Reduces 6. Fall 7. Average total 8. Increases 9. Profits 10. Increase 11. Increase 12. Enter 13. Rightward 14. Rises 15. Falls 16. Horizontal 17. Upward sloping 18. Fall 19. Profits 20. Expand 21. Below 22. Declined 23. Exit 24. Fall 25. Rises 26. Less 27. Equals 28. Maximum 29. Equal

Vocabulary Review

1. Increasing-costs industry 2. Long-run market supply curve 3. Long-run competitive equilibrium 4. Constant-costs industry

Skills Review

1. a.

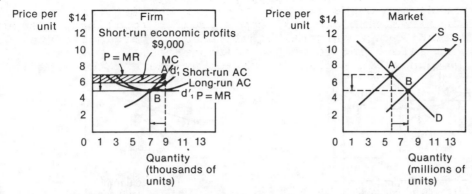

Price per unit

   b. (1) Profits, $9,000 (2) 9,000 units (3) $7 (4) 6 million
   c. (1) Entry, profit
       (2) On figure above
       (3) Entry, profits, fall; Entry, falls, profit
   d. Marginal cost, minimum possible average cost; possible average cost
       of production; zero, normal; $0, 7,000 units; $5, 8 million

2. a.

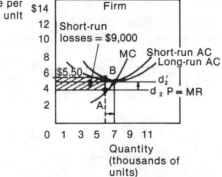

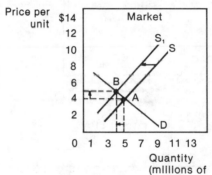

   b. (1) Loss, $9,000 (2) 6,000 units (3) $4 (4) 5 million
   c. (1) Exiting, losses
       (2) On figure above
       (3) Exiting, losses, fall; Exiting, rises, losses
   d. Marginal cost, minimum possible average cost; possible average cost
       of production; zero, normal; $0, 7,000 units; $5, 4 million

3. a.

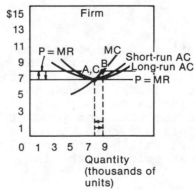

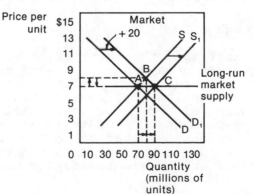

                Increases, $8, increases, 80 million
    b.   On figure above
    c.   On figure above, zero or horizontal

4. a.

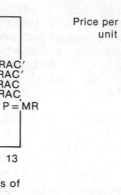 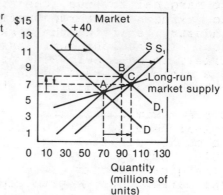

    b.   On figure above
    c.   On figure above
    d.   On figure above, positive

5. a.

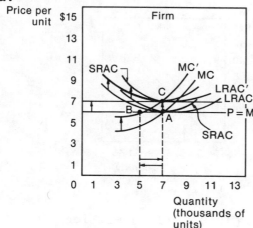 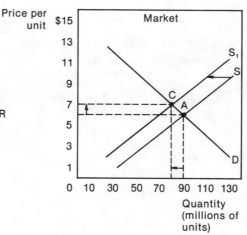

    b.   Losses; exit, increase, $1, $7, decrease, 80 million; rise, 100%

Self-Test for Mastery

1. e 2. b 3. d 4. d 5. b 6. c 7. d 8. a 9. b 10. c 11. c 12. c 13. b 14. c 15. d 16. b

Think it Through

1.   In the short run, the restriction of oil production reduces market supply relative to market demand and increases the price per barrel of oil. This results in greater short-run profits associated with the production of oil and in the long run results in firms entering the industry such as wildcats and other independent oil producers. It will also cause existing oil producers other than the members of OPEC to expand exploration and production efforts. The latter represents a movement up the supply curve in response to higher prices, and the former represents a rightward shift in the supply curve. As the supply curve shifts rightward, the market price in the long run will fall.

2.   Technological improvement increases the productivity of variable inputs, causing the marginal and average cost curves to shift downward. The minimum possible average cost of production likewise falls. As marginal costs fall relative to marginal revenue, the firm has an incentive to increase production in order to maximize short-run profits. But short-run profits induce entry into the industry, shifting the market supply curve rightward and reducing the market price. In the long run, (assuming a constant-costs industry) the market price is likely to fall below the original market price because price will fall to equal the minimum average cost, which has fallen below its original level due to the technological improvement.

3.   Consumers maximize utility by consuming goods to the point where price equals marginal benefit. Producers maximize profits by producing to the point where price equals marginal cost. The market equilibrium occurs where demand equals supply. But since a point on the market demand curve represents the consumer's marginal benefit of consuming an additional unit of a good and a point on the market supply curve represents the price necessary to just cover the firm's marginal cost, marginal benefits and marginal costs are equal where the market supply and demand curves intersect. When the market is in equilibrium, net gains to consumers and producers are maximized from the allocation of resources.

13
Monopoly

CHAPTER CHALLENGES

After studying your text, attending class, and completing this chapter, you should be able to:

1. Explain the concept of pure monopoly and how it can be maintained in a market.
2. Show how the demand curve for a product sold by a monopoly firm implies that the firm can control the market price.
3. Show how the marginal revenue from a monopolist's output is less than the price the monopolist charges for its product, and how the marginal revenue is related to the price elasticity of demand for the monopolist's product.
4. Show how a profit-maximizing monopoly seller chooses how much of its product to make available to buyers in markets, and demonstrate how the decision of how much to sell is inseparable from that of how much to charge.
5. Compare market outcomes under pure monopoly with those that would prevail under perfect competition.
6. Discuss the social cost and possible social benefit of monopoly.

IN BRIEF: CHAPTER SUMMARY

Fill in the blanks to summarize chapter content.

A pure monopoly exists when there is a single seller of a product or service for which there are (1)_____ (close, no close) substitutes. The monopolist controls the market price by restricting output and preventing entry into the industry. Barriers to entry include government franchises and licenses, patents and copyrights, (2)_____ (control of an important resource, government influence), and economies of scale made possible by large size. Some monopolies that exist because of economies of scale are regulated by government so that the economies associated with large-scale production can be passed on to consumers in the form of lower prices than would be possible if the industry were made up of many small firms operating inefficiently small plants. These monopolies are called (3)_____ (natural, pure) monopolies.

The monopolist faces (4)_____ (a horizontal, the market) demand curve because it is the only seller in the market. Because the market demand curve is downward sloping, prices must be lowered in order to increase sales. Therefore marginal revenue (5)_____(increases, falls) as output sold increases and is also (6)_____(less, greater) than the product price. A monopoly firm will maximize profits by finding the level of output where marginal revenue (7)_____ (is greater than, equals) marginal cost. Once the profit-maximizing level of output is found, the monopolist will set a price on the market demand curve at a level that will ensure that quantity of output will be sold. Because price (8)_____(equals, exceeds) marginal revenue and because at the profit-maximizing output marginal revenue equals marginal cost, price must also (9)_____ (equal, exceed) marginal cost. The monopolist will never operate where marginal revenue is negative. This means that the monopoly seller will operate on the (10)_____(inelastic, elastic) portion of the market demand curve where marginal revenue is positive and increases in output resulting from decreases in price will increase total revenue. No unique monopoly supply curve can be found because it is possible to have more than one price associated with the same level of monopoly output.

As compared to perfect competition, the monopolist charges a (11)_____ (higher, lower) price by (12)_____ (expanding output above, restricting output below) the level that would prevail in a competitive market. The monopolist's price (13)_____(equals, exceeds) marginal cost, whereas the competitive market results in a price (14)_____(equal to, greater than) marginal cost. Because of the presence of barriers to entry, the monopolist (15)_____(cannot, can) earn economic profits in the long run. With perfect competition, economic profits are competed away in the long run due to entry into the competitive industry. Further, the monopolist's price (16)_____ (equals, exceeds) the minimum possible average cost of production. Consumers pay more for the good than they would have to pay in a competitive market. Monopolization of markets in effect redistributes income from consumers to the owners of monopoly firms. Since price exceeds marginal cost, the marginal benefit to a consumer from the consumption of an additional unit of the monopolist's good will (17)_____ (be less than, exceed) the opportunity costs of the resources used to produce that good. Society's net gain (18)_____ (is, is not) maximized. That loss of potential net benefit is the (19)_____ (external, social) cost of monopoly and is measured by the triangular area between the demand and marginal cost curves from the monopolist's level of output to the level of output that would prevail in a perfectly competitive market.

Other comparisons between monopoly and perfect competition include analyses of the impact of taxes and price ceilings on a monopolist vs. a competitive firm and the effect of a price-discriminating monopolist on market quantity and price. An increase in a tax per unit of output increases the market price by an amount (20)_____(greater than, equal to) the increase in the tax for the case of perfect competition, but will result in an increase in price by (21)_____(less, greater) than the increase in the tax for a monopolist. A price ceiling (22)_____(increases, reduces) output in a perfectly competitive market, but (23)_____(increases, reduces) it in a monopoly. Price discrimination by a monopolist can result in a level of output (24)_____(greater than, equal to) that produced by a competitive market, but price will equal marginal cost (25)_____ (for all units, only for the last unit) of output sold. All other buyers have to pay a price in excess of marginal cost. Price discrimination is feasible if the firm can control the price, the good produced (26)_____(is, is not) resalable, and customers can be differentiated according to their willingness and ability to pay.

VOCABULARY REVIEW

Write the key term from the list below next to its definition.

Key Terms

Pure monopoly   Natural monopoly
Monopoly power   Social cost of monopoly
Barrier to entry   Price discrimination

Definitions

1. _____: the ability of a firm to influence the price of its product by making more or less of it available to buyers.

2. _____: a constraint that prevents additional sellers from entering a monopoly firm's market.

3. _____: a measure of the loss in potential net benefits from the reduced availability of a good stemming from monopoly control of price and supply.

4. _____: a firm that emerges as a single seller in the market because of cost or technological advantages contributing to lower average costs of production.

5. _____: occurs when there is a single seller of a product that has no close substitutes.

6. _____: the practice of selling a certain product of given quality and cost per unit at different prices to different buyers.

SKILLS REVIEW

Concept: Pure monopoly

1. List four characteristics of a pure monopoly.
   a. _____
   b. _____
   c. _____
   d. _____

Concept: A monopoly firm's demand, marginal revenue and total revenue

2. The following price and quantity demanded data are for a monopolistic market.

Price per Unit	Quantity Demanded (000s units)	Total Revenue	Marginal Revenue
$10	1	$ _____	
9	2	_____	$ _____
8	3	_____	_____
7	4	_____	_____
6	5	_____	_____
5	6	_____	_____
4	7	_____	_____

   a. Complete the marginal revenue and total revenue columns in the above table.

b. Plot the firm's total revenue curve in a in the figure below, and plot the demand and marginal revenue curves in b.

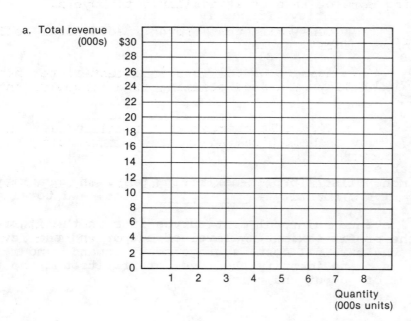

a. Total revenue
    (000s)

Quantity
(000s units)

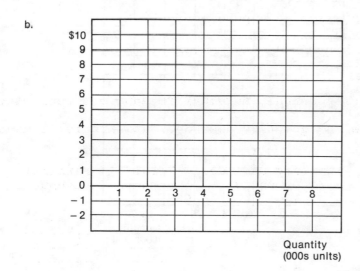

b.

Quantity
(000s units)

c. Total revenue _____ when marginal revenue is positive and _____ when marginal revenue is negative. The elastic segment of the demand curve is that section over the range of output where marginal revenue is _____ and total revenue is _____.

Concept: Profit maximization of a monopolist

3.   Consider the monopoly seller's cost and demand data in the table below.

Quantity Supplied (000s)	TC (000s)	AC	MC	Quantity Demanded (000s)	Price	TR (000s)	MR	Profit (Loss) (000s)
1	$12	$12.00		1	$10	$_____		$____
2	14	7.00	$2	2	9	_____	$____	____
3	17	5.67	3	3	8	_____	____	____
4	21	5.25	4	4	7	_____	____	____
5	26	5.20	5	5	6	_____	____	____
6	32	5.33	6	6	5	_____	____	____
7	39	5.57	7	7	4	_____	____	____

a.   Complete the table.
b.   Determine the monopolist's profit-maximizing price and quantity.
      Price = $_____, quantity = _____ units, and total profit
      = $_____.
c.   Plot the total revenue and total cost curves in a in the figure below
      and identify the profit-maximizing level of output and the level of
      profits. Plot the marginal cost, average cost, demand, and marginal
      revenue curves in b and identify the level of profits and the profit-
      maximizing level of output and price.

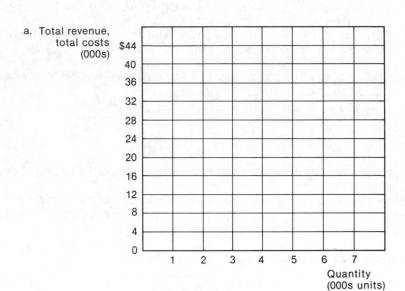

a. Total revenue, total costs (000s)

202

b.

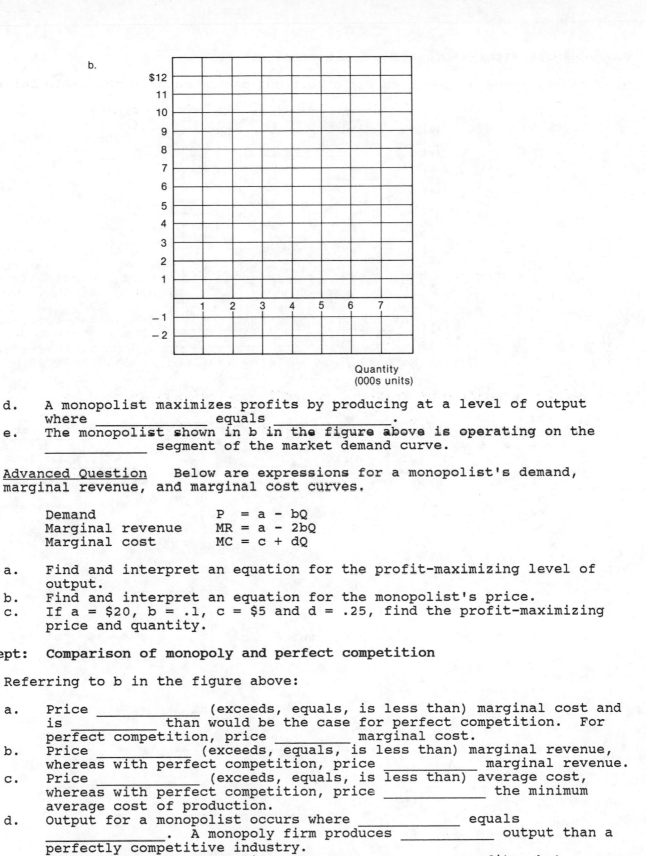

Quantity
(000s units)

d. A monopolist maximizes profits by producing at a level of output where _____ equals _____.

e. The monopolist shown in b in the figure above is operating on the _____ segment of the market demand curve.

4. <u>Advanced Question</u>   Below are expressions for a monopolist's demand, marginal revenue, and marginal cost curves.

Demand $P = a - bQ$
Marginal revenue $MR = a - 2bQ$
Marginal cost $MC = c + dQ$

a. Find and interpret an equation for the profit-maximizing level of output.

b. Find and interpret an equation for the monopolist's price.

c. If a = $20, b = .1, c = $5 and d = .25, find the profit-maximizing price and quantity.

Concept: **Comparison of monopoly and perfect competition**

5. Referring to b in the figure above:

a. Price _____ (exceeds, equals, is less than) marginal cost and is _____ than would be the case for perfect competition. For perfect competition, price _____ marginal cost.

b. Price _____ (exceeds, equals, is less than) marginal revenue, whereas with perfect competition, price _____ marginal revenue.

c. Price _____ (exceeds, equals, is less than) average cost, whereas with perfect competition, price _____ the minimum average cost of production.

d. Output for a monopolist occurs where _____ equals _____. A monopoly firm produces _____ output than a perfectly competitive industry.

e. In the long run, monopolists may earn _____ profits, but a perfectly competitive firm earns only _____ profits.

6. Suppose a tax of $1 per unit of output is levied on the monopolist shown in the figure below.

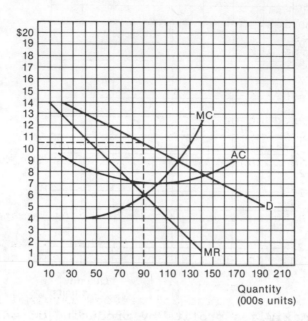

Quantity
(000s units)

a. Show the effect of a $1 per unit tax on the marginal and average cost curves above.
b. The profit-maximizing price _____ and the level of output _____. Price _____ (increases,decreases) _____ than the $1 tax. With perfect competition in long-run equilibrium, the price _____ (increases, decreases) by an amount _____ the $1 tax.

SELF-TEST FOR MASTERY

Select the best answer.

1. Which of the following is not a characteristic of a pure monopoly?

    a. Single seller
    b. No close substitutes
    c. Barriers to entry
    c. Control over price
    d. Operates on the inelastic portion of the demand curve

2. Which of the following are not barriers to entry?

    a. Government franchises and licenses
    b. Copyrights and patents
    c. Control of an important resource
    d. Advantages of government lobbying efforts
    e. Economies of scale

3.   Monopolies that are allowed to exist because of scale economy advantages but are regulated by the government are called:

   a.   Normal monopolies.
   b.   Natural monopolies.
   c.   Pure monopolies.
   d.   Regulated monopolies.
   e.   None of the above.

4.   A monopolist's marginal revenue is:

   a.   Equal to the product price.
   b.   Greater than the market price.
   c.   Less than the price on the market demand curve.
   d.   Measured by the change in output divided by the change in total revenue.
   e.   C and d.

5.   Marginal revenue is more steeply sloped than the demand curve because:

   a.   Price must be lowered in order to increase sales and the lower price pertains not just to the additional units sold but to the monopolist's total output.
   b.   The monopolist restricts output.
   c.   The monopolist raises price and reduces marginal revenue.
   d.   The monopolist restricts output and to do that it must raise price, which applies to all units sold.

6.   The monopolist maximizes profit when:

   a.   Marginal revenue equals average cost.
   b.   Price equals marginal revenue.
   c.   Marginal revenue equals marginal cost.
   d.   Price equals marginal cost.
   e.   Total revenue equals total cost.

7.   At the monopoly seller's profit-maximizing output:

   a.   Price exceeds marginal revenue.
   b.   Price exceeds marginal cost.
   c.   Price exceeds average cost.
   d.   Economic profits are being earned.
   e.   All of the above.

8.   A monopolist operates on the _____ portion of the market demand curve because that is where marginal revenue is _____ and total revenue is _____.

   a.   Elastic, positive, increasing
   b.   Elastic, negative, increasing
   c.   Inelastic, negative, decreasing
   d.   Inelastic, positive, decreasing

9.   A monopolist's supply curve:

   a.   Is the segment of its marginal cost curve above its average variable cost curve.
   b.   Is the market supply curve because the monopolist is the sole producer of output in the industry.
   c.   Is represented by the price - marginal revenue coordinates from a zero level of output to the level where price equals marginal cost.

d.   None of the above.

10. Compared to the case of perfect competition, a monopolist that does not
     experience significant economies of scale:

     a.   Charges a higher price.
     b.   Produces a lower level of output.
     c.   Earns long-run economic profits.
     d.   Operates at a level of output where average cost is not minimized.
     e.   All of the above.

11. The social cost of monopoly is the:

     a.   Sacrificed net benefit to society that results from the monopolist
          restricting output below the competitive output.
     b.   Cost incurred by the Justice Department to control monopoly behavior.
     c.   Income that consumers lose as a result of paying higher monopoly
          prices.
     d.   Explicit outlays by the monopolist to acquire scarce resources.

12. The social cost of monopoly is measured by:

     a.   The accounting costs of the monopolist's production.
     b.   The area underlying the marginal revenue curve.
     c.   The triangular area between the demand and marginal cost curves from
          the monopolist's level of output to the level of output that would
          prevail in a perfectly competitive market.
     d.   The area above the average cost curve and below the demand curve.

13. A per-unit tax on output _____ the monopolist's price by _____
     the tax.

     a.   Decreases, an amount equal to
     b.   Increases, an amount less than
     c.   Increases, an amount greater than
     d.   Increases, an amount equal to

14. A price ceiling _____ output in a competitive market but
     _____ it for a monopoly.

     a.   Decreases, increases
     b.   Decreases, decreases
     c.   Increases, decreases
     d.   Increases, increases

15. Price discrimination by a monopolist can result in a level of output
     _____ that produced by a competitive market, but price will equal
     marginal cost _____.

     a.   Greater than, only occasionally
     b.   Equal to, for all levels of output
     c.   Less than, for all levels of output
     d.   Equal to, only for the last unit of output sold

16. Which of the following best defines price discrimination?

     a.   Charging different prices on the basis of race
     b.   Charging different prices for goods with different costs of
          production
     c.   Selling a certain product of given quality and cost per unit at
          different prices to different buyers

d.   Charging different prices based upon cost-of-service differentials

17. Which of the following is not a condition necessary to enable a monopolist
     to engage in price discrimination?

     a.   Must operate on the inelastic portion of the demand curve
     b.   Must be able to set the price of the product
     c.   The product must not be resalable
     d.   Must be able to differentiate customers according to willingness and
           ability to pay

THINK IT THROUGH

1.   A monopolist produces a good for which no close substitutes exist. The
monopolist therefore faces an inelastic demand. True or false? Explain.

2.   Discuss the social cost of monopoly. How does society benefit from
efforts by government to reduce, eliminate, or regulate monopolies?

3.   Compare a perfectly competitive industry with one in which a monopolist is
engaged in price discrimination.

4.   Society is generally better off with perfect competition than with pure
monopoly. But why does government promote regulated monopolies or natural
monopolies in some industries rather than insist upon perfect competition?

CHAPTER ANSWERS

In Brief: Chapter Summary

1. No close 2. Control of an important resource 3. Natural 4. The market 5.
Falls 6. Less 7. Equals 8. Exceeds 9. Exceed 10. Elastic 11. Higher 12.
Restricting output below 13. Exceeds 14. Equal to 15. Can 16. Exceeds 17.
Exceed 18. Is not 19. Social 20. Equal to 21. Less 22. Reduces 23.
Increases 24. Equal to 25. Only for the last unit 26. Is not

Vocabulary Review

1. Monopoly power 2. Barrier to entry 3. Social cost of monopoly 4. Natural
monopoly 5. Pure monopoly 6. Price discrimination

Skills Review

1.   a. Single seller b. No close substitutes c. Can control price d.
     Barriers to entry

2.   a.   Total Revenue Marginal Revenue
                $10,000
                 18,000 $8
                 24,000   6
                 28,000   4
                 30,000   2
                 30,000   0
                 28,000   -2

b.

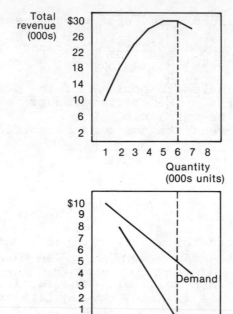

Total revenue (000s)

Quantity (000s units)

Demand

Marginal revenue

Quantity (000s units)

c. Increases, decreases; positive, rising

3. a.

TR	MR	Profit (loss)
$10,000		($2,000)
18,000	$8	4,000
24,000	6	7,000
28,000	4	7,000
30,000	2	4,000
30,000	0	(2,000)
28,000	-2	(11,000)

a. $7, 4,000 units, $7,000

c.

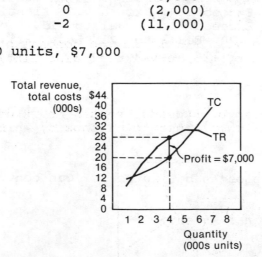

Total revenue, total costs (000s)

TC

TR

Profit = $7,000

Quantity (000s units)

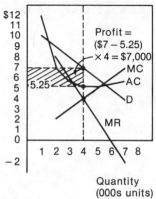

Quantity
(000s units)

d. Marginal revenue, marginal cost
e. Elastic

4. a. The profit-maximizing output equation can be found by first setting
        marginal revenue equal to marginal cost and then solving for output.

MR = MC
a - 2bQ = c + dQ

Q = (a - c)/(d + 2b)

An increase in a—an upward shift in the demand and marginal revenue
curves—will increase the profit-maximizing output. An increase in
c—an upshift in the marginal cost curve—will decrease the profit-
maximizing quantity. As can be seen in the denominator of the
quantity equation, changes in the slopes of the demand, marginal
revenue, and marginal cost curves will also influence the profit-
maximizing output.

b. Substituting the profit-maximizing quantity equation, Q, for Q in the
    demand curve yields the price required to maximize profit.

P = a - bQ
P = a - bQm   where Qm=(a - c)/(d + 2b)
P = [bc + a(b + d)]/(d + 2b)

An increase in c or a will result in the monopolist raising price.
Changes in the slopes of the curves will also likely affect the
monopolist's price.

c. Qm = 33.33 units; Pm = $16.67

5. a. Exceeds, greater; equals b. Exceeds, equals c. Exceeds, equals d.
    Marginal revenue, marginal cost; less e. Economic, normal

6. a.

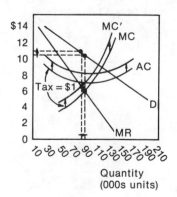

Quantity
(000s units)

209

b. Increases, decreases; less; increases, equal to

Self-Test for Mastery

1. d 2. d 3. b 4. c 5. a 6. c 7. e 8. a 9. d 10. e 11. a 12. c 13. b 14. a 15. d 16. c 17. a

Think it Through

1. False. The monopolist will never operate on the inelastic portion of the market demand curve because marginal revenue is negative and increases in production reduce total revenues while costs continue to increase.

2. The social cost of monopoly is the sacrificed net benefit that could have been realized if the market operated at the higher competitive level of output where price equals marginal cost. Social policies designed to replace monopoly with competition or to regulate monopolies such that output is not restricted and price equals marginal cost will allow society to realize the maximum net benefits from the allocation of resources. This assumes that the monopolies in question exist for reasons other than significant scale economies.

3. A price-discriminating monopolist produces at the same level of output as does a perfectly competitive industry--where price equals marginal cost, or in other words, where the market demand curve intersects the marginal cost curve. The monopolist, however, is able to redistribute the net gains to society of this level of output away from consumers to the monopolist's owners. Price equals marginal cost as it does for perfect competition, but only for the last unit of output sold.

4. Some monopolies exist largely because of scale economies. They must be large in order to realize an efficient use of plant and an efficient scale of operation. Even though economic profits are earned, a monopolist with significant scale economies might produce more output at a lower price than would be the case if the industry were made up of many small, inefficiently sized firms. States allow utilities such as electric power companies to exist as regional monopolies, but the states regulate prices so that the benefits of large-scale production can be passed on to consumers.

14

Monopolistic Competition and Oligopoly

CHAPTER CHALLENGES

After studying your text, attending class, and completing this chapter, you should be able to:

1. Explain the concept of monopolistic competition in markets and show how outcomes in such markets differ from those expected under perfect competition and pure monopoly.
2. Explain the concept of oligopoly and analyze market outcomes under oligopoly.
3. Explain the concept of a cartel and show how it differs from a pure monopoly.
4. Understand the impact of competition through advertising and improvements in product quality in imperfectly competitive markets, and explain how imperfectly competitive firms decide to price their products.

IN BRIEF: CHAPTER SUMMARY

Fill in the blanks to summarize chapter content.

Perfect competition and pure monopoly represent extreme market structures. Virtually all markets fall somewhere in between. Monopolistic competition and oligopoly are two such imperfectly competitive markets. Monopolistic competition is characterized by (a) (1)_____ (few firms, a large number of firms) with small market shares, (b) the production of goods that (2)_____ (are not, are) perfect substitutes, (c) (3)_____ (concern, lack of concern) regarding rivals' reactions to price and production policy, (d) relative freedom of entry and exit, and (e) (4)_____ (no, significant) opportunity or incentive to collude to limit competition.

In the short run, the monopolistic competitor finds the profit-maximizing price and quantity by producing at a level of output where (5)_____ (marginal revenue, price) equals marginal cost. The firm must set a price to achieve sales at this level of output because it faces a (6)_____ (market, downward-sloping) demand curve. The demand and marginal revenue curves are flatter or (7)_____ (less, more) elastic than in the case of monopoly because the goods in question, while not perfect substitutes, are nevertheless substitutes in consumption. In contrast, the monopolist produces a good for which there are no close substitutes. A perfectly competitive firm faces a horizontal demand curve because the goods produced in the market by various firms are perfect substitutes.

Short-run profits or losses will have the same effect on the monopolistic competitor as they do on the perfect competitor. Economic profits result in (8)_____ (exiting from, entry into) the industry, whereas losses result in (9)_____ (exiting from, entry into) the industry. (10)_____ (Profits, Losses) that cause firms to enter an industry will shift an existing firm's demand and marginal revenue curves leftward until they are just tangent to the firm's (11)_____(marginal, average) cost curve. (12)_____(Profits, Losses) cause exiting of firms in the long run and cause a rightward shift in a firm's demand and marginal revenue curves until they are again just tangent to the (13)_____(marginal, average) cost curve. In the long run, the monopolistically competitive firm will earn (14)_____ (zero economic, zero normal) profits and will charge a price (15)_____(greater than, equal to) average cost, but the price charged will (16)_____ (equal, exceed) both marginal cost and the minimum average cost of production. The industry operates in long-run equilibrium with too (17)_____(many, few) firms, each having (18)_____(insufficient, excess) capacity.

Whereas neither the perfectly competitive firm nor the monopolist has an incentive to advertise, the monopolistic competitor often uses substantial resources to advertise, establish brand names, and develop and improve products. In the short run, such efforts can shift the demand and marginal revenue curves (19)_____(rightward, leftward) and may even make them steeper or (20)_____(more, less) elastic. But the selling costs associated with product promotion and advertising increase average costs as well. In the long run, however, entry or exiting ensure that such efforts (21)_____ (produce, have no lasting effect on) economic profits. The consumer benefits from the information content in advertisements and the variety of products that are produced as firms try to differentiate their products. But prices (22)_____(may be higher, are always lower) as a result of the product promotion and differentiation.

(23)_____(Monopolistic competition, Oligopoly) is a market structure with (24)_____(a few, many) dominant firms having large market shares and producing either standardized or differentiated goods. Other characteristics include the necessity of considering rivals' reactions and the presence of barriers to entry. There is no single behavioral model of oligopoly. The oligopolistic market results in different outcomes depending upon how rivals react to a given oligopolist's decision to change price or promotion policy and other decisions. If each oligopolist assumes that rival oligopolists will not react to a price cut, then each firm believes it can increase market share by reducing price. This results in (25)_____ (price leadership, a price war), causing the price to fall to the (26)_____(average, marginal) cost of production. A (27)_____(cartel, contestable) market is one in which oligopolists reduce price to average cost in order to eliminate the incentive for new firms to enter the market.

Price warring and contestable markets benefit consumers through lower prices, but deplete economic profits. Since oligopolists have large market shares and are few in number, there is an incentive to collude to restrict industry output and increase market price and profit. In effect, there is an incentive to coordinate their activities such that they can jointly produce an outcome identical to that of (28)_____(monopoly, monopolistic competition). A (29)_____(cartel, contestable market) is created by an agreement among oligopolists to restrict market output and share in the sales and profits resulting from the higher market price. There is an incentive to form cartels if barriers to entry (30)_____(exist, do not exist), market and firm production targets can be agreed upon, and the agreement can be enforced. But once a cartel is formed, members have an incentive to cheat and to produce beyond their quota in order to increase profits. Cheating will work for a firm only if the change in market supply resulting from its increase in production (31)_____ (influences, does not influence) the market price and if it can be carried out undetected.

Two other models of oligopoly are the price leadership and price rigidity models. In a (32)_____ (price leadership, cartel) oligopoly, the dominant oligopolist takes the lead and establishes the market price and the less dominant firms follow shortly with similar prices. This behavior avoids price warring and brings some stability to the industry. Even though the dominant firm's price may not maximize the profits of the other oligopolists, the fear of predatory pricing by the dominant firm may be great enough to keep the other firms in a price follower pattern.

If oligopolists react to a price cut by reducing prices but do not match price increases, a kink in the demand curve results where there is a noticeable change in the elasticity of demand. Demand is more elastic above the kink and less elastic or even inelastic below the kink. A change in price above or below the kink will likely reduce total revenues. Therefore the price tends to (33)_____(be flexible, remain rigid) at the kink. Changes in costs that shift the marginal cost curve over a given range (34)_____(may not have any, always have an) impact on the profit-maximizing level of output and price and are another reason why the price is rigid.

VOCABULARY REVIEW

Write the key term from the list below next to its definition.

Key Terms

Imperfect competition	Oligopoly
Monopolistic competition	Price war
Product group	Contestable market
Excess capacity	Cartel
Selling costs	Price leader

Definitions

1. _____: exists when more than one seller competes for sales with other sellers of competitive products, each of whom has some control over price.

2. _____: represents several closely related, but not identical, items that serve the same general purpose for consumers.

3. _____: all costs incurred by a firm to influence the sales of its product.

4. _____: a market structure in which a few sellers dominate the sales of the product and where entry of new sellers is difficult or impossible.

5. _____: a market in which entry of sellers is easy and exit is not very costly.

6. _____: a group of firms acting together to coordinate and control price as if they were a single monopoly.

7. _____: exists when many sellers compete to sell a differentiated product in a market in which entry of new sellers is possible.

8. _____: the difference between the output corresponding to minimum possible average cost and that produced by the monopolistically competitive firm in the long run.

9. _____ : a bout of continual price cutting by rival firms in a market; one of many possible consequences of oligopolistic rivalry

10. _____ : one dominant firm in an industry that sets its price to maximize its own profits, after which other firms follow its lead by setting exactly the same price

SKILLS REVIEW

Concept: Monopolistic competition; comparison to perfect competition and pure monopoly

1. List five characteristics of a monopolistically competitive market.

   a. _____
   b. _____
   c. _____
   d. _____
   e. _____

2. The diagram below represents a monopolistically competitive firm in short-run equilibrium.

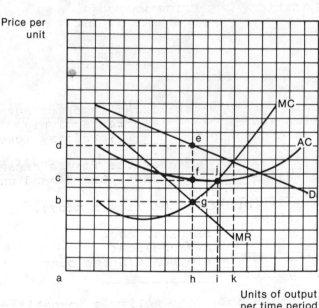

   a. Short-run profits are maximized where _____ equals _____. The profit-maximizing price = $_____, and quantity = _____ units.
   b. This firm has short-run economic _____ (profits, losses) equal to area _____ in the figure above.
   c. In the long run, _____ causes the firm's demand and marginal revenue curves to shift _____ until the demand curve is just tangent to the _____ curve.
   d. Show the long-run equilibrium on the figure above.

214

    e. In long-run equilibrium:
        (1) Price _____ marginal cost
        (2) Price _____ average cost
        (3) Price _____ minimum average cost
        (4) Economic profits = $ _____

3. The figure below represents a monopolistically competitive firm in short-run equilibrium.

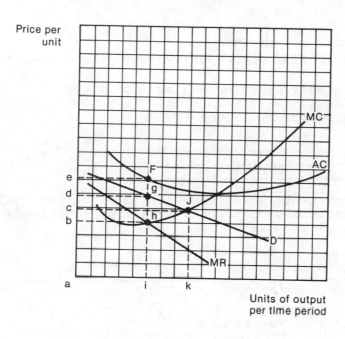

    a. The profit-maximizing or loss-minimizing level of output and price
        are _____ units and $ _____, respectively.
    b. The firm has short-run economic _____ (profits, losses) equal to
        area _____ in the figure above.
    c. In the long run, _____ causes the firm's demand and marginal
        revenue curves to shift _____ until the demand curve is just
        tangent to the _____ curve.
    d. Show the long-run equilibrium on the figure above.
    e. In long-run equilibrium:
        (1) Price _____ marginal cost
        (2) Price _____ average cost
        (3) Price _____ minimum average cost
        (4) Economic profit = $ _____

4. As compared to perfect competition, monopolistic competition results in:

    a. (Same, higher, lower) price.
    b. (Same, higher, lower) output.
    c. (Same, higher, lower) average cost.
    d. (Same, more efficient, less efficient) capacity utilization.
    e. (Same, more, less) economic profit.
    f. (Same, more, less) net benefits to society.
    g. (Same, more, less) product promotion and development.

5.   List four similarities and four dissimilarities between monopolistic
     competition in long-run equilibrium and pure monopoly.

     a.   Similarities
          (1) _____
          (2) _____
          (3) _____
          (4) _____
     b.   Dissimilarities
          (1) _____
          (2) _____
          (3) _____
          (4) _____

Concept: Oligopoly; oligopoly behavior and market outcomes

6.   List three characteristics of oligopoly.

     a.   _____
     b.   _____
     c.   _____

7.   The figure below represents an oligopolist in short-run equilibrium in an
     industry in which each oligopolist believes that a price decrease will <u>not</u>
     be matched by rival oligopolists.

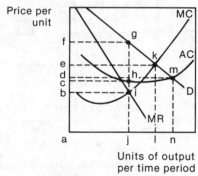

Units of output
per time period

     a.   The oligopolist maximizes profit by equating _____ and
          _____. Economic profits equal area _____, price
          = $_____, and quantity = _____ units.

b.   Suppose this oligopolist cuts price in order to increase market share.   Show the effect graphically in the figure below.

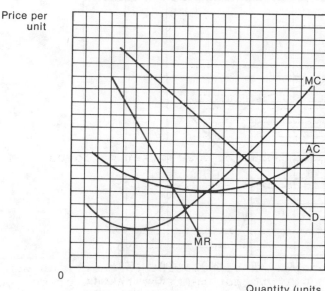

Price per unit

MC

AC

D

MR

0

Quantity (units per time period)

c.   If other oligopolists react by also cutting prices, the oligopolist that initiated the price reduction must _____ (match, not match) the price decrease in order to maintain market share. If a price war develops, price could potentially fall to a level equal to _____.   Show the effect of price warring in the figure above. What happens to economic profit?

d.   Price wars create an incentive for rival oligopolists to _____.   A formal agreement of output restriction and market sharing is known as a _____.   The intent of such a restriction and market sharing is to approximate the market outcome of a _____.

8.   Consider the following figure of an oligopolist.

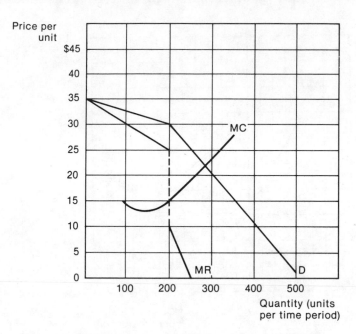

Price per unit / Quantity (units per time period)

a.   Explain the behavioral reactions of rival oligopolists that produce the "kink" in the demand curve.

b.   Profits are maximized at a level of output where _____ equals _____. Price = $_____ and quantity = _____ units.

c.   Show on the figure above the effect of an increase in marginal cost of $5 at each level of output and a decrease of $5. An increase in marginal cost of $5 at each level of output causes the profit-maximizing price and quantity to _____. A decrease in marginal cost of $5 at each level of output causes the profit-maximizing price and quantity to _____.

d.   Prices are _____ (rigid, flexible) given certain shifts in the marginal cost curve in the discontinuous section of the marginal revenue curve.

SELF-TEST FOR MASTERY

Select the best answer.

1.   Which of the following is not a characteristic associated with monopolistic competition?

a.   There is a large number of firms with small market shares.
b.   Goods produced by firms within the industry are not perfect substitutes.
c.   Firms are unconcerned with the reaction of rival firms.
d.   There are barriers to entry.
e.   There is no opportunity or incentive to collude to limit competition.

2. The demand and marginal revenue curves faced by a monopolistic competitor are flatter or more elastic than the demand and marginal revenue curves faced by a monopolist because:

    a. The demand for the good is very responsive to changes in income.
    b. The goods produced in the industry, while not perfect substitutes, are nevertheless close substitutes.
    c. The goods in the industry are unique and are not substitutes.
    d. Entry and exiting by firms makes consumers more responsive to price changes.

3. A monopolistically competitive firm maximizes profit at the level of output where:

    a. Price equals marginal revenue.
    b. Price equals marginal cost.
    c. Marginal cost equals average revenue.
    d. Marginal revenue equals marginal cost.

4. In the short run, economic profits cause _____ the monopolistically competitive industry and a _____ shift in the demand and marginal revenue curves.

    a. Entry into, leftward
    b. Entry into, rightward
    c. Exiting from, leftward
    d. Exiting from, rightward

5. In the short run, losses cause _____ the monopolistically competitive industry and a _____ shift in the demand and marginal revenue curves.

    a. Entry into, leftward
    b. Entry into, rightward
    c. Exiting from, leftward
    d. Exiting from, rightward

6. In a monopolistically competitive industry, short-run losses or economic profits will cause the demand curve to shift to the point where in long-run equilibrium, it:

    a. Intersects the supply curve.
    b. Intersects the average variable cost curve.
    c. Is just tangent to the average cost curve.
    d. Is just tangent to the marginal cost curve.

7. Monopolistic competition and perfect competition are similar in which of the following ways?

    a. In long-run equilibrium, economic profits are zero.
    b. Price exceeds marginal cost.
    c. Price equals minimum average cost.
    d. There is relative freedom of entry and exit.
    e. A and d.

8. Which of the following market structures is associated with significant advertising and product development?

    a. Perfect competition
    b. Pure monopoly
    c. Monopolistic competition

d. Oligopoly
e. C and d

9. Because the monopolistic competitor charges a price _____ marginal cost, net benefits to society _____.

   a. Equal to, are maximized
   b. Less than, are maximized
   c. Equal to, are not maximized
   d. Greater than, are not maximized

10. Which of the following is not a characteristic associated with oligopoly?

    a. Few firms
    b. Standardized or differentiated goods
    c. Lack of concern regarding a rival's behavior
    d. Large market shares
    e. Barriers to entry

11. If each oligopolist in a given industry believes that its rivals will not match price cuts:

    a. Price wars can develop resulting in economic profits for all but the smallest oligopolists.
    b. There is no incentive to reduce prices and risk a price war.
    c. A price war can develop, resulting in prices falling to a level equal to average cost.
    d. A kink appears in the oligopolist's demand and marginal revenue curves.

12. If each oligopolist in a given industry matches price cuts but does not match price increases:

    a. Price wars develop, resulting in zero economic profits.
    b. Prices become rigid at the intersection of the marginal revenue and average cost curves.
    c. Prices become flexible due to the price-cutting behavior.
    d. Prices become rigid at the kink in the demand curve.

13. Prices are rigid at the kink of an oligopolist's demand curve because:

    a. Of the distinct change in the elasticity of demand at the kink.
    b. Changes in fixed costs have no impact on the profit-maximizing price.
    c. Changes in marginal cost in the discontinuous section of the marginal revenue curve do not alter the profit-maximizing price and output.
    d. A and c.
    e. All of the above.

14. A contestable market is one in which

    a. There are significant transaction costs associated with exiting an industry.
    b. Entry is difficult, but exiting is costless.
    c. Entry is easy and exiting is not very costly.
    d. Rival oligopolists engage in predatory pricing.

15. In order to prevent entry into a contestable market, oligopolists:

    a. Set prices very high to earn monopoly profits.
    b. Set prices equal to marginal costs to maximize profits.
    c. Set prices to reduce normal profits to zero.

d.   Set prices at a level equal to average cost.

16.   Price warring creates an incentive by oligopolists to collude. A formal agreement to restrict output and share markets is called a:

a.   Pure monopoly.
b.   Restrictive oligopoly.
c.   Cartel.
d.   Quota.

17.   Which of the following conditions are necessary for a cartel to exist?

a.   Barriers to entry
b.   Agreement on total market production levels
c.   Agreement on individual firms' share of total output
d.   Ability to police and enforce the agreement
e.   All of the above

18.   An oligopolistic market in which the dominant oligopolist establishes the industry price, which subsequently is matched by the other oligopolists, is characterized by:

a.   Illegal collusion.
b.   Price leadership.
c.   Predatory pricing.
d.   Price discrimination.

THINK IT THROUGH

1.   Discuss the advantages and disadvantages of monopolistic competition relative to perfect competition.

2.   Which market structure best fits the video rental business in your community? Explain. What are your expectations for that industry as it attains long-run equilibrium?

3.   Discuss the natural forces that tend to make cartels unworkable over the long run.

4.   Why is it difficult to compare the market outcomes of oligopoly to those of other market structures?

POP QUIZ   Read the news brief at the of this chapter and answer the
                questions below.

1.   Using the information in the article, explain why OPEC is having difficulty maintaining the price of oil.

2.   According to the text, why are these difficulties expected?

CHAPTER ANSWERS

In Brief: Chapter Summary

1. A large number of firms 2. Are not 3. Lack of concern 4. No 5. Marginal revenue 6. Downward-sloping 7. More 8. Entry into 9. Exiting from 10. Profits 11. Average 12. Losses 13. Average 14. Zero economic 15. Equal to 16. Exceed 17. Many 18. Excess 19. Rightward 20. Less 21. Have no lasting effect on 22. May be higher 23. Oligopoly 24. A few 25. A price war 26. Average 27. Contestable 28. Monopoly 29. Cartel 30. Exist 31. Does not influence 32. Price leadership 33. Remain rigid 34. May not have any

Vocabulary Review

1. Imperfect competition 2. Product group 3. Selling costs 4. Oligopoly 5. Contestable market 6. Cartel 7. Monopolistic competition 8. Excess capacity 9. Price war 10. Price leader

Skills Review

1. a. There is a large number of firms with small market shares.
    b. Goods are close but not perfect substitutes.
    c. There is lack of concern regarding the reaction of rivals.
    d. There is freedom of entry and exit.
    e. There is no opportunity or incentive to collude to limit competition.

2. a. Marginal revenue, marginal cost; $ad, ah units
    b. Profits, cdef
    c. Entry, leftward, average cost

    d.

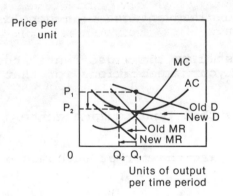

    e. (1) Exceeds (2) Equals (3) Exceeds (4) $0

3. a. ai units, $ad
    b. Losses, defg
    c. Exiting, rightward, average cost

d.

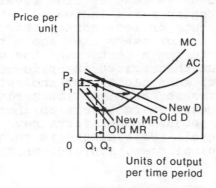

Price per unit

MC

AC

P₂
P₁

New D
Old D

New MR Old MR

0   Q₁ Q₂

Units of output per time period

e.   (1) Exceeds (2) Equals (3) Exceeds (4) $0

4.   a.   Higher b. Lower c. Higher d. Less efficient e. Same f. Less g. More

5.   a.   (1) Price exceeds minimum average cost.
         (2) Price exceeds marginal cost.
         (3) Price exceeds the competitive price.
         (4) Output is less than the competitive output.

     b.   (1) Price equals average cost for monopolistic competition, but exceeds average cost for a monopolist.
         (2) Economic profit is zero for the monopolistic competitor but positive for the monopolist.
         (3) Monopolistic competition is associated with ease of entry, whereas monopoly has barriers to entry.
         (4) Monopolistic competitors have incentives to advertise and engage in product development, whereas monopolists have little if any incentive to promote or improve their product.

6.   a.   Few firms with large market shares
     b.   Standardized or differentiated goods
     c.   Barriers to entry

7.   a.   Marginal revenue, marginal cost; cfgh, $af, aj units

     b.

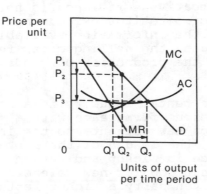

Price per unit

MC

AC

P₁
P₂
P₃

MR

D

0   Q₁ Q₂ Q₃

Units of output per time period

     c.   Match, average cost; economic profits fall to zero
     d.   Collude; cartel; monopolist

223

8.   a.   The kink in the demand curve results from rival oligopolists matching price cuts but not matching price increases. The logic is that the firm must match price cuts or lose market share. With price increases, a firm could increase market share by not matching the price increase and capturing a portion of the market share previously held by the oligopolist that raised its price. As a result, below the kink demand is much less elastic or inelastic because a price reduction does not increase sales very much since other oligopolists are also reducing prices. In contrast, an increase in price results in large sales losses because other firms have maintained their prices at the lower level. Here demand is much more elastic.

      b.   Marginal revenue, marginal cost, $30, 200 units

      c.

Price per unit / Quantity (units per time period) — graph showing MC_2, MC_1, MC_3, MR, and D curves.

        Not change, not change

      d.   Rigid

Self-Test for Mastery

1. d 2. b 3. d 4. a 5. d 6. c 7. e 8. e 9. d 10. c 11. c 12. d 13. d 14. c 15. d 16. c 17. e 18. b

Think it Through

1. Monopolistic competition results in product differentiation. Perfect competition is associated with a homogeneous good. Consumers benefit by having a greater variety of goods. Consumers, however, pay a higher price for less efficiently produced goods. Allocative efficiency is not achieved because the price charged by the monopolistic competitor exceeds marginal cost. While product advertising may increase the information available to consumers, resulting in more efficient choices, the selling costs represent resources that would otherwise be available for the production of goods in a perfectly competitive economy.

2. In a local market, the video rental industry is a monopolistically competitive market. The are numerous firms each with a small market share. Short-run economic profits attract new entrants to the industry. The product is differentiated by advertising, the length of the rental period, store hours, method of payment, and convenience in pickup and return. Even price discrimination is practiced in that popular new releases have a less elastic demand than older releases and often carry a higher rental fee. Because of the number of firms and the certainty of entry in response to economic profits, it would be very difficult to collude to limit competition. In the long run, the video rental business will have too many firms, each with excess capacity and earning only normal profits.

3.   The monopoly price resulting from a cartel's restriction of output will likely not be the price that maximizes profit for the individual cartel members. Each firm will probably have somewhat different average and marginal costs of production. Beyond the firm's share of cartel profits resulting from the sale of a specified level of output at the cartel price, the firm could increase profits even more by reducing prices to other buyers. This will work only if the increase in production does not affect market price and the cartel either does not detect the clandestine price cutting or cannot enforce the cartel agreement. If several of the members are doing this, market price will fall and the cartel will effectively be broken.

4.   The market outcomes of oligopoly depend, among other considerations, upon the reactions of rival oligopolists, the scope of the market--local, regional, national, or international--and the ease of entry and exit. An oligopolist may operate where price equals average cost or, because of scale economies, may even charge a price less than that of a perfectly competitive firm. On the other hand, an oligopolist may charge a price in excess of marginal and average cost and earn economic profits in the long run. There is no given model of oligopolistic behavior that fits all oligopolistic industries. Differences in firm behavior produce differences in outcomes. In order to assess oligopoly relative to other market structures, each oligopolistic market must be considered unique and studied individually.

Pop Quiz

1.   World oil prices have declined by as much as $4 per barrel since 1986. This is attributed to the world oil "glut" caused in part by increased production by certain members of OPEC. The United Arab Emirates have openly stated that they intend not adhere to their production quota. Instead, they intend to produce almost 50% more oil per day than their current quota of 948,000 barrels per day. Kuwait's output is up considerably as is the Saudi's production. It is estimated that total OPEC oil output is 20 million barrels per day, which is about 2 million barrels per day greater than required from the OPEC countries. Current OPEC members are scrambling for larger markets by increasing production and discounting prices. The OPEC cartel is having trouble maintaining the price of oil because it is having difficulty controlling the production of its own members.

2.   This behavior is not unexpected. If a cartel has no effective means of policing its members or erecting barriers to entry, the cartel will eventually break down as members disregard cartel agreements and pursue their own independent price-production strategy. If an individual OPEC country discounted oil prices on secret sales in excess of the quota and the increased production did not affect world oil prices, this country would likely be able to earn greater profits than under the OPEC agreement. If several countries are trying to do this, their combined production will likely decrease world oil prices, resulting in an effective breakdown of the cartel.

OPEC Output Jumps to Levels Of a Year Ago

Despite Glut, Price Decline, Daily Production Hits About 19 Million Barrels

By James Tanner
Staff Reporter of The Wall Street Journal

The Organization of Petroleum Exporting Countries suddenly is swelling the world oil glut by pumping out crude at the highest level in a year.

Trackers of the cartel's output say it now is up to 19 million barrels a day, despite the talk in OPEC about efforts to curb production excesses to stabilize deteriorating petroleum prices. Some authoritative estimates place output as high as 20 million barrels.

That is about 1.5 million barrels a day above OPEC's June level, and as much as two million barrels a day above the generally estimated need for OPEC oil for the third quarter.

Reasons for the spurting output—paced by OPEC's Middle East members, including Saudi Arabia—are not entirely clear. But, with petroleum storage tanks brimming world-wide, the production surge "helps explain the weakness in the oil market," a senior OPEC official conceded yesterday.

"We are not yet in a free-fall in prices, but we are seeing a free-for-all on OPEC production," added Lawrence Goldstein, the executive vice president of Petroleum Industry Research Foundation.

Few oil economists expect to see a repeat of the oil-price crash of early 1986. Nevertheless, petroleum markets remain stubbornly soft despite recurring signals of a possible turnaround, including major gains in petroleum demand and supply interruptions, such as last week's explosion that destroyed the Piper Alpha platform in the North Sea.

Prices Decline Again

On average, world oil prices are down more than $3 a barrel since Jan. 1 to the lowest level since 1986. They fell again yesterday, some by as much as $1 a barrel.

In volatile trading on European spot markets, prices of North Sea Brent crude dropped below $14 a barrel, down between 40 cents and 45 cents from day-earlier levels. On the U.S. futures market, West Texas Intermediate bounced off a 21-month low during the day to close at $14.72 a barrel, down only six cents.

However, major U.S. petroleum refiners—including Phillips Petroleum Co., Sun Co., USX Corp.'s Marathon Petroleum unit and Coastal Corp.—reduced their field postings for West Texas Intermediate crude by $1, to $14.25 a barrel. At such a posting, this U.S. benchmark crude is down nearly $6 a barrel from last year's peak price.

Significantly, OPEC crudes generally have dropped below $13 a barrel, which had been believed to be the "trigger" point at which Middle East producers would agree to some action to curb production. Dubai, an important United Arab Emirates crude, currently is being traded at $12.20 to $12.45 a barrel, depending on the delivery date.

Focus on Emirates

The Emirates are, in fact, a target of some OPEC efforts to restore production discipline. In recent weeks, the Emirates had proclaimed the country would ignore its OPEC quota of 948,000 barrels a day and would produce 1.5 million barrels a day.

As a result, Subroto, OPEC's new secretary-general and the former oil minister of Indonesia, plans to visit there to meet with the Emirates' president to discuss oil-market conditions. Yesterday, OPEC sources said Mr. Subroto won't arrive in the Emirates until after going to Saudi Arabia next week for the Hajj, the Moslem pilgrimage to Mecca.

Another effort that may be pursued by OPEC, as previously reported, would be a possible meeting of the price-monitoring committee. This group of five leading oil ministers is charged with monitoring world oil prices and can recommend a course of action including an emergency conference of OPEC. But yesterday, chances of a meeting of the price committee appeared to be fading.

"I don't think the meeting will take place," a senior OPEC official said. But he said several oil ministers will be in Saudi Arabia for the Hajj. "Maybe they will talk about oil," he said.

Saudi Arabia is one of the puzzles in the current outpouring of oil. Previously, the kingdom stuck to its OPEC quota of 4.3 million barrels a day, while urging others to adhere also to their production allotments. Now, there is some question as to whether the Saudis have become frustrated at the lack of restraint and whether the country, like the others, now sees the OPEC quotas as a floor for production, rather than a ceiling on output.

"The Saudis are aggressively discounting" prices, said Bryan Jacoboski, senior oil analyst at PaineWebber Inc.

Estimate Above Quota

It isn't unusual for Saudi production to be up in the first week of a month because of normal commercial commitments and then adjusted later. In the first week of July, however, Saudi Arabia exceeded its production quota by nearly one million barrels a day, according to Petro-Logistics of Geneva, Switzerland, which estimates total OPEC output at 20 million barrels a day.

"But it may be too early to draw the conclusion that Saudi policy is to produce more than quota on a regular basis," reports Petro-Logistics, which also puts Kuwait's output up sharply.

There are still differences between the current scramble for market share by OPEC's members and that which led to the 1986 price collapse. But one thing worrying oil economists this time is that Saudi Arabia, Kuwait and the Emirates seem to be going their separate ways. "The Persian Gulf players aren't coming together with a cohesive point of view," said Mr. Goldstein of Petroleum Industry Research Foundation.

Oligopoly Strategies and the Theory of Games

IN BRIEF: APPENDIX SUMMARY

Fill in the blanks to summarize appendix content.

Oligopolists (1)_____(are, are not) mutually interdependent. Strategies of one oligopolist (2)_____ (do not influence, influence) the strategies of other oligopolists. The theory of games analyzes the impact of decisions assuming various reactions on the part of rivals. The payoff matrix shows the expected gains or losses from each possible strategy (3)_____ (assuming firms are unconcerned with the reactions of rivals, given the reactions of rivals). Among many possible strategies, one possibility is to choose the strategy that (4)_____(minimizes, maximizes) the worst possible outcome of all possible strategies. This is known as the maximin strategy. If the decisions involve whether to cut price or leave it unchanged, and if each oligopolist hopes that a price cut will not induce rivals to also cut prices, a maximin strategy on the part of each firm that causes rivals to cut prices will result in a price war. Each firm (5)_____ (increases, loses) profit. This creates an obvious incentive to reduce the uncertainty by (6)_____ (colluding and agreeing to maintain, increasing) price.

VOCABULARY REVIEW

Write the key term from the list below next to its definition.

Key Terms

Theory of games
Payoff matrix
Maximin strategy

Definitions

1. _____: the strategy that maximizes the minimum (or worst) outcomes of all possible strategies.

2. _____: shows the gain or loss from each possible strategy for each possible reaction by the rival player of the game.

3. _____: analyzes the behavior of individuals or organizations with conflicting interests.

SKILLS REVIEW

Suppose there are two newspapers in a community-The Times and The Daily. The Times is trying to decide whether it should cut price. It expects to increase profits by 10% if The Daily does not react by cutting prices. If The Daily does match the price cut, it expects profits to fall by 4%. If The Times maintains price and The Daily cuts price, profits are expected to fall by 8%.

    a. Set up the payoff matrix.
    b. Assuming each firm employs the maximin strategy, what will The Times do? How will The Daily react? What are the long-run consequences for the local newspaper market?

SELF-TEST FOR MASTERY

Select the best answer.

1. The theory of games is useful:

    a. In understanding the operations of a monopolist.
    b. When the decisions of one firm are unrelated to the decisions of other firms.
    c. In understanding the behavior of monopolistic competitors.
    d. In understanding the behavior of oligopolists when their decisions are mutually interdependent.

2. The payoff matrix:

    a. Shows the potential profits or losses associated with a given price.
    b. Shows the gains or losses associated with various strategies given various reactions by rival firms.
    c. Ranks profitable strategies in descending order.
    d. Shows the relationship between oligopolistic profits and product price.

3. When each rival employs the maximin strategy to protect the level of profits:

    a. Monopolistic profits arise.
    b. Price wars develop, resulting in a decrease in profits and an incentive to collude.
    c. One oligopolist succeeds at the expense of the others and becomes the industry leader.
    d. Profits are maximized only when average-cost pricing accompanies the strategy.

APPENDIX ANSWERS

In Brief: Appendix Summary

1. Are 2. Influence 3. Given the reaction of rivals 4. Maximizes 5. Loses
6. Colluding and agreeing to maintain

Vocabulary Review

1. Maximim strategy 2. Payoff matrix 3. Theory of games

Skills Review

a.

		Times	
		Reduce price	No change
Daily	Reduce price	-4%	-8%
	No change	+10%	------

b. If both firms pursue the maximin strategy, they will cut prices, thus reducing profits and likely starting a price war. In the long run, the firms might decide that collusion is necessary to reduce the uncertainty and to protect profits.

Self-Test for Mastery

1. a 2. b 3. b

15

Antitrust Policy and Regulation of Markets

CHAPTER CHALLENGES

After studying your text, attending class, and completing this chapter, you should be able to:

1. Describe how governments use the law and the courts to prevent establishment of monopoly positions through unfair business practices. Also, discuss antitrust laws and how they affect business behavior and mergers.
2. Explain the characteristics of natural monopoly firms and discuss alternative policies of government control over the prices such firms are permitted to charge for their products. Also, demonstrate understanding of the concept of "fair-rate-of-return" pricing.
3. Describe the impact of government policies that limit the freedom of sellers to choose their own prices and to enter markets. Also, discuss the impact of eliminating government controls on prices and competition in markets.

IN BRIEF: CHAPTER SUMMARY

Fill in the blanks to summarize chapter content.

The goal of antitrust policy is to prevent abuses of market power in less competitive markets and to prevent the monopolization of markets that are presently competitive. The first antitrust law was the (1)_____ (Clayton, Sherman) Act of 1890. The intent of the law was to prohibit activities that restrain trade. The (2)_____ (Clayton, Sherman) Act of 1914 identified specific business practices that restrict competition, such as price discrimination, tying contracts, interlocking directorates, and anticompetitive mergers via the acquisition of corporate (3)_____ (assets, stock). The Federal Trade Commission, established in 1914, regulates methods of competition and today it (4)_____ (targets deceptive and false advertising, is mainly interested in violations of U.S. pricing statutes). The Robinson-Patman Act of 1936 was intended to protect small retailers from unfair competition from chain and discount stores. The Celler-Kefauver Act of 1950 closed a major loophole in the Clayton Act by making illegal the acquisition of (5)_____ (stock, assets) that lessens competition.

The antitrust laws have been interpreted in different ways by the courts over the years. In 1911, (6)_____ (U.S. Steel, Standard Oil) was broken up because it engaged in practices considered to constitute an intent to monopolize. In 1920, (7)_____ (U.S. Steel, Standard Oil) had a high market share but was not dissolved because it was found that it did not use its size to limit competition. In effect, the (8)_____ ("rule of reason," relevant market rule) was established in which it had to be shown that the monopolist or firm with a very large market share was a "bad" monopolist--

engaging in anticompetitive activities. This interpretation held until the Alcoa case of (9)_____ (1926, 1945). Alcoa had a 90% share of its market. It was found to have not engaged in anticompetitive activities, but it was found guilty of monopolization and broken up because its expansion of capacity was viewed as an attempt to monopolize the market. This essentially reversed the rule of reason--market share alone was enough to be convicted of monopolization. Another major interpretation relating to market share had to do with the concept of the "relevant" market. Although du Pont had a monopoly in the production of cellophane, if the definition of the relevant market was broadened to include all flexible wrappings, it had a much smaller market share. Du Pont was found (10)_____(guilty, innocent) of monopolization. Similar considerations were relevant when the Justice Department dropped its antitrust case against IBM in 1982.

Are high market concentration and profits evidence of monopoly power? In many cases the answer is yes, but not always. For instance, a firm may have a large market share because economies of scale require a large production run. The large firm may be large because it offers a superior product. High accounting profits do not necessarily mean high economic profits because implicit costs are not considered in accounting profit. If firms face competition from abroad, even firms with large domestic market shares must contend with numerous foreign firms. This tends to (11)_____ (lessen, increase) market power and the potential for market abuses. Concentration ratios can be misleading in that a firm with a small national concentration ratio may have a high ratio in some local or regional markets, allowing it to exercise market power.

An important portion of the market share concentration in business today is the result of mergers. Mergers can be horizontal, vertical, or conglomerate. (12)_____ (Horizontal, Vertical, Conglomerate) mergers occur between firms that operate at a given stage of production, such as refining in the oil industry, whereas (13)_____ (horizontal, vertical, conglomerate) mergers are between firms that operate at different stages of production, such as oil exploration and refining. (14)_____ (Horizontal, Vertical, Conglomerate) mergers are between firms in dissimilar industries.

Where economies of scale dictate the existence of a single producer and where the good or service is considered vital, the government allows the existence of the single firm, but regulates its profit and hence the rates or prices that it charges. These firms are called (15)_____ (oligopolies, natural monopolies). Marginal-cost pricing for such a firm is (16)_____ (unworkable, desirable) because a firm experiencing economies of scale has marginal costs that are below average costs. A price set below average cost would not allow the firm to realize enough normal profit to attract sufficient funds for expansion and modernization. Federal and state regulatory commissions today require utilities to employ (17)_____ (marginal-, average-) cost pricing to ensure that a "fair" rate of return is earned. The intent of this regulation is to ensure enough normal profits to allow the continuation of a vital service, but to not allow the utility to earn economic profits at the consumer's expense.

Regulation by federal and state governments in some industries such as airlines, railroads, and trucking, has actually prevented entry of potential new firms and prohibited price competition. The commissions set up to regulate these industries had the intent to ensure the continuation of a vital service at stable prices and to prevent monopolization. But in controlling service routes, rate structures, etc., they (18)_____ (promoted, in effect prevented potential) competition. Several of these industries have been deregulated, resulting in generally lower prices to the public, but in the airline industry there is concern regarding the quality of service and the threat of oligopolization as the market stabilizes.

VOCABULARY REVIEW

Write the key term from the list below next to its definition.

Key Terms

Antitrust statutes   Rule of reason
Horizontal merger   Vertical merger
Conglomerate merger

Definitions

1. _____: holds that acts beyond normal business practice that unduly restrain competition for the purpose of excluding rivals can be used to infer intent to monopolize an industry.

2. _____: seeks to prevent "unfair" business practices that give rise to monopoly power.

3. _____: a merger of a firm with its suppliers.

4. _____: occurs when competing sellers in the same market merge into a single firm.

5. _____: a merger of firms selling goods in unrelated markets.

SKILLS REVIEW

Concept: Antitrust laws

1. Identify the antitrust legislation designed to prevent each of the following activities.

   Law/Date
   a. _____ anticompetitive price discrimination
   b. _____ anticompetitive mergers resulting from the acquisition of corporate assets
   c. _____ anticompetitive mergers resulting from the acquisition of corporate stock
   d. _____ monopolization that results in a restraint of trade
   e. _____ false and deceptive advertising
   f. _____ chain stores taking over markets from independent retailers
   g. _____ tying contracts
   h. _____ interlocking directorates

2. Which antitrust cases are associated with the following?

   Case/Date

   a. _____ establishment of the rule of reason
   b. _____ market share itself or how it is acquired, whether or not the firm engages in anticompetitive activities, is evidence of intent to monopolize

c. _____ the "relevant" market must be identified in order
to use market share as evidence of monopolization

d. _____ mere size itself is not an offense

3. List five reasons why the presence of high market share and profits may
not be evidence of monopoly power.

a. _____

b. _____

c. _____

d. _____

e. _____

Concept: Regulation of natural monopolies

4. The figure below represents an electric power company located in a region
in which it is the sole supplier of electricity.

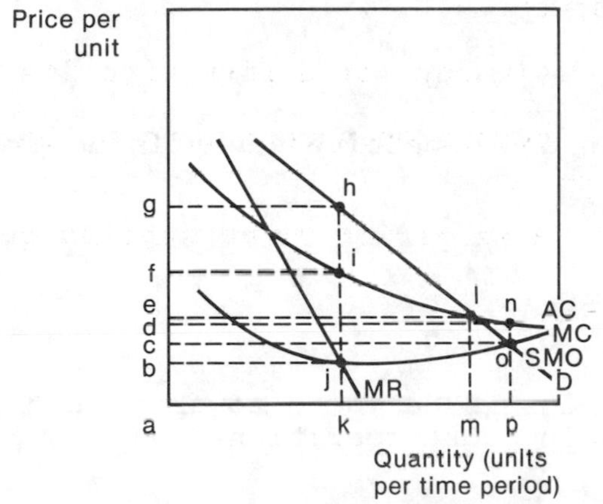

a. Identify the unregulated monopoly price, output, and economic
profits/losses. Price = $_____, output = _____ units,
profit/loss = $_____

b. Suppose you have just been elected to be a state regulatory
commissioner. Because you are aware that the net benefits to society
are maximized where price equals marginal cost, you decide to impose
marginal-cost pricing on the electric power company. Identify the
new price, quantity, and profit/loss. Price = $_____, output
= _____ units, profit/loss = $_____

c. An average-cost ("fair" rate-of-return) pricing scheme results in
price equal to $_____, quantity equal to _____ units,
and $_____ profit/loss.

d. Identify and discuss the problems associated with average-cost
pricing.

Concept: Deregulation of regulated industries

5. List four effects of the Airline Deregulation Act of 1978.

a. _____

b. _____

c. _____

d. _____

SELF-TEST FOR MASTERY

Select the best answer.

1. Which of the following acts made it illegal to "restrain trade"?

    a. Sherman Act of 1890
    b. Clayton Act of 1914
    c. Federal Trade Act of 1914
    d. Robinson-Patman Act of 1936
    e. Celler-Kefauver Act of 1950

2. Which of the following acts prohibited specific anticompetitive business practices such as price discrimination?

    a. Sherman Act of 1890
    b. Clayton Act of 1914
    c. Federal Trade Act of 1914
    d. Robinson-Patman Act of 1936
    e. Celler-Kefauver Act of 1950

3. Under which act is false and deceptive advertising prohibited?

    a. Sherman Act of 1890
    b. Clayton Act of 1914
    c. Federal Trade Act of 1914
    d. Robinson-Patman Act of 1936
    e. Celler-Kefauver Act of 1950

4. Which of the following acts is designed to protect small independent retailers from large chain store operations?

    a. Sherman Act of 1890
    b. Clayton Act of 1914
    c. Federal Trade Commission Act of 1914
    d. Robinson-Patman Act of 1936
    e. Celler-Kefauver Act of 1950

5. Which act prohibits anticompetitive mergers resulting from the acquisition of a firm's assets?

    a. Sherman Act of 1890
    b. Clayton Act of 1914
    c. Federal Trade Commission Act of 1914
    d. Robinson-Patman Act of 1936
    e. Celler-Kefauver Act of 1950

6. The "rule of reason":

    a. Holds that monopolists must be reasonably competitive when dealing with smaller rivals.
    b. Was established in the Alcoa case of 1920.
    c. Holds that acts beyond normal business practice that unduly restrain competition for the purpose of excluding rivals can be used to infer intent to monopolize an industry.
    d. Holds that the entire market must be considered rather than just the relevant market.

7. The "rule of reason" was established in which of the following cases?

   a. Standard Oil case of 1911
   b. U.S. Steel case of 1920
   c. Alcoa case of 1945
   d. Du Pont case of 1956

8. The concept that mere size was not an offense was established in the:

   a. Standard Oil case of 1911.
   b. U.S. Steel case of 1920.
   c. Alcoa case of 1945.
   d. Du Pont case of 1956.

9. The concept of the "relevant" market was important in which of the following cases?

   a. Standard Oil case of 1911
   b. Du Pont case of 1956
   c. IBM case, which was terminated in 1982
   d. U.S. Steel case of 1920
   e. B and c

10. High market concentration and profit are not necessarily evidence of monopoly power because:

    a. Of the presence of economies of scale.
    b. The firm may simply produce superior products.
    c. A firm with a high domestic concentration ratio might nevertheless face significant competition from imports.
    d. High accounting profits do not necessarily mean high economic profits.
    e. All of the above.

11. A merger of two firms operating in different markets producing dissimilar goods is called a:

    a. Horizontal merger.
    b. Vertical merger.
    c. Multinational merger.
    d. Conglomerate merger.

12. A merger of two firms operating in the same market is known as a:

    a. Horizontal merger.
    b. Vertical merger.
    c. Multinational merger.
    d. Conglomerate merger.

13. If marginal-cost pricing is imposed on a natural monopolist, one that experiences declining average costs of production:

    a. The firm will earn only normal profits.
    b. The firm is induced to produce the level of output that maximizes society's net benefits.
    c. Losses are imposed on the firm.
    d. The firm will have trouble attracting equity funds.
    e. C and d.

14. Average-cost (or "fair" rate-of-return) pricing

    a.   Allows the firm to realize normal profits but no economic profits.
    b.   Results in losses that have to be made up with tax revenue.
    c.   Results in the maximum net gain to society.
    d.   Creates an incentive for the firm to minimize average costs.

15. Which of the following is incorrect with respect to average cost pricing?

    a.   Average-cost pricing creates an incentive to be efficient and
         minimize average costs.
    b.   Average-cost pricing results in prices greater than marginal cost,
         meaning that society would experience a net gain if more of the good
         could be produced at a lower price.
    c.   Average-cost pricing results in the use of excess capital as a way of
         increasing the rate base in order to get higher rates or prices.
    d.   None of the above.

16. Some transportation industries, such as airlines, railroads, and trucking,
    were regulated:

    a.   Because violent unions required the government to intervene in order
         to establish stability.
    b.   To ensure or guarantee service and to prevent the monopolization of
         the industry.
    c.   Because such industries are considered natural monopolies.
    d.   To avoid the destructive effects of price wars.

17. Regulation in the transportation industries resulted in:

    a.   Price competition and freedom of entry and exit.
    b.   Lower prices.
    c.   The absence of both price competition and the freedom of entry and
         exit.
    d.   The establishment of the FTC as the major oversight body in charge of
         reviewing rate structures.
    e.   B and d.

18. The Airline Deregulation Act of 1978 has resulted in all but one of the
    following.

    a.   A reduction in fares
    b.   A more complex price structure
    c.   An increase in the quality of service
    d.   Increased entry to and exit from the industry

THINK IT THROUGH

1.   Discuss the how the interpretation of the antitrust laws has changed over
time and identify the important court cases associated with the changes.

2.   Large market share and high profits are evidence of the exercise of
monopoly power. True or false? Explain.

3.   If perfectly competitive markets result in allocative efficiency, then why
does the government grant exclusive operating rights to utilities? The
government is in effect sponsoring a monopoly.

4.   Interstate trucking was deregulated in the 1970s, but many states continue to regulate intrastate trucking. Discuss the intent or objectives of regulatory commissions. Can you think of any reasons why some of the strongest objections to the deregulation of intrastate trucking often come from trucking firms with dominant market shares rather than small firms?

POP QUIZ   Read the news brief at the end of this chapter and answer the questions below.

Certain industries are exempt from antitrust legislation. The insurance industry was exempted in 1944 by the McCarran-Ferguson Act. Critics of the insurance industry argue that the exemption should be removed. Why? How might society benefit?

CHAPTER ANSWERS

In Brief: Chapter Summary

1. Sherman 2. Clayton 3. Stock 4. Targets deceptive and false advertising 5. Assets 6. Standard Oil 7. U.S. Steel 8. "Rule of reason" 9. 1945 10. Innocent 11. Lessen 12. Horizontal 13. Vertical 14. Conglomerate 15. Natural monopolies 16. Unworkable 17. Average 18. In effect prevented potential

Vocabulary Review

1. Rule of reason 2. Antitrust statutes 3. Vertical merger 4. Horizontal merger 5. Conglomerate merger

Skills Review

1.   a. Clayton Act of 1914 b. Celler-Kefauver Act of 1950
     c. Clayton Act of 1914 d. Sherman Act of 1890 e. Federal Trade
     Commission Act of 1914 f. Robinson-Patman Act of 1936 g. Clayton Act of
     1914 h. Clayton Act of 1914

2.   a. Standard Oil (1911) b. Alcoa (1945) c. Alcoa (1945), du Pont
     (1956), IBM (suit terminated in 1982) d. U.S. Steel (1920)

3.   a. Economies of scale require a large production run and may result in a
         lower price than if the industry was made up of several inefficiently
         sized firms.
     b. The firm might produce a superior product.
     c. Accounting profit is likely to be larger than economic profit.
     d. The presence of foreign competition will likely result in more
         competition among firms having high domestic concentration ratios
         than among firms having lower ratios but no foreign competition.
     e. A firm may have a low national concentration ratio but have a
         regional monopoly.

4.   a. ag, ak, profit (fghi)
     b. ac, ap, loss (cdno)
     c. ae, am, 0
     d. Average-cost pricing does not create an incentive for a firm to
         minimize average costs, but rather creates an incentive to

overcapitalize--to build an inefficiently sized plant to pad the rate base in order to win higher rates from the regulatory commission.

5. a. Lower fares b. More complex fares c. Increased entry and exit d. Reduced quality of service

Self-Test for Mastery

1. a 2. b 3. c 4. d 5. e 6. c 7. a 8. b 9. e 10. e 11. d 12. a 13. e 14. a 15. a 16. b 17. c 18. c

Think it Through

1.   Standard Oil was found guilty in 1911 of monopolization and broken up. It engaged in business practices, in excess of those considered normal, that resulted in a restraint of trade. The "rule of reason" was established in which a firm could be found guilty of monopolization if it engaged in activities beyond normal business practices where the effect was to lessen competition. Although U.S. Steel was a firm with a large share of the market, in 1920 it was found innocent of monopolization because it did not engage in anticompetitive business practices. From 1920 until the Alcoa case of 1945, the interpretation of the antitrust laws was that size is itself not an offense, but anticompetitive business practices together with size were sufficient to show the intent to exercise market power. In 1945, this interpretation changed in the Alcoa case in that Alcoa was not found to have engaged in anticompetitive business practices, but was convicted of monopolization because of Alcoa's large market share and the way in which Alcoa's production capacity was acquired. The concept of the relevant market became important in the Alcoa case of 1945, the du Pont case of 1956, and the IBM case terminated in 1982. To be convicted of monopolization, the firm has to have a very high share in the relevant product market, not just a large market share in general.

2.   False. A large market share and high profits may many times indicate the exercise of monopoly power, but there are a number of reasons other than the exercise of market power why a firm could have a large market share and high profits. For instance, accounting costs do not include implicit costs and therefore accounting profits will likely always be higher than economic profits. A firm may have a low national market share but be a monopolist in regional or local markets. A firm with economies of scale may have a large market share in order to operate at an efficient level of production. Because of the scale economies, the firm may even charge a price lower than that charged by many small but inefficiently sized firms. A firm might have a large market share because of its reputation for quality and service.

3.   Utilities are natural monopolies--they realize significant economies of scale and require a high rate of production and hence a large market share in order to produce at low average cost. But they are still monopolies and will charge prices to maximize profits if unregulated. Their service or good is usually considered vital to the community. Regulatory commissions want to promote the continuation and stability of the utility's service or good, but they also want the cost advantages of a monopoly utility passed on to customers in the form of lower prices. Utilities must be allowed to earn at least a normal profit ("fair" rate of return) in order to attract equity funds for modernization and expansion. Therefore regulators choose a second-best option by imposing on utilities average-cost pricing rather than the socially preferable marginal-cost pricing.

4.   Objectives of regulation regarding the trucking industry include (a) ensuring the continuation of a vital service, and (b) avoiding price warring or monopolization that might threaten the availability of the regulated good or

service. Trucking regulation has been in the form of strict control over rates and service routes, thus prohibiting price competition and entry of new firms. Established firms, often having large market shares of the intrastate trucking business, are sheltered and protected by the very commissioners who are ostensibly acting in the public interest to promote lower rates and reliable and universal service. Thus the sheltered firm may have much to lose if the market is opened up to competitive pricing and entry.

Pop Quiz

The 1944 act exempting the insurance industry from antitrust prosecution and the 1980 prohibition against FTC investigation of the industry has given insurers license to operate together to jointly determine coverage and rates. Critics contend that the industry is a collusive oligopoly that in the mid-1980s dramatically cut liability coverage and raised rates. It is argued that the insurers were raising rates not because of mounting liability insurance losses, but because they were trying to increase profits. Although there are 1400 member insurers of the industry's trade association, only 8 to 12 of the 1400 effectively guide the "standards" established by the association. It is argued that these few insurers put undue pressure on the trade association to write into the standards certain restrictions such as pollution exclusions. It is also suspected that the insurers conspired to limit liability coverage and raise rates to induce state legislators to pass laws establishing maximum liability awards.

These critics further argue that the removal of the antitrust exemption would result in "...greater prudence at the companies and, ultimately, steadier competition in a broader array of products and price ranges." If, indeed, insurance companies are conspiring in the manner described in the article, subjecting them to antitrust prosecution would be desirable. Greater competition would likely result in greater product differentiation and product availability and would likely result in lower premiums or premiums that at least reflect past claims records.

Unaccustomed Risk

Insurers, Long Free Of Antitrust Curbs, Face Rising Challenges

Congress May Cut Immunity, And 19 States Are Suing; The Spark: Soaring Rates

Giant Firms' Dominant Role

By Peter Waldman

Staff Reporter of The Wall Street Journal.

The insurance industry has long held a cozy place in the heart of Congress.

In 1944, lawmakers exempted insurers from federal antitrust laws, allowing the state-regulated companies to share data and jointly fix premiums and policy provisions. In 1980, Congress broadened that immunity by prohibiting the Federal Trade Commission from investigating even non-antitrust aspects of the industry, squelching what had been a useful source of consumer information.

In return, the giant companies have long contributed generously to congressional campaigns.

Now, however, Congress is making the industry squirm. Faced with mounting evidence that some insurers have used their antitrust immunity to raise prices and limit coverage, the judiciary committees of both houses are considering bills to curtail that exemption. The bills still face several hurdles, but they could be signaling a shift in the regulatory winds.

'Committed' Congressman

"I've never seen [Rep. Peter] Rodino as committed to an antitrust issue as this," says one longtime congressional aide describing the attitude of the New Jersey Democrat who heads the House Judiciary Committee.

Documents obtained by The Wall Street Journal corroborate how the industry has worked in concert—perfectly legally—to fix prices, set restrictive policy terms and even influence legislation by reducing the availability of insurance. Congress granted the industry special immunity in the McCarran-Ferguson Act of 1944, which exempts the "business of insurance" from antitrust prosecution, provided the states regulate it. The immunity, however, specifically excludes acts of "boycott, coercion or intimidation."

Specifically, the suits charge that Insurance Services Offices Inc., a trade group based in New York, succumbed to pressure from a small group of member companies in 1984 and rewrote industrywide policy standards to exclude coverage for pollution damages and for "retroactive" losses—losses occurring before the starting date of a policy. These exclusions amounted to an illegal industry boycott, the suits charge.

The ISO says it began revising general-liability policy terms as early as 1977. Through the late 1970s and early 1980s, however, high interest rates were spurring a price-cutting frenzy among insurers striving to sell more policies and thereby raise capital for investment. Under those circumstances, proposals to adopt coverage restrictions that might have driven down premium income didn't get far.

"We have serious doubts about the fundamental soundness of an approach which is likely to create market problems," Lyman Baldwin Jr., a senior vice-president of the Hartford Fire Insurance unit of ITT Corp., wrote in a 1979 letter to ISO President Daniel McNamara.

But by 1983, interest rates had dropped, and many insurers were reeling from the price war. That year, the industry's profits on general-liability insurance plunged to just $118 million from $847 million in 1979, according to the federal General Accounting Office. Efforts to revise policies and raise rates began in earnest.

The seemingly small changes in coverage for pollution and retroactive losses severely hurt some municipalities, small businesses and nonprofit organizations, which suddenly were paying much higher premiums for less coverage.

Milford, Mass., for example, had to pay $125,000 for liability insurance in 1987, four times more than in 1984. Yet, under its new policy, Milford had no coverage for pollution-related accidents, such as gas or sewage leaks, nor for any claims reported after the policy expired, even if the damages occurred while it was in force.

Likewise, the Texas Easter Seal Society, which has never been sued for any reason, watched its liability premiums soar nearly tenfold in the past three years, to $117,000, for reduced coverage. That additional money spent on insurance could provide therapy services for 100 disabled people, says Lila Coughran, the chapter's executive director.

Many federal and state regulators have testified against that exemption before Congress. "It is not cynical to suspect that at least some insurers have taken advantage of McCarran-Ferguson immunity to harm consumers," Daniel Oliver, the FTC chairman, told the Senate Judiciary Committee last year.

The Insurance Crisis

Though critics have charged for years

that the industry's exemption allows a small cartel of dominant companies to manipulate the market, their cries for reform went largely unheeded until the insurance crisis of the mid-1980s. Then, seemingly overnight, insurers slashed coverage, jacked up premiums on many types of policies—and sparked heated debate.

Insurers, backed by the Reagan administration, blamed the crisis on a rash of unexpected court decisions that greatly expanded their liability for certain claims. In particular, some judges in the late 1970s reversed prior industry and judicial interpretations and decided that damages from gradual, long-term pollution leaks were covered under standard liability policies. Courts also stunned insurers by upholding their liability for unpredictable, so-called cumulative injuries such as asbestosis.

Traumatized by these and other decisions, the industry said it needed to move fast to rewrite policies and raise rates. If the public didn't like that, the companies reasoned, it could press for changes in state tort laws.

Critics' View

But consumer groups, trial lawyers and some politicians—with their own axes to grind—or pockets to fill—blame the crisis not on the courts but on collusion. Insurers, these critics contend, were merely exploiting their antitrust exemption to increase profits after years of reckless price-cutting. In 1986, when, for want of liability insurance, cities were curtailing services, directors were quitting corporate boards and charities were folding, the attorneys general of California, Texas and some other states launched a joint investigation of a possible conspiracy.

Their findings, lodged in antitrust suits filed last spring by 19 states against 32 insurer defendants, focus on the industry's cooperative practices expressly forbidden for most industries. Even the defendants' version of the facts of the case depicts a small old-boy network of giant-company executives who, by cajoling and sometimes bullying the industry's main trade group, jointly limited the liability insurance available in the U.S.

Seeking Common Goals

In addition to the state suits, other cases show how insurers use the antitrust exemption to fight for common goals. In one instance, several insurers, including the Aetna Casualty & Surety unit of Aetna Life & Casualty Co. and Fireman's Fund Insurance Co., agreed to interpret Pennsylvania's no-fault auto-insurance law in a way that barred work-loss benefits for survivors of auto-accident victims. The state's supreme court ruled against that interpretation in 1980, but not before the insurers had saved millions of dollars in payouts.

Subsequently, in 1981, the husband of an

Unaccustomed Risk: Insurers Face Possible Loss of Antitrust Shield

auto-accident victim filed an antitrust suit against the Pennsylvania insurers, but a federal district judge dismissed it. The judge ruled that the "wholly intra-industry agreement" was akin to rate-making and therefore exempt from the antitrust laws under the McCarran-Ferguson Act.

In another case, five medical-malpractice insurers, including St. Paul Fire & Marine Insurance Co. and Continental Casualty Co., simultaneously sent policy-cancellation letters to about 6,500 doctors, dentists, hospitals and clinics in West Virginia, after the state legislature passed a law they didn't like. Although that law, which was due to take effect in June 1986, limited awards in malpractice judgments, it also required insurers to base rates on policyholders' past claims records.

While both the law and the cancellations were pending, the state legislature, in a special session, repealed the rate-setting provision. West Virginia's attorney general filed an antitrust suit against the insurers and won a state-court order enjoining them from canceling policyholders en masse. The suit is still in litigation.

Multistate Suits

In the multistate suits, the states contend that four big U.S. insurers, along with several U.S. and British reinsurers, coerced the ISO into adopting the retroactivity and pollution exclusions in late 1984. Earlier that year, the ISO had issued standard forms without such restrictions.

Legal memorandums prepared for the ISO by its own attorneys indicate that some defendants used threats and other tactics to pressure the trade group into adopting the additional exclusions. Thomas Greene, a U.S. reinsurance broker who, the suits allege, was "enlisted" to pressure the ISO by defendants General Reinsurance Corp. and Hartford Fire Insurance, told the group's directors in June 1984 that without the added exclusions, the new policies "just [wouldn't] fly in the reinsurance market," according to an ISO memo. The broker added that there was "no chance" the reinsurers would "break ranks and give you what you want."

Reinsurers, many of whom are associated with Lloyd's of London, cover a portion of the risk underwritten by insurance companies and share in the premium. At the height of the alleged conspiracy, ISO documents show that senior ISO staff members traveled to London to confer with reinsurers about the new policy forms. At a dinner given by some British companies at London's posh Garrick Club, the ISO officials found their hosts "almost militant" in support of coverage restrictions in the new forms, the state complaints say.

ISO legal memorandums also show that in mid-1984, a senior ISO staffer tried to get Hartford Fire, a staunch proponent of added, industrywide restrictions, to compromise on less stringent provisions. But Hartford "refused to budge," according to the memorandums.

Coercion Denied

Hartford Fire and other defendants deny jointly coercing the ISO to adopt the narrower coverage. "We were proceeding to achieve Hartford's objectives for The Hartford"—to get a policy "tool we could use in a very difficult marketplace," says Stephen Martin, Hartford's vice president for government relations.

The defendants also argue that because any threats by reinsurers to boycott the U.S. market would have affected only other insurance companies, the state plaintiffs lack standing to sue. They add that the final policy revisions were scrutinized by state regulators, a few of whom rejected the new forms. Essentially, the defendants contend, the ISO did merely what state regulators expressly license it to do: It melded its members' needs and opinions into policy standards for the market.

"In any meeting where people have different views, it's only natural that people of similar views are going to line up and present their views together," says Robert Pike, the general counsel of defendant Allstate Insurance Co., a unit of Sears, Roebuck & Co.

But the very fact that such collusive actions may have been legal is exactly what makes the states' allegations so damning, industry critics say. Of the ISO's 1,400 member companies, the same eight to 12 insurers controlled its executive committee throughout the four years during which it rewrote the new liability forms, according to a complaint filed by Texas. Moreover, five of those same companies—Hartford, Aetna Life & Casualty, Liberty Mutual Insurance Co., Travelers Insurance Co. of Travelers Corp. and USF&G Corp.—served on all the major committees responsible for drafting the new policies, according to the complaint.

"Many companies don't have the resources to devote to the ISO function," Hartford's Mr. Martin explains.

ISO Staff's Influence Weak

Theoretically, the ISO's own independent staff is supposed to bridle committee members' self-interest. But ISO documents show how weak its influence really is. In the summer of 1984, for example, ISO President McNamara wrote a "staff recommendation" advising the trade group's leadership to postpone adoption of the coverage restrictions, pending further study. This suggestion was promptly rejected by the chairman of the ISO's Commercial Lines Committee, who feared more study would cause "unacceptable delay," according to ISO legal memorandums.

Critics of the McCarran-Ferguson immunity say the state suits, and other evidence of concerted action, show how the law has fostered a herdlike mentality in the insurance industry. Although few argue that its repeal will solve the underlying economic forces driving the industry's vicious market cycles, many critics contend that antitrust restrictions would spur greater prudence at the companies and, ultimately, steadier competition in a broader array of products and price ranges.

"Absent the implicit assumption that collective wisdom is favored over independent analysis, we would see less lock-step conformity," says John Van de Kamp, California's attorney general.

The congressional bills wouldn't wipe out the McCarran-Ferguson Act. Instead, they would repeal the industry's immunity for price-fixing and other "monopolistic" practices while safeguarding state regulation and certain "pro-competitive" joint activities such as collection of actuarial data. Overall, though, insurers would be held to a much tighter standard in matters of collusion.

That might not be so bad, some insurance executives say. Right or wrong, McCarran-Ferguson has become such an embarrassment that the exemption may well have outlived its usefulness, they concede. "We may have come to the time where the misconceptions that stem from the McCarran-Ferguson Act are more than the industry can tolerate," says the general counsel of one defendant in the state suits.

16

Market Failure and the Role of Government in Allocating Resources

CHAPTER CHALLENGES

After studying your text, attending class, and completing this chapter, you should be able to:

1. Explain the concept of an externality and show how externalities prevent free and competitive markets from allocating resources efficiently.
2. Describe the causes of externalities and show how government can help achieve efficiency by intervening in markets when externalities exist.
3. Explain the concept of a public good and show how provision of public goods by government can result in net gains to consumers.
4. Describe and evaluate social regulation by government to correct for market failure.

IN BRIEF: CHAPTER SUMMARY

Fill in the blanks to summarize chapter content.

Markets often fail to allocate resources efficiently. Governments may be able to correct the misallocation, thus enhancing society's well-being. Externalities are a common cause of market failure. (1)_____ (Positive, Negative) externalities are costs associated with the use of resources that are not reflected in price and are imposed on third parties--those other than the buyers or sellers of the good. Marginal social costs (2)_____ (are less than, exceed) the producer's marginal cost by the marginal external cost. Because profit-maximizing producers equate marginal cost and marginal revenue rather than the (3)_____ (higher, lower) marginal social cost and marginal revenue, too (4)_____ (much, little) is produced and market price (or marginal benefit) is (5)_____ (above, below) the marginal social cost. Thus society would benefit if (6)_____ (more, less) of the good were produced.

(7)_____ (Positive, Negative) externalities are benefits associated with the use of resources that are not reflected in price and accrue to third parties. Marginal social benefits (8)_____ (are less than, exceed) marginal benefits by the marginal external benefit. Since the market equates marginal benefit and marginal cost rather than the (9)_____ (lower, higher) marginal social benefit and marginal cost, the market (10)_____ (underproduces, overproduces) output, which results in a price that is too (11)_____ (high, low). It allocates too (12)_____ (many, few) resources to the production of the good. Society would gain if (13)_____ (more, less) of the good were produced.

Both negative and positive externalities result because (14)_____ (prices, property rights) either do not exist, are poorly defined, or are not enforced. Common property resources such as navigable rivers are often polluted in the absence of government regulation because no one individual has a property right to the river and therefore cannot prevent others from imposing external costs such as pollution on users of the river. The producer of a positive externality does not have a property right to the (15)_____ (benefits conferred, costs imposed) on others. There is no way to be compensated for these external benefits by the market.

Government can potentially correct an externality by internalizing the externality--forcing the external costs of negative externalities on those that generate them and requiring those that benefit from positive externalities to compensate the producer of the benefits. A (16)_____ (corrective subsidy, corrective tax) can be used to internalize a negative externality. A tax equal to the marginal (17)_____ (social, external) cost of some action will cause the firm's marginal cost to equal the marginal social cost. A profit-maximizing firm will be induced to (18)_____ (cut, increase) output and (19)_____ (lower, raise) price. The adjusted market price now equals the marginal social cost, and the level of output is the level that maximizes the net gain to society from the use of resources. The tax revenue can be used to compensate those that have suffered as a result of the negative externality.

A corrective (20)_____ (subsidy, tax) can be used to internalize a positive externality. A (21)_____ (subsidy, tax) to consumers equal to the marginal external benefit would cause the marginal benefit or demand curve to shift to the higher marginal social benefit curve. Consumers would be induced to purchase (22)_____ (less, more) of the subsidized good, ultimately causing market price and quantity to (23)_____ (decrease, increase). Price would (24)_____ (rise, fall) to equal marginal social benefit, which would also equal marginal cost. Again society's net benefit is maximized. Alternatively, a subsidy could be given to the producer, causing the producer to (25)_____ (increase, decrease) output, but price would (26)_____(rise, fall) and be less than the marginal social benefit. Subsidies can be financed via specific taxes levied on the beneficiaries of the positive externality. If the beneficiaries cannot be easily identified or the extent of the benefit cannot be precisely measured, then general tax revenues can be used.

Public goods are (27)_____ (rival, not rival) in consumption, are (28)_____ (subject, not subject) to the exclusion principle, and are associated with (29)_____ (zero, positive) marginal costs of production. If the public good is provided to one, it is provided to all and at zero marginal cost. A profit-maximizing firm equating price and marginal cost would not produce a good at zero price. Even if a positive price could be charged, there is no way to exclude nonpayers from enjoying the benefits of the good. The market will therefore (30)_____ (produce, not produce) public goods. Yet these goods bestow benefits on society.

Government can reallocate resources from private goods production to public goods production by taxing the private sector and using the tax revenues to purchase or produce public goods. In order to maximize net benefits from the use of resources, government should produce public goods up to the point at which marginal (31)_____ (social, external) benefits (the sum of individual marginal benefits) equal the marginal social cost of providing the public good. Beneficiaries can be forced to share the cost of the public good through taxation. Taxation is necessary because of the (32)_____ (democratic process, free-rider problem). If some people pay for the public good and it is provided, it is provided to all whether they pay or not. Since people can receive the benefits without having to contribute, many people have to be coerced to pay, and this is done via a mandatory tax.

Markets also fail in other areas, such as providing the socially desirable levels of product safety, occupational safety, and racial integration. Often these failures stem from lack of information or faulty information used by consumers and producers in making decisions. (33)_____ (Antitrust legislation, Social regulation) is the use of government power to intervene in markets to achieve social goals such as product and occupational safety, the absence of discrimination, and an equitable distribution of income.

VOCABULARY REVIEW

Write the key term from the list below next to its definition.

Key Terms

Negative externality
Marginal external cost
Positive externality
Marginal external benefit
Internalization of an
   externality

Corrective tax
Corrective subsidy
Private goods
Pure public good
Free rider
Social regulation

Definitions

1. _____: the extra benefit that accrues to third parties when a positive externality is present.

2. _____: a tax levied on polluters to simulate a charge equal to the marginal external cost of their actions.

3. _____: an amount paid to consumers or producers of a good equal to the marginal external benefit of the good.

4. _____: a good that provides benefits to all members of a community as soon as it is made available to any one person.

5. _____: the extra cost imposed on third parties when a negative externality is present.

6. _____: a benefit associated with the use of resources that is not reflected in prices. Also called external benefit.

7. _____: a person who seeks to enjoy the benefits of a public good without contributing to its costs.

8. _____: a cost associated with the use of resources that is not reflected in prices. Also called external cost.

9. _____: the use of government power to intervene in markets so as to reduce the risk of accidents and disease and to achieve other social goals such as equality of opportunity for all persons.

10. _____: goods whose benefits are rival in consumption and for which exclusion of those who refuse to pay is relatively easy.

11. _____: occurs when the marginal cost or marginal benefit of a good has been adjusted so that market sale of the item results in the efficient output.

SKILLS REVIEW

Concept: Externalities and government intervention in markets

1.   The diagram below represents the market for the propellant used in aerosol
     sprays. Aerosol use has been responsible for the release of fluorocarbons
     into the atmosphere, causing a depletion of the earth's protective ozone
     layer. It is speculated that this will increase the incidence of cancer.

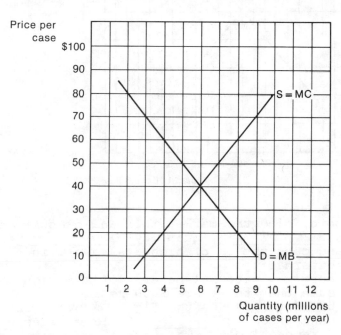

     a.   On the figure above, find the market price and quantity. Price =
          $_____, quantity = _____ cases
     b.   The production and use of aerosol propellants with fluorocarbons
          result in _____ externalities.
     c.   Assume that the marginal external cost is $10. Show the marginal
          social cost curve in the figure above. The efficient levels of
          output and price that maximize society's net benefits are
          _____ cases and $_____, respectively. The market
          _____ (overproduces, underproduces) the propellant and
          charges a price that is too _____ (low, high).
     d.   Society would be better off with an/a _____ in output and an/a
          _____ in price. Government could intervene to achieve this
          outcome by using a corrective _____ (tax, subsidy) equal to the
          marginal _____ (social, external) benefit of $_____.
          Show this graphically on the figure above.

2.   An urban highway is built in a metropolitan area through a portion of the
     city previously having poor access to the central business district. The
     direct beneficiaries are the users of the highway, who include the
     residents in the proximity of the highway. But the presence of the
     highway results in the development of commerce and industry near its major
     intersections, which benefits the local residents whether or not they use
     the highway. Assuming that highways are produced by the private sector,
     the metropolitan market for highways is shown in the figure below.

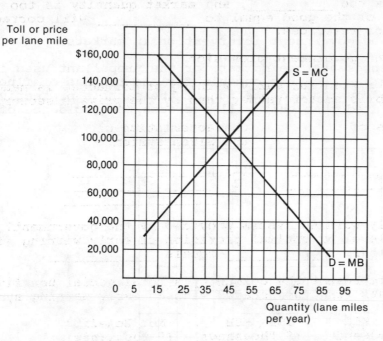

Toll or price per lane mile

Quantity (lane miles per year)

a. On the figure above, find the market toll and quantity of lane miles.
    Price or toll = $ _____, quantity = _____ lane miles

b. The production and consumption of highways result in a
    _____ externality.

c. Assume that the marginal external benefit of the highway per resident
    is $20. Also assume that there are 1000 residents. Show the
    marginal social benefit curve on the figure above. The efficient
    levels of output and price is _____ lane miles and
    $_____, respectively. The market _____
    (overproduces, underproduces) highways and charges a price that is
    too _____ (low, high).

d. The community would be better off with an/a _____ in lane
    miles and an/a _____ in tolls. Government could intervene in
    the market and use a corrective _____ (tax, subsidy) equal to the
    marginal _____ (social, external) benefit of $_____.
    Show this graphically on the figure above.

e. The _____ (tax could be levied on, subsidy could be
    given to) consumers equal to their individual marginal _____
    (social, external) benefit of $_____.

3. Advanced Question   The following equations are for a market in which a
    negative externality results from the production of the good.

        MB = a - bQ   (market demand)
        MC = c + dQ   (market supply)
        MEC = e   (marginal external cost)

        where   e is a positive constant
                       Q = output
                       P = price per unit
                       MC = marginal cost (private)
                       MB = marginal benefit = marginal social
                                                    benefit

a. Find the market equilibrium price and quantity equations.
b. Find the equations for the socially efficient price and quantity.

c. Market price is too _____, and market quantity is too _____.
d. A tax per unit of the good equal to _____ will correct the misallocation of resources.

Concept: **Public goods and government provision**

4. A community's siren system for early warning of tornadoes is made available by the public sector rather than by the private sector.

a. Characteristics of   Characteristics of
    a Private Good   the Siren System

    (1) _____   (1) _____
    (2) _____   (2) _____
                                    (3) _____

b. Why is the early warning system provided by the government?
c. The efficient level or optimal provision of early warning sirens is at that level where _____ equals _____.

5. The following data represent the community's total social benefits (TSB) and total social costs (TSC) associated with an early warning system.

Sirens per Square Mile	TSC ($ thousands)	MSC	TSB ($ thousands)	MSB	Net Benefit ($ thousands)
0	0		0		
1	3	____	30	____	____
2	9	____	54	____	____
3	18	____	72	____	____
4	30	____	84	____	____
5	45	____	90	____	____
6	63	____	90	____	____

a. Complete the table and plot the marginal social cost and marginal social benefit curves on the figure below.

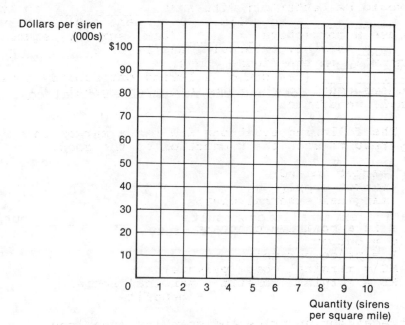

b.   The efficient provision of early warning capability is _____
     sirens. MSC = $_____, MSB = $_____. Show this
     graphically in the figure above.
c.   If there are 500 residents in the community and all benefit from the
     warning system, a voluntary contribution of $_____ per person
     could be used to finance the system.
d.   A voluntary contribution scheme will likely _____ (succeed,
     fail) because of the _____ problem. If a voluntary system
     will not work, how can the system be financed?

SELF-TEST FOR MASTERY

Select the best answer.

1.   A cost associated with the use of resources that is not reflected in price
     is known as a/an:

     a.   Positive externality.
     b.   External benefit.
     c.   Negative externality.
     d.   External cost.
     e.   C and d.

2.   A benefit associated with the use of resources that is not reflected in
     price is known as a/an:

     a.   Positive externality.
     b.   Public good.
     c.   External cost.
     d.   Negative externality.

3.   Which of the following must be added to marginal benefit in order to get
     marginal social benefit?

     a.   Marginal cost
     b.   Price
     c.   Marginal social cost
     d.   Marginal external benefit

4.   The sum of the firm's marginal cost and the marginal external cost is
     called:

     a.   Total cost.
     b.   Total marginal cost.
     c.   Marginal social benefit.
     d.   Marginal social cost.
     e.   Opportunity cost.

5.   The presence of negative externalities results in _____ output and
     a _____ price than is desirable for society.

     a.   More, higher
     b.   Less, lower
     c.   More, lower
     d.   Less, higher

6. The presence of positive externalities results in _____ output and a _____ price than is desirable for society.

    a. More, higher
    b. Less, lower
    c. More, lower
    d. Less, higher

7. Government can correct a negative externality by using _____, which result in a _____ market output and a _____ market price.

    a. Subsidies to consumers, larger, lower
    b. Corrective taxes, smaller, lower
    c. Corrective subsidies to suppliers, larger, higher
    d. Corrective taxes, smaller, higher

8. Government can correct a positive externality by using _____, which result in a _____ market output and a _____ market price.

    a. Corrective subsidies to consumers, larger, lower
    b. Corrective taxes, smaller, lower
    c. Corrective subsidies to suppliers, larger, lower
    d. Corrective subsidies to suppliers, larger, higher
    e. Corrective taxes, smaller, higher

9. Externalities are caused by:

    a. The absence of property rights.
    b. Poorly defined property rights, resulting in disputes.
    c. The lack of enforcement of existing property rights.
    d. All of the above.

10. A good whose benefits are rival in consumption and for which exclusion of those who refuse to pay is relatively easy is called a:

    a. Normal good.
    b. Rival good.
    c. Public good.
    d. Private good.

11. A good that provides benefits to all members of a community as soon as it is made available to any one member is called a:

    a. Pure public good.
    b. Rival good.
    c. Normal good.
    d. Private good.

12. Which of the following is not true of public goods?

    a. Public goods are not rival in consumption.
    b. Consumers cannot easily be excluded from the benefits of the good.
    c. Once the good is provided to one member of a community, it can be provided to each additional member at zero marginal cost.
    d. A system of voluntary financing of the public good can easily be established by those that benefit from the good.

13. The marginal social benefit of a public good:

    a. Is the difference between the marginal benefit and marginal cost.
    b. Is the sum of the individual marginal benefits enjoyed by all consumers.
    c. Is the marginal social benefit less the marginal social cost of a private good.
    d. Is the market demand curve for the public good.

14. Voluntary cost sharing by the beneficiaries of a public good will not work because:

    a. Income is insufficient to justify the good.
    b. Of the constant price problem.
    c. Of the free-rider problem.
    d. Of rising opportunity costs.
    e. None of the above.

15. The market system produces _____ pure public goods.

    a. Just the correct quantity of
    b. Excess quantities of
    c. Insufficient quantities of
    d. No

16. Market failure results from all but one of the following,:

    a. The absence of property rights
    b. The lack of information
    c. Inaccurate information
    d. Profits that are too low

17. Social regulation refers to:

    a. Specific antitrust statutes.
    b. Corrective taxes and subsidies.
    c. Government intervention in markets to achieve certain social goals, such as product and occupational safety.
    d. Government's "big brother" attempt to interfere with the efficient functioning of the free enterprise system.

THINK IT THROUGH

1. Explain the following statement. "The socially optimal or efficient level of pollution is not at a zero level."

2. Explain why the market will likely underallocate resources to the prevention of contagious diseases.

3. If a negative externality results from the lack of property rights or the lack of enforcement of those rights, what role can government play in reducing or eliminating externalities?

4. Explain how government can improve the efficiency of the economy's use of resources by providing information that either is not provided by the market or is provided in insufficient quantities or is misleading.

CHAPTER ANSWERS

In Brief: Chapter Summary

1. Negative 2. Exceed 3. Higher 4. Much 5. Below 6. Less 7. Positive 8. Exceeds 9. Higher 10. Underproduces 11. Low 12. Few 13. More 14. Property rights 15. Benefits conferred 16. Corrective tax 17. External 18. Cut 19. Raise 20. Subsidy 21. Subsidy 22. More 23. Increase 24. Rise 25. Increase 26. Fall 27. Not rival 28. Not subject 29. Zero 30. Not produce 31. Social 32. Free-rider problem 33. Social legislation

Vocabulary Review

1. Marginal external benefit 2. Corrective tax 3. Corrective subsidy 4. Pure public good 5. Marginal external cost 6. Positive externality 7. Free rider 8. Negative externality 9. Social regulation 10. Private good 11. Internalization of an externality

Skills Review

1.

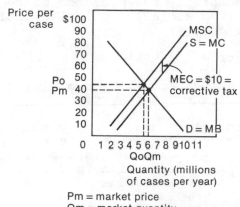

Pm = market price
Qm = market quantity
Po = socially optimal price
Qo = socially optimal quantity

a. $40, 6 million b. Negative c. 5.5 million, $45, overproduces, low
d. Decrease, increase, corrective tax, marginal external cost, $10

2.

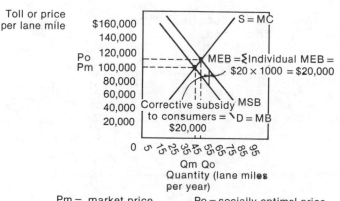

Pm = market price   Po = socially optimal price
Qm = market quantity   Qo = socially optimal quantity

a. $100,000; 45 b. Positive c. 50, $110,000; underproduces, low d. Increase, increase, corrective subsidy, marginal external benefit, $20,000
e. Subsidy could be given to, marginal external benefit, $20

3. a. Setting the marginal benefit and marginal cost equations equal to each other and solving for quantity yields

$$Q = (a - c)/(d + b)$$

Substituting the equilibrium quantity equation in place of Q in the marginal benefit equation gives the market price

$$P = (ad + bc)/(d + b)$$

b. Adding the MEC to the marginal cost equation gives

$$MC = (c + e) + dQ$$

Setting this equation equal to the marginal benefit equation and solving for P and Q as above results in

$$Q = (a - c - e)/(d + b)$$
$$P = (ad + bc + be)/(d + b)$$

Since e is a positive constant, the presence of negative externalities decreases the socially optimal quantity and increases the socially optimal price.

c. Low, high

d. Marginal external cost or e

4. a.

Characteristics of a Private Good	Characteristics of the Siren System
(1) Rival in consumption	(1) Nonrival in consumption
(2) Can exclude nonpayers	(2) Cannot exclude nonpayers
	(3) Zero marginal cost after provision to first individual

b. The siren system is provided by the public sector because a market cannot develop for a good that cannot be withheld from those that do not pay. Individuals have no incentive to purchase the good for a positive price because if it is purchased by one person, it is consumed by all others whether they pay or not.

c. Marginal social benefit, marginal social cost

5. a.

Sirens per Square Mile	MSC	MSB	Net Benefits
		($ thousands)	
0			0
1	3	30	27
2	6	24	43
3	9	18	54
4	12	12	54
5	15	6	45
6	18	0	27

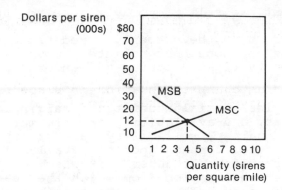

Dollars per siren
(000s)

Quantity (sirens
per square mile)

b.   4, $12,000, $12,000
c. $24
d.   Fail, free rider. A mandatory tax can be used to force the free
      riders to share the marginal social cost of the warning system.

Self-Test for Mastery

1. e 2. a 3. d 4. d 5. c 6. b 7. d 8. c 9. d 10. d 11. a 12. d 13.
b 14. c 15. d 16. d 17. c

Think it Through

1.   A good entailing a negative externality (pollution) is overproduced by the
market. A corrective tax equal to the marginal external cost will cause a
reduction in the market quantity of the good to the socially desired level but
will not necessarily result in zero pollution unless the tax provides
sufficient revenues for the cleanup of the pollution that continues to take
place as a result of the production of the good at the socially desirable
level. A producer in the long run might find that it is less costly to install
pollution abatement facilities than it is to pay the tax. But this involves a
comparison of the marginal benefits to the firm of pollution abatement with the
marginal costs of cleaning up the pollution. There is no reason to believe
that the firm's profit-maximizing level of pollution abatement will result in
zero pollution.

2.   The prevention of contagious diseases benefits the potential victims of
the disease in that they continue to be healthy and productive citizens.
Prevention also benefits society at large in that the economy and its
institutions function more fully and efficiently with healthy and productive
members of society than with individuals some of whom are out of the labor
force or are disabled or less productive because of diseases. Individuals in
the economy benefit from the economic activity and growth allowed in part by
the prevention of diseases even if those individuals would have never
contracted the disease. A market responds primarily to those who presently
have the disease and require treatment, not to potential victims and other
indirect beneficiaries. The marginal social benefits of disease prevention
exceed the marginal benefits reflected in the market. The market will
underproduce disease prevention.

3.   Government could reduce the incidence of externalities by clearly defining
and enforcing property rights where they exist and creating property rights
where they do not exist. The commonly owned environment--the atmosphere,
bodies of water, etc--is often polluted because no one individual has the right
to prevent some other individual from polluting it. Class action suits by
individuals without private property rights can enforce the collective property

rights of society. Also, government can sell property rights to the highest bidder or allot them on the basis of many allocation schemes. Government can exercise the collective property right in the commonly owned property by passing legislation to impose costs on those that pollute. Government provides a system of courts to resolve property right disputes and enforce property rights.

4.   The positions of both the marginal social benefit and marginal social cost curves depend in part on the accuracy and availability of information regarding, among other things, the quality, reliability, and safety of the good.   The efficiency of consumer choice depends upon the availability of complete and accurate product information.   Producers likewise require data for decisions but will produce only that information from which they can benefit. The market will not provide the necessary information to assess the extent of external costs or external benefits.   By providing accurate, timely, and comprehensive information in excess of that provided by the market, government can improve the choices made by consumers, the decisions made by business, and the resource reallocation decisions of the government.   Individual users of the government information benefit, but society as a whole benefits because of the more efficient use of scarce resources.   Governments provide information on the climate, product safety, the purity and safety of drugs and food, contagious diseases, demographics, and the economy.

17

Externalities and the Environment: Policy Analysis

CHAPTER CHALLENGES

After studying your text, attending class, and completing this chapter, you should be able to:

1. Explain the costs and benefits of pollution control and the tradeoffs involved in government policies designed to protect the environment.
2. Discuss some of the problems involved in estimating the costs and benefits of pollution control and in choosing policies that result in the efficient level of environmental protection.
3. Describe actual and proposed policies designed to control pollution, and evaluate their impact on the environment and resource allocation.
4. Describe economic incentives to use natural resources and discuss policies that prevent overuse or depletion of these resources.

IN BRIEF: CHAPTER SUMMARY

Fill in the blanks to summarize chapter content.

Pollution is an economic problem. It results in benefits to the polluter in the form of lower costs of production but imposes external costs on third parties. Pollution control creates benefits by reducing or eliminating the damage to resources that otherwise would occur. But scarce resources are required to clean up the pollution. Society's net benefit from environmental protection is maximized if pollution control is produced up to the level where the marginal social cost of controlling pollution (1)_____(is less than, just equals) the marginal social benefit to society. This would be the "efficient" level of pollution control. There is no reason to believe that this level of control (2)_____ (would not, would) eliminate pollution completely. In other words, an (3)_____ (efficient, inefficient) level of pollution is associated with an efficient level of pollution control.

Estimating the marginal benefits and costs of pollution control is (4)_____ (an, not an) easy task. Estimates of the marginal benefits must include the value of the benefits associated with the reduction in the incidence of pollution damage to people, material inputs, natural resources, and agricultural resources. If pollution causes death, a value must be placed on the reduction in death due to pollution control. If pollution affects the productivity or useability of resources, a value must be placed on the reduction in the incidence resource damage. In short, estimates of marginal benefits (5)_____(may not be, are) reliable, and it is likely that the public sector will choose a level of pollution control that is (6)_____(efficient, inefficient). The market will underproduce pollution control (or overproduce pollution), and government can improve upon the market's allocation of resources even if government is unable to precisely "maximize" net benefits.

Emission control policies include emission charges, regulation, and the use of property rights. An/A (7)_____ (emission charge, property right) is a charge per unit of pollution. The fee or charge can be set at a level where a profit-maximizing firm will be induced to clean up its emissions to some socially-desirable level. If a charge is high enough, it will be less costly to treat the emissions than to pollute and pay the charge. An effect of the emission charge is that it (8)_____ (allows, does not allow) firms flexibility in the methods used to clean up their discharge. A firm (9)_____ (does not have, has) an incentive to clean up pollution in the most efficient manner.

(10)_____ (Emission charges, Regulation) have/has been the dominant form of pollution control in the United States. The Environmental Protection Agency places limits on the amount of a pollutant that can be emitted. For instance, drinking water has a prescribed set of maximum chemical contaminant levels. If the emission limits are exceeded, a firm faces fines. The disadvantages of regulation are that there are no incentives to employ the most efficient pollution abatement techniques. The regulations also are often (11)_____ (flexible, inflexible) because they (12)_____ (allow several methods, prescribe a particular method) of compliance. In addition, firms have an incentive to just meet the allowed contaminant levels (13)_____ (but not, and often) to reduce emissions beyond that level. Therefore, if the marginal social benefits of pollution control vary regionally, inflexible national pollution standards are (14)_____(inefficient, efficient).

Another way to control pollution would be for government to assign, lease, or sell pollution rights. The right to pollute could be limited to achieve the socially-preferred level of pollution. If pollution rights are sold, the level of demand for those rights determines their price. Some firms would pay the price necessary to pollute, whereas others would find it less costly to clean up their emissions. (15)_____ (Disadvantages, Advantages) of pollution rights include the ability of government to strictly control the level of pollution through the issuance of pollution rights. In addition, firms would have the flexibility to purchase the right to pollute or to seek the most cost efficient method of pollution abatement.

The EPA has recently instituted new programs in an effort to make their regulations less rigid. In many regions of the country, emissions offsets are employed. A new firm entering a region has to pay other firms already established in the region to reduce their emissions. In this way, the increase in pollution caused by the new firm is "offset" by a decrease in the emissions of existing firms. This is equivalent to (16)_____ (emission charges, the sale of existing property rights). The EPA also allows firms to exceed some contaminant levels if they emit other contaminants in amounts less than the maximum allowable limits. In fact, a firm can earn credits for emitting less than the allowable limits. These credits can be used later if the firm wants to exceed the limits or can be sold.

In the short run, the amount of proven reserves of depletable resources depend upon (17)_____ (the profitability of extracting them and making them available to the market; the finite stock of resources). An increase in its price will bring forth a greater quantity of the resource, and in the long run will result in additional exploration and search for new deposits of the resource, resulting in increased (18)_____(supply, demand). In addition, price increases give users of the resource an incentive to substitute less expensive resources and to develop technologies not requiring as much of the resource or allowing the use of other resources. Demand for a resource may actually fall in the long run, as was the case with oil.

Resources may be overexploited in the short run, imposing external costs on society.   These external costs stem from a reduction in the future use of the resource. Common property resources are overused because
(19)_____(regulations, property rights) have not been established for the use of the resource.

VOCABULARY REVIEW

Write the key term from the list below next to its definition.

Key Terms

Pollution   Depletable resource
Emission charges   Renewable resource
Emission standards   Common property resource
Pollution right

Definitions

1. _____: prices established for the right to emit each unit of a pollutant.

2. _____: a government-issued certificate allowing a firm to emit a specified quantity of polluting waste.

3. _____: a resource (such as the ocean) whose use is not priced because property rights for payment of services have not been established.

4. _____: a natural resource that can be restocked over time, such as fish, timber, and wildlife.

5. _____: a resource for which there is a given amount of known reserves available at any point in time.

6. _____: limits established by government on the annual amounts and kinds of pollutants that can be emitted into the air or water by producers or users of certain products.

7. _____: waste that has been disposed of in the air, in water, or on land that reduces the value of those resources in alternative uses.

SKILLS REVIEW

Concept: Efficient level of environmental protection

1. You are an administrator with the EPA and are responsible for determining the efficient level of pollution control (sulphur removal) from smokestack emissions of coal-fired electric power plants. These emissions result in acid rain and the deterioration of forests and lakes.

    a. What are some of the benefits associated with controlling smokestack emissions?

b. The costs of controlling the emissions is the _____ cost of the resources used for pollution control in their next-best use. Explain.

c. Below are total social benefits and costs associated with reducing sulphur emissions.

Percent Reduction Sulphur Emissions	Total Social Benefits ($millions)	MSB	Total Social Costs ($millions)	MSC	Net Benefit
0%	0		0		
10	180		60		_____
20	350	_____	140	_____	_____
30	510	_____	240	_____	_____
40	660	_____	360	_____	_____
50	800	_____	500	_____	_____
60	930	_____	660	_____	_____
70	1,050	_____	840	_____	_____
80	1,160	_____	1,040	_____	_____
90	1,260	_____	1,260	_____	_____
100	1,350	_____	1,500	_____	_____

(1) Complete the table.
(2) Plot the marginal social benefit and marginal social cost curves on the graph below.

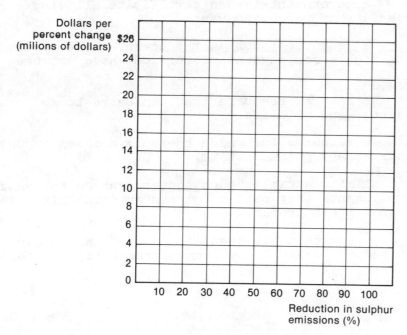

Dollars per percent change (milions of dollars)

Reduction in sulphur emissions (%)

(3) The efficient level of pollution control is a _____ % reduction where _____ equals _____ and

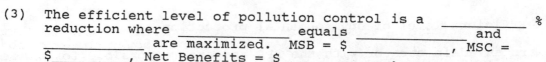

_____ are maximized.   MSB = $_____, MSC = $_____, Net Benefits = $_____.
(4) Identify the efficient level of pollution control on the graph above.

Concept: Pollution policies

2.   Assume that for the example above each firm faces identical costs
     associated with removing a given percentage of sulphur from smokestack
     emissions.   Below are pollution control data for a representative electric
     power company.

Sulphur Reduction Percent	Units	Total Cost ($thousands)	MC per Unit Removed
0%	0	0	
10	50	25	
20	100	60	_____
30	150	105	_____
40	200	160	_____
50	250	225	_____
60	300	300	_____
70	350	385	_____
80	400	480	_____
90	450	585	_____
100	500	700	_____

a.   Complete the table.
b.   Plot the firm's marginal cost of pollution removal on the following
     graph.

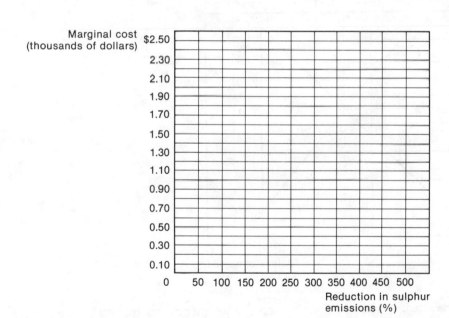

c.   From question 1, it was found that the socially-desirable level of
     sulphur reduction was _____ %.   For the power company above, this
     means reducing sulphur emissions by _____ units.   An emission
     charge of $_____ would induce the power company to reduce
     emissions to the efficient level.   Explain.
d.   Show the emissions charge on the figure above and identify the
     efficient level of pollution (emission of sulphur).
e.   If, because of new and more accurate estimates of the marginal social
     benefits of emission control, the EPA decided to reduce emissions
     further, it could _____ the emission charge.

3. List three advantages of using emissions charges as a means of controlling pollution.

   a. _____
   b. _____
   c. _____

4. List three disadvantages associated with regulation as a means of controlling pollution.

   a. _____
   b. _____
   c. _____

5. List two advantages associated with the assignment or sale of property rights as a means of controlling pollution.

   a. _____
   b. _____

Concept: Depletable and renewable resources

6. The market for oil, a depletable resource, is shown in the figure below.

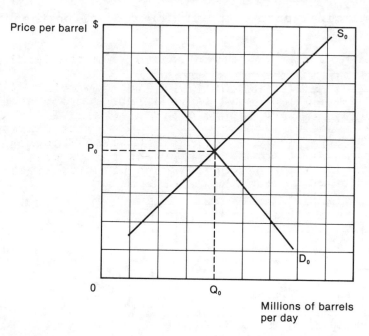

Price per barrel $

P_0

S_0

D_0

0   Q_0

Millions of barrels per day

   a. At the current market price of oil, Po, the current quantity of oil demanded will eventually cause the supply of the depletable resource, oil, to _____. Show graphically. This causes the price of oil to _____.

   b. The _____ in the price of oil will, in the long run, likely result in an/a _____ in supply, thus causing the market price to _____. Explain.

   c. How will consumers of oil react in the long run to the increase in the price of oil today, and what are the implications for the market price and quantity?

7. The marginal benefits associated with catching fish from a common-property lake (one in which property rights do not exist) is shown below.

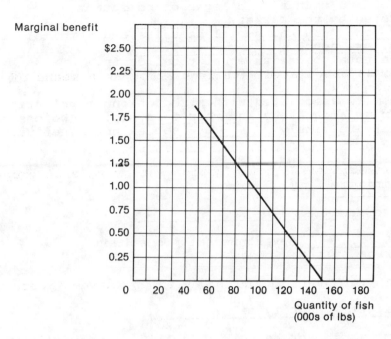

Marginal benefit

a. What quantity of fish will fishermen remove from the lake? _____ lbs. Why?
b. In order to maintain a given quantity of fish for future fishermen, a maximum catch of 80,000 lbs would leave a reproduction stock of fish just large enough to achieve future desired levels of fish production. The current catch of _____ lbs represents an _____ (overuse, underuse) of the renewable resource. Explain how property rights could be used to correct the problem.
c. Show on the graph above the effect of using property rights to correct the inefficient use of the lake.

SELF-TEST FOR MASTERY

Select the best answer.

1. Pollution is an/a:

   a. Public good.
   b. Negative externality.
   c. Positive externality.
   d. Opportunity cost.

2. An emission creates pollution :

   a. All of the time.
   b. When the efficient level of pollution is reached.
   c. When the emission causes damage to resources.
   d. If it is emitted into the atmosphere.

3. The efficient level of pollution control is :

   a. That level associated with a zero level of pollution.
   b. That level produced by the market.
   c. That level where the marginal social benefits and marginal social costs of control are equal.
   d. At a level where total benefits equal total costs.
   e. None of the above.

4. Estimates of the benefits associated with a reduction in pollution are _____ to determine accurately and result in social choices regarding pollution control that are likely _____ social net benefits.

   a. Easy, to maximize
   b. Easy, not to maximize
   c. Difficult, to minimize
   d. Difficult, to maximize
   e. Difficult, not to maximize

5. The market will _____ environmental protection.

   a. Underproduce
   b. Not produce
   c. Overproduce
   d. Produce the efficient quantity of

6. Which of the following would not be used in pollution control?

   a. Corrective subsidies
   b. Regulation
   c. Emission charges
   d. Property rights

7. Which of the following is considered an advantage of emission charges?

   a. The charge can be set at a level to induce a profit-maximizing firm to either clean up or restrict pollution to the desired level.
   b. The firm has an incentive to employ the most efficient technique of pollution cleanup.
   c. Charges allow flexibility by firms in various regions to deal with the pollution problem in the most appropriate way.
   d. All of the above.

8. The predominant method of pollution control in the United States:

   a. Is regulation.
   b. Is emission charges.
   c. Is property rights sales.
   d. Is corrective taxes.

9. Regulation as a means of eliminating or reducing pollution:

   a. Is efficient because it results in the maximum net benefits to society.
   b. Is inefficient because it is often inflexible, requiring a single method of compliance rather than allowing the firm to seek the cost efficient method of pollution abatement.
   c. Is effective because it creates incentives by firms to reduce pollution by more than the allowable limits.
   d. Is the only practical method of pollution control when the point

source of pollution can be identified and the emission can be easily measured.

10. Common property resources are often polluted:

    a. Because emission charges are set too low.
    b. Because regulation needs to be extended to include more than privately owned property.
    c. Because of the absence of property rights.
    d. Because of industrialization.

11. The efficient level of pollution control can be achieved by imposing an/a_____ on the polluter _____ the polluter's marginal cost of pollution cleanup at the socially-desired level of pollution reduction.

    a. Regulation, increasing
    b. Regulation, decreasing
    c. Corrective subsidy, greater than
    d. Emission charge, greater than
    e. emission charge, equal to

12. The EPA's emission offset is equivalent

    a. to an emission charge.
    b. to a subsidy.
    c. to a tax.
    d. In effect to a sale of property rights.

13. Under which EPA program can a firm earn credits for emitting less than the allowable limits of pollution? The credits can be used by the firm to exceed the limits in the future or can be sold to other firms.

    a. Emission charge
    b. Emission offset
    c. The "bubble"
    d. Leasing of property rights

14. The supply of proven reserves of a depletable resource depends

    a. Upon the profitability of extracting the resource and making it available to the market.
    b. Exclusively upon the technological ability to extract the resource.
    c. Only on the finite supply of the resource.
    d. On the reserves presently being mined and the yet undiscovered reserves.

15. Other things constant, the supply of a depletable resource will in time _____, causing the price of the resource to _____, which in turn causes new exploration and the use of new extraction techniques and in the long run causes the supply of the resource to_____.

    a. Increase, rise, increase
    b. Increase, fall, decrease
    c. Decrease, rise, decrease
    d. Decrease, rise, increase
    e. Increase, fall, increase

16. Which of the following property resources are likely to be overused?

    a. A private lake
    b. Your backyard

c. A rancher's stock pond
d. Ocean fisheries

17. Common property resources are overexploited because:

    a. Of the absence of regulation.
    b. Of the absence of corrective subsidies.
    c. Of the absence of property rights.
    d. Of competing regional interests.
    e. None of the above.

THINK IT THROUGH

1. An environmentalist might argue that any emissions beyond that which can be safely absorbed by the natural environment reduces society's well-being. Do you agree? Explain.

2. Discuss the dominant approach to pollution control in the United States. What alternative approaches could be used? What are the advantages of these other methods of pollution control?

3. Can you think of any reason why it is necessary for federal and state governments to "manage" wildlife populations? Explain. What alternatives could be employed other than game limits?

CHAPTER ANSWERS

In Brief: Chapter Summary

1. Just equals 2. Would 3. Efficient 4. Not an 5. May not be 6. Inefficient 7. Emission charge 8. Allows 9. Has 10. Regulation 11. Inflexible 12. Prescribe a particular method 13. But not 14. Inefficient 15. Advantages 16. The sale of existing property rights 17. The profitability of extracting them and making them available to the market 18. Supply 19. Property rights

Vocabulary Review

1. Emission charges 2. Pollution right 3. Common property resource 4. Renewable resource 5. Depletable resource 6. Emission standards 7. Pollution

Skills Review

1. a. A reduction in sulphur emissions will reduce the incidence of acid rain, which will reduce the deterioration of lakes and forests. The benefits of controlling sulphur emissions are the commercial and recreational values of lakes and forests, which would have otherwise diminished as a result of pollution.
    b. Opportunity. Controlling pollution involves the use of scarce resources that have value in alternative uses.

c. (1)

Sulphur Reduction	MSB	MSC	Net Benefits
		($ millions)	
0%			$ 0
10	18	6	120
20	17	8	210
30	16	10	270
40	15	12	300
50	14	14	300
60	13	16	270
70	12	18	210
80	11	20	120
90	10	22	0
100	9	24	-150

(2)

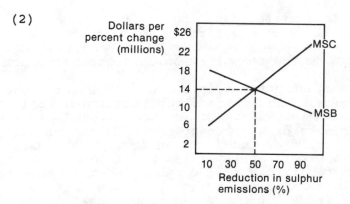

(3) 50, MSB, MSC, Net Benefits; $14 million, $14 million; $300 million

(4) See figure above.

2. a.

Units	MC ($ thousands)
0	
50	0.5
100	0.7
150	0.9
200	1.1
250	1.3
300	1.5
350	1.7
400	1.9
450	2.1
500	2.3

b.

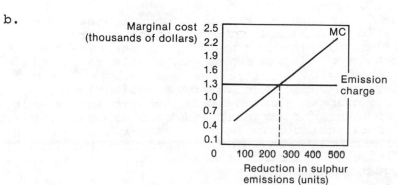

c. 50, 250; $1,300. As long as the charge exceeds the marginal cost of cleanup, a profit-maximizing firm will treat the effluent rather than pollute and pay the charge. If marginal cost exceeds the emission charge, the least-cost strategy would be to pollute and pay the charge. Therefore, a firm has an incentive to treat its discharge up to the point at which the emission charge equals the marginal cost of pollution treatment.

d. See figure above.

e. Increase

3. a. Emission charges can be set a level to achieve the desired level of pollution reduction.

    b. Firms have the flexibility to employ techniques of pollution treatment that best fit their unique situation.

    c. Firms have an incentive to minimize costs of cleanup that improve the economy's resource allocation.

4. a. Regulations are often inflexible requiring a single method of compliance rather than allowing the firm to seek the most cost-efficient solution.

    b. Firms have no incentive to reduce pollution below the emission standards set by the EPA.

    c. Regulations that are uniform nationally do not allow for regional variations in the marginal social benefits of pollution control.

5. a. Issuance of property rights or government certificates granting the right to pollute can be sold or issued in an amount that will limit pollution to the socially-desired level.

    b. A market for these limited rights will develop in which some firms will find it more profitable to treat their effluent before discharge than to pay the market price for the right to pollute. Thus firms have an incentive to minimize costs associated with reducing emissions.

6. a. Decrease; increase

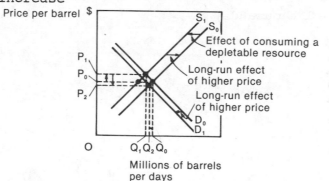

7. a. 150,000 lbs. With no cost or price associated with the use of the resource, fishermen will catch fish up to the point where their total

    b. Increase, increase, fall. In the long run, there will be more exploration as a result of the higher prices, and new extraction technologies will likely be employed both of which increase the supply of oil. Other things being constant, this will reduce the price of oil.

    c. Users of resources respond to rising prices by substituting relatively less costly resources and developing production techniques or products allowing the use of more plentiful and less costly resources. As in the case of oil, the higher short-run price of oil causes a movement up the demand curve in the short run, but it will also shift the demand curve leftward in the long run, causing long-run market price and quantity to fall.

benefits are maximized, that is, where the marginal benefit curve intersects the quantity axis at a level of zero marginal benefits.

b. 150,000 lbs, overuse. Government certificates allowing the right to extract 80,000 lbs of fish annually could be sold. Assuming all benefits associated with fishing are private and there are no social goals involved other than preventing the overuse of the resource, the property rights scheme will result in the highest and best use of the resource (assuming competitive markets).

c.

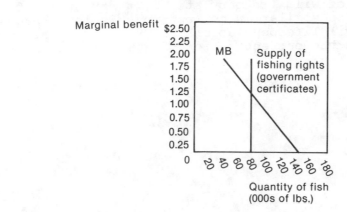

Self-Test for Mastery

1. b 2. c 3. c 4. e 5. a 6. a 7. d 8. a 9. b 10. c 11. e 12. d 13. c 14. a 15. d 16. d 17. c

Think it Through

1. Emissions are a by-product of production. The production of goods benefits society. But if emissions result in pollution, there is an external cost that is not reflected in the firm's costs of production. The firm will allocate too many resources to the production of the good. It is "efficient" to require the firm to reduce pollution only up to the level that maximizes social net benefits. Requiring the firm to reduce pollution to zero will likely mean that the opportunity costs of the pollution control resources will exceed the benefits to society from the reduction in pollution.

2. Regulation is the dominant method of pollution control in the United States. Emissions standards are established for various pollutants, and fines are imposed if the standards are violated. The regulations tend to be inflexible and do not allow firms to respond in the most efficient manner to emission reduction. Emission charges could be used giving firms the incentive to seek the most cost efficient method of pollution reduction. They are flexible and can vary by firm and region. Property rights could be established and sold, giving those in the market for pollution rights the incentive to seek the least-cost solutions to pollution reduction. The quantity of those rights can be set to achieve the desired level of pollution.

3. It is necessary to regulate or manage wildlife populations because of the fear that breeding stocks would eventually be depleted, reducing the commercial and recreational values associated with hunting and fishing for future generations. Private landowners can prevent excessive hunting--they have a legal remedy. Public lands and lakes are common property resources for which no individuals own property rights. In the absence of government involvement, public lands would be overhunted and public lakes would be overfished as individuals hunt and fish to the point where their marginal benefits equal zero. This assumes that no price or any other cost is associated with the use of the resource.

The traditional approach to preventing overexploitation of wildlife populations is by regulation and establishing game limits. If the limits are exceeded, fines are imposed. Property rights are used to a limited extent. Certain hunting grounds may be opened only to a limited number of hunters. The rights to hunt are generally allocated on a lottery basis rather than sold in markets. User charges are used in the form of a license or stamp fee, but these are inflexible in the sense that they are not set to achieve specific game limits for each given species of game. If there are no social goals other than preventing the overexploitation of wildlife populations, a market for property rights or a hunting or fishing fee similar in concept to emission charges would achieve the desirable level of wildlife populations; furthermore, this would achieve it more efficiently than the current system of game limits and fines.

18

Subsidizing Agriculture and Industries: The Economics of Special-Interest Groups

CHAPTER CHALLENGES

After studying your text, attending class, and completing this chapter, you should be able to:

1. Discuss special interest groups, their goals, and the impact on prices and resource allocation of programs that benefit these interests.
2. Describe the process of rent seeking in which people compete for government subsidies and other programs that increase their incomes.
3. Evaluate the impact of agricultural policies that subsidize farmers in the United States.

IN BRIEF: CHAPTER SUMMARY

Fill in the blanks to summarize chapter content.

(1)_____ (Special interest groups, Lobbying associations), such as in agriculture, seek expenditures or special benefits from government that result in an increase in income. The costs of the benefits are dispersed over many millions of taxpayers and add little to a taxpayer's tax liability. Therefore, special interest legislation often encounters little resistance from the general public. Many individuals seek to use the power of government to increase their earnings above their opportunity costs. These people are (2)_____(income, rent) seekers. (3)_____(Wages, Rents) are receipts in excess of opportunity costs that can be created by government by limiting the right to perform a given activity. Agricultural allotments and exclusive franchises are created by government policy and have the effect of (4)-_____(decreasing farm incomes, creating rents).

Agriculture is a major special interest group in the United States. In 1933, the (5)_____(Agricultural Adjustment Act, Farm Price Support Act) was passed, controlling acreage in both production and prices. The primary goal of the Act was to prevent surpluses of agricultural commodities in order to keep prices and framers' incomes from falling. More specifically, the goal was to keep the purchasing power of the farmers' income from falling. This is accomplished if the price of agricultural products rise at a rate fast enough to compensate for the (6)_____(cost increases associated with producing the commodities; rise in the prices of the goods and services consumed by farmers). This is known as (7)_____(parity, a price support). As of the mid-1980s, the parity price ratio was at an all time (8)_____(low of under 60%, high of just over 90%).

Government price supports and acreage control programs are intended to increase farm incomes. Government agricultural price supports increase farm incomes but result in (9)_____ (shortages, surpluses) if the price supports exceed market prices. Prices are supported through the loan support program through which a farmer can borrow from the government at a specified price per bushel.

The agricultural commodity is used as collateral for the loan. The loan rate is generally set (10)_____(below, above) the market price per bushel. The farmer can choose to let the government keep the grain or repay the loan. The farmer will repay the loan only if the market price (11)_____(exceeds, is less than) the loan rate. Acreage control programs involve payments to farmers to (12)_____(expand, take land out of) production. The idea is to (13)_____(reduce, increase) supply and to keep market price, and hence farm incomes, at a higher level.

The government holds a large portion of the grain that it acquires off the market to prevent depressing prices and incomes. There are large storage costs and other costs associated with reducing these stocks of commodities. The (14)_____ (Target Price, Payment-in-Kind) program was an attempt to control farm production and to reduce government stocks of grain at the same time. Farmers that took acreage out of production were paid in kind with the government's stock of commodities.

Current methods of supporting farm incomes include (15)_____ (target prices, payment-in-kind) and direct subsidies. Target prices are government guaranteed prices. Farmers are generally required to restrict acreage in order to qualify for the Target Price program. If the guaranteed price exceeds the market price, farmers sell all of their output at the market price and the difference between the market and target price is made up by the government. Surpluses (16)_____ (develop, do not develop), but the acreage restrictions (17)_____ (do not necessarily, necessarily) limit or fix supply. The program, in effect, transfers income from taxpayers to farmers. Target prices result in (18)_____ (higher, lower) market prices than with traditional farm policies, but prices are not necessarily lower than would prevail in a competitive market.

Government policies can benefit special interest groups with direct subsidies and tax breaks. Subsidies increase the market price and quantity of the subsidized good if given to (19)_____ (consumers, producers), but they decrease market prices if given to (20)_____ (consumers, producers). The net price paid by consumers and received by producers is exactly the same, regardless if subsidies are given to producers or consumers. Both consumers and producers of the subsidized good benefit, as well as those that supply specialized inputs to the subsidized industry.

In addition to direct payments, subsidies can be in the form of (21)_____ (excise taxes, tax preferences). Certain activities, such as home ownership, are given preference in the tax code, which in effect "subsidizes" the activity through a lower tax liability. The losses in government tax revenues from the tax breaks are called (22)_____(tax expenditures, tax losses). Tax preferences benefit both buyers and sellers in the preferred markets, including the resource suppliers to those markets.

Some subsidies are "hidden" because they indirectly benefit certain groups. Examples of "hidden" subsidies include (23)_____ (agricultural loan supports, government loan guarantees) and government-provided insurance (flood insurance, for example). By transferring some of the risks associated with production in the private sector to the public sector, in effect the government is subsidizing business growth and development.

VOCABULARY REVIEW

Write the key term from the list below next to its definition.

Key Terms

Special interest group
Rent seeking
Parity price ratio
Acreage control program
Tax preference

Economic rents
Parity
Target price
Tax credit
Tax expenditure

Definitions

1. _____: an organization that seeks to increase government expenditures or induce government to take other actions that benefit particular people.

2. _____: the ratio of an average of the prices of goods sold by farmers to an average of the prices of goods on which farmers spend their incomes.

3. _____: an exemption, deduction, or exclusion from income or other taxable items in computing tax liability.

4. _____: the idea that the prices of agricultural commodities must rise as fast as the prices of goods and services on which farmers spend their incomes.

5. _____: a reduction in the tax liability for a person or corporation making certain purchases or engaging in certain activities.

6. _____: the process by which people compete to obtain government favors that increase the economic rents they can earn.

7. _____: guarantees sellers a minimum price per unit of output.

8. _____: earnings that exceed the opportunity cost of an activity.

9. _____: provide cash payments to farmers who agree to take some of their land out of production for certain crops.

10. _____: the losses in revenue to the federal government as a result of tax breaks granted to individuals and corporations.

SKILLS REVIEW

Concept: Special interest programs--Agriculture

1. The diagram below represents a market for an agricultural commodity in the absence of government intervention.

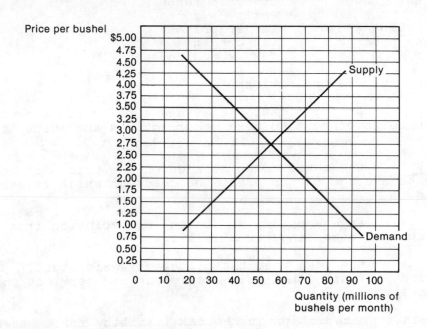

Price per bushel

Quantity (millions of bushels per month)

a. The current market price and quantity are $_____ and _____ bushels, respectively. Assume that the current market price results in a parity price ratio of 100%.

b. Because of improvements in production techniques, the supply of the commodity increases 10 million bushels at each price. Show this in the graph above and label the new supply curve, S1. After the change in supply, market price and quantity are $_____ and _____ bushels, respectively. Assuming all other prices are unchanged, the parity price ratio _____ (increases, decreases), which means that the farmers' purchasing power has _____ (increased, decreased).

c. Assume that farmers are able to win legislation ensuring a parity price ratio of 100%. This is accomplished through a commodity loan program that effectively establishes a price support. The supported price must equal $_____. At the supported price, quantity demanded equals _____ bushels and quantity supplied equals _____ bushels resulting in a _____ (shortage, surplus) of _____ bushels. Show graphically in the figure above.

d. The cost to the taxpayer of the _____ (shortage, surplus) is $_____. Shade in the area representing that cost in the figure above.

e. The price support program results in _____ prices to consumers and _____ taxes incurred or_____ government services received by society.

f. An acreage restriction program could also be used to achieve a price sufficient to yield a parity price ratio of 100%. How much would supply have to be reduced at each price? _____ bushels. This program results in either _____ taxes or _____ government

272

services and _____ prices to consumers as well as _____
(shortages, surpluses).

2. The market below is for an agricultural commodity for which there is no
government intervention.

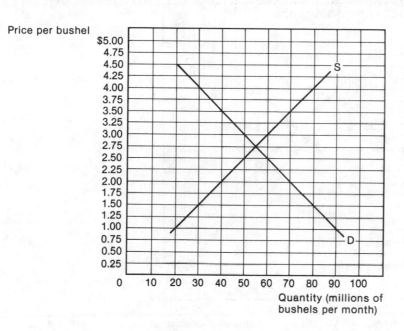

Price per bushel

Quantity (millions of
bushels per month)

a. The current market price and quantity are $_____ and _____
bushels, respectively.

b. Because the market price is considered by farmers to be too low, farm
lobbies are able to win special interest legislation guaranteeing a
price per bushel--a target price which is above the prevailing market
equilibrium price. To qualify for the program, farmers must restrict
acreage. Suppose the acreage restriction phase of the program
reduces quantity supplied at each price by 25 million bushels. Show
the new supply curve in the figure above and label it, S1. Market
price _____ to $_____ and market quantity _____ to
_____ bushels.

c. At a target price of $4 per bushel, farmers will produce and make
available to the market _____ bushels and will receive a market
price per bushel of $_____ and a subsidy per bushel of
$_____. Show in the figure above. Consumers will pay a price of
$_____, and taxpayers will pay a total subsidy of $_____.
Quantity demanded will _____ quantity supplied.

d. As compared to price supports or acreage restriction programs, the
Target Price program results in a _____ price to the consumer.
As compared to a competitive market without government intervention,
the Target Price program above results in _____ price to
the consumer.

e. Target price programs, in effect, transfer income from _____
to _____.

Concept: Effects of subsidies, tax breaks

3.   The diagram below represents a competitive market for a good.

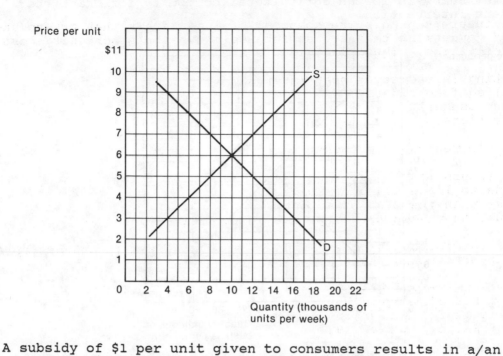

Price per unit

Quantity (thousands of
units per week)

a.   A subsidy of $1 per unit given to consumers results in a/an
     _____ in demand.   Show in the diagram above.
b.   Market price _____ to $_____ and market quantity _____
     to _____ units.   The net price (after deducting the subsidy) to
     the consumer at the new market quantity is $_____ .
c.   Given the initial demand curve, D, show the effect graphically in the
     diagram if the $1 subsidy is given to producers instead of consumers.
d.   Market price _____ to $_____ and market quantity
     _____ to _____ units.   The net price (after the subsidy
     is added) received by the producer is $_____ .
e.   Subsidies to consumers, as compared to subsidies to producers, result
     in _____ market prices.   The net price paid by consumers and
     the net price received by producers are _____ for
     subsidies to consumers or for subsidies to producers.

4.   List two indirect subsidies and give an example of each.

     a.   _____
     b.   _____

5.   Give two examples of hidden subsidies.

     a.   _____
     b.   _____

274

SELF-TEST FOR MASTERY

Select the best answer.

1. Special interest groups are composed of individuals that try to use the power of government to increase incomes above the opportunity cost of their activities. These individuals are:

   a. Acting in society's best interest.
   b. Called free riders.
   c. Rent seekers.
   d. Irrational.

2. An economic rent is a payment:

   a. In excess of the opportunity cost of an activity.
   b. Made to lease building space.
   c. Less than the cost of an activity.
   d. Equal to the opportunity cost of an activity.

3. Which of the following acts sought to maintain farm income by implementing price supports and acreage restrictions?

   a. Payment-in-Kind program of 1933
   b. Food Security Wheat Reserve Act of 1933
   c. Agricultural Adjustment Act of 1933
   d. Rent Seekers Act of 1933

4. Which of the following is not a goal of U.S. farm policy?

   a. Maintaining farming as a free and independent business
   b. Maintaining an adequate supply of food at reasonable prices
   c. Encouraging agricultural exports
   d. Reducing the size of family farms and increasing their numbers

5. The concept of parity:

   a. An equitable distribution of income among farmers.
   b. That farm commodity prices must keep in step with other prices in order to keep the farmers' purchasing power from falling.
   c. That a commodity price must be set above the market equilibrium price.
   d. None of the above.

6. As of the mid-1980s, the parity price ratio:

   a. Is at an all time low of 20%.
   b. Is at an all time high of 90%.
   c. Has risen above the 80% level.
   d. Is at an all time low of less than 60%.
   e. Has fallen to just below 80%.

7. Price supports result in _____ and _____ prices to consumers.

   a. Shortages, higher
   b. Shortages, lower
   c. Surpluses, higher
   d. Surpluses, lower

8. Acreage restriction programs are similar to price support programs in that prices to consumers are _____ than unregulated market prices, but they are different in that quantity supplied _____ quantity demanded.

   a. Lower, exceeds
   b. Higher, exceeds
   c. Lower, equals
   d. Higher, equals

9. Which of the following programs pays farmers with government stocks of commodities to restrict acreage?

   a. Target price program
   b. Price support program
   c. Government commodity program
   d. Payment-in-kind program
   e. Acreage allotment program

10. Which of the following programs guarantees farmers a price per bushel but allows market supply and demand to determine the market price?

    a. Target price program
    b. Price support program
    c. Government commodity program
    d. Payment-in-kind program
    e. Acreage allotment program

11. Which of the following programs effectively transfers income from taxpayers to farmers without necessarily resulting in commodity prices lower than would prevail in a competitive market?

    a. Target price program
    b. Price support program
    c. Government commodity program
    d. Payment-in-kind program
    e. Acreage allotment program

12. Subsidies given to consumers result in an/a _____ market price and an/a _____ in market quantity.

    a. Decrease, increase
    b. Increase, decrease
    c. Decrease, decrease
    d. Increase, increase

13. Subsidies given to producers result in an/a _____ in market price and an/a _____ in market quantity.

    a. Decrease, increase
    b. Increase, increase
    c. Decrease, decrease
    d. Increase, increase

14. The net price paid by a consumer under a consumer subsidy program is
_____ the net price paid by the consumer under a producer subsidy
program.

   a.   Equal to
   b.   Greater than
   c.   Less than
   d.   Equal to or less than
   e.   Equal to or greater than

15. Which of the following is a deduction, exemption, or exclusion from income
in computing taxes?

   a.   Tax credit
   b.   Tax liability
   c.   Tax preference
   d.   Tax expenditure

16. Which of the following is a reduction in tax liability resulting from
engaging in some activity?

   a.   Tax credit
   b.   Tax liability
   c.   Tax preference
   d.   Tax expenditure

17. Which of the following is the loss in government tax revenue resulting
from a tax break?

   a.   Tax credit
   b.   Tax liability
   c.   Tax preference
   d.   Tax expenditure

18. Government loan guarantees are an example of a/an:

   a.   Direct subsidy.
   b.   Indirect subsidy.
   c.   Lost subsidy.
   d.   Hidden subsidy.

THINK IT THROUGH

1.   Discuss the advantages of a target price program as compared to a price
support program.

2.   You are on the staff of a U.S. congressman and have been asked to prepare
a statement regarding the gains and losses associated with a subsidy program.
Identify the typical benefits and costs as well as the gainers and losers.

3.   Can you think of any reasons why a tax expenditure rather than a direct
subsidy would be employed to promote a given activity?

POP QUIZ   Read the news brief at the end of this chapter and answer the
                  following questions.

1.   One of the goals of U.S. farm policy is to ensure adequate supplies of
farm commodities at reasonable prices. According to the article, how has
government contributed to the reduction in the soybean crop and the increase in
soybean prices?

2.   Discuss how the special interest lobby, the American Soybean Association,
contributed to the impending soybean shortages.

CHAPTER ANSWERS

In Brief: Chapter Summary

1. Special interest groups 2. Rent 3. Rents 4. Creating rents 5.
Agricultural Adjustment Act 6. Rise in the prices of the goods and services
consumed by farmers 7. Parity 8. Low of under 60% 9. Surpluses 10. Above
11. Exceeds 12. Take land out of 13. Reduce 14. Payment-in-Kind 15. Target
prices 16. Do not develop 17. Do not necessarily 18. Lower 19. Consumers
20. Producers 21. Tax preference 22. Tax expenditures 23. Government loan
guarantees

Vocabulary Review

1.   Special interest group 2. Parity price ratio 3. Tax preference 4.
Parity 5. Tax credit 6. Rent seeking 7. Target price 8. Economic rents 9.
Acreage control programs 10. Tax expenditure

Skills Review

1.   a. $2.75, 55 million

     b.

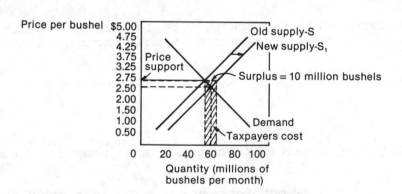

          $2.50, 60 million, decreases, decreased
     c. $2.75, 55 million, 65 million, surplus, 10 million
     d.   Surplus, $27.5 million
     e.   Higher, higher, fewer
     f.   10 million; higher, fewer, higher, an equality between quantity
          supplied and quantity demanded

2. a. $2.75, 55 million
    b.

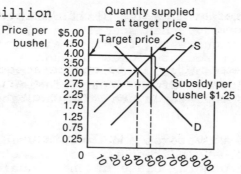

Increases, $3.38, decreases, 42.5 million
    c.   55 million, $2.75, $1.25; $2.75, $68.75 million; equal
    d.   Lower, the same
    e.   Taxpayers, farmers

3. a.   Increase

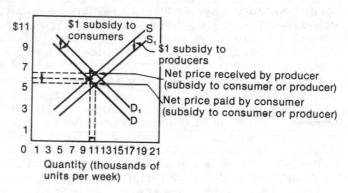

    b.   Increases, $6.50, increases, 11,000, $5.50
    c.   Shown in the graph above.
    d.   Decreases, $5.50, increases, 11,000, $6.50
    e.   Higher, the same

4. a.   Tax credits: investment tax credits, child care tax credits
    b.   Tax preferences: interest exemption on home mortgage interest

5. a.   Government loan guarantees
    b.   Government provided insurance, such as flood insurance

Self-Test for Mastery

1. c 2. a 3. c 4. d 5. b 6. d 7. c 8. d 9. d 10. a 11. a 12. d 13.
a 14. a 15. c 16. a 17. d 18. d

Think it Through

1.   A target price program does not result in surpluses, as is the case with
price supports. Government does not have any costs associated with purchasing,
storing, and disposing of surplus farm commodities. The commodity prices paid
by consumers are likely to be less with the target price program and may even
be as low as would prevail in an unregulated market. Nevertheless, with a
target price program, taxes must be used pay the farm subsidies. The program
redistributes income from taxpayers to farmers.

2.   The beneficiaries of a subsidy include the consumers of the good, the
producers of the good, and the resource suppliers to the subsidized industry.

If the subsidy is intended to correct a market misallocation of resources resulting from a positive externality, then society as a whole benefits as well. Because subsidy programs require tax funding, either taxpayers lose because of an increase in taxes or society loses through a reduction in government services. Income is effectively transferred from taxpayers to the beneficiaries of the subsidized good. If the beneficiaries of the subsidy have, on average, higher incomes than taxpayers, the distribution of income may become more unequal.

3. A direct subsidy is visible to voters, and beneficiaries usually can be readily identified. In contrast, an indirect subsidy is not as obvious to voters, and the benefits go to a general class of individuals or institutions engaging in certain activities. Furthermore, the tax expenditures resulting from these tax breaks are not appropriated on an annual basis, once enacted, there is no limit to the extent of the subsidy over time nor are there any criteria as to whether the tax expenditures have accomplished their goals. Also, tax expenditures do not show up in government budgets as expenditures-- they represent lost tax revenues that are not clearly visible to the general public. In short, it is politically easier and more expedient to encourage activities through the tax system than risk the annual public debates associated with annual program appropriations in Congress.

Pop Quiz

1. By the mid-1980s, U.S. farm policy was giving lavish subsidies in the form of price support loans and marketing loans to growers of certain crops in return for restricting acreage. These crops included corn, wheat, rice, and cotton. In contrast, soybean support prices were low, there were no marketing loans, and farmers were prohibited from growing soybeans on "set-asides" from other crop programs. It was simply more profitable to produce the crops with the more generous government subsidies than to produce soybeans. Soybean prices are strong and demand is growing, but shortages of soybeans are expected and the loss of foreign export markets anticipated. U.S. buyers of soybeans are making plans to import soy even though there is "idle" land from the set-asides that could be planted in soy. As recently as the 1970s, soybeans were America's major export crop. As of 1982, the United States was responsible for 86% of the world trade in soybeans. This share of the world market is expected to decline to 60% in 1989, in large part because of U.S. farm policy. As noted in the text, one of the goals of farm policy is to encourage exports.

2. The soybean lobby, the American Soybean Association, is not a powerful or cohesive lobby. There is regional factionalism regarding the proper policy. Southern farmers want marketing loans but no expansion of acreage. Midwestern farmers want to expand acreage without being penalized but oppose marketing loans. The soybean lobby previously supported limited acreage restrictions in hopes of reaping gains from rising market prices. The soybean lobby contributed to the shortages because it was not effective enough in maintaining the status of soybeans relative to other crops in terms of U.S. farm subsidies.

Coming a Cropper

Farm-Policy Fumbling On Soybeans Shrinks U.S. Share of Market

Despite the Demand, Farmers Idle Their Land and Grow Other Crops for Subsidies

Next: Chickens From Brazil?

By SCOTT KILMAN
And BRUCE INGERSOLL
Staff Reporters of THE WALL STREET JOURNAL

CAMERON, S.C.—On Cemetery Road, at the edge of this farming community of 536 people in Calhoun County, lies a pile of rubble—all that is left of a soybean processing plant that until last year had been the town's biggest employer. The cause of its demise: a 50% plunge in the size of the county's biggest cash crop, soybeans, over the past five years.

Here and elsewhere, in places from the Deep South to the Great Plains, the American soybean boom has gone bust.

Once the "miracle bean" stood as the brightest hope of American agriculture. Now U.S. output is falling for the third consecutive year; yesterday, the Agriculture Department forecast a 23% drop in the 1988 crop. This means that for the first time since American breeders redesigned the Manchurian native to thrive on these shores, America will have grown less than half the world's soybeans. With millions of fertile acres idle, the U.S. is close to running out of its second most valuable crop, after corn.

"We are just realizing that the U.S. isn't the only ball game in town," says John Hane, a Fort Motte, S.C., farmer. South American growers, he says, "are taking away our crop from us and making us look like asses."

Inflation and Shortages

Don't blame market prices or demand. On the contrary, prices for processed soybean products are strong and, partly because of the drought, headed higher; some farmers who use the beans for feed may lose money on their hogs and chickens. By the fall of 1989, there may be shortages of soybeans, used in cooking oils and other human food as well as in animal feed.

Despite all this, farmers seem reluctant to grow the crop without government assistance—help they frittered away in a splintered lobbying effort.

Foreign farmers are fast plowing new acreage for soybeans to meet demand around the world. American processors are laying plans to *import* soybeans that won't be grown on the U.S.'s idle acreage. At the Chicago Board of Trade, speculators swap rumors of bargeloads of South

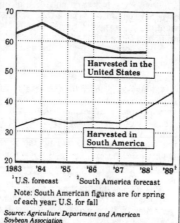

The Decline in U.S. Soybeans

(In millions of acres)

Harvested in the United States

Harvested in South America

1983 '84 '85 '86 '87 '88[1] '89[2]

[1] U.S. forecast   [2] South America forecast

Note: South American figures are for spring of each year; U.S. for fall.

Source: Agriculture Department and American Soybean Association

American soybean oil moving up the Mississippi River.

If all this seems weird, it is. The short, if cynical, explanation is that producers of corn, wheat, rice and cotton command powerful and cohesive lobbies. Soybean growers do not. But that is oversimple. The growers themselves, hoping to enjoy the best of both the subsidized and free-market worlds, pitched their own wrenches into the agricultural policy machinery and now suffer the consequences.

Trusting the Market

By 1984, policy makers were eager to refloat a floundering farm economy with lavish subsidies for corn, wheat, rice and cotton—which farmers call program crops. Income-support payments and price-support loans guaranteed growers of these crops profits in return for setting aside big chunks of their usual planting acreage. For rice and cotton growers came a bonus in the form of marketing loans, costly export subsidies that compensate farmers and exporters for selling U.S. commodities abroad at low prices.

Soybean growers lacked a consensus toward subsidies. For years, in fact, their strongest lobby had looked askance at subsidies, confident that market demand for the wondrous protein source would ensure higher profits. In the farm legislation that took effect in 1985, soybean support prices were low. No marketing loans were offered. Nor were farmers permitted to plant soybeans on land idled by corn, wheat and cotton "set-asides." Because government subsidies are based on an average of five consecutive harvests, planting soybeans for one season on program cropland would penalize a farmer for several years.

Since then, U.S. soybean acreage has shrunk by 15%. On world markets, American agriculture has been made to look much like General Motors in the 1970s, a lumbering giant slow to size up its competition. The vast, empty refining vats amid the rubble of Cameron's former Continental Grain Co. plant attest to the cost.

The plant sprang up in the 1960s, a few years before the buff-colored bean was engineered into a new source of protein for a hungry world. While U.S. farmers had planted a few soybeans in the past, processors lifted the crop from obscurity in the 1970s and made it America's biggest farm export. Its champions, ranging from farmers and processors to Agriculture Department officials, put technicians to work on recipes for tofu, meat lookalikes, gravies and bread—all made from soybeans.

"When you start thinking about future applications of soy protein, it can boggle the mind," gushed a promotional brochure by Archer Daniels Midland Co., the leading U.S. processor.

At the same time, costly overseas promotion made the soybean a staple of diets in Japan, Korea, West Germany and elsewhere. Prices in the 1970s doubled, showering farmers with cash they invested to double their production by 1979 to 2.26 billion bushels, the biggest crop ever. The American Soybean Association, a farmer lobby, chose to risk price swings in the market in order to avoid limiting production and exports.

Then came the farm crisis of the early 1980s and the 1985 farm act. By early 1988, the stage was set for a soybean shortage. In February, Rep. Jerry Huckaby, a Louisiana Democrat, tried to help soybean growers by introducing a bill to provide them with a marketing loan. Rep. Dan Glickman, a Kansas Democrat who chairs the House Agriculture subcommittee on wheat, soybeans and feed grains, held hearings on the soybean industry's dilemma, and he and others pressed ahead with legislation designed to increase soybean acreage.

Coming a Cropper: Farm-Policy Fumbling Shrinks U.S. Output and Growers' Share of Soybean Market

That began a political fiasco that killed the industry's chances for a 1988 recovery. In what a congressional aide called "the North-South war," the soybean association split along regional lines. Southern soybean farmers sought a marketing loan in hopes of lifting exports but wanted no expansion of soybean acreage, which might depress prices. At the same time, growers in the Midwest, where soybean yields are 50% higher, mostly wanted a chance to plant more beans without their subsidies being penalized. But they opposed a marketing loan for precisely the same reason the Southerners objected to increase acreage: It might depress prices.

"The politics of soybeans are very confused," says Illinois Rep. Edward Madigan, the ranking Republican on the House Agriculture Committee. Says soybean-association President James Lee Adams, of Camilla, Ga., "We were in a terrible quandary at the time."

After flip-flopping on the issue, the growers' group declared itself opposed to both a marketing loan *and* an acreage expansion in 1988. The waffling outraged legislators and doomed efforts to expand production. By then it was March, too late to change the farm program in time for 1988 plantings. "It would have just added to the confusion," Mr. Adams says.

Jumping Ship

Nevertheless, he concedes, "we haven't had our act together. . . . Making policy for the American Soybean Association is a lot like trying to load a wheelbarrow full of frogs. We get a few of us on board, and others start jumping ship."

With soybean stockpiles now expected to fall to a dangerously low three weeks' supply by next summer, the government has since sweetened the pot. Under the $3.9 billion drought-relief package enacted last month, farmers can without penalty shift at least 10% of their land from program crops into soybeans for one year, and perhaps as much as 25% at the Agriculture Secretary's discretion.

Changes in the farm program may be too little and too late. Some 14 million acres of U.S. soybeans have effectively shifted to South America. There, the plant-ing season begins next month, and Argentina and Brazil are expected to increase their plantings by 20% and 15%.

In the U.S., corn subsidies are still so attractive that LeRoy, Minn., farmer Russell Roe plans to switch only 15% of his corn acreage to soybeans. U.S. soybean plantings are expected to rise by only two million to three million acres next spring, half the increase expected in competing South American nations.

Losing Market Share

Bit players such as Australia are weighing into soybeans, and nations unsuited to growing them are planting alternative crops. Heavily subsidized rapeseed production in Western Europe has risen 60% in the past four years, lessening the European Economic Community's dependence of U.S. soybean meal and strengthening it as a competitor in world vegetable oil.

The decline in America's share of the world soybean trade, totaling $10 billion a year now, will be tough to end. The U.S. share is expected to tumble to less than 60% in the coming year from 86% in 1982. The number of domestic processing plants—crushers and refiners—has fallen 28% in the past 10 years, to 88.

More are on the verge of closing. Decatur, Ill., a processing town deep in the Farm Belt, has conceded its title of "the soybean capital of the world." Ponta Grossa, Brazil, and Rosario, Argentina, are new contenders.

Here in Cameron and the rest of the Southeast, a major soybean-producing region, the cost of farm-policy machinations has run especially high. Mr. Hane, the Fort Motte farmer, planted only 250 acres in soybeans this spring, just one-third as much as six years ago. "When you plant soybeans, you are totally on your own," Mr. Hane says. "With the others, the government protects you from low prices."

Soybean seed sales skidded last spring in South Carolina, and dealers were forced to destroy tens of thousands of bags. Luther Wannamaker, president of his family's seed business, is glum about the prospects for soybeans. Farmers have planted pine trees on many former soybean fields under a government program that pays them $45 an acre each year to idle land. Other acreage is in subsidized crops such as cotton. "Program crops are too attractive," Mr. Wannamaker says.

Only two of the five soybean processing plants within 100 miles of Calhoun County are still crushing soybeans. Lessened demand from the processors is further dulling the local price on beans, further dulling farmers' incentive to grow them here. Yet the drought, reduced competition and higher transportation costs have worked to increase the prices on soybean products. Livestock raisers are smarting from an 80% increase in the cost of soybean meal, a principal feed ingredient.

Steve Pittman, a Fort Motte, S.C. farmer, says rising feed costs will wipe out profit on his 450-hog operation this year. The plant closing is "a sad waste," he says. "We lost a golden opportunity."

Southeastern poultry producers fear withering soybean supplies will force up prices on other commodities. Joe Hatfield, president of Fieldale Farms Corp., a Baldwin, Ga., poultry grower, says the cost of feeding soybean meal to chickens could make them too expensive to export.

He also worries that Brazil might take advantage of its expanding soybean crop to develop its poultry industry—and exports. "We could be facing South American competition for chickens," he says.

At Sylvia's restaurant in downtown St. Matthews, the seat of Calhoun County, a knot of farmers mulls international trade issues over lunch. "We fought low prices. Then the weather," says Pallie Wiles, a soybean farmer in a John Deere cap. "Now it's the South Americans."

The closing of the Cameron plant dashed farmers' hopes of expanding markets for their promising new crop. With the plant vanished the jobs of 58 residents and the line of trucks that snaked into town during the annual harvest. Along Cemetery Road, "it's going to be right quiet this fall," says David Summers, president of the Golden Kernel Pecan Co., across the road from the plant site.

Says Mr. Wiles, "It's a tragedy, what's happening."

19

The Government Sector of the Economy:
Expenditures, Revenues, and Public Choice

CHAPTER CHALLENGES

After studying your text, attending class, and completing this chapter, you should be able to:

1. Describe the economic functions of modern governments.
2. Explain how governments raise revenue and describe the major catagories of expenditure for the federal, state, and local governments in the United States.
3. Explain the principles used to evaluate taxes.
4. Explain the process of public choice under majority rule.

IN BRIEF: CHAPTER SUMMARY

Fill in the blanks to summarize chapter content.

The (1)_____(democratic, federal government) system consists of various levels of government, each with its own powers to provide services and to regulate the private sector. The basic functions of government include (a) the establishment of rights to use productive resources and the regulation of private actions, (b) provision of goods and services, (c) redistribution of income, and (d) (2)_____ (stabilization of the economy, provision of armed forces). Government-provided goods and services can be categorized in two basic ways. Some publicly provided goods are made available free of charge to all members of society, and the cost is financed with taxes or through borrowing. National defense, public health, and (3)_____(national parks, welfare benefits) are some examples of this type of good. Some tax-financed government goods and services are made available only to some individuals meeting certain eligibility criteria. Examples include education, Social Security pensions, and (4)_____(national parks, welfare benefits).

At the federal level of government, as of 1987, national defense spending was the (5)_____(largest, second largest) component of federal spending. Social Security benefits are also a major federal government outlay. State and local governments spend just over (6)_____ (two thirds, half) of the amount spent by the federal government. At the state and local levels of government, (7)_____(welfare, education) accounts for more than one third of all expenditures, followed by income support, social insurance, and welfare as the second major type of expenditure. Road maintenance and transportation is also an important function at the state and local levels of government.

In 1987, federal government tax revenues (8)_____ (exceeded, fell short of) expenditures by $152.6 billion. This is referred to as a budget deficit. Deficits have to be financed by borrowing. The U.S. Treasury does this by issuing U.S. government securities. Major federal taxes in order of importance include the personal income tax, (9)_____ (the payroll tax, sales taxes), corporate profits taxes and excise taxes.   State and local governments

incurred a budget (10)_____(deficit, surplus) of $45.5 billion in 1987.
Major state and local sources of revenue by order of importance include
(11)_____(income, sales) taxes, property taxes, federal grants,
(12)_____(income, sales) taxes, fees and charges, and payroll taxes.

Taxes are evaluated on the basis of efficiency and equity. Taxes can be levied
on the basis of the taxpayer's ability to pay or the benefits received from the
government good or service. A person with a higher income may pay more taxes
than an individual with a lower income, and yet the tax can still be a
(13)_____ (progressive, regressive) tax in which individuals with
higher incomes pay a smaller percentage of their incomes in taxes than lower-
income persons. A (14)_____ (progressive, regressive) tax, such as the
personal income tax, requires individuals with higher incomes to pay a larger
percentage of their incomes in taxes.   A flat-rate tax is an example of a
(15)_____(regressive, proportional) tax in which persons with
different incomes pay the same percentage of their income in taxes.

Economic decisions are based on (16)_____ (marginal, average) tax rates
rather than (17)_____ (marginal, average) tax rates. Whether or not an
individual engages in an activity or a change in some activity depends in part
on the after-tax net gains. The decision to work an extra hour depends on the
net take-home wage. What is important is not the worker's average tax per
dollar earned, but the increase in tax associated with an additional hour of
work. Taxes can result in efficiency losses from less employment, less
productivity, and less saving and capital growth. This efficiency loss or
(18)_____ (excess burden, tax loss) of a tax is the loss in net benefits
from resource use caused by the distortion in choices resulting from taxation.

Public choices are made through voting. Under simple majority rule, as
individuals pursue their most-preferred political outcome, a political
equilibrium is reached at the median most-preferred outcome. This is known as
the (19)_____ (plurality, median-voter) rule. A competitive market
provision of goods allows consumers to purchase goods up to the point at which
marginal benefits equal price. (20_____ (Consumers cannot, Each
consumer can) maximize utility. But with politically supplied goods, only the
median voter maximizes satisfaction. Some citizens will receive more of the
public good than they desire and some less.

VOCABULARY REVIEW

Write the key term from the list below next to its definition.

Key Terms

Taxes	Marginal tax rate
Federal system	Excess burden
of government	Public choices
Government transfers	Simple majority rule
Budget deficit	Most-preferred political
Budget surplus	outcome
Regressive tax	Political equilibrium
Progressive tax	Median voter
Proportional tax	Median voter rule
Average tax rate	Government failure

Definitions

1. _____: payments that are financed by taxes and made directly to certain citizens or organizations for which no good or service is received in return at that time.

2. _____: that alternative for which the marginal benefit just equals the tax a voter would pay if he were able to purchase the good or service in a market at a price equal to his assigned tax per unit.

3. _____: a tax for which the percentage of income paid in taxes is the same no matter what the taxpayer's income.

4. _____: the loss in net benefits from resource use caused by the distortion in choices resulting from taxation.

5. _____: the extra tax paid on extra income or the extra dollar value of any other taxed item.

6. _____: the amount of taxes paid divided by the dollar value of the item taxed.

7. _____: choices made by voting.

8. _____: a tax for which the fraction of income used to pay it increases as income increases.

9. _____: a means for reaching public choices that enacts a proposal if it obtains affirmative votes from more than half the voters casting ballots in an election.

10. _____: a tax for which the fraction of income used to pay it decreases as income increases.

11. _____: an agreement on the quantity of a public good to supply through government, given the rule for making the public choice and given the taxes per unit of the public good for each voter.

12. _____: an excess of government revenues over government expenditures in a given year.

13. _____: given an odd number of voters, the voter whose most-preferred outcome is the median of all the most-preferred outcomes.

14. _____: the amount by which government expenditures exceed government revenues in a given year.

15. _____: states that when the marginal benefit of a pure public good declines for each voter as more of the good is made available, the political equilibrium under majority rule always corresponds to the median most-preferred outcome when there is an odd number of voters.

16. _____: numerous levels of government, each with its own powers, exist to provide services and regulate private affairs.

17. _____: exists when voters approve programs for which marginal costs exceed marginal benefits.

18. _____: compulsory payments associated with income, consumption, or holding of property that persons and corporations are required to make each year to governments.

SKILLS REVIEW

Concept: Economic functions of government

1. List four functions of government and give an example of each.

   a. _____
   b. _____
   c. _____
   d. _____

2. Government goods and services can be classified as (1) goods that are made available to all citizens free of charge and (2) goods and services that are available only to certain citizens based on specific eligibility criteria. For each of the goods or services below, indicate whether the good or service is of the first or second category. Use (1) for the first category and (2) for the second category.

a.	_____ National defense		b.	_____ Medicaid
c.	_____ Roads		d.	_____ Fire protection
e.	_____ Food stamps		f.	_____ National parks
g.	_____ Police		h.	_____ Social security
i.	_____ Education			

Concept: Government revenues and expenditures

3. List the federal government's tax revenues in order of importance.

   a. _____
   b. _____
   c. _____
   d. _____

4. List the federal government's expenditures in order of importance.

   a. _____
   b. _____
   c. _____
   d. _____
   e. _____

5. List state and local revenue sources in order of importance.

   a. _____
   b. _____
   c. _____
   d. _____
   e. _____
   f. _____

6. List major categories of state and local expenditures in order of importance.

   a. _____
   b. _____
   c. _____

Concept: Principles used to evaluate taxation

7. Taxes are generally considered equitable if taxpayers pay taxes on the basis of their _____ or the _____ from the public good or service consumed.

8. Indicate for the taxes below whether they are progressive, regressive, or proportional taxes.

    a. _____ Federal personal income tax
    b. _____ Sales tax
    c. _____ Payroll tax (FICA)
    d. _____ Flat-rate tax
    e. _____ Cigarette excise tax

Concept: Public choice and voting

9. Below are the marginal benefits associated with various quantities of a public good for five voters. Assume that the public choice rule is the majority vote and the tax cost per voter per year is $100.

Marginal Benefits ($)

Units of the Public Good	A	B	C	D	E
0					
1	200	140	80	125	110
2	180	130	70	100	105
3	160	120	60	75	100
4	140	110	50	50	95
5	120	100	40	25	90
6	100	90	30	0	85
7	80	80	20	-25	80

a. If each voter maximizes his net benefits, what is the most-preferred political outcome for each voter?

Voter	Units
A	_____
B	_____
C	_____
D	_____
E	_____

b. At the following levels of public goods provision, indicate the vote for and against and whether the vote fails or passes.

Units	For	Against	Pass/Fail
0	___	___	___
1	___	___	___
2	___	___	___
3	___	___	___
4	___	___	___
5	___	___	___
6	___	___	___
7	___	___	___

c. Political equilibrium is achieved at what level of public goods provision? _____ units This quantity is the most-preferred political outcome of which voter?_____ This voter is called the _____ voter.

SELF-TEST FOR MASTERY

Select the best answer.

1. Welfare payments fall under which of the following government functions?

    a. Establishment of rights to use resources and the regulation of private actions
    b. Provision of goods and services
    c. Redistribution of income
    d. Stabilization of the economy

2. Education expenditures fall under which of the following government functions?

    a. Establishment of rights to use resources and the regulation of private actions
    b. Provision of goods and services
    c. Redistribution of income
    d. Stabilization of income

3. Payments made by government to certain persons or organizations for which no good or service is currently received in return are called:

    a. Government spending
    b. Welfare benefits
    c. Government off-budget expenditures
    d. Government transfer payments

4. Which of the following was the largest federal government expenditure in 1987?

    a. Income security
    b. Social Security
    c. National parks
    d. National defense
    e. Education

5. Which of the following was the largest source of tax revenue for the federal government in 1987?

    a. Excise tax
    b. Corporate profits tax
    c. Sales tax
    d. Payroll tax
    e. Income tax

6. Which of the following was the largest category of spending at the state and local levels of government in 1986?

    a. Highways
    b. Education
    c. Welfare

d.   Police and fire protection
e.   Hospitals

7. Which of the following was the largest source of state and local
    government revenue in 1987?

    a.   Sales tax
    b.   Income tax
    c.   Gross production tax
    d.   Excise tax
    f.   Property tax

8. Two concepts of equity in taxation are the _____ and _____
    concepts.

    a.   Egalitarian, utopian
    b.   Ability-to-pay, benefits received
    c.   Democratic, Republican
    d.   Progressive, regressive

9. A tax for which the fraction of income used to pay it decreases as income
    increases is called a:

    a.   Progressive tax.
    b.   Regressive tax.
    c.   Proportional tax.
    d.   Flat-rate tax.

10 A tax for which the fraction of income used to pay it increases as income
    increases is called a:

    a.   Progressive tax.
    b.   Regressive tax.
    c.   Proportional tax.
    d.   Value-added tax.

11. A flat-rate tax is an example of :

    a.   A progressive tax.
    b.   A regressive tax.
    c.   A proportional tax.
    d.   The U.S. income tax.

12. The appropriate tax concept to be used in marginal analysis is:

    a.   The total tax liability from the full extent of an activity.
    b.   The marginal tax rate.
    c.   The average tax rate.
    d.   The ability-to-pay concept.

13. A voter's most-preferred political outcome is:

    a.   When taxes are shared equally by all voters.
    b.   When total benefits equal the total cost of the public good.
    c.   At the level of public goods provision where the voter's marginal
         benefit just equals his tax share per unit of the public good.
    d.   Always satisfied more efficiently in the market.

14. If the public choice rule is the majority vote rule and voters know their respective tax shares and maximize net benefits, political equilibrium:

   a. Occurs at a level of provision where the median voter maximizes net benefits.
   b. Occurs at the same level of provision as would be the case for a competitive market equilibrium.
   c. Occurs at a level of provision where all voters maximize net benefits.
   d. None of the above.

15. An advantage of having nonpublic goods produced by the market rather than by government is that:

   a. Consumers can consume goods up to the point at which their net benefits are maximized.
   b. Taxes will be lower.
   c. Consumers can consume goods up to the point at which their marginal benefits equal the price of the good.
   d. A and c.
   e. None of the above.

16. _____ exists when voters approve programs for which marginal costs exceed marginal benefits.

   a. Anarchy
   b. Market failure
   c. The most-preferred political outcome
   d. Government failure

THINK IT THROUGH

1. Compare and contrast the expenditures and revenue sources of the federal government with those of the state and local levels of government.

2. Describe what is meant by efficiency and equity in taxation.

3. Explain why it is possible under a majority vote system for voters to pass legislation on single issues where voter contentment with legislative outcomes can range from a broad consensus to a great deal of dissatisfaction.

POP QUIZ   Read the news brief at the end of this chapter and answer the questions below.

1. What is the excess burden of a tax?
2. What is a major cost of compliance with the federal income tax? Do you think that the compliance cost of the federal income tax is a significant component of the excess burden associated with the tax? Explain.

CHAPTER ANSWERS

In Brief: Chapter Summary

1. Federal government 2. Stabilization of the economy 3. National parks 4. Welfare benefits 5. Largest 6. Half 7. Education 8. Fell short of 9. The payroll tax 10. Surplus 11. Sales 12. Income 13. Regressive 14. Progressive 15. Proportional 16. Marginal 17. Average 18. Excess burden 19. Median voter 20. Each consumer can

Vocabulary Review

1. Government transfers 2. Most-preferred political outcome 3. Proportional tax 4. Excess burden 5. Marginal tax rate 6. Average tax rate 7. Public choices 8. Progressive taxes 9. Simple majority rule 10. Regressive tax 11. Political equilibrium 12. Budget surplus 13. Median voter 14. Budget deficit 15. Median voter rule 16. Federal system of government 17. Government failure 18. Taxes

Skills Review

1. a. The establishment of rights to use resources and the regulation of private actions
   b. Provision of goods and services
   c. Redistribution of income
   d. Stabilization of the economy

2. a. 1 b. 2 c. 1 d. 1 e. 2 f. 1 g. 1 h. 2 i. 2

3. a. Personal income tax b. Payroll taxes c. Corporate profits taxes d. Excise taxes

4. a. National defense b. Social Security c. Interest payments d. Income security e. Medicare

5. a. Sales taxes b. Property taxes c. Federal grants d. Income taxes e. Fees and charges f. Payroll taxes

6. a. Education b. Income support, social insurance, and welfare c. Road maintenance and transportation

7. Ability-to-pay, benefits received

8. a. Progressive b. Regressive c. Regressive d. Proportional e. Regressive

9. a.
Voter	Units
A	6
B	5
C	0
D	2
E	3

   b.
For	Against	Pass/Fail
1	4	Fail
4	1	Pass
4	1	Pass
3	2	Pass
2	3	Fail
2	3	Fail

```
        1    4              Fail
        0    5              Fail
```

    c.   3 units, voter E, median

Self-Test for Mastery

1. c 2. b 3. d 4. d 5. e 6. b 7. a 8. b 9. b 10. a 11. c 12. b 13. c 14. a 15. d 16. d

Think it Through

1.   The federal government provides national defense, Social Security, income security, interest payments on the public debt, and Medicare as well as other goods and services. These are financed with personal income taxes, payroll taxes, corporate profits taxes, and excise taxes. State and local governments provide education, income support, social insurance, welfare, road maintenance and transportation, police and fire protection, and other goods and services. State and local levels of government finance their activities with sales taxes, property taxes, federal grants, income taxes, fees and charges, and payroll taxes. The largest federal expenditure as a percentage of total spending is for national defense, whereas the largest state and local expenditure is for education. Sales taxes are the major revenue source at the state and local levels of government, but personal income taxes provide the most revenue to the federal government.

2.   Taxes can create an excess burden when there are tax-caused changes in individual and business behavior resulting from changes in net wages, net interest rates, and other prices or incomes. Efficiency can be improved if the tax is used to correct a negative externality. An efficient tax is one that raises tax revenue without causing an excess burden. The two basic concepts of equity in taxation are the ability-to-pay and benefits received concepts. The benefits received principle cannot be used where the benefits cannot be closely correlated with an individual's activity. The ability-to-pay criterion states that a fair tax is one for which an individual's tax liability is correlated with his or her ability to pay. Thus, higher income persons should pay more in taxes than those with lower incomes. This criterion does not indicate whether proportional, progressive, or regressive taxes are preferable, because ability-to-pay can be measured in absolute dollars or as a percentage of income.

3.   If the marginal benefits from a public good for most taxpayers are similar with little variability and the tax share per taxpayer is the same, the majority vote rule will result in a political equilibrium in which many or most voters have most-preferred political outcomes that are very close to the median voter outcome. Only the median voter achieves the most-preferred political outcome, but the extent of dissatisfaction with the vote is much less than if there is considerable dispersion of marginal benefits. If a larger percentage of voters have most-preferred political outcomes that depart widely from the median voter outcome, there will be far more dissatisfaction with the vote.

Pop Quiz

1.   The excess burden of a tax is the loss in net benefits from resource use caused by the distortion in choices resulting from taxation.

2.   According to Rose Gutfeld's article, a 3-year study funded by the IRS found that taxpayers used a total of 5.3 billion hours for filing federal income tax returns in 1986. This is unquestionably the major cost of compliance and is an important component of the excess burden associated with federal income taxes. The opportunity cost of compliance is the value of these billions of hours in their next-best alternative uses in either work or

leisure. The resources used for tax filing would have been used for other activities that increase total social benefits. The tax-compliance loss must be added to other distortions caused by the income tax in order to determine the extent of its excess burden. In fact, one of the objectives of the Tax Reform Act of 1986 was to simplify the tax-compliance process in order to reduce this aspect of the excess burden.

It Seems Like Days, but IRS Estimates Tax Filing Takes Only About Nine Hours

By Rose Gutfeld

Staff Reporter of The Wall Street Journal

WASHINGTON—Take heart, taxpayers. Filing a return may be unpleasant, but the Internal Revenue Service has found the task takes the average person a mere nine hours and five minutes.

Starting next year, estimates of the average time taxpayers spend on record keeping, learning about the tax law, preparing forms, copying them and sending them to the IRS will be printed on the instructions accompanying the returns and schedules. The nine-hour-plus estimate is for someone filing a 1040 without any schedules such as those for interest and dividend income.

Understated Burden

The agency has been required to come up with these so-called burden estimates for several years, but in the past it strenuously resisted efforts to have them listed on forms or instructions. Officials argued, among other things, that doing so would encourage tax protesters and others to stop working on their returns as soon as they had put in the stated time, whether they had completed the forms or not. Moreover, the estimates could be discouraging even to willing filers who found themselves spending more time than average.

At a news conference yesterday, though, Arthur Altman, chairman of the agency's forms coordinating committee, said previous reluctance reflected concerns that past agency estimates, which included only time needed for preparation, understated the burden on taxpayers. He said the agency doesn't think the new estimates will encourage protesters or be frustrating for slow filers.

The times released yesterday reflect the results of a three-year study conducted for the IRS by Arthur D. Little Inc. The study found that Americans, including individuals and businesses, spent a total of 5.3 billion hours on tax filings for 1986, with two-thirds of the burden falling on business taxpayers.

The study involved focus-group interviews, studies of taxpayer diaries and nationwide surveys of taxpayers. It found that for 1986 returns, taxpayers spent 1.5 billion hours on preparation alone, up from 796 million hours according to previous IRS estimates.

Tax Times

Estimated average times needed to complete and file the following tax forms

FORM	RECORD KEEPING	LEARNING ABOUT THE LAW OR THE FORM	PREPARING THE FORM	COPYING, ASSEMBLING AND SENDING THE FORM TO IRS
1040	3 hrs., 7 min.	2 hrs., 22 min.	3 hrs., 1 min.	35 min.
Sch. A (1040)	2 hrs., 47 min.	26 min.	1 hr., 1 min.	20 min.
Sch. B (1040)	33 min.	8 min.	16 min.	20 min.
Sch. C (1040)	7 hrs., 4 min.	1 hr., 11 min.	2 hrs., 9 min.	25 min.
Sch. D (1040)	1 hr., 2 min.	45 min.	54 min.	35 min.
Sch. E (1040)	3 hrs., 12 min.	1 hr., 2 min.	1 hr., 22 min.	35 min.
Sch. F (1040)	10 hrs., 53 min.	2 hrs., 2 min.	4 hrs., 10 min.	35 min.
Sch. R (1040)	20 min.	16 min.	22 min.	35 min.
Sch. SE (1040)				
Short	20 min.	11 min.	13 min.	14 min.
Long	26 min.	22 min.	37 min.	20 min.

Source: Internal Revenue Service

People with vivid memories of the 1988 filing season may be surprised to learn that, according to the IRS, they spent less time, on average, filling out tax forms this year, the first year of filing under the new law, than they did a year earlier. Among other reasons, under the new tax law, fewer people itemize their deductions, so more can use the simpler 1040A and 1040EZ forms. The time estimate for the 1040 form increased slightly under the new law.

Several professional tax preparers say they think the new time estimates generally are accurate, but they say a few are too low. "I wouldn't argue with many of those estimates," says David J. Silverman, a New York tax consultant. "But I would dispute the record keeping. Out of every 10 people who come into my office, seven have to go back and dig up additional stuff that's missing. That takes time."

A spokesman for H&R Block Inc. says people spend more than the estimated time on learning about the form. "You have to read a lot just to see if it applies to you," he says.

Of the main individual forms, the longest estimate applied to Schedule F, where farm income is listed. Record keeping alone for the form is put at 10 hours, 53 minutes, with the total time needed estimated at 17 hours, 40 minutes.

Schedule A, for itemized deductions, is supposed to take four hours and 34 minutes, while Schedule B, where interest and dividend income is listed, takes one hour, 17 minutes. The form for capital gains income or loss, Schedule D, should take three hours, 16 minutes.

Seeking Feedback

On next year's tax forms, the IRS also will solicit public comment on the time estimates and suggestions for simplifying the forms. Mr. Altman says the forms contain only subtle changes from this year's versions.

John D. Johnson, an assistant IRS commissioner, says the agency plans additional research into making tax forms as accessible as possible to taxpayers. The agency will attempt to measure filers' "tax literacy"—that is, how much of the tax forms they actually understand. Forms currently are aimed at people with a 10th-grade reading level. The agency also will consider the possibility of converting the tax forms to a more visual approach, through the use of flow charts or question-and-answer formats.

20

Input Markets and the Demand for Resources

CHAPTER CHALLENGES

After studying your text, attending class, and completing this chapter, you should be able to:

1. Explain the concept of a perfectly competitive input market.
2. Show how much of a particular input, like labor, a profit-maximizing firm chooses to buy over a certain period in a competitive market.
3. Show how a firm's demand for an input depends on the productivity of the input and on the price the firm receives from selling the product of the input.
4. Show how the market price of an input depends on its supply and demand.

IN BRIEF: CHAPTER SUMMARY

Fill in the blanks to summarize chapter content.

A competitive input market is one in which there is (1)_____ (lack of free, free) entry and exit of sellers of inputs, where the owners of resources (2)_____ (can, cannot) shift their resources to different locations in response to differences in input prices, and where buyers and sellers of resources (3)_____ (have, have no) control over resource prices. In competitive input markets, the forces of supply and demand determine market input prices and quantities employed.

The demand for an input is a derived demand--derived from the demand for the product produced by the input. The demand curve for an input is the (4)_____(marginal revenue product, marginal product) curve. Marginal revenue product is the input's marginal product times (5)_____ (average cost, marginal revenue). Marginal product is the extra production that results from the use of one additional unit of an input. For the case of a perfectly competitive product market, marginal revenue (6)_____ (is less than, equals) price. Therefore, for competitive input markets, marginal revenue product (7)_____ (is less than, equals) product price times the input's marginal product. Marginal revenue product is the contribution by an extra unit of an input to the firm's total revenue.

A profit-maximizing firm will employ an input up to the point at which the additional benefit from doing so (the marginal revenue product) (8)_____ (is greater than, equals) the additional costs (or marginal input costs). For the case of labor, a firm will employ labor up to the point at which the marginal revenue product of labor equals the wage, assuming a competitive input market. A firm's demand curve for labor is the marginal revenue product curve with the wage rate plotted on the vertical axis. Each point on the curve represents a profit-maximizing quantity of labor demanded at that wage rate.

An input demand curve will shift if the demand for the firm's output changes, if the prices of substitute or complementary inputs change, or if changes in technology affect the marginal product of the input. The demand for an input will increase (the demand curve will shift to the right) if the price of the product produced by the input (9)_____ (increases, decreases), if technological improvement (10)_____ (increases, decreases) the input's marginal product, if the price of a substitute input (11)_____ (increases, decreases), or if the price of a complementary input (12)_____ (increases, decreases). The opposite changes will cause the demand for an input to decrease and the input demand curve to shift to the left.

For the case of a monopoly product market, marginal revenue is (13)_____ (equal to, less than) price at each level of output, causing the monopolist's marginal revenue product curve for an input to lie (14)_____ (outside, inside) the market input demand for competitive firms. As a result, at a given wage the monopolist will maximize profit by hiring (15)_____ (more, fewer) units of the input than would be the case for competitive firms.

The market demand curve for an input is a summation of the individual firm-level demand curves for the input. It is downward sloping, as is the case for the firm's input demand curve. The supply curve for an input is upward sloping because higher input prices are necessary to cover (16)_____ (rising, falling) marginal costs associated with supplying the input. The market supply of and demand for an input determine the market price and quantity of the input. For example, if the demand for an input increases or supply decreases or some combination of the two, market input prices will (17)_____ (increase, decrease).

Economic rent exists when the market price of an input (18)_____ (equals, exceeds) the minimum price that sellers of the input will take. It represents a surplus over the opportunity costs associated with producing and providing an input and can be taxed away (19)_____ (reducing, without reducing) the quantity of inputs offered at the market price. Key facts regarding input markets include: (a) the prices of inputs are determined by the forces of supply and demand, (b) the price of an input equals its marginal revenue product for the case of competitive input markets, (c) the demand for an input is a derived demand, (d) productivity is a major determinant of input prices, and (e) for the case of competitive input markets, attempts by employers to pay less than the going market input price will fail.

VOCABULARY REVIEW

Write the key term from the list below next to its definition.

Key Terms

Input market   Marginal input cost
Competitive input market   Change in input demand
Derived demand   Market demand for an input
Marginal revenue product   Market supply of an input

Definitions

1. _____: a relationship between the price of an input and the quantity supplied for employment in all industries and other uses.

2. _____: the change in total revenue that results when one more unit of that input is hired.

3. _____: the sum of the quantities demanded by all industries and other employers using that input at any given price.

4. _____: the demand for an input that is derived from the demand for the product that the input is used to produce.

5. _____: a shift of an entire input demand curve caused by a change in one of the determinants of input demand other than price.

6. _____: a market in which neither individual buyers nor individual sellers can influence the prices of input services.

7. _____: the extra cost associated with hiring one more unit of an input.

8. _____: a market used to trade the services of productive resources for income payments.

SKILLS REVIEW

Concept: Perfectly competitive input markets

1. List the characteristics of a perfectly competitive input market.

    a. _____
    b. _____
    c. _____

Concept: Demand for an input by a profit-maximizing competitive firm

2. Company X is a profit-maximizing firm selling in a competitive product market and hiring in a competitive input market. Company X uses semi-skilled labor to produce dampers used in office building ventilation systems. Below are data regarding labor productivity for the firm. Assume that the current market price per damper is $500.

Workers	Total Product (dampers/week)	Marginal Product	Marginal Revenue Product
0	0		
10	15	_____	$_____
20	28	_____	_____
30	39	_____	_____
40	48	_____	_____
50	55	_____	_____
60	60	_____	_____

a. Complete the table and plot the marginal revenue product curve in the diagram below.

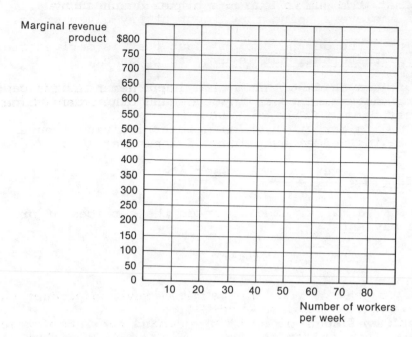

Marginal revenue product $800 ... 0

10 20 30 40 50 60 70 80

Number of workers per week

b. Assume that the prevailing weekly salary per semi-skilled worker is $550. Company X would employ _____ workers. The profit-maximizing level of employment occurs where _____ equals _____.

c. Suppose the market wage fell from $550 per week to $450 per week. Company X would employ _____ workers. If the market wage increased to $650, Company X would employ _____ workers.

d. Plot the quantities of labor demanded by Company X at the three wages considered in parts a and c in the figure below. For Company X, the input demand curve for semi-skilled labor is the _____ curve.

Wage per week $800 750 700 650 600 550 500 450 400 350 300 250 200 150 100 50 0

10 20 30 40 50 60 70 80

Quantity of labor demanded per week

298

Concept: Determinants of a competitive firm's input demand

3.   List three factors that will shift a firm's input demand curve.

    a. _____
    b. _____
    c. _____

4.   Given the data in question 2 above, show what happens to the firm's
    marginal revenue product schedule and curve and its input demand curve for
    labor if the price per damper falls to $400.

Workers	Marginal Revenue Product
0	
10	$_____
20	_____
30	_____
40	_____
50	_____
60	_____

    a.   Complete the table.
    b.   On the first figure shown, plot the marginal revenue product curve
        associated with a price per damper of $400.
    c.   On the second figure shown, plot the new demand for labor curve.
    d.   The input demand curve shifts to the _____ (left,right).
    e.   At a wage of $550 per week, would Company X continue to hire the same
        number of workers given the reduction in the price of dampers?
        Explain.
    f.   The demand for an input is a _____ demand.

Concept: The demand for an input by a profit-maximizing monopolist

5.   The product and employment data below are for an entire market.

Q	Ql	Pc	Pm	MRm	MPL	MRPc	MRPm
0	0	$2	$2.00				
1	5	2	1.80	$____	____	$____	$____
2	11	2	1.60	____	____	____	____
3	18	2	1.40	____	____	____	____
4	26	2	1.20	____	____	____	____
5	35	2	1.00	____	____	____	____

    Q = thousands of units of output per week
    Ql = workers
    Pc = competitive firm's product price
    Pm = monopolist's product price
    MRm = monopolist's marginal revenue
    MPL = marginal product of labor
    MRPc = competitive firm's marginal revenue product
    MRPm = monopolist's marginal revenue product

    a.   Complete the table.

b. Plot the competitive market input demand curve on the figure below.

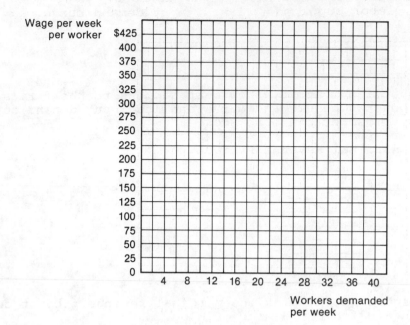

Wage per week per worker

Workers demanded per week

c. Plot the monopolist's input demand curve on the above figure.
d. At a wage of $250 per week, competitive firms will employ a total of _____ workers. At the same wage a monopolist will hire between _____ and _____ workers. Show this in the figure above. A monopolist hires _____ workers than a competitive firm.

Concept: Market input prices and quantities

6. The competitive market for skilled workers is shown below. The companies hiring skilled labor are selling output in competitive markets.

Hourly Wage	Quantity of Labor Demanded	Quantity of Labor Supplied
	(millions of labor hours per day)	
$10.00	30	105
9.75	35	95
9.50	40	85
9.25	45	75
9.00	50	65
8.75	55	55
8.50	60	45
8.25	65	35
8.00	70	25

a. In the diagram below, plot the demand and supply curves for labor and identify the market wage and level of employment. Wage = $_____, labor supplied _____ hours.

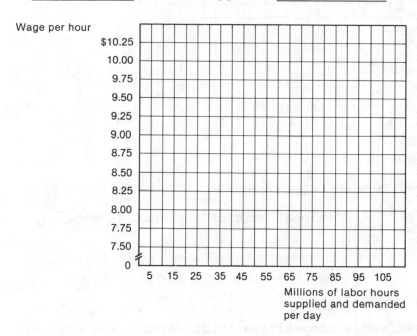

b. On the figure above, show the effect of an increase in the market demand for labor. Market wage rates _____ and employment _____.

c. On the figure above, show the effect of an increase in the market supply of labor. Market wage rates _____ and employment _____.

d. For those workers willing to work for a wage no less than $8.25 per hour but who receive the market wage of $_____, economic rent per labor hour equals $_____. A maximum tax per hour of $_____ could be levied on worker income without affecting the quantity of labor supplied.

e. An increase in labor productivity will shift the _____ curve to the _____ (right, left) and will cause the market wage to _____ and market employment to _____.

f. A decrease in the market prices of the goods produced by the employers of skilled labor will shift the _____ curve to the _____ (right, left) and will cause the market wage to _____ and market employment to _____.

SELF-TEST FOR MASTERY

Select the best answer.

1. Which of the following is not a characteristic of a competitive input market?

    a. There is an absence of close substitute resources.
    b. Both buyers and sellers of inputs are price takers.
    c. There is freedom of entry into and exit from input markets.

d.   Resources are mobile in that they can be used in other employments and in other locations.

2.   The demand for an input is a/an _____ demand.

     a.   Normal
     b.   Individual
     c.   Derived
     d.   Market

3.   Which of the following concepts represents the extra revenue a firm receives from the services of an additional unit of an input?

     a.   Total revenue
     b.   Marginal revenue
     c.   Marginal product of an input
     d.   Marginal revenue product of an input

4.   The cost of employing an additional unit of an input is called:

     a.   Input cost.
     b.   Income.
     c.   Marginal revenue product.
     d.   Marginal cost.
     e.   Marginal input cost.

5.   For the case of a perfectly competitive input market, the marginal input cost equals:

     a.   The total cost of the input.
     b.   The price of the input.
     c.   The average cost of the input.
     d.   Marginal cost.

6.   For the case of a perfectly competitive product market, the marginal revenue product equals:

     a.   Revenue times marginal product.
     b.   Price times total product.
     c.   Marginal revenue times average product.
     d.   Price times marginal product.

7.   If at a firm's current level of employment the marginal revenue product of the last worker employed exceeds the marginal cost of labor, the firm should:

     a.   Decrease employment.
     b.   Maintain the existing level of employment.
     c.   Increase employment.
     d.   Produce less output and hire fewer workers.

8.   A profit-maximizing competitive firm will hire labor in a competitive labor market up to the point at which the _____ equals the _____.

     a.   Average revenue product, product price
     b.   Total product, wage
     c.   Marginal revenue product, wage
     d.   Marginal input cost, wage

9. A firm's demand curve for an input is its:

    a. Marginal cost curve.
    b. Market demand curve.
    c. Marginal product curve.
    d. Marginal revenue product curve.
    e. None of the above.

10. An increase in the demand for the product produced by an input:

    a. Will increase the supply of the input.
    b. Will decrease the supply of the input.
    c. Will increase the demand for the input.
    d. Will decrease the demand for the input.

11. If labor and capital are substitute resources in production, an increase
    in the price of capital will:

    a. Increase, the demand for labor.
    b. Increase, the supply of labor.
    c. Decrease, the demand for labor.
    d. Decrease, the supply of labor.

12. Technological innovation that increases the marginal product of labor
    will:

    a. Increase, the demand for labor.
    b. Increase, the supply of labor.
    c. Decrease, the demand for labor.
    d. Decrease, the supply of labor.

13. A monopolist's marginal revenue product curve :

    a. Is the monopolist's demand for an input.
    b. Equals marginal revenue times marginal product.
    c. Lies inside a competitive industry's demand curve for an input.
    d. Is equated to the marginal cost of labor in order to maximize profits
        from the employment of a variable input.
    e. All of the above.

14. The market supply of an input is upward sloping because:

    a. A supply curve must be upward sloping.
    b. Input suppliers face rising marginal costs as they make more of an
        input available to the market.
    c. Price and quantity supplied are inversely related.
    d. Price and quantity demanded are inversely related.

15. Economic rent is:

    a. A payment to landlords.
    b. The difference between what a resource supplier earns in the market
        and the minimum amount of income required by the resource supplier to
        maintain the same quantity of the input supplied.
    c. The maximum wage required by labor less the market wage.
    d. The minimum wage required by labor less the market wage.

16. What portion of an input supplier's income can be taxed away without affecting the quantity of inputs made available to the market?

    a.   0%
    b.   100%
    c.   A portion equal to economic rent
    d.   A portion equal to the input supplier's opportunity cost
    e.   None of the above

17. An increase in the market demand for an input _____ market input price and _____ employment of the input.

    a.   Increases, increases
    b.   Decreases, decreases
    c.   Increases, decreases
    d.   Decreases, increases

18. An increase in the market supply of an input _____ market input price and _____ employment of an input.

    a.   Increases, increases
    b.   Decreases, decreases
    c.   Increases, decreases
    d.   Decreases, increases

19. If education increases the productivity of labor, the market _____ curve will shift _____ and cause the market wage to _____.

    a.   Supply, leftward, increase
    b.   Demand, leftward, increase
    c.   Supply, rightward, decrease
    d.   Demand, rightward, increase
    e.   Demand, leftward, decrease

THINK IT THROUGH

1.   Discuss intuitively how competitive input markets equalize wages of a given type of labor.

2.   In the 1980s, the world price of oil fell dramatically. Discuss the likely impacts on input markets in the energy-producing regions of the United States.

3.   Explain why movie or sports stars could have a much larger share of their income taxed than is currently the case without reducing the quantities of their services supplied.

4.   Discuss the five key facts about input markets.

POP QUIZ   Read the news brief at the end of this chapter and answer the following questions.

1.   According to the article, why are incomes of those with a bachelor's degree "exploding" in the 1980s?

2. Using the analysis of this chapter, can you explain why college education results in higher income?

CHAPTER ANSWERS

In Brief: Chapter Summary

1. Free 2. Can 3. Have no 4. Marginal revenue product 5. Marginal revenue
6. Equals 7. Product price 8. Equals 9. Increases 10. Increases 11.
Increases 12. Decreases 13. Less than 14. Inside 15. Fewer 16. Rising 17.
Increase 18. Exceeds 19. Without reducing

Vocabulary Review

1. Market supply of an input 2. Marginal revenue product 3. Market demand for
an input 4. Derived demand 5. Change in input demand 6. Competitive input
market 7. Marginal input cost 8. Input market

Skills Review

1.   a.   Buyers and sellers of inputs are price takers
     b.   There is free entry into and exit of sellers from input markets.
     c.   Economic resources can be transferred to different
          employments and to different locations.

2.   a.   Marginal Product   Marginal Revenue Product
                1.5 $750
                1.3   650
                1.1   550
                 .9   450
                 .7   350
                 .5   250

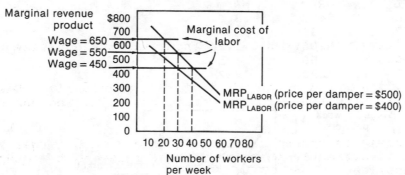

     b.   30; marginal revenue product of labor, wage per week per
          employee
     c.   40; 20
     d.   Marginal revenue product

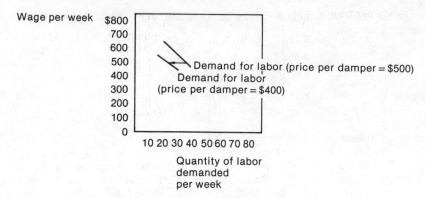

Wage per week

Quantity of labor
demanded
per week

3. a. A change in the demand for the output produced by the input
    b. Changes in the productivity of an input
    c. Technological changes affecting the marginal product of an input

4. a. Marginal Revenue Product
            $600
             520
             440
             360
             280
             200
    b. Answer on the first figure above.
    c. Answer on the second figure above.
    d. Left
    e. No. A decline in the price of dampers reduces the marginal revenue
        product relative to the marginal cost of labor. A profit-maximizing
        firm, by reducing employment, lowers labor costs more than revenues,
        thus increasing profit.
    f. Derived

5. a.

MRm	MPL	MRPc	MRPm
$1.80	200	$400	$360
1.40	167	334	234
1.00	143	286	143
.60	125	250	75
.20	111	222	22

    b.

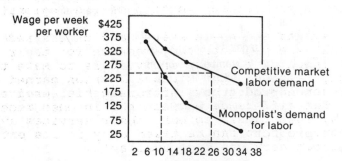

Wage per week
per worker

Workers demanded
per week

    c. Answer in figure above.
    d. 26; 5, 11; fewer

6. a. $8.75, 55 million

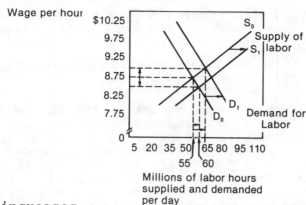

Wage per hour

Millions of labor hours supplied and demanded per day

b.   Rise, increases
c.   Fall, increases
d. $8.75, $.50; $.50
e.   Labor demand, right, rise, increase
f.   Labor demand, left, fall, decrease

Self-Test for Mastery

1. a 2. c 3. d 4. e 5. b 6. d 7. c 8. c 9. d 10. c 11. a 12. a 13. e 14. b 15. b 16. c 17. a 18. d 19. d

Think it Through

1.   Assuming free entry into and exit from a given labor market and the mobility of labor, if wages in region A exceeded wages for identical labor in region B, some workers would leave the low-wage region and move to the high-wage region in pursuit of higher wages. This would cause a reduction in the supply of labor in region B and an increase in the supply of labor in region A. Assuming given labor demand curves for the two regions, market wages in region A will fall while market wages in region B will rise. These changes will continue until there are no further gains by labor from moving from one region to the other. This occurs where the wage rates in the two regions for the given type of labor are equalized.

2.   The large decline in oil prices reduced the marginal revenue products of labor and other inputs used by the oil industry. As the marginal revenue product of an input falls relative to the marginal cost of the input, profit-maximizing firms reduce employment. The oil industry reduced employment and cut production, causing regional recessions in those areas of the nation where the oil industry represents a significant portion of the regional economy.

3.   Some top executives, sports and movie stars, and others receive such enormous annual incomes that the payments they receive for their services far exceed the minimum amount required by these individuals to make their services available. It was recently reported that Michael Jackson earned $97 million last year. Do you think that he would have withdrawn his services if he had earned only $87 million? The difference between the incomes received and the minimum incomes required by individuals to make their services available is called economic rent. Economic rent can be taxed away in its entirety without reducing the quantity of input services made available.

4.   Simple conclusions emerge regarding competitive input markets. The prices of inputs used in production are determined by supply and demand. The price of an input equals the input's marginal revenue product--an input is paid an income equal to its contribution to the firm's revenues. The demand for an input is derived from the demand for the output produced by the input. Influences affecting product demand curves therefore influence input demand

curves. An input's productivity is an important determinant affecting input prices. In competitive input markets, firms are input price takers--attempts to pay an input price below the market price and marginal revenue product will fail.

Pop Quiz

1.   Income growth in the 1980s can in part be attributed to the increase in the number of men and women in the labor force having college degrees. The income gap between those having bachelor's degrees and those having just finished high school is widening in the 1980s. This gap is widening even faster among those with some years of job experience in addition to a college degree. Over the last 10 years, the work force has expanded faster than the number of new entrants with college degrees. Given the increasing emphasis on education in the high-tech workplace, bachelor's degrees are in strong demand. From the supply side of the labor market, the payback time from earning a degree is falling, thus increasing the perceived economic value of the degree to students. More people are responding to this incentive and the realization that education is increasingly necessary and are enrolling in universities.

2.   The price received by an input in a competitive labor market is equal to the input's marginal revenue product. Marginal revenue product equals the price of the output produced by the input times the input's marginal product. Anything that increases labor productivity will increase labor's marginal revenue product. If labor productivity increases, competitive firms hiring in competitive labor markets will increase employment. The market demand for labor rises, causing the market wage and level of employment to increase. It could be argued that a bachelor's degree (or rather the level of educational proficiency attained) increases labor productivity. With the widespread perception on the part of employers that bachelor's degrees are increasingly necessary and with more members of the labor force earning degrees, the demand for individuals with bachelor's degrees will increase, putting upward pressure on salaries.

Benefit of B.A. Is Greater Than Ever

Latest Data Show College Degree Greatly Increases Earnings Power

YOUR

MONEY

MATTERS

By GARY PUTKA

Staff Reporter of THE WALL STREET JOURNAL

There may be something rising faster than the price of going to college, after all.

The price of not going.

In a ritual well known to strapped parents, the College Board recently released its annual survey showing tuitions rising faster than inflation. As is customary, the big admissions group gave no explanation for the 7% increase for 1988-89, the eighth year in a row that the rise in college tuition has outpaced inflation.

Pressed by Congress and others for the reasons, colleges have in the past blamed the need for more scholarships and higher faculty salaries. But a growing body of research suggests a more markets-like answer: College costs more because the product is worth more.

Measured in terms of income, returns on a bachelor's degree "have been exploding in the '80s," says Finis Welch, an economics professor at the University of California at Los Angeles who specializes in the labor market. Mr. Welch and other analysts, using census data, see a dramatic rise in the amount of income gained by going to college over a time period roughly coinciding with the big tuition increases.

Salary Gap

Male college graduates in the work force made 39.2% more than high school graduates in 1986, the latest year of Census Bureau reports, compared with 23.8% in 1979. For women, the difference rose to 40.5% from 27.9%.

More recent data, derived by University of Michigan economist Jonathan Bound from computer tapes of the Census Bureau's monthly surveys, indicate that the differences were more pronounced in 1987. Mr. Bound's figures show that the gap last year was 70% for women in their first 10 working years and 46% for males of that experience. Economists caution that when data for all workers is reported by the Census Bureau, the unusually large gap for women will probably shrink, though it still will be above the 1986 figure.

Moreover, Mr. Bound says the figures don't reflect another benefit of college, namely that the college educated are less likely to be unemployed than high school graduates. And Mr. Welch's research shows that the gap between more-seasoned workers is widening even faster, peaking at about 20 years' experience and remaining steady afterward.

No one is sure what's behind the growing income gap, but some economists point to a drop in high-paying factory jobs among high school graduates. Another reason may be the growing importance of high-tech employment demanding more education. Also, while the number of new college graduates has edged up only about 5% in the past 10 years to about 980,000 a year, the work force has expanded much faster. This has given a sheepskin a rarity value unimagined in the 1970s, when the well-educated flooded the labor market and the cabbie with a doctorate drove his way into national folklore.

"It's rather remarkable," says Richard Freeman, an economist whose 1976 book, "The Overeducated American," presented evidence on the decline of a diploma's value. Now director of labor studies at the National Bureau for Economic Research in Boston, Mr. Freeman says he had expected college's value to make a comeback, "but no one anticipated the magnitude" of the gains for college graduates.

Census data show that the median income of the college-educated man in 1986 was $34,391 versus $24,701 for those without college. That means that the college "payback time"—the number of years it takes a worker to recoup four years of tuition and lost earnings—has shrunk despite the soaring tuitions. Using tuition figures for public colleges, which educate about 77% of all students, the payback time is down to about 11 years, from about 17 in 1979, before the big tuition mark-ups.

Economists don't suggest that high school seniors are delving through census data and punching calculators before deciding whether or not to attend college. But they do say students and parents know what's going on around them—and act accordingly.

"People see some of the kind of job creation that's going on, and they realize without a college education they're up a tree," says Louis Morrell, treasurer of Radcliffe College, Cambridge, Mass. "People want it and they're willing to pay for it."

Relatively stable annual enrollment of about 12 million students in the 1980s wouldn't seem to support the idea of more clamoring for college. But enrollment has

The College Edge

Comparing the median income of college-educated men and women and high-school educated men and women. (In thousands of dollars)

■ College
▨ High school

Men

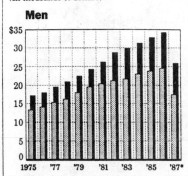

Women

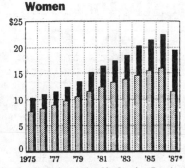

*Includes only workers out of school 10 years or less, based on census data analyzed by Jonathan Bound, University of Michigan.
Source: Bureau of the Census

held steady in the face of a 16% decline in the number of high school graduates since 1977. More college freshmen than ever say they're there to make more money, and according to the most recent Gallup survey on the subject, 64% of Americans rate a college education as "very important" in getting ahead, up from 36% in 1978.

"Costs have escalated at the very moment in history when more people believe that (college) is worth it," says Terry Hartle, education aide to Sen. Edward Kennedy of Massachusetts. "I don't think it's unrelated."

Market Forces

The figures tend to support the economic value of college. But they also suggest that prices in higher education are more subject to market forces than universities have generally acknowledged. Richard Rosser, president of the National Association of Independent Colleges and Universities, says many colleges struggle to hold the line on costs without sacrificing quality. And he adds that tuitions cover only a portion of total costs, with the balance coming from governments, private donations and investment earnings. "Colleges agonize over tuition decisions," he says. "What they're doing is simply covering the real cost of running our universities."

With soaring applications, officials of Ivy League and other top private colleges have long contended that they could raise tuitions by more than they have, and still retain enrollments. They say they have resisted doing so because of concern about the ability of some people to pay.

As for the future?

High Cost of College

Average annual price of four-year colleges

	TUITION AND FEES	
	PUBLIC	PRIVATE
1977-78	$ 621	$2,476
1978-79	651	2,647
1979-80	680	2,923
1980-81	706	3,279
1981-82	819	3,709
1982-83	979	4,021
1983-84	1,105	4,627
1984-85	1,126	5,016
1985-86	1,242	5,418
1986-87	1,337	5,793
1987-88*	1,359	7,110
1988-89*	1,566	7,693

NOTE: Figures are as reported in year of survey
*Weighted averages; all others unweighted
Source: College Board

Higher tuitions still, say the economists who study higher education, until quality, or at least the economic value of higher education, is perceived to decline. "Colleges will act like businessmen on a board," says Mr. Morrell of Radcliffe. "They price themselves according to what the value of the good is perceived to be, and they'll continue to do that until the market says it won't accept it."

21

Labor Markets, Labor Productivity, and Personnel Management

CHAPTER CHALLENGES

After studying your text, attending class, and completing this chapter, you should be able to:

1. Analyze the choice to work and show how a person's labor supply curve depends on his preferences and other influences, such as nonlabor sources of income.
2. Show how the market supply of labor services is influenced by population and other demographic variables.
3. Explain why different wages are paid for different jobs, occupations, or skills.
4. Show how labor productivity is a key determinant of the average level of wages in a nation.
5. Show how personnel management techniques can be used to motivate workers and increase the marginal revenue product of labor.

IN BRIEF: CHAPTER SUMMARY

Fill in the blanks to summarize chapter content.

An individual's decision to work an additional hour depends on the additional gains versus additional losses from doing so. The (1)_____(marginal benefits, marginal costs) of an additional hour of work include the extra monetary and nonmonetary satisfaction received. The additional cost of an hour of work is the (2)_____ (wage, value of a forgone hour of leisure). The opportunity cost of leisure time increases as the individual works more hours. As a result, higher wages or other nonmonetary benefits are (3)_____ (necessary, unnecessary) to compensate the worker for the rising opportunity cost of leisure time. The individual's labor supply curve is upward sloping if an increase in wages, or an increase in the marginal (4)_____ (benefits, costs) relative to the marginal cost of work, induces the individual to work additional hours.

There are both substitution and income effects associated with a change in the wage. An increase in the wage makes an hour of work more valuable in terms of the goods and services that can be purchased with the higher income earned. This causes the opportunity cost of an hour of leisure to increase. An individual will substitute an hour of work for an hour of leisure. The substitution effect results in (5)_____(less, more) hours worked as wages rise. The income effect has just the opposite impact on hours worked. An increase in wages means that the worker can consume the same quantities of goods and services with (6)_____ (fewer, more) hours worked. If the substitution effect outweighs the income effect, the supply curve of labor is (7)_____ (upward sloping, backward bending). If the income effect outweighs the substitution effect, the labor supply curve is (8)_____ (backward bending, upward sloping). If the income and substitution effects just offset each other, the labor supply curve is (9)_____ (positively sloped, vertical).

Market wages depend upon the supply of and demand for labor. The supply of labor is influenced by population and the rate of participation in the labor force. Birth and death rates, immigration, and emigration all influence the supply of labor. Labor productivity is a key determinant of the demand for labor. Increases in a nation's labor productivity (10)_____ (increase, decrease) labor incomes.

Differences in wages among workers and jobs can be explained by productivity or quality differences. Differences in quality are influenced by natural abilities or other characteristics of the individual and by the extent of training or education. Differences in wages can also be attributed to working conditions. Some jobs have negative (11)_____ (externalities, nonpecuniary wages) in that nonmonetary aspects of the job make it less desirable than another job paying exactly the same wage. In order to induce people to accept employment in less desirable occupations, a compensating wage differential must be paid to the worker to make the total compensation from the job (12)_____ (equal to, greater than) to other jobs paying a lower wage but having higher nonmonetary benefits. Some jobs have nonpecuniary benefits that are greater than those for other jobs. These jobs pay a lower wage in order to equalize the total compensation among jobs.

An objective of (13)_____ (production, personnel) management is to adjust the monetary and nonmonetary characteristics of a job in order to increase the marginal revenue product of labor. But first, personnel managers must hire and train workers. The signals from the job seeker's resume and interview offer an (14)_____ (efficient, low-cost; inefficient, high-cost) method of screening. Once hired, the worker has to be trained. This is often a costly process, and firms tend to give only firm-specific training. Where possible firms promote from within in order to avoid some of these training costs. A firm must monitor the actions of its workers to ensure that the owner's desires are met. Owners want to maximize profits, but when workers seek to maximize personal objectives that do not coincide with the owner's goal of profit maximization, workers shirk on the job. They engage in activities that increase their satisfaction (15)_____ (but that increase, and lower) production costs and (16)_____ (increase, lower) worker productivity. One way to reduce shirking is to design and implement compensation systems tying together the interests of workers, managers, and owners. Profit sharing and stock options are two examples.

VOCABULARY REVIEW

Write the key term from the list below next to its definition.

Key Terms

Nonwage money income   Nonpecuniary wages
Marginal cost of work   Compensating wage differential
Marginal benefit of work   Staffing
Labor supply curve   Signals
Substitution effect of a   Screening
   wage change   Internal labor market
Income effect of a wage   Shirking
   change   Backward-bending labor supply
Human capital   curve

Definitions

1. _____: represents the skills and qualifications of workers that stem from education and training.

2. _____: the nonmonetary aspects of a job that must be added to or subtracted from money wages to obtain total compensation per hour of work.

3. _____: implies that the substitution effect on a worker's labor services outweighs the income effect only at relatively low wages.

4. _____: a difference in money wages necessary to make total compensation for similar jobs equal when nonpecuniary wages are not equal to zero.

5. _____: the change in hours worked stemming from the change in income caused by the wage change.

6. _____: indicators displayed by job applicants and used by employers to predict the future satisfaction and productivity of a worker.

7. _____: the change in hours worked resulting only from a change in the opportunity cost of an hour of leisure.

8. _____: the process of recruiting and hiring workers to perform the various tasks required to produce goods and services.

9. _____: shows a relationship between a worker's hourly wages and labor hours supplied for work over a given period.

10. _____: a process in which an employer limits the number of applicants for a job to those it believes are the most likely to succeed in the company.

11. _____: the extra income received from extra work, including any nonmonetary satisfaction obtained from a job.

12. _____: behavior by workers that prevents a firm from achieving the maximum possible marginal product of labor over a given period.

13. _____: the value of extra leisure time given up to work.

14. _____: exists within a firm when it fills positions by hiring its own employees, rather than new employees, to fill all but the lowest-level positions.

15. _____: includes pensions, welfare payments and subsidies, interest, dividends, allowances, and any other type of income that is available independent of work.

SKILLS REVIEW

Concept: An individual's choice to work and labor supply curve

1. Fred's marginal benefits and marginal costs associated with additional
    hours of work are shown below. Assume Fred's marginal benefit from a hour
    of labor is the market wage and that after 8 hours of sleep, Fred has 16
    hours per day to allocate between work and leisure.

Hours per Day	Marginal Benefit	Marginal Cost
0		
1	$9	$1.50
2	9	3.00
3	9	4.50
4	9	6.00
5	9	7.50
6	9	9.00
7	9	10.50
8	9	12.00
9	9	13.50
10	9	15.00

a. Plot the marginal costs and marginal benefits on the figure below.

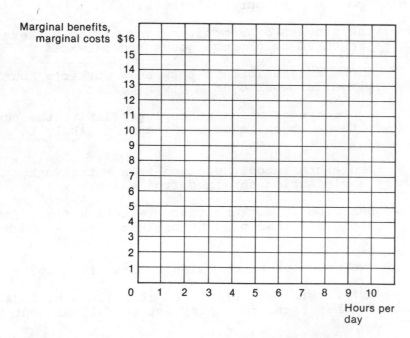

b. Fred maximizes net benefits from work by working _____ hours and
    consuming _____ hours of leisure. Show this in the figure
    above.
c. If the market wage increases to $12 per hour, Fred maximizes net
    benefits by working _____ hours and consuming _____
    hours of leisure. Show this in the figure above.
d. If the market wage falls to $6 per hour, Fred maximizes net benefits
    by working _____ hours and consuming _____ hours of leisure.
    Show this in the figure above.
e. Plot Fred's labor supply curve in the figure below using market
    wages of $6, $9, and $12.

314

Wage

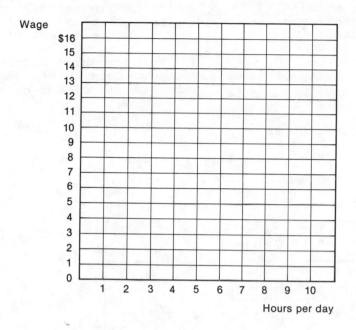

Hours per day

f. Fred's labor supply curve is his _____ curve.

2. <u>Advanced Question</u> Suppose Fred's marginal cost and marginal benefit can be expressed as follows:

MB = Wo
MC = a + bH   where Wo represents the given market wage and H is the number of hours worked

a. Derive an expression for the number of hours worked that maximizes net benefits.
b. What happens to the net benefit-maximizing level of hours worked given changes in a, b, and W? Interpret.
c. If a wage tax, t, is levied on the hourly wage, what happens to the benefit-maximizing level of hours worked? (Assume that t is greater than zero but less than 1.)

3. Answer the following questions on the basis of the figure below.

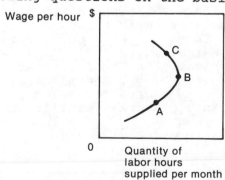

Wage per hour $

0   Quantity of
     labor hours
     supplied per month

a. At point A, there is _____ relationship between the hourly wage and the quantity of labor supplied. This is because the substitution effect _____ the income effect of a wage change.

b. At point B, there is _____ relationship between the hourly wage and the quantity of labor supplied. This is because the substitution effect _____ the income effect of a wage change.

c. At point C, there is _____ relationship between the hourly wage and the quantity of labor supplied. This is because the substitution effect _____ the income effect of a wage change.

Concept: Determinants of market wages

4. What factors influence the market supply of labor? Give an example of each.

    a. _____

    b. _____

5. Below is a market for sales clerks.

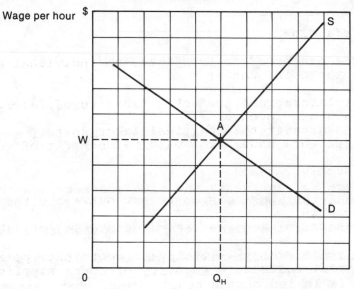

Wage per hour $

W

A

0   Q_H

Quantity of
labor hours supplied
and demanded
per week

a. Assume that because of an increase in the birth rate some years ago, there is currently a large increase in the number of teenagers entering the labor force. The _____ curve for sales clerks shifts _____. Market wages _____, and employment _____. Show this graphically in the figure above.

b. Assume that because of new technology, the marginal products of sales clerks increase. The _____ curve for sales clerks shifts _____. Given the initial market equilibrium at point A, wages _____ and employment _____. Show this graphically in the figure above. Worker productivity and wage rates are _____ related.

316

SELF TEST FOR MASTERY

Select the best answer.

1. Which of the following is a definition for the marginal cost of work?

    a. The value of the time and toil involved in a job
    b. The wage
    c. The value of extra leisure time given up to work
    d. The additional production costs associated with the use of an additional unit of labor

2. The extra income received from extra work, including any nonmonetary satisfaction obtained from a job, is called:

    a. Total pecuniary benefits.
    b. The marginal benefit of work.
    c. External benefits.
    d. The wage rate.
    e. Nonpecuniary satisfaction.

3. In order to maximize the net benefits from work, an individual should work additional hours up to the point where:

    a. The total costs of labor equal the total benefits of labor.
    b. The wage equals marginal revenue.
    c. Marginal revenue is greater than marginal labor cost.
    d. The marginal cost of work equals the marginal benefit of work.

4. An individual's labor supply curve:

    a. Is upward sloping if the substitution effect outweighs the income effect of a wage change.
    b. Represents combinations of wage rates and quantities of labor hours supplied.
    c. Is an equilibrium relationship in that each coordinate point on the curve is a net benefit-maximizing quantity of hours supplied at that wage rate.
    d. May have sections that are upward sloping, downward sloping and even vertical.
    e. All of the above.

5. If the market wage rises such that an individual's wage exceeds the marginal cost of work and assuming that the substitution effect is dominant, the individual will maximize net benefits from work by:

    a. Working additional hours.
    b. Working fewer hours.
    c. Consuming more leisure.
    d. Consuming the same quantity of leisure.

6. The backward-bending portion of a labor supply curve occurs:

    a. When wages equal the firm's marginal product.
    b. Where the substitution effect outweighs the income effect.
    c. Only rarely and at low levels of income.
    d. Where the income effect outweighs the substitution effect.

7. Which of the following is a determinant of the market supply curve for labor?

    a. Population growth
    b. Rate of labor force participation
    c. Birth rate
    d. Extent of immigration
    e. All of the above

8. Investment in capital _____ labor productivity, resulting in a _____ shift in the market _____ curve for labor.

    a. Decreases, leftward, supply
    b. Decreases, rightward, demand
    c. Increases, rightward, demand
    d. Increases, leftward, demand

9. The "baby boom" caused the market _____ curve for labor to shift _____, resulting in a/an _____ in market wages, others things held constant.

    a. Supply, rightward, decrease
    b. Demand, leftward, increase
    c. Supply, leftward, increase
    d. Demand, rightward, decrease

10. Training and education:

    a. Are investments in human capital.
    b. Increase the productivity of labor.
    c. Increase a nation's living standards because of the increase in labor productivity.
    d. Are one explanation for wage differences between different jobs and workers.
    e. All of the above.

11. Which of the following is an example of nonpecuniary wages?

    a. Hourly wage rate
    b. Air-conditioned workplace
    c. Health and retirement benefits
    d. Stock options

12. Which of the following is an example of nonpecuniary job benefits?

    a. Flexible work hours
    b. Opportunities for advancement
    c. Nonhazardous job
    d. Pleasant job or local amenities
    e. All of the above

13. If two jobs, job A and job B, are identical with the exception that job B is associated with nonpecuniary job benefits, job A will pay _____ job B.

    a. A higher wage than
    b. A lower wage than
    c. The same wage as
    d. None of the above

14. Firms often have a preference for promoting existing employees to fill new or vacant positions. Which of the following terms represents this concept?

    a. Staffing
    b. Signals
    c. Screening
    d. Internal labor market

15. Shirking by management and labor results when:

    a. Lazy employees are hired.
    b. The interests of owners, management, and workers coincide.
    c. Goods and services are produced by government but never when private firms produce output.
    d. The interests of owners, management, and workers do not coincide.

16. Shirking on the job:

    a. Is a problem unless a compensation system is devised in which managers and workers are induced to pursue the owner's goals for the firm.
    b. Is an insignificant problem because monitoring eliminates it.
    c. Is most efficiently reduced with monitoring.
    d. Is most efficiently reduced by compensation systems such as stock options and profit sharing, particularly if monitoring is costly.
    e. A and d.

THINK IT THROUGH

1. Why does the opportunity cost of leisure rise as an individual works additional hours per day?

2. If two occupations located in the same city and requiring the same skills, education, and experience pay different wage rates, there must be discrimination. True or false? Explain.

3. If two individuals working in the same occupation receive different wage rates, there must be discrimination. True or false? Explain.

4. If workers and managers have goals other than the owner's goal of profit maximization, explain how shirking arises and its implications for the firm and for the economy's allocation of resources. How can owners deal with the shirking problem?

POP QUIZ

Read the news brief at the end of this chapter and answer the questions below.

1. According to the article, why has real hourly pay of blue-collar and clerical workers remained roughly constant over the last 15 years? (Indicate the influences affecting the demand for and supply of labor.)

2. Explain, in terms of supply of and demand for labor, why real wages are expected to rise in the future.

CHAPTER ANSWERS

In Brief: Chapter Summary

1. Marginal benefits 2. Value of a forgone hour of leisure 3. Necessary 4. Benefits 5. More 6. Less 7. Upward sloping 8. Backward bending 9. Vertical 10. Increase 11. Nonpecuniary wages 12. Equal to 13. Personnel 14. Efficient, low-cost 15. But that increases 16. Lower

Vocabulary Review

1. Human capital 2. Nonpecuniary wages 3. Backward-Bending labor supply curve 4. Compensating wage differential 5. Income effect of a wage change 6. Signals 7. Substitution effect of a wage change 8. Staffing 9. Labor supply curve 10. Screening 11. Marginal benefit of work 12. Shirking 13. Marginal cost of work 14. Internal labor market 15. Nonwage money income

Skills Review

1. a.

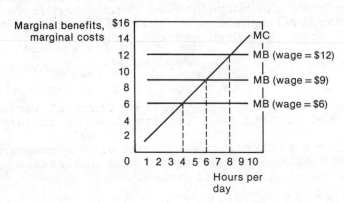

   b.   10, 6 c. 8, 8 d. 4, 12

   e.

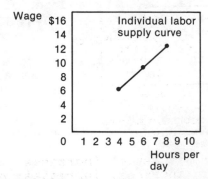

   f.   Marginal cost of work

2. a. Net benefits from work are maximized where the marginal cost of work equals the marginal benefit of work. Setting MB equal to MC and solving for H yields the net benefit-maximizing level of hours worked.

   $$H = (W1 - a)/b$$

   b. A change in a shifts the marginal cost of work curve, whereas a change in b changes the slope of the curve. An increase in a or b decreases hours worked. Anything that causes Fred's marginal cost of work to increase relative to the prevailing wage will cause Fred to work less and vice versa. For instance, if Fred receives news that he has a terminal illness, the value of extra leisure time given up to work would increase. The marginal cost curve would shift upward, and Fred would work less. An increase in the market wage will increase Fred's hours worked and vice versa.

   c.   Fred's willingness to work an additional hour is based on the wage received and available for expenditure. Taxes reduce spendable wages. It is necessary to reduce the before-tax wage by the amount of the tax.

$$Wa = \text{After-tax wage} = (1 - t)W1$$

Inserting Wa in the expression above for the net benefit-maximizing hours worked gives

$$H = [(1 - t)W1 - a]/b$$

Since t is a positive fraction, Fred's hours worked after taxes are imposed are less than the hours worked before the imposition of a wage tax. The marginal benefits of work fall relative to the marginal cost of work, and Fred reduces hours worked.

3.   a.   Positive, outweighs b. No, just offsets the c. Inverse, is less than

4.   a.   Population. The "baby boom" affects the number of workers entering the labor force and results in a rightward shift in labor supply curves.

   b.   Rates of labor force participation. Even with a constant population, if more people are entering the labor force and seeking employment, labor supply curves will shift rightward.

5.   a.

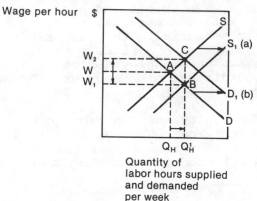

Wage per hour $

Quantity of labor hours supplied and demanded per week

       Market supply, rightward; decrease, increases

   b.   Market demand, rightward; increase, increases; positively

Self-Test for Mastery

1. c 2. b 3. d 4. e 5. a 6. d 7. e 8. c 9. a 10. e 11. b 12. e 13. a 14. d 15. d 16. e

Think it Through

1.   Assuming an individual sleeps 8 hours per day, there are 16 hours to be allocated between work and leisure. An additional hour worked means that an additional hour of leisure is sacrificed. Because of diminishing marginal utility (or benefits), the value of an hour of leisure rises as less leisure

time is available. Therefore the opportunity cost of an hour worked rises as more hours are worked and fewer hours are available for leisure.

2.   There may be discrimination, but the difference in wage could be due to compensating wage differentials paid to compensate the worker for undesirable aspects of the job or because of the presence of nonpecuniary job benefits that allow employers to pay a lower wage. In both cases, total compensation received by the worker is the same even though wages differ. The individual working in the job with nonpecuniary job benefits receives a portion of his total compensation from the pleasant or desirable nonmonetary benefits of the job.

3.   There may be discrimination, but a wage differential between two workers in the same occupation could also be due to differences in the productivity or quality of the two workers. It could also be due to regional differences in labor markets, including regional differences in product prices that may affect marginal revenue products. Regional amenities (weather, sports, fine arts, education, etc.) vary, thus affecting the nonpecuniary benefits associated with a given occupation located in different regions.

4.   Assume that individuals maximize utility whether they are owners, workers, or managers. Owners maximize utility in part by maximizing the return to their invested resources--by maximizing profits. Workers and managers maximize utility by engaging in activities that give satisfaction. This may include earning income, consuming goods and services, exercising power, achieving job security, achieving prestige, and so on. If a firm's compensation system is not designed to encourage both workers and managers to seek the owner's goal of profit maximization, workers and managers will shirk on the job. They will, within the constraints of the job, engage in activities that enhance their welfare but do not necessarily maximize the firm's profits. Managers may decorate their offices with expensive furniture and art and hire attractive but possibly inefficient secretaries. Workers will likely not maximize their effort per hour worked in earning a wage income and assuring themselves of job security and promotion opportunities. The marginal products of managers and workers alike will not be at their potential. The firm's costs of production will be higher, and owners will not receive maximum profit. The economy is less efficient in that resources are underemployed because maximum output is not being achieved from a given complement of resources. The economy is inside its production possibilities curve.

A firm can use stock options or an employment contract to encourage a manager to increase profits. If the manager's compensation is tied to the firm's profits, the manager will make more decisions consistent with the interests of the owner. Workers also can be motivated to seek the owner's profit goals with profit-sharing wage contracts.

Pop Quiz

1.   A number of factors have been responsible for the lack of growth in the real hourly wages of blue-collar and clerical workers over the last 15 years. On the supply side of the labor markets, the baby-boom generation increased the supply of labor and the labor force participation rate increased due to the entry of teenagers and women. Further, the decline in union power meant that unions were decreasingly able to manipulate the supply side of labor markets. On the demand side of the labor markets, the economy at times has been stagnant, resulting in a reduction in the demand for labor. Increased competition in international markets and deregulation held down prices and marginal revenue products. The rate of saving and investment in capital decreased, reducing the marginal products of labor. In short, the supply of labor was increasing faster than the demand for labor, keeping real hourly wages from rising.

2.   Real wages are expected to rise over the next few years because the labor force is expected to grow less rapidly due to a decline in population growth and immigration laws preventing the entry of illegal aliens. Another cause of the expected increase in real wages is an anticipated increase in saving and capital investment. The supply of labor is expected to fall relative to the demand for labor, causing wages to rise.

Wage Stagnation May Be Ending

By WILLIAM A. COX

The presumed American birthright of rising living standards has been on hold for 15 years. Average hourly pay of blue-collar and clerical workers is slightly lower in purchasing power now than it was in 1973 and has made no progress even in the prosperous mid-1980s. Counting managers, professionals, other self-employed people, and the rising share of employee compensation received as fringe benefits, real earnings per hour have increased only 0.7% a year from 1973 through 1987.

Income per capita has risen faster than income per hour because a larger share of the adult population is working more hours per capita. In other words, we are working harder for it, and this has its cost in leisure, child care, and home-cooked meals. Per-capita income also rose faster than hourly pay because of the faster rise in interest income and Social Security.

The reasons for stagnant real wages will be much debated in this election year. But this epoch may now be ending, regardless of who becomes the next president.

Erosion of Unions

The world's postwar economic boom foundered in the 1970s just when the U.S. labor force was growing at a pace unmatched since early in the century. Pay fell behind oil-fueled price rises partly because plentiful young workers were a drag on productivity. Young and other marginal workers, including swelling ranks of low-income single mothers, lost ground rapidly relative to others in the general retrenchment in the 1980s.

Intense foreign competition, due mainly to exchange-rate maladjustments, held down wages (as well as prices and profits) in the mid-1980s in all industries exposed to international competition. Some of the lag in average wages stemmed from erosion of union wage scales that were out of line with the rest of the economy. Union wages in manufacturing, construction and transportation have been undermined by spreading nonunion competition. Federal deregulation of the airline and trucking industries accelerated the breakdown of their sheltered wage and price structures by allowing new competition in markets that for decades had been protected.

An important fact explaining the stagnation of productivity and real wages is that bumper crops of new workers were not matched by faster additions to capital. Total hours worked in the private economy grew by only 0.5% a year from 1950 through 1968 but three times as fast from 1969 through 1986. But the wherewithal and motivation for business investment did not suddenly increase with swelling labor supplies. According to the Commerce Department, the net stock of fixed capital in private business expanded more slowly in the later period, as economic growth slowed and profitability declined. Since its peak postwar growth rates of the mid-1960s, net private capital has grown more slowly in each successive business upswing, including the present one. The amount of capital per hour worked has continued to grow, but only about half as fast as before 1968.

Given the drop in domestic saving and extremely high real interest rates since 1979, it is remarkable investment has not slowed by more. Private saving as a share of gross national product was sustained in the 1970s by rising corporate saving (undistributed profits), which offset the decline in personal saving. But corporate saving plunged during the 1980-82 recession and never recovered, while personal saving, after rising in 1978-81, resumed its fall.

The federal government, moreover, had deficits (dissaving) that averaged 0.1% of GNP from 1950 through 1969; during that period, deficits exceeded 1% of GNP only during five years of recession or war. But in 13 of the 19 years from 1970 to date, deficits have been at least 2% of GNP and usually much larger. Since 1980 they have averaged 4%.

As a result, net national saving—the sum of personal, corporate and government saving—which averaged 8% of GNP from 1950 to 1979, has fallen to 3.1% from 1980 through 1987. Partly for this reason, real interest rates (represented here by Treasury bill rates minus concurrent consumer inflation), which ranged between 1% and 2% traditionally and were negative during most of the 1970s, averaged 3.7% from 1979 through 1987.

Starting in 1979, the number of teenagers reaching working age began to fall. Labor-force growth plummeted from 2.9% annually in 1978 and 1979, peak years of the last business cycle, to 1.7% in 1985 through 1987. This scarcity of newly trained young workers will intensify until the mid-1990s, with little relief even then. The 1986 immigration law, moreover, limits labor-force growth further by curtailing illegal aliens' access to jobs.

The Labor Department recently forecast that labor-force growth will average only 1.2% annually from 1986 through 2000, assuming that the new law is partially effective in curtailing illegal workers. This means a return to labor-supply conditions of the 1950s, except that many more of the future new workers will be minority and female workers.

With labor scarcity wages will rise, especially for entry-level workers, regardless of minimum-wage legislation. Employers

---

Opportunities for inexperienced and poorly educated workers will be revolutionized. Conditions favor a reduction in the poverty rate among female-headed households.

---

will have to take much more vigorous measures to recruit and train workers. Firms incurring those "start-up" costs will improve amenities to retain people. Opportunities for inexperienced and poorly educated workers will be revolutionized. This makes a shift from welfare to workfare very timely and suggests that improved child-care and work-sharing arrangements are the wave of the future. Conditions favor a reduction in the high rate of poverty among female-headed households.

Effects on wages of the deregulation moves of the late 1970s have nearly run their course. The exchange-rate maladjustment, which depressed U.S. industries, has now been corrected, and American producers are coming back strong. Thus wage catch-up is likely to replace wage givebacks as labor's agenda in the future.

The $64 billion question is whether supplies of home-grown saving available for investment will recover. The federal deficit has been reduced from 5.2% of GNP in 1983 to about 3.2% in 1988, although the improvement was more than offset by the remarkable drying up of private saving. The Gramm-Rudman-Hollings law requires the deficit to be eliminated, and steadily rising surpluses in the Social Security trust fund suggest that the overall budget may in fact be balanced sometime in the 1990s and could move into surplus for 20 years or so.

A big question mark hangs over the future of private savings, corporate as well as personal, both of which are at historic lows. But there may be hope. Corporate saving did not recover from its plunge of the early 1980s because of poor profits in industries facing international competition and woe in the financial sector. Profitability in manufacturing, insurance and commercial banking is now being restored. Even the personal saving rate could rise gradually as the baby-boomers finish acquiring initial stocks of automobiles, housing and equipment, and move into a stage of life characterized by greater saving.

A shift toward scarcer labor and more plentiful capital—the reverse of conditions that marked the past 15 years—would raise returns to labor relative to capital. Scarcity of labor is an imminent certainty. A rise in domestic saving, evolving over several years, could result in a long-term decline in real interest rates from today's inordinate levels. Rising wages and lower capital costs would strengthen incentives for labor-saving investment, boosting capital-labor ratios and productivity. Faster growing productivity is the missing link to convert faster rising wages into rising real living standards.

Foreign Debt

With today's global capital markets, however, an increase in American saving could flow into investments abroad if returns are higher there. The earnings would help to cover payments on the recent buildup of foreign-held assets in this country, but the productivity and wage gains would go to foreigners. The extent to which savings will flow abroad depends in part on the extent to which technology development creates attractive new investment opportunities in this country.

The bill to service the foreign-debt buildup of the 1980s is coming due. This will divert some future income gains abroad. How large this burden will become depends on two interrelated factors: How fast the U.S. saving rate rises and how fast the trade deficit declines. In any event, faster-growing productivity and real wages would make the burden easier to bear and leave more for renewed gains in American living standards.

Mr. Cox was deputy chief economist at the Commerce Department, 1978-81, and now specializes in economic policy at the Congressional Research Service.

22

Imperfectively Competitive Input Markets: Labor Unions, Monopsony, and Bilateral Monopoly

CHAPTER CHALLENGES

After studying your text, attending class, and completing this chapter, you should be able to:

1. Describe the goals and purposes of labor unions.
2. Show how labor union practices can influence wages and affect the productivity of workers.
3. Describe the hiring practices of a monopsony firm and show how such a firm sets input prices.
4. Show how conflicts in input markets arise when monopoly and monopsony are simultaneously present.

IN BRIEF: CHAPTER SUMMARY

Fill in the blanks to summarize chapter content.

Labor unions engage in collective bargaining to win higher wages and better working conditions and to achieve other goals. In (1)_____ (imperfectly competitive, competitive) product markets, labor unions can only succeed in getting higher wages if the entire industry is unionized. A union must erect barriers to entry to jobs for which it has been able to raise wages. It must also be able to prevent workers from making side agreements with employers.

The earliest unions in the United States were (2)_____ (craft, industrial) unions. The modern union movement began in 1886 with the (3)_____ (Congress of Industrial Organizations, CIO; American Federation of Labor, AFL), which included craft unions composed of skilled workers. In 1935, the (4)_____ (Congress of Industrial Organizations, CIO; American Federation of Labor, AFL) organized industrial unions. A/An (5)_____ (craft, industrial) union organizes all types of labor within an industry, regardless of skill level. In 1955, the AFL and CIO merged. Federal legislation prohibits closed shops and featherbedding, but allows states to pass right-to-work laws. The federal government can intervene and issue an injunction to delay a strike for a period of time. The labor movement has (6)_____ (declined since it peaked, expanded since it bottomed out) in the 1950s. As of 1984, only (7)_____ (35%, 16.1%) of U.S. workers belonged to unions.

Unions try to increase wages by (8)_____ (expanding, restricting) the supply of labor or imposing an above-market equilibrium wage through the collective bargaining process. Unions (9)_____ (can also; cannot, however,) raise wages by promoting demand for the products they produce. If collective bargaining ends in stalemate, arbitrators will be used to mediate the issues. Evidence indicates that the average wage differential between unionized and nonunionized industries is between (10)_____ (25% and 33%,

10% and 20%) with the differential being much larger for certain industries or occupations. Evidence also indicates that a unionized work force is (11)_____ (more, less) stable, reliable, and productive than a nonunionized work force.

A pure (12)_____ (monopoly, monopsony) exists when there is a single buyer of an input that has few if any alternative employment opportunities. A monopsonist can set wage rates and other input prices. Because the monopsonist is the sole employer of the market supply of an input, it must pay higher input prices to induce input suppliers to make additional inputs available. But the higher input prices have to be paid not only to the new employees but to all existing employees as well. The monopsonist's marginal input cost (13)_____ (equals, exceeds) the wage rate (or average input cost). A profit-maximizing monopsonist will hire inputs up to the point at which the (14)_____ (marginal cost of an input, wage) equals the input's marginal revenue product. A monopsonist pays a wage (15)_____ (equal to, below) the marginal input cost of labor and the worker's marginal revenue product. The (16)_____ (competitive labor market, monopsonist) hires fewer workers and pays a lower wage than employers in a (17)_____ (competitive, monopsonistic) labor market.

A (18)_____ (bilateral monopoly, pure monopsony) exists when the demand side of an input market is represented by a monopsonist and the supply side is represented by a monopoly seller. Through the collective bargaining process a monopoly seller of an input such as a labor union can win a wage above the wage desired by the monopsonist, resulting in (19)_____ (less, higher) employment and higher wages that are closer to or equal to the worker's marginal revenue product.

VOCABULARY REVIEW

Write the key term from the list below next to its definition.

Key Terms

Labor union   Pure monopsony
Monopsony   Monopsony power
Collective bargaining   Marginal input cost
Craft union   Average input cost
Industrial union   Bilateral monopoly
Closed shop

Definitions

1. _____: exists when only one buyer and one seller trade input (or output) services in a market.

2. _____: a union that represents all workers in a particular industry, regardless of their craft or skill.

3. _____: a single firm that buys the entire market supply of an input that has few if any alternative employment opportunities.

4. _____: an organization of workers in a particular skilled job, such as plumbers, electricians, carpenters, or musicians.

5. _____: the ability of a single buyer to influence the prices of some of the input services it purchases.

6. _____: the process of negotiating for wages and
   improvements in working conditions between a labor union and employers.

7. _____: the change in total input cost associated with a
   change in input services hired.

8. _____: a single buyer with no rivals in an input market.

9. _____: the price of an input.

10. _____: an organization formed to represent the interests
    of workers in bargaining with employers for contracts concerning wages,
    fringe benefits, and working conditions.

11. _____: a union arrangement with an employer that permits
    hiring only of union members.

SKILLS REVIEW

Concept: Labor union practices

1. Match the union legislation listed below to the following descriptions.

        Norris-LaGuardia Act (1932)
        Wagner Act (1935)
        Fair Labor Standards Act (1938)
        Taft-Hartley Act (1947)

    a. _____   allowed states to establish right-to-work laws
    b. _____   outlawed featherbedding
    c. _____   outlawed child labor
    d. _____   limited the power of federal courts to intervene in
                         labor disputes
    e. _____   prohibited closed shops
    f. _____   was established to protect workers against unfair
                         labor practices
    g. _____   gave courts the right to issue injunctions to delay
                         strikes
    h. _____   guaranteed workers the right to form unions

2. The diagram below represents a competitive labor market with Wc and Lc representing the market wage rate and the level of employment, respectively.

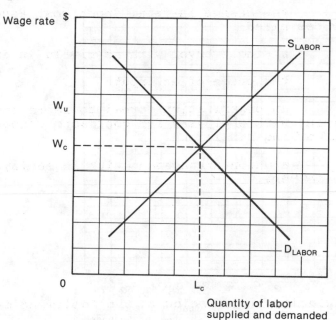

Wage rate $

S_{LABOR}

W_u

W_c

D_{LABOR}

0   L_c

Quantity of labor
supplied and demanded
per week

a. Show on the figure above the effect of a union-imposed wage rate of Wu. Employment is _____ (higher, lower) than for the case of a competitive labor market.

b. Show on the figure above the effect of an union policy of limiting the quantity of labor supplied in order to increase wages to Wu. Employment is _____ (higher, lower) than for the case of a competitive labor market.

c. The union-desired wage of Wu could alternatively be achieved by promoting or advertising the product produced by the union's members. Show on the figure above the effect of this approach. Employment is _____ (higher, lower) than for the case of a competitive labor market.

Concept: Hiring practices of a monopsonist

3. A large textile firm has a plant located in a small rural town and is virtually the town's only employer. Residents of the town are too far away from other communities to commute to a job. Therefore they have no alternative employment opportunities. Below are data for the town's labor supply and the textile firm's marginal revenue product schedule.

Wages per Day	Labor Hours Supplied per Day	Total Cost of Labor	Marginal Input Cost of Labor	Marginal Revenue Product
$50	600	$_____		
55	700	_____	$_____	$175
60	800	_____	_____	155
65	900	_____	_____	135
70	1,000	_____	_____	115
75	1,100	_____	_____	95
80	1,200	_____	_____	75

329

a. Complete the table above and plot the marginal input cost of labor, labor supply, and marginal revenue product curves in the figure below.

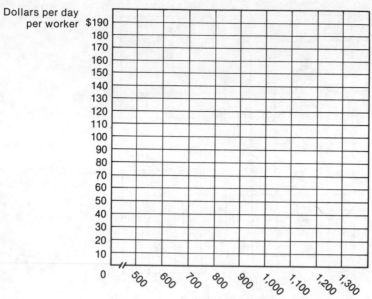

Dollars per day per worker

$190
180
170
160
150
140
130
120
110
100
90
80
70
60
50
40
30
20
10
0

500 600 700 800 900 1,000 1,100 1,200 1,300

Quantity of labor supplied and demanded per day

b. A profit-maximizing monopsonist will equate _____ and _____ and hire _____ workers and pay a wage equal to $_____.

c. The monopsonist's wage _____ the worker's marginal revenue product.

d. Assume that the labor market above is a competitive labor market having the same demand for labor as the textile firm. As compared to a perfectly competitive labor market, a monopsonist pays a _____ wage and hires _____ workers. Show this in the figure above.

Concept: Simultaneous presence of monopoly and monopsony in input markets

4. Assume that a monopsonist such as the one in the preceding problem is confronted by a union representing all workers in the town. The monopsony labor market is shown below.

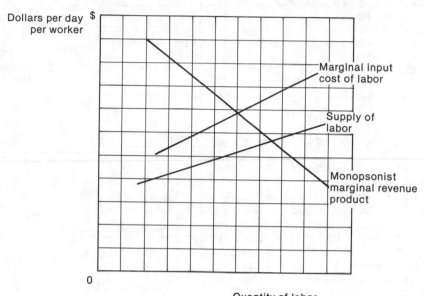

Dollars per day $
per worker

Marginal input
cost of labor

Supply of
labor

Monopsonist
marginal revenue
product

0

Quantity of labor
supplied and demanded
per day

    a. Suppose now that a monopoly union is able to win a union-desired wage of Wu, which is above the wage preferred by the monopsonist, Wm. On the figure above identify the monopsony wage and employment and label them Wm and Lm, respectively. Show the effect on employment of a union wage, Wu, greater than Wm.
    b. For the case of bilateral monopoly, the wage will equal labor's marginal revenue product if the union wage is equal to or greater than the wage at which the _____ curve intersects the _____ curve.

SELF-TEST FOR MASTERY

Select the best answer.

1. An organization formed to represent the interests of workers is called a/an:

    a. Trade association.
    b. Monopsony.
    c. Labor union.
    d. Industrial organization.

2. A goal or objective of unions is to:

    a. Improve job safety.
    b. Increase wages.
    c. Achieve job security.
    d. All of the above.

3. If a union is successful in raising wages for some firms in a perfectly competitive industry:

    a. The firms will exit the industry in the long run.
    b. The firms will not be covering normal profits.
    c. The gains in wages by workers will be short lived.
    d. All of the above.

4. Which of the following acts outlawed child labor?

    a. Norris-LaGuardia Act of 1932
    b. Wagner Act of 1935
    c. Fair Labor Standards Act of 1938
    d. Taft-Hartley Act of 1947

5. Which of the following acts prohibited closed shops?

    a. Norris-LaGuardia Act of 1932
    b. Wagner Act of 1935
    c. Fair Labor Standards Act of 1938
    d. Taft-Hartley Act of 1947

6. Labor was guaranteed the right to form unions by the:

    a. Norris-LaGuardia Act of 1932.
    b. Wagner Act of 1935.
    c. Fair Labor Standards Act of 1938.
    d. Taft-Hartley Act of 1947.

7. Which of the following organizations is a federation of unions representing skilled labor as well as all types of labor in given industries?

    a. American Federation of Labor
    b. United Mine Workers
    c. United Rubber Workers
    d. Congress of Industrial Unions
    e. AFL-CIO

8. Union membership peaked in the _____, but was _____% of all workers in 1984.

    a. 1920s, 20%
    b. 1930s, 40%
    c. 1940s, 18.1%
    d. 1950s, 16.1%
    e. 1960s, 24.2%

9. Which of the following is not usually practiced by unions as a means to raise wages?

    a. Investing in capital to increase worker productivity
    b. Restricting the supply of labor
    c. Imposing a union wage through the collective bargaining process
    d. Advertising or promoting the product produced with union labor

10. If unions increase wages by restricting the supply of labor or by getting a higher wage through negotiation:

    a. Labor is unquestionably better off.
    b. Industry employment actually increases.

c.   Industry employment decreases.
d.   Total wages received by labor as a group must increase.

11. A union may support a restrictive tariff on the import of foreign products because:

a.   Domestic product prices are likely to increase.
b.   The marginal revenue product of labor in the protected industries will increase.
c.   Wages paid in the protected industries will rise.
d.   All of the above.

12. Empirical evidence indicates that unions have raised average wages in unionized as compared to nonunionized industries by:

a.   5% to 50%.
b.   10% to 20%.
c.   25% to 33%.
d.   16.1% to 24%.
e.   13%.

13. Evidence indicates that union work forces are _____ reliable and stable than nonunionized work forces and collective bargaining may _____ labor productivity.

a.   Less, decrease
b.   More, decrease
c.   Less, increase
d.   More, increase

14. A single firm that buys the entire market supply of an input is called:

a.   A monopolist.
b.   An oligopoly.
c.   A multinational firm.
d.   A labor federation.
e.   A pure monopsonist.

15. A monopsonist pays a wage that is _____ than the marginal cost of labor and is _____ than the worker's marginal revenue product.

a.   Less, less
b.   Greater, less
c.   Greater, greater
d.   Less, greater

16. As compared to a competitive input market, a monopsonist pays a _____ wage and employs _____ workers.

a.   Lower, more
b.   Higher, fewer
c.   Lower, fewer
d.   Higher, more

17. A monopsonist employs an input up to the point at which the _____ equals the _____.

a.   Wage, supply curve
b.   Marginal cost, marginal product
c.   Wage, marginal cost
d.   Marginal input cost, marginal revenue product of the input

e.   None of the above

18. The marginal input cost curve of a monopsonist:

a.   Lies above the market input supply curve.
b.   Is more steeply sloped than the market input supply curve.
c.   Differs from the input supply curve because the monopsonist must not only pay higher input prices to attract additional inputs, but must also pay these higher prices to the suppliers of inputs currently employed.
d.   Together with the marginal revenue product curve determines the profit-maximizing level of employment.
e.   All of the above.

19. Which of the following best defines a market in which only one buyer and one seller trade input services?

a.   Monopoly
b.   Monopsony
c.   Bilateral monopsony
d.   Bilateral monopoly

20. With bilateral monopoly, if unions can _____ wages, employment will _____ and the wage will come closer to or even equal the worker's _____.

a.   Increase, decrease, marginal input cost
b.   Increase, increase, marginal product
c.   Increase, increase, marginal revenue product
d.   Increase, decrease, marginal revenue product

THINK IT THROUGH

1.   Explain why union attempts to raise wages in competitive firms will fail unless the entire competitive industry is unionized.

2.   Compare and contrast the case of a monopsonist selling in a competitive product market with the case of a monopsonist that is also a monopolist in its product market.

3.   Is it possible for the power of a monopoly union to just offset the power of a monopsonist such that wage and employment levels are the same as they would be in a competitive labor market? Explain.

4.   Discuss the social gains and losses associated with unionism.

CHAPTER ANSWERS

In Brief: Chapter Summary

1. Competitive 2. Craft 3. American Federation of Labor, AFL 4. Congress of Industrial Organizations, CIO 5. Industrial 6. Declined since it peaked 7. 16.1% 8. Restricting 9. Can also 10. 10% and 20% 11. More 12. Monopsony 13. Exceeds 14. Marginal cost of an input 15. Below 16. Monopsonist 17. Competitive 18. Bilateral monopoly 19. Higher

Vocabulary Review

1. Bilateral monopoly 2. Industrial union 3. Pure monopsony 4. Craft union
5. Monopsony power 6. Collective bargaining 7. Marginal input cost 8.
Monopsony 9. Average input cost 10. Labor union 11. Closed shop

Skills Review

1. a. Taft-Hartley Act b. Taft-Hartley Act c. Fair Labor Standards Act d.
    Norris-LaGuardia Act e. Taft-Hartley Act f. Wagner Act g. Taft-Hartley
    Act h. Wagner Act

2.

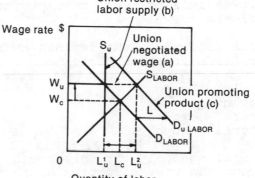

    a. lower b. lower c. higher

3. a.

Total Cost of Labor	Marginal Input Cost of Labor
$30,000	$
38,500	85
48,000	95
58,500	105
70,000	115
82,500	125
96,000	135

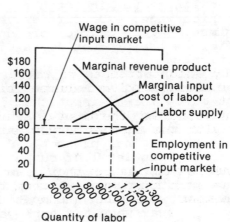

    b. Marginal input cost of labor, marginal revenue product of labor,
        1,000, $70
    c. Is less than
    d. Lower, fewer

4.   a.

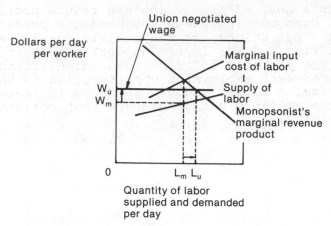

Dollars per day per worker

Union negotiated wage

Marginal input cost of labor

Supply of labor

Monopsonist's marginal revenue product

W_u
W_m

0   L_m L_u

Quantity of labor supplied and demanded per day

   b.   Labor supply curve, marginal revenue product curve

Self-Test for Mastery

1. c   2. d   3. d   4. c   5. d   6. b   7. e   8. d   9. a   10. c   11. d   12. b   13. d   14. e   15. a   16. c   17. d   18. e   19. d   20. c

Think it Through

1.   In competitive long-run equilibrium, the firm is just earning normal profits and zero economic profits. If a union is successful in raising wages in a few of the industry's firms but not the entire industry, these firms will continue to sell at the prevailing market price but will have higher costs of production. The owners will not earn sufficient normal profits to keep them in the industry. In time, they will exit the industry and their employees will be unemployed or no longer working at the union wage. If all firms in the industry face a higher union wage, each firm's average cost and marginal cost curves rise. The minimum average cost of production is at a higher level, and in long-run equilibrium the product price will rise to equal the minimum average cost of production.

2.   A monopsonist selling in a competitive product market has a marginal revenue product curve for an input that is found by multiplying product price times the input's marginal product. A monopsonist that is also a monopolist in its product market derives its marginal revenue product curve by multiplying marginal revenue by marginal product. Since marginal revenue is less than product price at a given level of output, the monopoly monopsonist will have a marginal revenue product curve that lies inside the competitive monopsonist's marginal revenue product curve. A competitive monopsonist pays a lower wage and employs fewer workers than a competitive input market. But a monopoly monopsonist pays a lower wage and employs even fewer workers than a competitive monopsonist.

3.   Interestingly, it is possible to achieve the competitive market wage and level of employment in the case of a bilateral monopoly if the collective bargaining process results in a negotiated wage above the monopsonist wage such that the negotiated wage is at a level that equates the supply of and demand for labor (where the labor supply curve intersects the marginal revenue product curve). This assumes that competitive employers have the same aggregate marginal revenue product as the monopsonist. Wages and employment are at their competitive levels, and the wage equals the worker's marginal revenue product.

4.   Unions add to a firm's cost of production and reduce profits received by the owners of the firm. Consumers purchase the products produced by union members at higher prices. But unions are responsible for increasing average wages in unionized industries and for improving working conditions. Wages in nonunionized industries are probably lower because unionization results in fewer jobs. The unemployed seek employment opportunities in the nonunionized labor markets, thus depressing market wages. Evidence indicates, however, that union work forces are more reliable and stable and that collective bargaining increases worker productivity.

23
Interest, Rents, and Profit

After studying your text, attending class, and completing this chapter, you should be able to:

1. Explain the concepts of capital and investment and show how the interest rate represents a crucial price influencing investment in new capital.
2. Analyze investment decisions and show how the interest rate affects those decisions.
3. Outline the influences on the supply of and demand for loanable funds that affect the equilibrium interest rate for various types of loans in a competitive market.
4. Explain how land rents are determined in competitive markets.
5. Understand how profit opportunities arise in an economy and how entrepreneurs seize those opportunities for personal gain.

IN BRIEF: CHAPTER SUMMARY

Fill in the blanks to summarize chapter content.

In addition to wages, other types of income include rents, interest, and profit. (1)_____ (Interest, Rent, Profit) is a payment for the use of borrowed funds. (2)_____ (Interest is, Rents are, Profits are) paid to acquire land. (3)_____ (Interest arises, Rents arise, Profits arise) from the production and sale of output and accrues to the owners of businesses.

Businesses invest in (4)_____ (stocks, physical capital) either to replace worn-out capital or to expand capacity. Individuals invest in (5)_____ (financial assets, human capital) to increase their productivity and value in the market place. (6)_____ (Saving, Borrowing) is the income not consumed during the year that is available for capital investment. Investment in capital will take place up to the point at which the marginal revenue product from additional capital is (7)_____ (greater than, just equal to) the marginal input cost of capital. Expressed in percentage terms, investment will take place up to the point at which the (8)_____ (marginal return on investment, marginal revenue product of an investment) is just equal to the market rate of interest.

The loanable funds market determines the market rate of interest which, in turn, determines the profit-maximizing level of investment. A/An (9)_____ (decrease, increase) in the demand for loanable funds increases the market interest rate above the marginal return on investment and results in a/an (10)_____ (decrease, increase) in investment and vice versa. The expected marginal return on an investment is the present value of the stream of expected returns over the life of the investment project expressed as a percentage return. Future returns must be discounted to obtain their current or present value because dollars received in the future (11)_____ (are not worth as much as, are worth more than) the same amount of dollars received today. Dollars today could be invested at the prevailing market rate of interest, resulting in more future dollars. The (12)_____ (present value, cost) of an investment project is the sum of the discounted future returns over the life of the project. An increase in the interest rate (13)_____ (increases, reduces) the present value, whereas a decrease in the interest rate (14)_____ (increases, reduces) the present value. Firms will find it profitable to invest if the present value of an investment project (15)_____ (exceeds, is just equal to) its present cost. In perfectly competitive capital markets, the price of a capital asset is (16)_____ (less than, equal to) the present value of the asset.

The demand for and supply of loanable funds determine the market rate of interest and thus influence the present value of an investment project, affecting its profitability or desirability. The demand for loanable funds is (17)_____ (downward sloping, upward sloping) and can shift in response to changes in business expectations regarding future sales as well as improvements in technology that affect the marginal revenue product of new capital. Households and government likewise demand loanable funds, but for different reasons. The market supply of loanable funds is (18)_____ (downward sloping, upward sloping) because people require more than a dollar of future consumption for each dollar saved (or not consumed). The additional compensation is in the form of higher interest rates. Also higher interest rates increase the opportunity cost to firms of holding idle funds or using those funds internally. As businesses minimize their holdings of idle balances and internal funds in response to higher interest rates, more funds are made available to the loanable funds market.

While the general level of interest rates is determined by the supply of and demand for loanable funds, specific rates of interest are affected by such factors as the risk associated with an investment or a loan, the length of a loan or maturity of a bond, the amount of collateral pledged to a lender, and the tax treatment of the asset. Higher risk requires (19)_____ (lower, higher) interest rates to compensate risk-averse individuals; otherwise they will invest in less risky projects. A lender may charge a (20)_____ (lower, higher) interest rate on a personal loan that is not collateralized as compensation for a greater exposure to risk of default. A tax-exempt bond with a low interest rate can still compete with taxed financial assets having higher yields for a portion of the available pool of savings because the after-tax yields are the same for both assets.

Rents are determined by the supply of and demand for usable land. Demand for land is determined by the (21)_____ (marginal revenue product, marginal cost) of land. The supply of land, however, is fixed--the market supply curve is perfectly (22)_____ (elastic, inelastic). Market rents are determined entirely by the market demand for land. Anything that changes the price of a good produced with land or alters the marginal productivity of land, such as climate, location, and access to water, utilities, or highways, will affect the (23)_____ (marginal revenue product, marginal cost) of land and cause the market rent to change. In central cities, land is fixed in supply and the highest bidders for the central parcels will put the land to its highest-valued use--such as with high-rise office buildings. Land at the periphery of an urban area is too far from the central city to be used as office space. The bidders for outlying parcels will be farmers, ranchers, and residential developers. The land will be allocated to the highest bidder based on the use that has the (24)_____ (highest, lowest) marginal revenue product. Because rent is a payment in excess of that which is necessary to bring forth the current quantity of land supplied (the current quantity of land is fixed regardless of rent), landlords could be taxed the full amount of their rent received (25)_____ (reducing, without altering) the quantity of land made available.

Profit is the return or reward to the owner. (26)_____ (Economic, Normal) profit is a payment equal to the opportunity cost of the owner's self-owned resources. Normal profits are necessary in order to keep the owner from exiting the industry--from taking his self-owned resources elsewhere. Economic profit and losses allocate resources among industries as some industries expand and some decline. (27)_____ (Economic, Normal) profit results from innovations and anticipation of consumer demands, risk taking, and the exercise of monopoly power.

VOCABULARY REVIEW

Write the key term from the list below next to its definition.

Key Terms

Rent	Marginal return on investment
Capital	Discounted present value
Investment	Risk
Depreciation	Risk averse
Saving	

Definitions

1. _____: the amount of income not consumed in a given year.

2. _____: the percentage rate of return on investment of additional sums used to purchase more capital.

3. _____: the rate at which machines and structures wear out.

4. _____: the current value of funds to be received in future periods.

5. _____: the process of replenishing or adding to capital stock.

6. _____: measures the variation of actual outcomes from expected outcomes.

7. _____: an input created by people for the purpose of producing goods and services. It consists of tools, machinery, vehicles, structures, raw material, inventories, and human skills.

8. _____: describes an investor who, if given equal expected returns, would choose an investment with lower risk.

9. _____: the price that is paid for the use of land

SKILLS REVIEW

Concept: **Investment decisions and the interest rate**

1. The Awax Paint Company is considering whether or not to install a new metering device for 1 year. The cost of the system is $95,000. The expected return from the metering device at the end of the year is $15,000 plus a resale value of $90,000 for the used metering device.

   a. The marginal return to the investment is expected to be _____ %. If the market rate of interest is 8%, Awax _____ (will, will not) install the new metering system.

   b. If the market rate of interest rises to 13%, Awax _____ (will, will not) install the device.

2. If Awax's metering device had a useful life of 5 years and did not have any resale value at the end of this period, determine the present value of the measuring system from the data given below.

	Expected Return	PV (10%)	PV (5%)
Year 1	$15,000	_____	_____
2	35,000	_____	_____
3	30,000	_____	_____
4	25,000	_____	_____
5	10,000	_____	_____

   Total PV (10%) = $_____   Total PV (5%) = $_____

   a. Complete the table.

   b. At a present cost of $95,000 and a market rate of interest of 10%, Awax _____ (will, will not) install the device because the present value of the system _____ the present cost.

   c. If the market rate of interest falls to 5%, Awax _____ (will, will not) install the device because the present value of the system _____ the present cost.

   d. The present value of a capital asset and the interest rate are _____ related.

   e. A decrease in the interest rate _____ the present value of proposed investment projects and results in a/an _____ in the volume of investment.

341

3. The diagram below represents the market for loanable funds and a given firm's marginal return on investment.

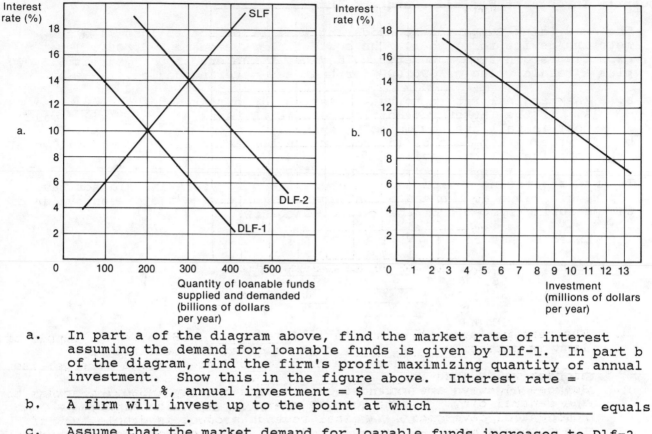

a.

Loanable Funds Market

Interest rate (%)

Quantity of loanable funds supplied and demanded (billions of dollars per year)

b.

Firm's Investment Demand

Interest rate (%)

Investment (millions of dollars per year)

a. In part a of the diagram above, find the market rate of interest assuming the demand for loanable funds is given by Dlf-1. In part b of the diagram, find the firm's profit maximizing quantity of annual investment. Show this in the figure above. Interest rate = _____ %, annual investment = $_____

b. A firm will invest up to the point at which _____ equals _____.

c. Assume that the market demand for loanable funds increases to Dlf-2. Find the new interest rate and the firm's annual level of investment. Show on the above figure. Interest rate = _____ %, annual investment = $_____

d. An increase in the supply of loanable funds given the demand for loanable funds _____ the market rate of interest, causing a firm's current marginal return on investment to _____ the interest rate and resulting in a/an _____ in investment.

Concept: Rent determination in competitive markets

4. A large parcel of land exists at the periphery of an urban area, but is still used by farmers to grow crops. The data below represent the quantity of land supplied and demanded by farmers at this site.

Rent per Acre	Acres Supplied (per year)	Marginal Revenue Product (MRP)	Acres Employed
$100	1,000	$100	1,400
200	1,000	200	1,200
300	1,000	300	1,000
400	1,000	400	800
500	1,000	500	600
600	1,000	600	400
700	1,000	700	200

342

a.   Plot the farmer's marginal revenue product schedule and supply curve on the figure below.

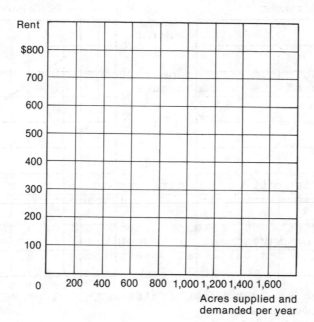

b.   The rent per acre at this site is $_____ . Because the supply of land is perfectly _____ , rent is determined entirely by _____ . If there are no other bidders for the acreage, its highest-valued use is _____ .

c.   Suppose highways are extended to the site greatly improving access to the central city. Assume that at every acreage size employed a residential developer's marginal revenue product is double that of the farmer's marginal revenue product. Show the developer's marginal revenue product curve on the figure above. The market rent per acre _____ to $_____ , and it highest-valued use changes from _____ to _____ .

d.   Rent is a payment _____ of the payment necessary to bring forth a resource. For the case above, the developer pays a total rent of $_____ . What percentage of this amount could be taxed without affecting the quantity of land supplied or its highest-valued use? _____ %

SELF-TEST FOR MASTERY

Select the best answer.

1.   A payment for the use of funds lent by one person for the use of others is called:

a.   Rent.
b.   Interest.
c.   Profit.
d.   Wage.

2. A payment for the services of land is called:

    a. Rent.
    b. Interest.
    c. Profit.
    d. Wage.

3. _____ is/are a return to entrepreneurs for risks associated with the introduction of new products or techniques.

    a. Rents
    b. Interest
    c. Profits
    d. Wages

4. A profit-maximizing firm will add capital up to the point at which the _____ equals the _____.

    a. Marginal revenue product, marginal input cost of capital
    b. Marginal return on investment, interest rate
    c. Present value of a capital asset, present cost
    d. All of the above

5. Which of the following concepts best explains the slope of the marginal return on investment curve?

    a. Profit maximization
    b. Law of diminishing marginal returns
    c. Law of increasing returns
    d. Equimarginal principle
    d. Diminishing marginal revenue

6. Present value can be defined as:

    a. The total return associated with a project.
    b. The end-of-the-period return discounted to its future value.
    c. The sum of the discounted future returns associated with a capital asset.
    d. The cost of the project.
    e. The sum of the discounted future profits associated with a capital asset.

7. The interest rate and the present value of a capital asset are:

    a. Independent of each other.
    b. Positively related.
    c. Inversely related.
    d. Unrelated.
    e. Unimportant in investment decisions.

8. An increase in the market demand for loanable funds _____ the market rate of interest causing the interest rate to _____ the current marginal return on investment and resulting in an/a _____ in investment.

    a. Decreases, fall below, increase
    b. Increases, equal, decrease
    c. Decreases, fall below, decrease
    d. Increases, rise above, decrease

9. An increase in the market supply of loanable funds _____ the market rate of interest, causing the interest rate to _____ the current marginal return on investment and resulting in an/a _____ in investment.

   a. Decreases, fall below, increase
   b. Increases, equal, decrease
   c. Decreases, fall below, decrease
   d. Increases, rise above, decrease

10. Of the following factors influencing interest rates, which one does not result in higher interest rates?

    a. Higher risk
    b. Less collateral pledged against a loan
    c. Longer-term loan or bond
    d. Tax-exempt status

11. The supply of land:

    a. Reflects the law of supply.
    b. Is perfectly elastic.
    c. Is upward sloping.
    d. Is perfectly inelastic.
    e. Is downward sloping.

12. A firm's demand for land:

    a. Is downward sloping.
    b. Is the firm's marginal revenue product curve for land.
    c. Shifts if the price of the product produced with the land changes.
    d. Determines the rent.
    e. All of the above.

13. Rent is determined:

    a. By the landlord.
    b. By shifts in supply of and demand for land.
    c. Entirely by the demand for land.
    d. Entirely by the supply of land.

14. The highest-valued use to which land is put is dependent upon:

    a. The marginal cost curves of the bidding firms.
    b. The marginal revenue curves of the bidding firms.
    c. The use desired by the supplier of land.
    d. The marginal revenue product curves of the bidding firms.

15. A tax on land rents:

    a. Will reduce the quantity of land supplied.
    b. Will result in an increase in rents.
    c. Will be passed forward to consumers.
    d. Will not affect the quantity of land supplied, nor will it increase rents.

16. Which of the following is defined as the opportunity cost of owner-supplied resources?

    a. Total cost
    b. Profit

c. Normal profit
d. Economic profit

17. The profit reported by business:

    a. Is greater than economic profit.
    b. Includes normal profit.
    c. Accounts for some of the opportunity costs of owner-supplied resources.
    d. All of the above.

18. Which of the following is not a source of economic profit?

    a. Innovations and anticipation of consumer demands
    b. Risk taking
    c. Exercise of monopoly power
    d. The owner's stock of self-owned resources

THINK IT THROUGH

1. Discuss intuitively how the principles of investment discussed in this chapter can be used in deciding whether or not to pursue a university degree.

2. Suppose that consumers are heavily indebted and have reached a point at which they must reduce their demand for loanable funds. Discuss the implications for the loanable funds market and for the level of business investment in physical capital.

3. If the market supply of and demand for loanable funds determine the market rate of interest, then why are there many different rates of interest at any one time?

4. Taxes levied on land are considered more efficient than taxes levied on improvements on the land (such as structures). Can you think of any reasons why?

CHAPTER ANSWERS

In Brief: Chapter Summary

1. Interest 2. Rents arise 3. Profits arise 4. physical capital 5. Human capital 6. Saving 7. Just equal to 8. Marginal return on investment 9. Increase 10. Decrease 11. Not worth as much 12. Present value 13. Reduces 14. Increases 15. Exceeds 16. Equal to 17. Downward sloping 18. Upward sloping 19. Higher 20. Higher 21. Marginal revenue product 22. Inelastic 23. Marginal revenue product 24. Highest 25. Without altering 27. Economic

Vocabulary Review

1. Saving 2. Marginal return on investment 3. Depreciation 4. Discounted present value 5. Investment 6. Risk 7. Capital 8. Risk averse 9. Rent

Skills Review

1. a. 10.53%, will   b. Will not

2. a.

PV (10%)	PV (5%)
$13,636.36	$14,285.71
38,925.62	31,746.03
22,539.44	25,915.12
17,075.34	20,567.56
6,209.25	7,835.26
$88,386.01	$100,349.68

   b. Will not; is less than
   c. Will; is greater than
   d. Inversely   e. Increases, increase

3. a.

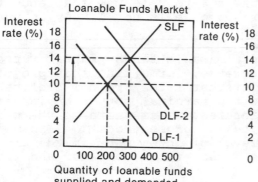 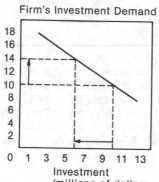

      10%, $10 million
   b. Marginal return on investment, the market rate of interest
   c. 14%, $6 million
   d. Decrease, exceed, increase

4. a.

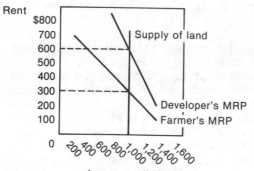

   b. $300; inelastic, the demand for land; in agricultural production
   c. Increases, $600, agriculture, residential development
   d. In excess of, $600,000; 100%

Self-Test for Mastery

1. b   2. a   3. c   4. d   5. b   6. c   7. c   8. d   9. a   10. d   11. d   12. e   13. c   14. d   15. d   16. c   17. d   18. d

Think it Through

1.   An investment in a college degree generates a stream of benefits over time
and involves the explicit outlays of tuition, room, and board but also includes
as a cost the forgone income that could have been earned if the individual had
worked rather than attended college. Future benefits of a college degree
include both pecuniary and nonpecuniary benefits. A net benefit-maximizing
individual will compare the present value (or the sum of the discounted future
returns) resulting from a college degree to the present costs, which include
the forgone income mentioned above. If the present value of a degree is less
than the present cost, the individual will not invest in a degree. If the
present value is greater than the present cost, the individual will invest in a
degree. For instance, assuming only pecuniary benefits are considered, a very
highly paid executive will not likely take a 4-year leave of absence to earn a
degree. The present value of a bachelor's degree is not likely to outweigh the
current sacrifice of income.

2.   If consumers reduce their demand for loanable funds, market rates of
interest decrease. As interest rates decrease, firms find that projects that
were previously unprofitable at higher interest rates are now profitable
because interest rates have fallen below the marginal return on investment for
many projects. Alternatively, falling interest rates increase the present
value of an investment project relative to its present cost. Firms will
increase investment, and the aggregate level of investment in the economy may
rise or fall depending upon the relative sizes of the consumer and firm
effects.

3.   The average level of interest rates is determined by the demand for and
supply of loanable funds. Because different loans and financial assets have
different characteristics, they command different rates of interest at any
point in time. Interest rates are higher on financial assets that are riskier,
involve a longer term to maturity, are less collateralized, and do not receive
favorable tax treatment. Nevertheless, when the average rate of interest
changes, these specific rates of interest are likewise changing in the same
direction but with different lags and rates of change.

4.   Efficient taxes are able to raise tax revenues without distorting resource
allocation--without altering the allocation of resources that would prevail in
the absence of the tax. Because land is fixed in supply and the payment to
acquire land is economic rent, land could be taxed without altering the present
quantity of land supplied or the use to which it is put. Landlords cannot
escape the tax by taking their land elsewhere. Nor can the owner of the land
pass the tax to the renter in the form of higher rents. If this was tried, the
renter would find that the rent exceeded his marginal revenue product for the
land and would leave. But the land owner needs the land employed in its most
productive use in order to earn the highest rents to cover the tax.

Taxes on structures distort economic choices and resource allocation. Taxes on
improvements result in an allocation of resources that differs from what would
prevail in the market without taxes. Some improvements and structures are
mobile. A tax can be avoided by moving the improvements to an area with a
lower tax or no tax. In the long run, structures may be allowed to
deteriorate, thus reducing the productivity of the land upon which the
structure is located.

348

24

The Distribution of Income and the Economics of Poverty

CHAPTER CHALLENGES

After studying your text, attending class, and completing this chapter, you should be able to:

1. Discuss the facts about income distribution in the United States.
2. Document the extent of poverty in the United States.
3. Discuss government assistance programs to the poor and the impact of these programs on incentives and well-being of recipients.
4. Explain the causes of income inequality and evaluate the impact of policies designed to reduce poverty and alter income distribution.

IN BRIEF: CHAPTER SUMMARY

Fill in the blanks to summarize chapter content.

Income in the United States is not distributed equally. As a percentage of total money income, the lowest 20% of families in 1984 received (1)_____ (5%, 15%) of the nation's income, whereas the richest 20% of families received almost (2)_____ (43%, 33%) of total money income. The degree of inequality as reflected in the distribution of income has (3)_____ (decreased, remained relatively unchanged) from 1947 to 1984. The (4)_____ (welfare, Lorenz) curve is a useful tool for showing the degree of income inequality. The line of income equality results if a given percentage of families receive (5)_____ (that same, a greater) percentage of the nation's money income. For the United States the line is bowed outward, meaning that the distribution of income is skewed to the higher-income families. Policies designed to reduce the inequality will shift the Lorenz curve (6)_____ (away from, inward toward) the line of income equality.

As of 1985, about (7)_____ (6%, 14%) of the U.S. population were counted as poor--having incomes below the poverty income threshold. (8)_____ (The poverty threshold is, Welfare benefits are) determined by estimating the minimally acceptable food budget for a family of a certain size and multiplying by three. By this measure of poverty, the incidence of poverty fell dramatically from 1959 to the end of the 1970s (9)_____ (and continued to decline, but increased) in the early 1980s. Estimates of poverty do not take into account forms of government assistance other than cash assistance. If noncash government benefits were included, it is estimated that the poverty rate would fall to about (10)_____ (2%, 10%).

The incidence of poverty is (11)_____ (higher, lower) among blacks and Hispanics, female-headed households, and children than for the population as a whole. The (12)_____ (Hispanic minorities, elderly) have experienced the largest gains in reducing poverty, largely because of more generous private and public pensions (such as Social Security).

Programs designed to assist the poor are called welfare programs. Recipients must qualify for the programs based on a means test. Government assists the poor with cash and in-kind assistance. (13)_____ (Cash, In-kind) assistance programs include the AFDC and SSI programs. AFDC benefits vary widely by state and are at a level considerably below the poverty line. Examples of (14)_____ (cash, in-kind) assistance include Medicaid, food stamps, and housing assistance. In 1986, AFDC and SSI benefits equaled $20 billion and in-kind assistance totaled $55 billion.

A disadvantage of the assistance programs mentioned above is that there are considerable work disincentives. As the welfare recipient works and earns income, welfare benefits drop such that it is not uncommon for a welfare mother, for instance, to lose 80 cents in cash and in-kind benefits for every dollar earned. The losses in production from these disincentives are one form of inefficiency associated with assistance programs. Another form of inefficiency results from the (15)_____ (resource underemployment, distortion of choices) caused by in-kind transfers. If a poor family prefers less food than it could purchase with the food stamps, the stamps are less highly valued than an equivalent amount of cash. If the family received cash instead, it would purchase the desired amount of food and other goods and attain a higher level of utility. However, this apparently is not a big problem because food stamp benefits are low and most families would probably consume more food than allowed by their food stamps. Medicaid is offered to the poor at a zero price. This results in (16)_____ (overconsumption, underconsumption) of medical services, which probably raises the prices of health care services to all consumers.

There are equity-efficiency tradeoffs in the welfare system. Increasing welfare benefits require additional tax revenues. If tax rates are increased, incentives to work, save, and invest are reduced. Improving the equity of the distribution of income results in some efficiency (17)_____ (gains, losses). Apparently, the United States has chosen over the years to minimize the efficiency losses and has shifted the Lorenz curve inward toward greater income equality (18)_____ (by a considerable, by only a very modest) amount. The (19)_____ (antipoverty, negative) income tax proposal has been suggested as a way to reduce poverty without creating efficiency losses as large as is presently the case. Politically, it is not likely to be seriously considered because it involves transferring income to the nonpoor and would require high tax rates.

Because poverty results from the lack of marketable skills or the inability to work, government can do a number of things to increase worker productivity and opportunities to work. The government could provide educational opportunities or subsidies. Economic growth could be promoted as well as worker training. Where discrimination exists it can be reduced or eliminated. Evidence indicates that some of the wage or income differentials observed are probably the result of discrimination, (20)_____ (but a significant share, and only a very small percentage) of the differentials can be attributed to factors other than discrimination, such as education or work experience.

VOCABULARY REVIEW

Write the key term from the list below next to its definition.

Key Terms

Lorenz curve   Means test
Poverty income threshold   Negative income tax
Welfare programs   Discrimination in
                                 labor markets

Definitions

1. _____: occurs when minority-group workers with skills, experience, and training comparable to those of workers in other groups are paid lower wages and have less opportunity for employment and advancement.

2. _____: government programs to assist the poor in the United States who are unable to work.

3. _____: the income level below which a person or family is classified as being poor.

4. _____: provides for government payments to people whose income falls below certain levels.

5. _____: establishes the fact that people in the groups eligible for welfare payments have incomes below the amounts that are minimally acceptable.

6. _____: a plotting of data showing the percentage of income enjoyed by each percentage of households ranked according to their incomes.

SKILLS REVIEW

Concept: **Distribution of income, poverty and the poverty threshold income**

1. Given the data below on the distribution of family income, answers the questions below.

Percentage of Families	Percentage of Total Income
Highest 20%	43%
4th 20%	24%
3rd 20%	17%
2nd 20%	11%
Lowest 20%	5%

a.   On the figure below, plot the Lorenz curve for the data above.

Percent of total income

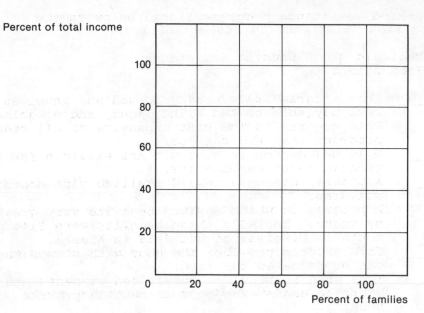

Percent of families

b.   On the figure above, identify the line of income equality.
c.   On figure above, show the effect on the current distribution of
     family income of policies that reduce income inequality.

2.   Which groups of individuals in the United States in 1984 had the highest
     incidence of poverty?

Group	Percentage of the Group Classified as Poor
a. _____	_____ %
b. _____	_____
c. _____	_____
d. _____	_____

3.   If the federal government determines that the minimally acceptable food
     expenditure is $3 per person per day, determine the poverty threshold
     income for a:

a.   Family of 2. $_____
b.   Family of 3. $_____
c.   Family of 4. $_____
d.   Given the following distribution of four-person families, determine
     the poverty rate. (The poverty rate is the percentage of four-person
     families having incomes below the poverty-threshold income.)

Income	Families of Four
$51,000 and above	2 million
Below $51,000	27 million
Below $27,640	19 million
Below $13,140	3 million
Below $ 6,280	1 million

     Poverty rate = _____ %

Concept: Programs to aid the poor

4.   Match the cash and in-kind assistance programs listed below to the
     statements below.

            AFDC   Medicaid   Housing assistance
            SSI   Food stamps

     a.   _____   This program is federally funded and involves
                                cash payments to the blind, aged, and disabled.
     b.   _____   This program is the most expensive of all federal
                                programs that aid the poor.
     c.   _____   Only one person in four who are eligible for this
                                program receives benefits.
     d.   _____   A program designed to aid families with dependent
                                children.
     e.   _____   A program in which maximum benefits vary greatly
                                by state. In 1987, these benefits were $144 per
                                month in Mississippi but $833 in Alaska.
     f.   _____   This program provides the poor with stamps that
                                can be redeemed for food.
     g.   _____   This program provides subsidized payments and
                                rents to assist the poor in renting private
                                housing.
     h.   _____   This program involves a service rendered for
                                which the poor pay a zero price.

5.   In the long run, government must pursue certain fundamental policies if
     poverty is to be reduced or eliminated.   What are they?

     a.   _____
     b.   _____
     c.   _____
     d.   _____

SELF-TEST FOR MASTERY

Select the best answer.

1.   What percentage of the U.S population was classified as poor in 1985?

     a.   5%
     b.   9%
     c.   14%
     d.   18%
     e.   22%

2.   In 1984, the highest 20% of the families in the income distribution
     received what percentage of total income?

     a.   20%
     b.   43%
     c.   67%
     d.   53%
     e.   38%

3. In 1984, the lowest 20% of the families in the income distribution received what percentage of total income?

   a. 14%
   b. 21%
   c. 8%
   d. 5%
   e. 12%

4. The distribution of income in the United States from 1947 to 1984:

   a. Has become more unequal.
   b. Has become significantly more equal.
   c. Has been stable.
   d. Has coincided with the line of income equality.

5. Which of the following is a plotting of data showing the percentage of income enjoyed by each percentage of households ranked according to their incomes?

   a. Income curve
   b. Distribution curve
   c. Phillips curve
   d. Lorenz curve

6. If a nation's Lorenz curve lies below the line of income equality:

   a. Proportionately more of the nation's income is received by the highest 20% of families than the lowest 20%.
   b. The income received by each 20% of families is 20% of the total income.
   c. Proportionately more of the nation's income is received by the lowest 20% of families than the highest 20%.
   d. Income is equally distributed.

7. Poverty in the United States is defined as:

   a. Unwholesome living conditions.
   b. A level of income below the median income for all families.
   c. A level of income below the minimally acceptable annual food budget of a family of a given size times three.
   d. An income below 20% of the average family income.

8. The percentage of the U.S. population living in households having incomes below the poverty threshold level has _____ from 1959 to 1984.

   a. Decreased
   b. Increased
   c. Remained remarkably stable
   d. Increased for 2 decades and fallen for 5 years

9. Which of the following groups does not have a high incidence of poverty--a rate of poverty above the rate for the population as a whole?

   a. The elderly
   b. Female-headed households
   c. Blacks
   d. Hispanics
   e. Children

10. Which of the following groups has experienced the largest drop since 1959 in the percentage of its members who are poor?

    a. The elderly
    b. Female-headed households
    c. Blacks
    d. Hispanics
    e. Children

11. Which of the following assistance programs to the poor is not an in-kind assistance program?

    a. Food stamps
    b. Medicaid
    c. Housing
    d. AFDC

12. The most costly program to aid the poor is:

    a. The food stamp program.
    b. Medicaid.
    c. Federal housing assistance.
    d. SSI.

13. A Census Bureau study found that if income was defined as including money income and in-kind transfers, the percentage of the population having incomes below the poverty threshold level would be about:

    a. 0%.
    b. 5%.
    c. 8%.
    d. 10%.
    e. 14%.

14. Which of the following best illustrates the work disincentives present in the current welfare system?

    a. The vicious circle of welfare teaches children to be lazy.
    b. For each additional dollar earned, a welfare recipient may lose as much as 80 cents in welfare assistance.
    c. Even though the poor are able-bodied, they choose to not work in order to rip off the welfare system.
    d. An average welfare recipient faces a tax rate of 15%.

15. Policies that increase welfare benefits and require tax rate increases to fund the expanded programs

    a. Increase both equity and efficiency.
    b. Decrease both equity and efficiency.
    c. Increase efficiency, but decrease equity.
    d. Increase equity, but decrease efficiency.

16. The negative income tax proposal:

    a. Provides for a minimum-guaranteed income.
    b. Involves high tax rates.
    c. Transfers income to higher-income families than currently receive benefits under existing welfare programs.
    d. Is very costly.
    e. All of the above.

17. Which of the following policies should be undertaken by government in order to reduce or eliminate poverty?

    a. Programs that support equality of opportunity
    b. Programs the promote economic growth
    c. Programs that encourage or provide education
    d. Programs that encourage or provide training
    e. All of the above

18. Which of the following acts outlawed discrimination on the basis of race, religion, sex, or national origin?

    a. The Anti-discrimination Statute of 1955
    b. The Equal Rights Amendment of 1982
    c. The Civil Liberties Union Act of 1978
    d. The Civil Rights Act of 1964

THINK IT THROUGH

1. Discuss how poverty is measured. Can you think of any limitations of the current method of defining poverty?

2. Discuss the nature of the efficiency-equity tradeoff associated with efforts to redistribute income.

3. Briefly discuss current programs to aid the poor and discuss the effectiveness of the programs in terms of the level of poverty and the distribution of income.

4. If poverty results from the lack of marketable skills, inability to work, or the lack of opportunity to work or attain skills, discuss the types of policies that government must pursue if it is to successfully reduce poverty.

POP QUIZ   Read the news brief at the end of this chapter and answer the following question.

Evidence indicates that some of the wage differential between males and females is likely the result of discrimination. Discrimination can be of the direct type where an employer exercises a sex bias in promotion, employment, and pay, or it can be a more subtle form of discrimination that still has the same consequences in terms of relative pay. According to the article, what is one source of this subtle discrimination, and how does it affect the pay of women?

CHAPTER ANSWERS

In Brief: Chapter Summary

1. 5% 2. 43% 3. Remained relatively unchanged 4. Lorenz 5. That same 6. Inward toward 7. 14% 8. Poverty threshold is 9. But increased 10. 10% 11. Higher 12. Elderly 13. Cash 14. In-kind 15. Distortion of choices 16. Overconsumption 17. Losses 18. Only by a very modest 19. Negative 20. But a significant share

Vocabulary Review

1. Discrimination in labor markets 2. Welfare programs 3. Poverty income threshold 4. Negative income tax 5. Means test 6. Lorenz curve

Skills Review

1.

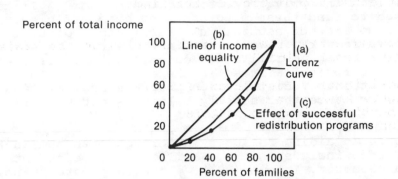

Percent of total income

(b) Line of income equality
(a) Lorenz curve
(c) Effect of successful redistribution programs

Percent of families

2. a. Female-headed households with dependent children; 34%
    b. Blacks; 33.8%
    c. Hispanics; 28.4%
    d. Children; 20%

3. a. $6,570 b. $9,855 c. $13,140 d. 7.69%

4. a. SSI
    b. Medicaid
    c. Housing assistance
    d. AFDC
    e. AFDC
    f. Food stamps
    g. Housing assistance
    h. Medicaid

5. a. Promote equal opportunity
    b. Promote economic growth
    c. Provide or subsidize education
    d. Provide, encourage, or subsidize training

Self-Test for Mastery

1. c 2. b 3. d 4. c 5. d 6. a 7. c 8. a 9. a 10. a 11. d 12. b 13. d 14. b 15. d 16. e 17. e 18. d

Think it Through

1.   The poverty rate of a given group or population in the United States is the percentage of the group or population having incomes below the poverty income threshold. The poverty income threshold is determined by estimating the minimally acceptable food expenditure per day per person and multiplying that amount by three. Therefore the poverty income threshold for a family depends on the size of the family. One limitation of this measure of poverty is that it does not include in-kind goods or services received by households. If these benefits were included, it is estimated that the poverty rate for the entire population would fall to 10%. Another limitation is that the measure is an absolute rather than a relative measure of poverty. Over time more families might have incomes above the poverty income threshold but still retain their

relative place in the distribution of income. In other words, they are likely to feel just as poor even though their absolute income level has risen.

2.   Programs designed to reduce poverty and redistribute income, if successful, will improve equity (assuming that society feels that some redistribution is socially desirable). However, programs require resources that must be withdrawn from the private sector of the economy. If tax rates are ultimately increased to fund these programs, economic efficiency is reduced. Since most taxes are not neutral in their impact, distortions will occur in decisions regarding work, saving, and investment. The economy is operating inside its production possibilities curve. But this is the tradeoff-- the opportunity cost of improving fairness in the economy is a lower level of production. The very fact that redistribution programs and tax laws have been in place for decades is evidence that society believes that some redistribution should take place.

3.   The current approach to aiding the poor is through cash and in-kind transfers. Cash assistance includes Aid to Families with Dependent Children (AFDC) and Supplemental Security Income (SSI). In-kind programs include Medicaid, which is the most expensive program for the poor, housing assistance, and food stamps. The nation's poverty rate fell in the 1960s and until the end of the 1970s. In the early 1980s, the poverty rate increased substantially and has fallen to the present but still remains above the all-time lows of the late 1970s. From the answer to question 1 above, note that improvements in absolute income levels do not guarantee that a family's relative position in the distribution of income will improve. In fact, the Lorenz curve has shifted inward only a slight amount since the advent of these poverty programs. In the 1980s, the distribution of income has likely become less rather than more equal.

4.   The government needs to treat the disease in addition to the symptoms. Poverty is the result of the lack of purchasing power. But the lack of purchasing power is related to the absence of marketable skills, the lack of opportunity to attain those skills or find employment, and both overt and subtle forms of discrimination. Evidence suggests that a considerable portion of the wage differentials among workers can be attributed to differences in skills, education, or experience. But there is an unexplained component of these differentials that may be due to discrimination. Government programs that assure equal opportunity, not only to education and training, but also to the workplace and that increase workers' marginal products, such as programs designed to encourage the consumption of additional training and education, will in the long run be more effective in combatting poverty than short-term cash or in-kind transfers.

Pop Quiz

There is evidence of subtle discrimination or bias while females are in school- -from first grade through the university level. Females are given less attention than males, and are less likely to be praised by teachers. This impairs a female's self esteem and affects her expectations regarding her future. As a result, women are socially trained to be less assertive and more risk averse. They will not likely "...present themselves as effective managers." Boys receive more scolding in school than girls but this increases their aggressiveness and assertiveness. In college, females enroll in courses with large female enrollments to avoid being intimidated by male-dominated classes. Female-dominated courses often lead to some of the lower-paying occupations. In short, the socialization process "tracks" females into occupations that are crowded with women and consequently involve low pay.

Studies Link Subtle Sex Bias in Schools With Women's Behavior in the Workplace

By SHARON E. EPPERSON

Staff Reporter of THE WALL STREET JOURNAL

What's holding women back as they climb the success ladder?

Classrooms may be partly to blame.

Overt discrimination it isn't, for schools are increasingly offering equal opportunities to girls and boys in both formal courses and extracurricular activities, including sports. But several studies suggest that, from first grade through college, female students are the victims of subtle biases. As a result, they are often given less nurturing attention than males.

Consider these findings from studies at schools in the U.S. and Britain. Compared with girls, boys are:

—Five times as likely to receive the most attention from teachers.

—Eight times as likely to call out in class, which helps to explain why they out-talk girls there by a ratio of 3 to 1. (When the teacher is female and the majority of the class is male, boys are 12 times as likely to speak up.)

—Twice as likely to demand help or attention from the teacher, to be seen as model students or to be called on or praised by teachers.

Researchers maintain that a chilly climate for women in the classroom undermines self-esteem and damages morale. They believe, too, that some of these patterns of student-teacher interaction may help set the stage for expectations and interactions later in the workplace.

Emotional Baggage

"Females aren't taught to be risk takers; they don't have the same autonomy as males," asserts Jane Ayer, associate dean of education and professor of counseling psychology at the University of Wisconsin, Madison. "And you take what you've learned about yourself in the classroom into the workplace."

In coed schools, researchers find that girls receive considerably less direct attention than boys. For instance, a study of teachers' interactions with pupils in more than a hundred fourth-, sixth- and eighth-grade math and language-arts classes found that boys receive significantly more praise, criticism and remedial help.

Reactions of both male and female teachers to their female students "aren't that great," says David Sadker, an American University professor of education who conducted the four-year study with his wife, Myra, also an education professor at American. Teachers often accept the girls' responses without offering constructive comment, Mr. Sadker explains.

"In the workplace," he argues, "women are less likely to present themselves as effective managers. A lot of it deals with passive roles" they assume at school.

In lower grades, other researchers have found, boys often also receive more attention through disciplinary action. These scoldings for disruptive activity can make boys "less sensitive to negative feedback from teachers" and may further their aggressive behavior, says Marlaine Lockheed, a senior research scientist for the World Bank who studied the matter while working for the Educational Testing Service in Princeton, N.J.

Yet another study, begun in 1981 by two researchers at the University of Illinois, has measured the self-confidence of 80 high-school valedictorians, salutatorians and honor students. The study found that, upon graduation, 23% of the men and 21% of the women believed they were "far above average" in intelligence. As college sophomores, only 4% of the women said they felt far above average, while 22% of the men rated themselves that way. By senior year in college, none of the women reported feeling far above average, compared with 25% of the men.

This apparent lack of self-esteem on the part of the women appears to be rooted in classroom interaction, says Bernice Sandler, executive director of the Association of American Colleges' project on the status and education of women. Researchers, she notes, have found that even in college classes "men receive more eye contact from their professors than women, are called on more often and receive informal coaching from their instructors."

Racial prejudice can make the situation even worse. "Minority women in higher education frequently face double discrimination—once for being female and once for being racially or ethnically different," noted a 1986 report by the college association's project on women. "For example, intellectual competence and leadership ability, along with other primary academic qualities, are associated not only with males but with white males."

A More Comfortable Setting

Researchers say sexual bias leads some women to opt for courses with a large female enrollment, where they will feel more comfortable voicing their opinions. Bertha French, a junior at the University of Virginia, Charlottesville, agrees. She notes that women usually dominate discussions in her mostly female French classes; the two or three male students don't speak up so much. "I think it's because it's not considered a masculine major," she says. In her male-dominated government classes, she adds, she and other female students sometimes feel intimidated.

At many schools, students, teachers and administrators often seem unaware of everyday inequities in the classroom. Faculty members may consider themselves too evenhanded to discriminate.

For example, the Sadkers' study included a math teacher who was active in the National Organization for Women. She told the Sadkers she probably wouldn't benefit from their training sessions on sexism in the classroom because she had been concerned about the issue for years. After viewing videotapes of her classroom interaction, however, she said she was "stunned" to find that she was talking to boys more than twice as much as to girls, and praising them four times as much.

Such disparities are the reason some educators stress the usefulness of single-sex schools, which are nonetheless on the decline. All-girl schools and women's colleges "create a more positive learning environment for females, who don't have to fear failing in front of males," maintains the University of Wisconsin's Ms. Ayer. She says she believes the schools help females to get away from traditional social conditioning and give them freedom "to show what they can do."

25

International Trade, Productivity, and the Economics of Less Developed Countries

CHAPTER CHALLENGES

After studying your text, attending class, and completing this chapter, you should be able to:

1. Understand the underlying basis for international trade and the gains in well-being possible from free trade with foreign nations.
2. Discuss the principle of comparative advantage and show how productivity changes in specific industries can affect their comparative advantage in international trade.
3. Discuss controversies regarding free trade vs. protection of U.S. industries from foreign competition in light of the basic theory of international trade.
4. Analyze the impact on the economy of tariffs, import quotas, and other trade restrictions.
5. Discuss some of the unique economic problems of less developed countries and the causes of low per capita income and slow economic growth in those nations.

IN BRIEF: CHAPTER SUMMARY

Fill in the blanks to summarize chapter content.

Nations engage in international trade because it is mutually beneficial for all trading nations to do so; otherwise they would not trade. Some nations may have a/an (1)_____ (comparative, absolute) advantage in producing goods, meaning that with a given complement of resources, one nation can produce more of an item than another nation with the same quantity of resources. But the presence of an absolute advantage in the production of an item does not indicate whether a nation should specialize in and export that good or whether the good should be imported. A country should specialize in and export those goods for which it has an/a (2)_____ (absolute, comparative) advantage and import those goods for which other countries have a comparative advantage. A nation has a comparative advantage in the production of a good relative to another nation if it produces the good at (3)_____ (lower, higher) opportunity cost than its trading partner.

Nations that trade on the basis of comparative advantage (4)_____ (gain at the expense of their rivals, mutually gain from trade). On an international scale, resources are used more efficiently as nations produce output based upon comparative advantages. World output, income, and living standards are (5)_____ (higher, lower) as a result of specialization and trade than would be the case in the absence of trade. All trading partners gain, although not equally. The distribution of the gains from trade is determined by the (6)_____ (foreign exchange rate, terms of trade)--the rate at which goods can be traded or exchanged for one another on international markets. A nation will be induced to trade goods for which it has a comparative advantage

for import goods if it can obtain the imported goods at prices below the
domestic opportunity cost of production. The real terms of trade are
determined by (7)_____ (government, world demand and supply). For
trade incentives to exist, the terms of trade must be (8)_____ (below,
above) the opportunity cost of producing each additional unit of the good a
nation desires to import. When countries specialize in and export those goods
for which they have a comparative advantage and import goods for which other
nations have a comparative advantage, the consumption possibilities curve of
each nation lies (9)_____ (outside, inside) the production possibilities
curve.

Changes in productivity can affect a nation's competitiveness in international
markets. If a nation experiences slower technological growth or lower levels
of investment in human and physical capital relative to those of its trading
partners, in time it may lose its (10)_____ (absolute, comparative)
advantage in those industries where international competitiveness requires
improvements in productivity. The nation that invests more heavily in things
that enhance productivity will eventually (11)_____ (gain, lose) a
comparative advantage relative to the lagging nation and will capture a share
of the international market that it previously did not have. Productivity
growth (growth in output per labor hour) in the United States from 1981-1985
was among the (12)_____ (highest, lowest) for industrialized nations at
about (13)_____ (10%, 1%) per year. This has been cited as a reason for the
decline in the competitiveness of some U.S. export industries. The primary
cause of the low productivity growth is believed to be the low rate of annual
(14)_____ (government, investment) spending as a percentage of domestic
production relative to other nations, particularly Japan. Increased government
regulation and (15)_____ (a liberal Congress, higher energy prices)
have also been cited as factors contributing to the productivity decline of the
1970s.

As comparative advantage changes, nations losing the comparative advantage in a
good no longer export that good. Industry sales and output fall, causing some
workers with specialized skills to become unemployed and other suppliers of
specialized inputs to experience a decline in income. Both the owners of the
declining industry and its input suppliers are harmed. But this has to be
balanced against the widespread gains to society when a nation produces on the
basis of comparative advantage. Changes in comparative advantage are painful
in the short run, but nations are better off in the long run by specializing in
and exporting those goods for which they have a comparative advantage and
trading for those goods for which they do not.

Several arguments, however, have been advanced for protecting domestic
industries. It is argued that some industries may need to be protected from
international competition to maintain production capacity (16)_____
(vital to national security, necessary to be self-sufficient). Protecting
(17)_____ (large and established industries, new and emerging "infant"
industries) from the rigors of international competition is considered a way of
allowing an industry to grow in a sheltered environment until it attains
sufficient economies of scale to compete internationally. Industries
experiencing changes in comparative advantage can be spared some of the short
run costs to specialized input suppliers and owners by receiving some
protection from foreign rivals. Some industries are protected from what is
viewed as unfair competition by foreign governments that subsidize their export
industries. Arguments against free trade derive from changes in the
(18)_____ (distribution of income that occur, efficiency with which
goods are produced) as some industries fail and lose their comparative
advantage.

Two methods of import protection are import tariffs and import quotas. A
(19)_____ (quota, tariff) is a tax on an imported good. The intention is

to reduce imports and increase the sales of domestic products. A tariff
(20)_____ (raises, lowers) the price of the imported good to the consumer,
(21)_____ (increases, reduces) the net price to the foreign producer, and
generates tax revenue for the government. A/An (22)_____ (tariff, import
quota) is a limit on the quantity of foreign goods that can be sold in a
nation's domestic market. Like the tariff, an import quota (23)_____
(increases, reduces) the quantity of imported goods sold and (24)_____
(raises, lowers) the price to the consumer, but unlike a tariff, the import
quota also (25)_____ (lowers, raises) the price received by the foreign
producer. If the demand for the imported good is inelastic, the foreign
producer (26)_____(is always worse off, may be better off) operating with
a quota. Further, quotas raise no revenue for government. But protectionism
invites retaliation from trading partners. If a nation's trading partners also
impose import tariffs and quotas, all of the trading nations (27)_____
(lose, gain) because the level of international trade is lower and consumers in
each country are paying higher prices than necessary.

(28)_____ [Newly industrialized countries, Less developed
countries (LDCs)] have very low real per capita GNPs. This is because of (a)
(29)_____ (high, low) rates of saving and capital accumulation, (b) poorly
skilled and educated workers, (c) lagging technological know-how, (d)
(30)_____ (high, low) population growth and unemployment, and (e) political
instability and government policies that discourage production. These nations
are dependent on foreign trade to acquire capital and technology necessary for
increases in their standard of living. But unless they export enough to
acquire the foreign exchange to purchase the imported goods, these nations will
not be able to advance significantly without the help of gifts or loans from
foreign nations.

VOCABULARY REVIEW

Write the key term from the list below next to its definition.

Key Terms

Specialization   Consumption possibilities
Mutual gains from   curve
  international trade   Tariff
Absolute advantage   Import quota
Comparative advantage   Real per capita output
Real terms of trade   Less developed country
                                  (LDC)

Definitions

1. _____: shows combinations of two goods a nation can
consume given its resources, technology, and international trade.

2. _____: the actual market exchange rate of one good for
another in international trade.

3. _____: a tax on imported goods.

4. _____: a nation has a comparative advantage over a
trading partner in the production of an item if it produces that item at
lower opportunity cost per unit than its partner does.

5. _____: a limit on the quantity of foreign goods that can be sold in a nation's domestic markets.

6. _____: a nation has an absolute advantage over other nations in the production of an item if it can produce more of the item over a certain period with a given amount of resources than the other nations can.

7. _____: a measure of output per person in a nation; calculated by dividing real GNP by population.

8. _____: on average, citizens in all trading nations gain from exchanging goods in international markets.

9. _____: a country whose real GNP per capita is generally much less than $1000 per year.

10. _____: use of labor and other resources in a nation to produce the goods and services for which those resources are best adapted.

SKILLS REVIEW

Concept: Absolute vs. comparative advantage, terms of trade, gains from trade

1. The domestic production possibilities of two nations, nation A and nation B, for two goods, cases of wine and boxes of cheese, are shown below.

Production Possibilities

	Nation A	Nation B
Wine (cases)	1 million	600,000
Cheese (boxes)	500,000	400,000

a. Plot the production possibilities curve for each nation in a and b in the figure below.

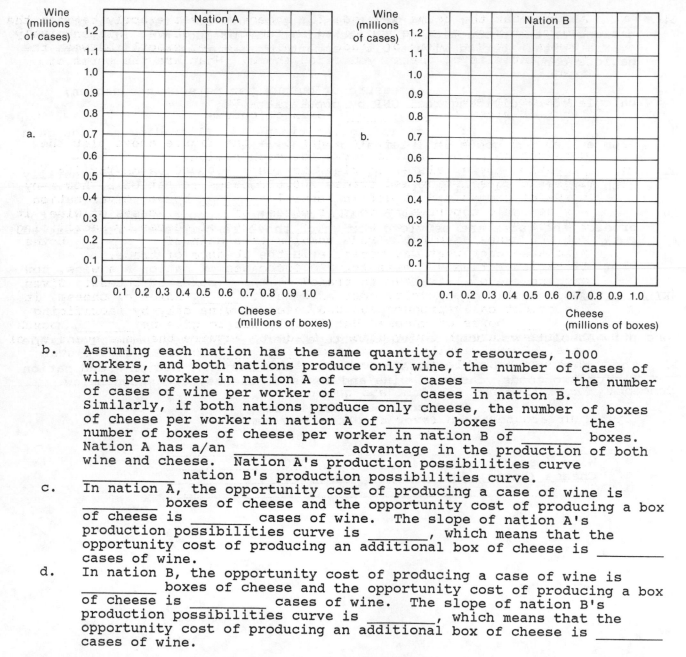

Wine (millions of cases) — Nation A — Cheese (millions of boxes)

Wine (millions of cases) — Nation B — Cheese (millions of boxes)

a.

b.

b. Assuming each nation has the same quantity of resources, 1000 workers, and both nations produce only wine, the number of cases of wine per worker in nation A of _____ cases _____ the number of cases of wine per worker of _____ cases in nation B. Similarly, if both nations produce only cheese, the number of boxes of cheese per worker in nation A of _____ boxes _____ the number of boxes of cheese per worker in nation B of _____ boxes. Nation A has a/an _____ advantage in the production of both wine and cheese. Nation A's production possibilities curve _____ nation B's production possibilities curve.

c. In nation A, the opportunity cost of producing a case of wine is _____ boxes of cheese and the opportunity cost of producing a box of cheese is _____ cases of wine. The slope of nation A's production possibilities curve is _____, which means that the opportunity cost of producing an additional box of cheese is _____ cases of wine.

d. In nation B, the opportunity cost of producing a case of wine is _____ boxes of cheese and the opportunity cost of producing a box of cheese is _____ cases of wine. The slope of nation B's production possibilities curve is _____, which means that the opportunity cost of producing an additional box of cheese is _____ cases of wine.

2. Regarding the problem above, nation A has a comparative advantage in the production of _____, whereas nation B has a comparative advantage in the production of _____. Nation A should specialize in and export _____ and should import _____. Nation B should specialize in and export _____ and should import _____. For nation A to be induced to trade for _____, it must give up less _____ than that implied by its domestic opportunity cost of _____. For nation B to be induced to trade for _____, it must give up less _____ than that implied by its domestic opportunity cost of _____. Trade will be mutually beneficial to both nations if 1 box of cheese trades for between

_____ and _____ cases of wine. Alternatively, trade will result if 1 case of wine trades for between _____ and _____ boxes of cheese.

3. a. Assume that the terms of trade for cheese are set exactly between the two quantities of wine you cited in question 2 above. Alternatively, assume that the terms of trade for wine are set exactly between the two quantities of cheese you cited above. What are the terms of trade?

    1 box of cheese = _____ cases of wine
    1 box of wine   = _____ boxes of cheese

    b. Given the terms of trade, in a and b in the figure above plot the consumption possibilities curve for each nation.
    c. If nation A specializes in wine and keeps 800,000 cases for its domestic consumption and trades 200,000 cases to nation B, how many boxes of cheese can it get in return? _____ boxes Given nation A's domestic opportunity cost of cheese of _____ cases of wine, it can domestically produce only _____ boxes of cheese by sacrificing 200,000 cases of wine. Trade results in a gain of _____ boxes of cheese over what was possible in the absence of trade.
    d. If nation B trades cheese for 200,000 cases of nation A's wine, how much cheese will it have to trade? _____ boxes of cheese. Given B's domestic opportunity cost of wine of _____ boxes of cheese, it can domestically produce 200,000 cases of wine only by sacrificing _____ boxes of cheese, but it only has to give up _____ boxes of cheese through international trade to acquire the same quantity of wine. Trade results in a gain of _____ boxes of cheese over what was possible in the absence of trade.

Concept: Protectionism, tariffs, and quotas

4. List four arguments in favor of protectionism.

    a. _____
    b. _____
    c. _____
    d. _____

5. In a and b in the figure below are shown the domestic and import markets
    for shoes.

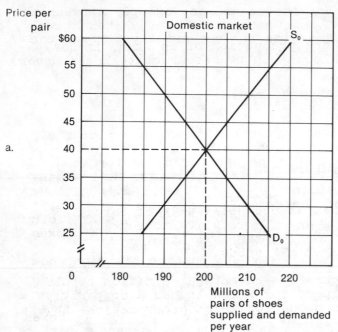

a.

Price per pair — Domestic market — S_0, D_0 — Millions of pairs of shoes supplied and demanded per year

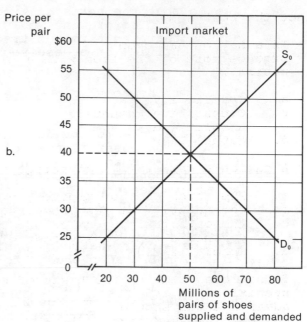

b.

Price per pair — Import market — S_0, D_0 — Millions of pairs of shoes supplied and demanded per year

a. Suppose that domestic shoe manufacturers and their input suppliers
    are able to win an import tariff of $10 per pair of imported shoes.
    Show the new import supply curve in b above. The $10 tariff causes
    the price to the consumer to _____ to $_____ and the net price
    to foreign shoe manufacturers to _____ to $_____. Sales of
    imported shoes _____ to _____ million pairs. The tariff has
    raised tax revenue of $_____. Show these effects in b.

b. In a, assume that the decline in import sales causes an increase in
    domestic shoe demand by an equal amount at each price level. The
    domestic demand for shoes shifts _____ by _____ million pairs
    of shoes. Domestic shoe prices _____ to $_____ and sales
    _____ to _____ million pairs.

c. In effect, the tariff redistributes income from _____ and
    _____ to the owners and input suppliers of the protected
    domestic shoe industry.

d. If an import quota had been used instead to achieve the lower level
    of import sales that you found in part a above, the price of
    imported shoes paid by the consumer and received by the foreign
    producer _____ to $_____. The domestic market price of shoes
    _____ to $_____, and sales _____ to _____ million
    pairs of shoes. In this case, the government receives _____ tax
    revenue and the foreign producer may experience a/an _____ in
    total revenue if the demand for imported shoes is sufficiently
    inelastic. Show the case of an import quota in b in the figure
    above.

SELF-TEST FOR MASTERY

Select the best answer.

1. If a nation has a/an _____ in the production of an item, it can produce more of the item with a given quantity of resources than can other nations.

    a. Special advantage
    b. Comparative advantage
    c. Absolute advantage
    d. Mutual gain

2. A nation's comparative advantage is determined by:

    a. The total cost of production.
    b. The quantity of resources required to produce a unit of output.
    c. The opportunity cost of producing an item relative to a trading partner's opportunity cost of producing the same item.
    d. Specialization in the production of all goods.

3. If nations trade on the basis of comparative advantage, a nation should specialize in and _____ those goods for which it has a comparative advantage and should _____ those goods for which other nations have a comparative advantage.

    a. Export, import
    b. Import, export
    c. Export, export
    d. Import, import

4. If nations trade on the basis of comparative advantage:

    a. A nation can gain only at the expense of trading partners.
    b. Exporting nations gain and importing nations lose.
    c. Importing nations gain and exporting nations lose.
    d. All trading partners mutually gain.

5. A nation will be induced to trade for imported goods if the nation can give up _____ goods through international trade for the imported item than implied by its domestic _____ cost of production.

    a. More, total
    b. More, opportunity
    c. Fewer, variable
    d. Fewer, opportunity

6. Which of the following refers to the rate at which goods are exchanged for one another in international markets?

    a. Exchange rate
    b. Terms of trade
    c. Specialization
    d. Opportunity cost
    e. None of the above

7. If nations trade on the basis of _____ advantage, the consumption possibilities curve lies _____ the production possibilities curve.

   a. Absolute, inside
   b. A unique, parallel to
   c. Comparative, parallel to
   d. Comparative, outside

8. When a nation's productivity growth lags behind that of its trading partners, in time it may:

   a. Lose its comparative advantage in some industries.
   b. Gain a comparative advantage as a result of the lag in productivity growth.
   c. Diversify with "infant" industries.
   d. Experience a reduction in the opportunity cost of producing the good.

9. Lagging productivity growth of a nation relative to its trading partners:

   a. Results in a loss of comparative advantage in some industries.
   b. Results in an increase in the opportunity cost of producing some goods relative to that of foreign rivals.
   c. Results in a loss of income to the owners and specialized input suppliers in the industries experiencing lagging productivity growth.
   d. All of the above.

10. The United States from 1981 to 1985 experienced an average rate of growth of _____% in its output per worker, which was among the _____ for industrialized nations.

    a. 1, lowest
    b. 3.5, lowest
    c. 10, highest
    d. 8, highest

11. Which of the following have been cited as reasons for the slow productivity growth in the United States in the 1970s?

    a. Average annual net investment of 6% of domestic production
    b. Increased government regulation to improve working conditions and the environment
    c. Rising energy prices
    d. All of the above
    e. None of the above

12. Which of the following is not an argument in favor of protectionism?

    a. National security
    b. Reducing structural unemployment
    c. Protecting infant industries
    d. Protecting U.S. industries against subsidized foreign producers
    e. Goal of self-sufficiency

13. Which of the following is a tax on an imported good?

    a. Income tax
    b. Import quota
    c. Rationing tax
    d. Tariff

14. A tariff does which of the following?

   a. Increases the price of the imported good to the consumer
   b. Decreases the net price received by the foreign producer
   c. Increases the price of the domestic good
   d. Redistributes income from domestic consumers and foreign producers to the protected industry
   e. All of the above

15. Which of the following places a limit on the quantity of a foreign good that can be imported into a domestic market?

   a. Import capacity limit
   b. Import quota
   c. Export quota
   d. Tariff

16. An import quota does which of the following?

   a. Increases the price of the imported good to the consumer
   b. Increases the price received by the foreign producer
   c. Increases the price of the domestic good
   d. Redistributes income from domestic consumers to the protected domestic exporter
   e. All of the above

17. Which of the following is a country whose real GNP per capita is generally less than $1000 per year?

   a. A newly industrialized country
   b. A less developed country
   c. An industrialized country
   d. A socialist state

18. Which of the following is not a reason for low per capita output in a country?

   a. Low rates of saving and investment
   b. Poorly skilled and educated workers
   c. High population growth and unemployment
   d. Lagging technology
   e. Socialism

THINK IT THROUGH

1. "In international trade, one nation's trade surplus (exports in excess of imports) must be another nation's trade deficit (imports in excess of exports). Therefore the mercantilists must be correct in saying that a nation should encourage exports and discourage imports." Evaluate this statement.

2. The United States has lost its international competitiveness in some basic industries, particularly those that produce standardized goods with large economies of scale. Can you think of any reasons why?

3. If a nation employs protectionist measures such as tariffs or quotas and trading partners retaliate in kind, discuss some likely consequences.

369

POP QUIZ   Read the news brief at the end of this chapter and answer the
                  questions below.

1.   In the first half of 1988, the U.S. trade deficit was $70 billion, but it
narrowed from $84.45 billion in the first half of 1987. In June of 1988, the
trade deficit widened to $12.54 billion from $9.76 billion the previous month.
Discuss the changes in imports and exports for the month of June that produced
this widening gap.

2.   How did the U.S. trade deficit change with major trading partners? In
light of this chapter, discuss how the United States benefits from trade even
though its deficit with several major trading partners widened in June of 1988.

CHAPTER ANSWERS

In Brief: Chapter Summary

1. Absolute 2. Comparative 3. Lower 4. Mutually gain from trade 5. Higher
6. Terms of trade 7. World demand and supply 8. Below 9. Outside 10.
Comparative 11. Gain 12. Lowest 13. 1% 14. Investment 15. Higher energy
prices 16. Vital to national security 17. New and emerging "infant"
industries 18. Distribution of income that occur 19. Tariff 20. Raises 21.
Reduces 22. Import quota 23. Reduces 24. Raises 25. Raises 26. May be
better off 27. Lose 28. Less developed countries (LDCs) 29. Low 30. High

Vocabulary Review

1. Consumption possibilities curve 2. Real terms of trade 3. Tariff 4.
Comparative advantage 5. Import quota 6. Absolute advantage 7. Real per
capita output 8. Mutual gains from international trade 9. Less developed
countries (LDCs) 10. Specialization

Skills Review

1.   a.

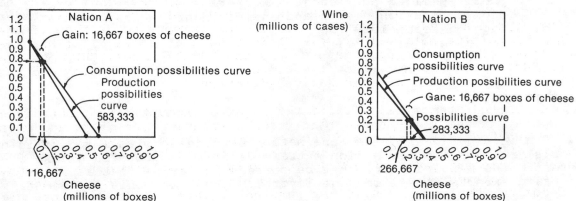

     b.   1,000, exceeds, 600; 500, exceeds, 400; absolute; lies farther from
          the origin than
     c.   1/2, 2; -2, 2
     d.   2/3, 1.5; -1.5, 1.5

2.   Wine, cheese; wine, cheese; cheese, wine; cheese, wine, cheese; wine,
     cheese, wine; 1.5, 2; 1/2, 2/3

3. a. 1.75 cases of wine, 7/12 box of cheese
    b. Shown on figure above
    c. 116,667; 2, 100,000; 16,667
    d. 116,667; 2/3, 133,333; 116,667; 16,667

4. a. National security
    b. Protect infant industries
    c. Reduce structural unemployment
    d. Protect U.S. industries against subsidized foreign producers

5. a.
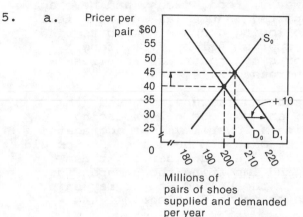

Millions of
pairs of shoes
supplied and demanded
per year

Millions of
pairs of shoes
supplied and demanded
per year

    Rise, $45, fall, $35; fall, 40; $400 million
    b. Rightward, 10; increase, $45, rise, 205
    c. Consumers, foreign producers
    d. Increase, $45; increases, $45, rise, 205; no, increase

Self-Test for Mastery

1. c 2. c 3. a 4. d 5. d 6. b 7. d 8. a 9. d 10. a 11. d 12. e 13.
d 14. e 15. b 16. e 17. b 18. e

Think It Through

1. A nation's wealth is not defined in terms of the foreign currency (or gold
during the mercantilist era) earned from trade surpluses, but by the total
goods consumed by the nation in part as a result of international trade. A
nation may run a trade deficit yet still consume more goods than if the nation
engaged in no international trade. It is true that a trade deficit means a
lower level of domestic aggregate demand and level of real GNP, but that level
of real GNP may be higher than it would have been if the nation did not produce
and trade on the basis of comparative advantage.

2. The United States has experienced lagging productivity growth in several
of its heavy industries--those that produce standardized goods and whose firms
realize substantial economies of scale. Other nations have had more rapid
productivity growth in some of these industries, taking away the comparative
advantage once enjoyed by the U.S. industries. New techniques of production
were being introduced abroad at a time during which many U.S. plants were aging
and becoming obsolete. U.S. firms were not investing enough in new plant and
equipment and technology to maintain their relatively lower opportunity cost of
production. Several foreign nations that have captured the comparative
advantage from the United States have done so by investing a greater percentage
of their domestic production in physical capital and technology. They also
have an advantage in having a relatively less costly labor force.

3. If all trading nations are engaging in protectionist measures, all lose in
that the volume of international trade will be lower, the level of world output

and living standards will be lower, and household real incomes will be lower because the prices of imported and domestic goods will be higher than in the absence of trade restrictions.

Pop Quiz

1.   The U.S. trade deficit increased in June because imports for the month exceeded exports. Imports increased by 5.7% and included the following changes: imports of capital goods increased by 10%, imports of consumer goods increased 8%, auto imports increased 12.5%; however, food, feeds, and beverage imports fell 4%, oil imports fell 9.3%, and imported industrial supplies fell 2.8%. Exports fell by 2.4% and included the following changes: exports of capital goods fell by 6%, auto and auto parts exports fell by 7.3%, food, feeds, and beverage exports fell 7.2%, but exports of industrial supplies increased 3.2% and exports of consumer goods increased 2.4%.

2.   Although the U.S. trade deficits with Canada and Taiwan increased, the U.S. trade deficits with Japan, Western Europe, and various oil-producing nations declined. The U.S. trade deficit implies a lower level of aggregate demand and equilibrium real GNP than would be the case if the United States did not have a trade deficit. However, by specializing in and exporting those goods for which it has a comparative advantage and importing those goods for which other nations have a comparative advantage, the United States may enjoy higher domestic standards of living even with a trade deficit than if the nation engaged in no international trade.

U.S. Trade Gap Widened in June To $12.54 Billion

Result, After 42-Month Low In May, Came as Imports Rose 5.7% to a Record

By David Wessel

Staff Reporter of The Wall Street Journal

WASHINGTON—The nation's merchandise trade deficit worsened in June, as a strong U.S. economy boosted imports to a record.

The Commerce Department put the deficit at $12.54 billion, substantially widened

Markets Rebound

Stock and bond markets and the U.S. dollar initially fell on the trade-gap news, but rebounded through the day. The Dow Jones Industrial Average rose 17.24 to 2021.51. Bonds wound up with small gains, as did the dollar, after a day of volatile trading. See related stories on pages 41, 26 and 33.

from the revised $9.76 billion reported for May. The May gap was a 42-month low.

Imports rose 5.7% to $39.35 billion in June as Americans bought more foreign-made capital goods, consumer products and autos. Exports fell by a modest 2.4% to $26.81 billion, but they remain well above year-earlier levels. The deficit worsened with all major trading partners.

Slow and Difficult

Although the U.S. trade picture still appears brighter than last year, the report underscores how slow and difficult the process of closing the trade gap will be. "The June deficit confirms . . . the willingness of the U.S. to consume more than we can actually afford," said James Howell, a Bank of Boston economist.

"Our economy is drawing a larger-than-expected quantity of goods into the coun-

try, and we're probably running into bottlenecks in getting goods out of the country," said James Cochrane, an economist with Texas Commerce Bancshares Inc. in Houston.

Surging imports suggest that the Federal Reserve Board, which already has pushed interest rates higher, is likely to force them still higher, economists said. "We're going to have to keep import demand slow and that means more of a lift for short-term interest rates," warned Robert Barbera, a Shearson Lehman Hutton Inc. economist.

Monthly trade figures can be misleading because they are volatile. Commerce Secretary C. William Verity insisted that the underlying trend in the U.S. trade position "remains favorable," noting that the trade deficit in the second quarter was narrower than those in each of the preceeding three quarters.

First Half

In the first half of this year, the U.S. trade deficit was $70 billion, narrowed from $84.45 billion in the first half of 1987. The trade figures are adjusted for usual seasonal fluctuations, but not for higher prices. If the effects of higher prices are removed, the improvement in the trade deficit is far more impressive, Mr. Verity said.

The Commerce Department said U.S. imports of capital goods rose 10% in June to $9.22 billion, a reflection of the continued U.S. boom in capital spending. Imports of consumer goods were up 8.5% to $8.68 billion. And auto imports rose 12.5% to $7.51 billion, mainly because of more imported Canadian cars.

Imports of food, feeds and beverages fell 4% in June to $2.08 billion, and imports of industrial supplies dropped 2.8% to $10.74 billion. Oil imports, which aren't adjusted for seasonal fluctuations, fell 9.3% to $3.57 billion, as both the volume of imports and the price declined.

On the export side, the Commerce Department said exports of capital goods dropped 6% in June to $8.69 billion. Ex-

ports of autos and parts fell 7.3% to $2.25 billion. And exports of foods, feeds and beverages declined 7.2% to $2.72 billion. But exports of industrial supplies were up 3.2% to $7.37 billion and consumer-goods exports rose 2.4% to $1.97 billion.

Major Partners

The trade deficit with major U.S. trading partners widened in June, but the deficits with Japan, Western Europe, the Organization of Petroleum Exporting Countries and the newly industrializing countries of Asia all were lower than in June 1987.

The trade deficit with Canada, America's largest trading partner, rose to $1.4 billion in June from $1.04 billion in May and was more than double its $530.5 million level in June 1987. An increase in imports of Canadian autos and parts accounted for much of the change. The auto industry's trade deficit with Canada widened to $826.1 million in June from $621 million in May and $226.9 million in June 1987.

But Commerce Department officials warned that for the past several months Canadian customs data—upon which the U.S. relies—have understated U.S. exports, forcing subsequent revisions in the department's reports. The figure for U.S. exports to Canada in May was revised up by $300 million.

The trade deficit with Taiwan widened a substantial 30% in June to $1.23 billion, and is now larger than the U.S. deficit with any single country except Japan and Canada. This occurred even though Taiwan bought $200 million of non-monetary gold in June, and $300 million in May, in what U.S. officials have described as a "gimmick" to shrink its reported trade surplus with the U.S. Taiwanese central-bank officials said in July they were suspending the gold purchases.

The seasonally adjusted trade deficit for May originally was estimated at $10.93 billion. Before seasonal adjustments, the Commerce Department said the trade deficit in June was $12.62 billion, up from $9.51 billion in May.

U.S. Merchandise Trade Deficits

(In billions of U.S. dollars, not seasonally adjusted)

	JUNE '88	MAY '88	JUNE '87
Japan	$4.40	$4.12	$5.35
Canada	1.40	1.04	0.53
Western Europe	1.91	1.20	2.93
NICs*	2.72	2.35	3.70

*Newly industrialized economies, including Singapore, Hong Kong, Taiwan, South Korea

Source: Commerce Department

Tracking the Trade Deficit

(In billions of dollars, seasonally adjusted)

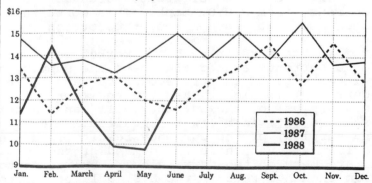

Note: Monthly figures for 1986 aren't adjusted for undocumented exports to Canada

Source: Commerce Department

26

The Economics of Foreign Exchange and the
Balance of International Trade

After studying your text, attending class, and completing this chapter, you should be able to:

1. Understand how international transactions between the United States and the rest of the world involve the exchange of dollars for units of foreign currency.
2. Use supply and demand analysis to show how exchange rates of one currency into another are established in foreign exchange markets.
3. Use aggregate supply and demand analysis to show the impact of changes in the real exchange rate of the dollar on macroeconomic equilibrium.
4. Explain the causes of currency appreciation and depreciation in foreign exchange markets and discuss the evolution of the current international monetary system.
5. Understand how a balance of trade deficit in the United States in a given year implies an increase in net foreign acquisition of U.S. financial and other assets in that year.

IN BRIEF: CHAPTER SUMMARY

Fill in the blanks to summarize chapter content.

International trade requires the exchange of currencies. The (1)_____ (foreign exchange rate is, terms of trade are) the price of one nation's monetary unit in terms of the monetary unit of another nation. The (2)_____ (stock market, foreign exchange market) is a market in which currencies are exchanged. Here the forces of supply and demand determine the rate at which any two currencies are exchanged. For example, a U.S. importer wants to purchase foreign goods with dollars but foreign exporters want to be paid in their own currencies. An exchange of currency must take place. For a fee, the importer can use dollars to purchase a bank draft denominated in foreign currency from a U.S. bank. This constitutes (3)_____ (a demand for, an increase in the supply of) the foreign currency.

Equilibrium in the foreign exchange market occurs where the supply of and demand for a currency are equal--where the supply and demand curves for a currency intersect. If the price of a currency (expressed in terms of units of another currency) is higher than the equilibrium exchange rate, a (4)_____ (shortage, surplus) of the currency will cause a decline in the exchange rate. If the exchange rate is below the equilibrium exchange rate, a (5)_____ (shortage, surplus) of the currency results in an increase in the exchange rate. Influences that shift the demand or supply curves will alter the exchange rate between two currencies. Several factors can affect the equilibrium exchange rate of the U.S. dollar: (a) foreign demand for U.S. exports, (b) U.S. demand for imports, (c) real interest rates in the United States relative to those in foreign nations, (d) profitability of direct investment in U.S. businesses and real estate relative to profitability of similar investments in foreign nations, (e) expectations of an increase in the price of the dollar in terms of foreign currency, and (f) the price level (6)_____ (established by the Bretton Woods agreement; in the United States) relative to the price levels in foreign nations.

If real interest rates in the United States rise relative to interest rates in Great Britain, for instance, the British will increase their (7)_____ (supply of, demand for) U.S. dollars in the foreign exchange markets in order to purchase higher-yielding U.S. financial assets. As the demand for dollars rises relative to the supply of dollars, the exchange rate of the dollar (8)_____ (falls, rises). The dollar will be exchanged for more British pounds than previously. Conversely, the British pound will be exchanged for (9)_____ (more, fewer) U.S. dollars. The dollar (10)_____ (depreciates, appreciates) and the pound (11)_____ (depreciates, appreciates). British goods valued in dollars fall in price, and U.S. goods valued in British pounds increase in price. As a result, U.S. goods exported to Great Britain become (12)_____ (more, less) price competitive with British domestic output. Likewise, in the United States, British imported goods become (13)_____ (more, less) expensive relative to U.S. domestic output.

A higher rate of interest in the United States increases the real exchange rate between the pound and dollar, causing U.S. exports to Britain to (14)_____ (rise, fall) and U.S. imports from Britain to rise. U.S. net exports (15)_____ (fall, rise), causing the aggregate demand curve to shift (16)_____ (rightward, leftward). But an appreciation of the dollar also reduces the dollar prices of imported raw materials and other inputs, which shifts the aggregate supply curve (17)_____ (rightward, leftward). It is expected that the change in aggregate demand is larger than the change in aggregate supply, causing equilibrium real GNP and the price level to (18)_____ (rise, fall).

Conversely, a depreciation of the dollar makes U.S. goods (19)_____ (more, less) price competitive abroad while increasing the relative prices of imports to the United States. U.S. exports (20)_____ (fall, rise) and imports (21)_____ (fall, rise), causing net exports to rise. An increase in net exports shifts the aggregate demand curve (22)_____ (rightward, leftward). The aggregate supply curve shifts leftward because the prices of imported inputs (23)_____ (decrease, increase). On net, the increase in aggregate demand will outweigh the decrease in aggregate supply, causing equilibrium real GNP and the price level to (24)_____ (fall, rise). These changes may take some time to develop. Empirical evidence indicates that it may take up to 2 years before changes in exchange rates significantly affect import prices. This, of course, depends upon the profit goals of foreign producers. If foreign producers wish to maintain prices in foreign markets, they may absorb most of the change in exchange rates as lower profits. If import prices remain unchanged relative to other prices, there is no reason for net exports to change.

The foreign exchange market described above is a free market often referred to as a (25)_____ (fixed, floating or flexible) exchange rate market. Prior to the 1930s, however, exchange rates were fixed within narrow limits. This was accomplished by the gold standard, under which currencies were convertible into (26)_____ (gold, the U.S. dollar) at fixed rates. This meant that each currency had (27)_____ (several exchange rates, a unique exchange rate) relative to every other currency. Exchange rates remained fixed as long as the gold price of each currency remained (28)_____ (flexible, unchanged). Nations concerned with domestic macroeconomic problems would often devalue their currency rather than allow an outflow of gold that would reduce the nation's money stock. Devaluation alters exchange rates, however. This system was replaced in 1944 by the (29)_____ (managed float, Bretton Woods system) in which the values of foreign currencies were tied to the U.S.

dollar rather than to gold. The United States abandoned its role as the guarantor of exchange rate stability when it chose to suspend convertibility of the dollar into gold in (30)_____ (1971, 1961). In 1973, the United States and other nations abandoned the fixed exchange rate system in favor of the (31)_____ (modified gold standard, flexible exchange rate system). Today the foreign exchange market is characterized as a managed float rather than a freely floating or flexible exchange rate system. The Federal Reserve System and foreign central banks intervene in the market to effect desirable changes in exchange rates.

The balance of payments for a nation shows the net exchange of the nation's currency for foreign currencies from all transactions between that nation and foreign nations in a given year. In the United States the balance of payments consists of the current account and the capital account. The (32)_____ (capital, current) account shows the effect of the volume of goods and services traded on international markets, including changes in investment income and other miscellaneous transactions. The balance (33)_____ (on the current account, of trade) represents the difference between the value of merchandise exports and imports. The balance (34)_____ (on the current account, of trade) is more comprehensive in that it measures U.S. net exports for the year, including transactions involving services, investment income, and transfers. As recently as 1981, the United States had a surplus in its current account balance but had a large merchandise trade deficit.

In 1985, the current account registered a (35)_____ (deficit, surplus) of over $117 billion. This means U.S. citizens supplied $117 billion more to foreigners than foreigners supplied in foreign currencies to Americans. A net outflow must be offset (financed). When the current account is in deficit, the United States must sell assets or borrow to finance the deficit. These transactions are shown in the (36)_____ (capital, current) account. As foreigners purchase U.S. financial and real assets at a rate greater than U.S. citizens purchase those assets abroad, the net inflow of dollars just offsets the current account deficit.

VOCABULARY REVIEW

Write the key term from the list below next to its definition.

Key Terms

Foreign exchange rate
Foreign exchange market
Foreign exchange
Currency appreciation
Currency depreciation
Purchasing power parity
Gold standard
Balance on current account
  of the balance of
  payments

Bretton Woods system
International Monetary
  Fund (IMF)
Special drawing right (SDR)
International balance of
  payments
Balance of trade
Managed float
Real exchange rate
Nominal exchange rate

Definition

1. _____: the price of a unit of one nation's currency in terms of a unit of a foreign currency.

2. _____: the price of one nation's monetary unit in terms of the monetary unit of another nation.

3. _____: the sacrifice of goods and services that foreign buyers must make when they use their own currency to purchase goods of the first nation worth one unit of that nation's currency.

4. _____: a market in which buyers and sellers of bank deposits denominated in the monetary units of many nations exchange their funds.

5. _____: an international monetary system that required that currencies be converted into gold at a fixed price.

6. _____: the money of one nation held by citizens of another nation either as currency or as deposits in banks.

7. _____: describes the current international monetary system, under which central banks affect supply of and demand for currencies in ways that influence equilibrium in foreign exchange markets.

8. _____: occurs when there is an increase in the number of units of one nation's currency that must be given up to purchase each unit of another nation's currency.

9. _____: established under the Bretton Woods agreement; set rules for the international monetary system to make loans to nations that lack international reserves of dollars.

10. _____: occurs when there is a decrease in the number of units of one nation's currency that must be given up to purchase each unit of another nation's currency.

11. _____: an international monetary system developed in 1944 and based on fixed exchange rates, with the value of foreign currencies tied to the U.S. dollar.

12. _____: a principle that states that the exchange rate between any two currencies tends to adjust to reflect changes in the price levels in the two nations.

13. _____: a paper substitute for gold that is created by the International Monetary Fund and is distributed to member nations to use as international reserves.

14. _____: a statement showing the net exchange rate of a nation's currency for foreign currencies from all transactions between that nation and foreign nations in a given year.

15. _____: the difference between the value of merchandise exported by a nation's firms and the nation's imports of foreign-produced goods.

16. _____: measures U.S. net exports for the year, including transactions involving services, investment income, and transfers.

SKILLS REVIEW

Concept: Foreign exchange rates and foreign exchange markets

1.   The figure below represents a foreign exchange market for the U.S. dollar
      and the Canadian dollar.

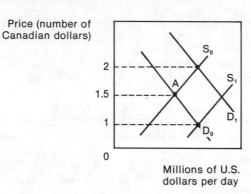

Price (number of
Canadian dollars)

Millions of U.S.
dollars per day

   a.   Given demand curve Do and supply curve So, the equilibrium exchange
         rate between the Canadian and U.S. dollar is 1 U.S. dollar =
         _____ Canadian dollars or alternatively, 1 Canadian dollar =
         _____ U.S. dollars.
   b.   A U.S. good valued at $1000 in U.S. dollars would cost _____
         Canadian dollars. A Canadian good valued at 100 Canadian dollars
         would cost _____ U.S. dollars.

2.   List six factors that influence the exchange rate of the dollar.

      a. _____
      b. _____
      c. _____
      d. _____
      e. _____
      f. _____

3.   Referring to the figure above, suppose real interest rates in the United
      States rise relative to interest rates abroad, causing the demand for
      dollars to increase to D1.

   a.   What are the new exchange rates?

         (1) 1 U.S. dollar = _____ Canadian dollars
         (2) 1 Canadian dollar = _____ U.S. dollars

   b.   The U.S. dollar has _____, and the Canadian dollar has
         _____.
   c.   A U.S. good valued at 1000 U.S. dollars now costs _____ Canadian
         dollars. A Canadian good valued at 100 Canadian dollars now costs
         _____ U.S. dollars.
   d.   U.S. goods become _____ price competitive in Canada, and Canadian
         goods become _____ price competitive in the United States.

378

4. Referring to the figure above, given the initial demand curve, Do, assume that U.S. firms increase their imports from Canada, causing the supply of U.S. dollars to shift to S1.

   a. What are the new exchange rates?

      (1) 1 U.S. dollar = _____ Canadian dollars
      (2) 1 Canadian dollar = _____ U.S. dollar

   b. The U.S. dollar has _____, and the Canadian dollar has _____.

   c. A U.S. good valued at 1000 U.S. dollars now costs _____ Canadian dollars. A Canadian good valued at 100 Canadian dollars now costs _____ U.S. dollars.

   d. U.S. goods become _____ price competitive in Canada, and Canadian goods become _____ price competitive in the United States.

Concept: **Changes in real exchange rates and equilibrium real GNP and the price level**

5. The figure below represents an economy.

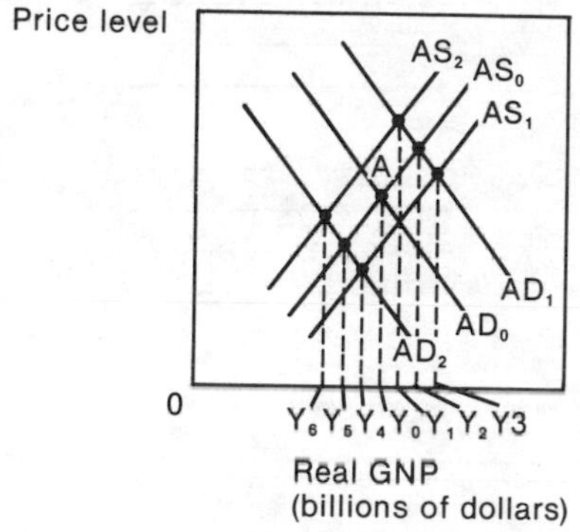

Price level

AS₂ AS₀
AS₁
A
AD₁
AD₀
AD₂

0   Y₆Y₅Y₄Y₀Y₁Y₂Y3

Real GNP
(billions of dollars)

   a. A depreciation of the U.S. dollar relative to the Canadian dollar makes U.S. goods _____ price competitive in Canada and Canadian goods _____ price competitive in the United States. U.S. exports _____, imports _____, and net exports _____.

   b. Given the initial aggregate demand and supply curves, ADo and ASo, the change in net exports indicated above shifts the AD curve to _____ (AD1, AD2).

   c. The price of imported inputs in U.S. dollars _____, causing the AS curve to shift to _____ (AS1, AS2).

   d. Equilibrium real GNP _____ from Yo to _____.

6. Refer to the figure above in answering this question.

   a. An appreciation of the U.S. dollar relative to the Canadian dollar makes U.S. goods _____ price competitive in Canada and Canadian goods _____ price competitive in the United States. U.S. exports _____, imports _____, and net exports _____.

   b. Given the initial aggregate demand and supply curves, ADo and ASo, the change in net exports indicated in part a above shifts the AD curve to _____ (AD1, AD2).

   c. The prices of imported inputs in U.S. dollars _____, causing the AS curve to shift to _____ (AS1, AS2).

   d. Equilibrium real GNP _____ from Yo to _____.

379

Concept: International balance of payments

7. Identify which of the following represent a <u>capital account</u> and which represent a <u>current account</u> transaction in the balance of payments and state whether the transaction results in an <u>inflow</u> or <u>outflow</u> of U.S. dollars.

   a. U.S. exports of services increase.
   b. Foreigners purchase U.S. Treasury bills.
   c. Automobile imports into the United States decrease.
   d. Transfers to foreigners increase.
   e. U.S. firms purchase factories abroad.
   f. Rich oil sheiks purchase Texas ranch land.
   g. Hitachi receives income from its U.S. plants.
   h. Foreigners increase imports of U.S. merchandise goods.
   i. U.S. citizens purchase stock in foreign enterprises.

Capital or Current Account?	Inflow or Outflow?
a. _____	_____
b. _____	_____
c. _____	_____
d. _____	_____
e. _____	_____
f. _____	_____
g. _____	_____
h. _____	_____
i. _____	_____

SELF-TEST FOR MASTERY

Select the best answer.

1. A market in which buyers and sellers of bank deposits denominated in the monetary units of many nations exchange their funds is known as:

   a. The loanable funds market.
   b. The money market.
   c. The capital market.
   d. The foreign exchange market.

2. If the price of a dollar in terms of units of a foreign currency is above the equilibrium exchange rate, a _____ exists, which will put _____ pressure on the equilibrium exchange rate of the dollar.

   a. Shortage, downward
   b. Shortage, upward
   c. Surplus, downward
   d. Surplus, upward

3.   If a $10,000 U.S.-made automobile is sold in France and the exchange rate
     between the dollar and the franc is $1 = 8 francs, the U.S. automobile
     sold in France will cost _____ francs.

     a.   20,000
     b.   40,000
     c.   60,000
     d.   80,000
     e.   100,000

4.   The exchange rate between the dollar and the franc is $1 = 8 francs, and
     the price of a bottle of imported French wine is $5. If the exchange rate
     changes to $1 = 4 francs, the dollar price of the French wine _____ to
     $_____.

     a.   Falls, $2.50
     b.   Rises, $10
     c.   Rises, $20
     d.   Does not change

5.   An increase in foreign demand for U.S. exports will _____ demand for
     the dollar, causing the dollar to _____.

     a.   Decrease, appreciate
     b.   Increase, depreciate
     c.   Increase, appreciate
     d.   Decrease, depreciate

6.   An increase in U.S. demand for imports will _____ the _____
     U.S. dollars, causing the dollar to _____.

     a.   Increase, demand for, appreciate
     b.   Increase, supply of, appreciate
     c.   Decrease, supply of, depreciate
     d.   Decrease, demand for, appreciate
     e.   Increase, supply of, depreciate

7.   If real interest rates in the United States rise relative to interest
     rates abroad, the _____ dollars will _____, causing the dollar to
     _____.

     a.   Demand for, increase, appreciate
     b.   Demand for, increase, depreciate
     c.   Supply of, decrease, depreciate
     d.   Supply of, increase, appreciate

8.   If the rate of inflation in the United States rises relative to the rate
     of inflation in foreign nations, U.S. exports _____ and imports
     _____, causing the demand for dollars to _____ and the supply of
     dollars to _____.

     a.   Increase, decrease, rise, fall
     b.   Decrease, increase, fall, rise
     c.   Increase, increase, fall, fall
     d.   Decrease, decrease, rise, rise

9.   The price of a unit of one nation's currency in terms of a unit of a
     foreign currency is called:

     a.   The nominal exchange rate.
     b.   The real exchange rate.

c.   Foreign exchange.
d.   Purchasing power parity.
e.   None of the above.

10. Empirical evidence suggests that:

a.   Import prices respond very quickly to changes in exchange rates.
b.   Net exports respond within a year to changes in the exchange rate of the dollar.
c.   Import prices are slow to respond to changes in exchange rates, taking up to 2 years to be affected.
d.   There is an immediate link between exchange rates and import prices.

11. An increase in the real exchange rate of the dollar causes aggregate demand to _____ and aggregate supply to _____, resulting in a/an _____ in real GNP.

a.   Decrease, decrease, decrease
b.   Increase, increase, increase
c.   Increase, decrease, decrease
d.   Increase, increase, decrease
e.   Decrease, increase, decrease

12. A depreciation of the dollar causes aggregate demand to _____ and aggregate supply to _____, resulting in a/an _____ in real GNP.

a.   Decrease, decrease, decrease
b.   Increase, increase, increase
c.   Increase, decrease, increase
d.   Increase, increase, decrease
e.   Decrease, increase, decrease

13. The Bretton Woods agreement:

a.   Represented a new international monetary system.
b.   Tied the value of foreign currencies not to gold but to the dollar.
c.   Was established in 1944.
d.   Also established the International Monetary Fund.
e.   All of the above.

14. The present international monetary system is best described as a:

a.   Fixed exchange rate system.
b.   Purchasing power parity system.
c.   Flexible exchange rate system.
d.   Managed float.

15. Which of the following summarizes the transactions involving the international exchange of goods and services, investment income, and other miscellaneous transactions?

a.   Balance of trade
b.   Statistical discrepancy
c.   Current account
d.   Capital account

16. Which of the following is the difference between the value of merchandise exported and merchandise imported?

    a. Balance of trade
    b. Balance on the current account
    c. Budget balance
    d. Balance of payments

17. Which of the following measures net exports for the year, including transactions involving services, investment income, and transfers?

    a. Balance of trade
    b. Balance on the current account
    c. Budget balance
    d. Balance of payments

18. When the current account is in deficit, the capital account must

    a. Be balanced.
    b. Be zero.
    c. Not add to the deficit.
    d. Have an equal and offsetting surplus.

THINK IT THROUGH

1. How can the Fed, through domestic monetary policy, cause the U.S. dollar to depreciate?

2. How can the Fed, through direct intervention in foreign exchange markets, cause the U.S. dollar to depreciate?

3. If the U.S. dollar depreciates, what are the likely economic consequences?

POP QUIZ   Read the news brief at the end of this chapter and answer the questions below.

1. Lindley Clark cites two reasons for the recent climb in the exchange rate of the U.S. dollar. What are they?

2. According to the article, why would Japan, Britain, and West Germany be hesitant to intervene to slow the appreciation of the dollar?

CHAPTER ANSWERS

In Brief: Chapter Summary

1. Foreign exchange rate is 2. Foreign exchange market 3. A demand for 4. Surplus 5. Shortage 6. In the United States 7. Demand for 8. Rises 9. Fewer 10. Appreciates 11. Depreciates 12. Less 13. Less 14. Fall 15. Fall 16. Leftward 17. Rightward 18. Fall 19. More 20. Rise 21. Fall 22. Rightward 23. Increase 24. Rise 25. Floating or flexible 26. Gold 27. A unique exchange rate 28. Unchanged 29. Bretton Woods system 30. 1971 31.

Flexible exchange rate system 32. Current 33. Of trade 34. On the current account 35. Deficit 36. Capital

Vocabulary Review

1. Nominal exchange rate 2. Foreign exchange rate 3. Real exchange rate 4. Foreign exchange market 5. Gold standard 6. Foreign exchange 7. Managed float 8. Currency appreciation 9. International Monetary Fund (IMF) 10. Currency depreciation 11. Bretton Woods system 12. Purchasing power parity 13. Special drawing right (SDR) 14. International balance of payments 15. Balance of trade 16. Balance on the current account of the balance of payments

Skills Review

1. a. 1.5, 2/3
    b. 1,500, $66.67

2. a. Foreign demand for U.S. exports
    b. U.S. demand for imports
    c. Real interest rates in the United States relative to those in foreign nations
    d. Profitability of direct investment in U.S. businesses and real estate relative to profitability of similar investments in foreign nations
    e. Expectations of an increase in the price of the dollar in terms of foreign currency
    f. The price level in the United States relative to the price levels in foreign nations

3. a. 2, 1/2
    b. Appreciated, depreciated
    c. 2,000; 50
    d. Less, more

4. a. 1, 1
    b. Depreciated, appreciated
    c. 1,000; 100
    d. More, less

5. a. More, less; rise, fall, increase
    b. AD_1
    c. Rises, AS_2
    d. Increases, Y_1

6. a. Less, more; fall, rise, decrease
    b. AD_2
    c. Falls, AS_1
    d. Decreases, Y_4

7. a. Current, inflow
    b. Capital, inflow
    c. Current, outflow
    d. Current, outflow
    e. Capital, outflow
    f. Capital, inflow
    g. Current, outflow
    h. Current, inflow
    i. Capital, outflow

Self-Test for Mastery

1. d 2. c 3. d 4. b 5. c 6. e 7. a 8. b 9. a 10. c 11. e 12. c 13. e 14. d 15. c 16. a 17. b 18. d

Think It Through

1.   If the Fed pursues an expansionary monetary policy that reduces the real rate of interest in the United States relative to interest rates abroad, Americans will increase their demand for foreign currencies by supplying more dollars to the international foreign exchange markets in order to purchase higher-yielding foreign financial assets. The increase in the supply of dollars relative to demand will cause the dollar to depreciate. The expansionary monetary policy will also increase the nation's income, causing imports to increase. In order to increase imports, Americans must supply dollars to acquire foreign exchange to purchase the foreign goods. This too will cause the dollar to depreciate. If the expansionary monetary policy is also inflationary such that the rate of inflation in the United States rises relative to foreign rates of inflation, U.S. exports will fall and imports will rise. This will cause foreign demand for the dollar to fall and the supply of dollars to increase, also resulting in depreciation of the dollar.

2.   If the Fed wished to depreciate the dollar, it could purchase foreign currencies with its dollar holdings, causing the demand for foreign currencies to rise and the supply of dollars to increase. This in turn would cause the dollar to depreciate relative to the foreign currencies purchased by the Fed.

3.   If the dollar depreciates, U.S. goods become less costly in foreign currencies, increasing their price competitiveness in foreign markets. Likewise, foreign goods become more costly in dollars, decreasing their price competitiveness in the United States. U.S. imports of foreign goods decrease, and U.S. exports to foreign nations increase. The increase in net exports causes the aggregate demand curve to shift rightward. But foreign inputs now cost more in dollars. As production costs rise, the aggregate supply curve shifts leftward. On net, however, real GNP increases.

Pop Quiz

1.   According to the article, the dollar has appreciated because the U.S. downing of an Iranian airliner in the Persian Gulf raised fears of a possible international crisis. Money tends to flow to "safe-haven" currencies such as the dollar when there are mounting fears of international instability. It is noted that increases in U.S. exports and foreign investors' optimism regarding the inflation outlook in the United States were also responsible for the rise in the exchange rate of the dollar. Exports create a demand for the dollar, causing its exchange rate to rise. If foreign investors expect U.S. inflation to remain stable, they will be more likely to invest in U.S. dollar-denominated securities. This too creates a demand for the dollar, causing it to appreciate.

2.   All of these nations are enjoying strong economies. If they intervened in foreign exchange markets to prevent the appreciation of the dollar, they would have to purchase their own currencies with their dollar holdings. The increase in the supply of dollars keeps the dollar from appreciating, and the increased demand for foreign currencies prevents the foreign currencies from depreciating relative to the dollar. These actions, however, keep foreign currencies from depreciating and foreign export industries from becoming more price competitive in the United States. "Defending" the dollar against appreciation means that foreign nations sacrifice an increase in net exports and income.

The Outlook

Should the Dollar Find Its Own Market Level?

NEW YORK

Anyone who wonders why Japan hesitates to let the yen become an international currency should consider the continuing convolutions of the U.S. dollar. Not only the U.S. but most major countries want to manage the dollar to suit their own convenience. Japan may be an industrial giant, but it has no desire to subject the yen to that sort of nonsense.

The dollar has been climbing lately, at least temporarily reversing the drop that began in February 1985. Early last week, the dollar spurted on foreign markets for reasons entirely separate from U.S. economic management. The accidental U.S. downing of an Iranian passenger plane in the Persian Gulf, killing all 290 persons aboard, raised fears of a new international crisis. In an international crisis, investors seek a safe-haven currency, and the dollar still is perceived to be the best around.

The rise in the dollar stems in large part from the increase in U.S. exports, which has shrunk the merchandise trade deficit. The dollar's rise, moreover, lessens inflation fears, since it tends to make imports less expensive. An analysis by Lawrence H. Meyer & Associates of St. Louis notes that the rise leads foreign investors to become more optimistic about the dollar's future and thus more willing to buy dollar securities, helping to push the dollar higher. "A stronger dollar," the firm says, "hints that the dollar may have bottomed."

Jerry L. Jordan, chief economist of First Interstate Bank of Los Angeles, is convinced that the dollar "has seen its lows for this cycle." He says Federal Reserve Chairman Alan Greenspan "is building up credibility as an inflation-fighter. He hasn't quite moved into the spot Paul Volcker held as the second most powerful man in the U.S., but he's making progress."

Some analysts argue that the stronger dollar will end the upsurge of U.S. exports, just as the weaker dollar started it. A few contend that the dollar not only will have to fall but will have to drop sharply to continue the improvement in the U.S. trade balance. The fact is that no one can be absolutely certain what level of the dollar is needed to sustain exports—or just what the future level of the dollar will be. The dollar's current strength is based heavily on a foreign perception that the U.S. is beginning to get its house in order. Evidence to the contrary could send the dollar down.

All of this is happening, it should be noted, when neither the Federal Reserve nor any other major central bank has much appetite to push the dollar significantly lower or higher. The Fed prefers peace and quiet in presidential election years, so its preference presumably would be a dollar that stabilized at about the current level—at least, between now and November. So far, Fed Chairman Greenspan has commented only that he sees no reason for the dollar to go lower. The U.S. hope obviously is that the dollar now is low enough to permit continued strength in U.S. exports.

Some central banks have sold dollars in an effort to slow the gains of the U.S. currency, but others are hesitant. If the Bank of Japan sells dollars it soaks up yen, tending to weaken the Japanese economy, now in the midst of a consumer-fueled boom. Japan knows it may eventually have to tighten credit to cool off the boom, but presumably it would prefer to base the timing on its domestic needs, not on the buoyant dollar.

The British and West Germans also have strong economies, which could be weakened by new dollar sales. Some foreigners find the current situation strange. A German banker quoted in this newspaper last week said he found it hard to believe that Germany would have to defend its mark when it has a low inflation rate, high current account surpluses and a booming export economy.

For the present, market factors seem to be working in favor of the dollar. "The question is how foreign net demand for our assets will compare with our net demand for foreign goods," Mr. Jordan says. "Our net demand for foreign goods is going down, while net foreign demand for our assets has picked up sharply." The U.S. is still bringing assets home from abroad, while foreigners continue to buy assets here.

One reason the outlook for sales of assets to foreigners is strong is that the inflation rates seem to be moving in our favor. The foreign perception is that U.S. inflation has stabilized, at a time when other major industrial countries are worrying about rising inflation.

Time will tell. The U.S. has found that a nation with an international currency can largely ignore inflation, trade deficits and budget deficits for a long time without disaster. But no one can ignore such fundamental factors forever.

For the near term, the Federal Reserve needs to continue to provide investors, foreign and domestic, assurance of its determination to prevent a surge of inflation, a task that is complicated by higher food prices stemming from the Midwest drought. It's unlikely that much reduction of the budget deficit will be forthcoming until after the election, if then, but it would be helpful if the presidential candidates gave more evidence that they appreciated the seriousness of the problem.

In the long run, the fundamental factors must prevail. But it's no wonder that Japan prefers to keep the yen out of the uncertainties that persist until the fundamentals assert themselves. What is surprising is that government officials don't remember that the exchange rate is a market price and thus decide to let the dollar find its own level.

—LINDLEY H. CLARK JR.

27

Economics and Ideology: Socialism vs. Capitalism

CHAPTER CHALLENGES

After studying your text, attending class, and completing this chapter, you should be able to:

1. Discuss the ideas of Karl Marx and the ideological underpinnings of socialism.
2. Discuss modern socialist economies, particularly that of the Soviet Union.
3. Explain central planning as a means of allocating resources in a command economy.
4. Discuss issues involved in evaluating economic performance in modern economies.

IN BRIEF: CHAPTER SUMMARY

Fill in the blanks to complete the chapter summary.

(1)_____ (Capitalism, Socialism) is associated with private ownership of resources, freedom of enterprise, and an economy in which markets allocate resources. (2)_____ (Capitalism, Socialism), in contrast, is associated with government ownership of productive resources and central planning. Prices and resource allocation are determined by central planners rather than by markets.

According to Karl Marx, only (3)_____ (labor, capital) produces value. Even capital is the past product of labor. Marx argued that capitalists hire labor at subsistence wages, generating a (4)_____ (marginal revenue product, surplus value)--the wages paid to labor are less than the value of the worker's production. Capitalists therefore exploit workers and will continue to do so until the working class revolts and establishes a socialist state. Most workers, however, earn incomes well above a subsistence level in market economies. Marx did not foresee the enormous gains made in (5)_____ (profits, labor productivity) as a result of technology and capital formation. Over time, the (6)_____ (supply of, demand for) labor has outpaced the (7)_____ (supply of, demand for) labor, resulting in increases in real wages. The working class has not revolted in a manner envisioned by Marx because of gains in real living standards and social policy designed to alleviate some of the failures of market systems.

The Soviet Union is a (8)_____ (market, command) economy in which resources are allocated by central planners who set production goals. The (9)_____ (Gosplan, Politburo) is the central planning board for the Soviet Union and drafts 5-year plans listing production goals for the economy. The government sets prices to ensure the satisfaction of the output goals. Prices of many goods have been kept artificially low as a way of subsidizing consumption. But when prices are set below the level that equates supply and demand, (10)_____ (surpluses, shortages) become a problem. Shortages can be eliminated with a (11)_____ (lump sum, turnover) tax if it is equal to the difference between the price that would equate supply and demand and the lower subsidized price. Shortages are reduced, but only from a reduction in quantity demanded. Quantity supplied remains fixed at the planners' production target.

As of January 1, 1988, the Soviet economy began to institute reforms such as putting (12)_____ (10%, 60%) of Soviet enterprises on a self-financing basis. These firms are required to earn a profit or they will be shut down. Managers (13)_____ (will be, will not be) able to decide what is to be produced and how to produce it. In fact, many prices will be determined by markets rather than by central planning. Even prior to these reforms, farmers were allowed to sell produce in markets from private plots. These plots are considerably more productive than collective farms in producing food, accounting for as much as (14)_____ (25%, 75%) of Soviet agricultural output. Economic incentives are also used to motivate Soviet labor and existed prior to the reforms instituted at the beginning of 1988. In 1987, private enterprise was legalized in 29 areas, primarily in crafts and services. These changes will be beneficial to the Soviet economy. Managers will no longer have incentives to just meet output targets or exceed those targets, but will now have incentives to minimize costs in order to generate profits. This will result in a (15)_____ (less, more) efficient use of resources.

Other socialist systems vary in the degree to which central planning and markets are relied upon to allocate resources. In (16)_____ (North Korea, Yugoslavia), for example, most businesses are state owned but worker managed. Profits from these firms are used for investment in the enterprise or are divided among the firm's workers. In other nations, such as Great Britain, some large industrial enterprises are publicly owned, but the remainder of the economy is organized as a market economy.

In evaluating capitalism and socialism, important considerations include: (a) the extent to which the pursuit of self-interest and market exchange of goods and services produce results that coincide with a general consensus regarding national goals, (b) the way an economic system distributes well-being among members of a society, (c) the achievement of technological efficiency, (d) freedom of choice and responsiveness to consumer demands, and (e) economic growth and fluctuations.

VOCABULARY REVIEW

Write the key term from the list below next to its definition.

Key Terms

Economic system   Gosplan
Socialism   Materials balance
Labor theory of value   Consumer sovereignty
Surplus value   Turnover tax
Command economy   Indicative planning
Centrally planned economy

Definitions

1. _____: an economy in which politically appointed committees plan production and manage the economy to achieve political goals.

2. _____: the central planning board for the Soviet Union.

3. _____: an economy in which resource allocation decisions are determined largely by the central planning authorities who set production goals.

4. _____: exists when the supply of each intermediate product equals its demand as an input in some other productive process.

5. _____: defined by Karl Marx as the difference between a worker's subsistence wage and the value of the worker's production over a period.

6. _____: the responsiveness of the market economy to changes in consumer demand.

7. _____: maintains that only labor can produce something worth paying for.

8. _____: a sales tax used to raise revenue for the government; often used in planned economies to eliminate shortages in consumer markets.

9. _____: an economic system that is usually associated with government ownership of resources and central planning to determine prices and resource use.

10. _____: a system in which government encourages voluntary compliance by industrial and labor interests to coordinate economic decisions so as to achieve politically determined objectives.

11. _____: an accepted way of organizing production, establishing rights to ownership and use of productive resources, and governing economic transactions in a society.

SKILLS REVIEW

Concept: **Production targets, shortages, the turnover tax, and black markets**

A competitive market for a good is shown in the figure below.

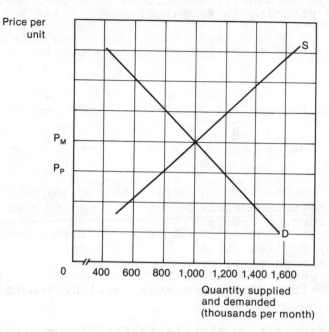

a.   Assume that this market economy now becomes a command economy in which central planners set production targets. Show the effect of a production target of 800,000 units where planners establish a price of Pp per unit. At the controlled price of Pp, there exists a _____ of _____ units.

b.   If the official government price is raised to the previous market level of Pm, there exists a _____ of _____ units.

c.   In order to eliminate the _____ and still maintain the production target of 800,000 units, a turnover tax equal to the difference between _____ and the _____ could be used. However, if a turnover tax is used in this manner, consumers in the command economy pay _____ prices and consume _____ output than they did previously in the market economy.

d.   Black markets will likely develop because some consumers will be willing to pay _____ prices than a government price like Pp in order to have additional units of the good. Even if a turnover tax eliminates shortages, black markets will likely still exist because the marginal cost of supplying an additional unit of a good will likely be _____ than the government price that eliminates shortages.

SELF-TEST FOR MASTERY

Select the best answer.

1. An economic system that is usually associated with government ownership of resources and central planning is known as:

   a. Capitalism.
   b. Fascism.
   c. Socialism.
   d. A market system.

2. Which of the following individuals argued that only workers create value?

   a. Adam Smith
   b. George Bush
   c. Karl Marx
   d. Karl Menninger

3. Marx argued that capitalists exploit workers by paying them a
   _____ in order to create _____.

   a. Subsistence wage, surplus value
   b. Wage equal to their marginal product, profits
   c. Portion of their profits, good will
   d. Wage less than their profit per worker, maximum growth for their enterprises

4. What main factor did Marx not foresee in making his prediction that workers would not rise above a subsistence standard of living?

   a. Population growth
   b. Growth in household consumption
   c. Growth in labor productivity
   d. Advances in technology
   e. C and d

5. The Soviet Union is an example of a:

   a. Market economy.
   b. Mixed-market system.
   c. Democratic socialist state.
   d. Command economy.

6. Which of the following is the Soviet Union's central planning board?

   a. Ministry of Industry
   b. Soviet Monetary Alliance
   c. _Perestroika_
   d. Gosplan

7. As of January 1, 1988, economic reforms were initiated in the Soviet Union. Which of the following is an economic reform?

   a. Requiring some soviet enterprises to earn a profit
   b. Allowing managers of some enterprises to decide what to produce and how to produce it
   c. Allowing many prices to be determined by markets
   d. All of the above

8. A turnover tax is:

    a. Used to reduce surpluses.
    b. Used to finance the Soviet economic reforms.
    c. Used to reduce shortages.
    d. The difference between the cost of a good and the price that
        equates supply and demand.

9. One advantage of a planned economy is that:

    a. It is more efficient.
    b. It responds more rapidly to changes in consumers' desires.
    c. It has achieved the highest living standards in the world.
    d. It can avoid fluctuations in aggregate demand and thus avoid the
        costs associated with business cycles.

10. Which of the following is true regarding private enterprise in the Soviet
    Union?

    a. The Soviet economic reforms have privatized collective farms.
    b. Private farm plots account for as much as 25% of the Soviet Union's
        total agricultural output.
    c. In 1987, private business was legalized in 29 areas.
    d. Most individuals engaged in private enterprise are in crafts or
        services.
    e. B, c, and d

11. In which of the following nations is a majority of enterprises state
    owned but worker managed?

    a. People's Republic of China
    b. France
    c. Yugoslavia
    d. Argentina

12. In which of the following nations is government ownership of or financial
    interest in large industrial enterprises common?

    a. United Kingdom
    b. France
    c. Italy
    d. All of the above
    e. A and c

13. Which of the following nations uses indicative planning--where private
    industry cooperates with the government to achieve political goals?

    a. Great Britain
    b. Yugoslavia
    c. Soviet Union
    d. United States
    e. France

14. In assessing the merits of capitalism vs. socialism, which of the following considerations are important?

    a. The extent to which the pursuit of self-interest and market exchange of goods and services produce results that coincide with a general political consensus regarding national goals

    b. The way an economic system distributes well-being among members of a society

    c. The achievement of technological efficiency

    d. Freedom of choice and responsiveness to consumer demands

    e. All of the above

THINK IT THROUGH

1. Identify and briefly discuss some of the main differences between capitalism and socialism.

2. Several nations have returned state-owned enterprises to the private sector, whereas other socialist nations have instituted major market-based reforms. Can you think of any reasons why?

POP QUIZ   Read the news brief at the end of this chapter and answer the questions below.

1. Outline Angola's new economic plan. What is Angola's motivation for employing market-based reforms?

2. How do Angolans cope with the lack of product quantity and variety at state stores and a virtually worthless currency?

CHAPTER ANSWERS

In Brief: Chapter Summary

1. Capitalism 2. Socialism 3. Labor 4. Surplus value 5. Labor productivity
6. Demand for 7. Supply of 8. Command 9. Gosplan 10. Shortages 11.
Turnover 12. 60% 13. Will be 14. 25% 15. More 16. Yugoslavia

Vocabulary Review

1. Centrally planned economy 2. Gosplan 3. Command economy 4. Materials
balance 5. Surplus value 6. Consumer sovereignty 7. Labor theory of value
8. Turnover tax 9. Socialism 10. Indicative planning 11. Economic system

Skills Review

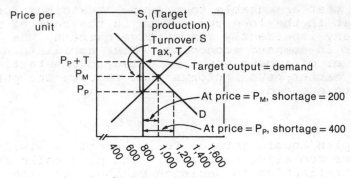

Price per unit

$P_P + T$
P_M
P_P

S₁ (Target production)

Turnover S
Tax, T

Target output = demand

At price = P_M, shortage = 200

D

At price = P_P, shortage = 400

400 600 800 1,000 1,200 1,400 1,600

Quantity supplied
and demanded
(thousands per month)

a. Shortage, 400,000
b. Shortage, 200,000
c. Shortage, the subsidized price, price that would equate supply and
    demand; higher, less
d. Higher, less

Self-Test for Mastery

1. c 2. c 3. a 4. e 5. d 6. d 7. d 8. c 9. d 10. e 11. c 12. d 13.
e 14. e

Think It Through

1.   Capitalism relies on self-interest, private ownership, and markets to
allocate resources. Socialism is distrustful of self-interest (the profit
motive) and in the extreme case of a command economy, resources are allocated
with extensive central planning. Capitalism rewards input suppliers on the
basis of the quantity and productivity of inputs supplied. This is not
necessarily so if markets are imperfectly competitive. A socialist state earns
a profit from state-owned resources and redistributes it to workers in the form
of wages and services. Modern mixed economies try to achieve equity in the
distribution of income through transfer payments. In a competitive market
economy, firms have an incentive to keep costs as low as possible, resulting in
technological efficiency. Managers in socialist states often confront a much
different set of costs and incentives, which reward managers not for minimizing
costs, but for meeting production targets. In capitalist economies with
competitive markets, consumers are sovereign. There is free choice in
consumption, the employment of inputs, and the production of output. In a
socialist state, individual freedoms are much less important than the
achievement of political goals. A capitalist system is subject to recurrent
ups and downs in real GNP and the rate of unemployment. The incidence of
business cycles can be lessened considerably in command economies because
aggregate demand is strictly controlled. If there are ups and downs in
production, they are likely the result of supply-side shocks rather than
fluctuations in aggregate demand.

2.   Competitive economies that rely on markets to allocate resources realize a
higher level of technological efficiency than economies that rely on central
planning. In a market system, self-interest coordinates decisions such that
resources are allocated to their most productive employments. Workers are free
to offer their labor services to the highest bidder. Entrepreneurs bring
resources together to produce goods desired by consumers in hopes of earning a
profit. Economic survival in a competitive economy requires technological

394

efficiency. Firms that are unable to produce at minimum possible unit costs will exit the market in the long run. Even in the case of modern mixed economies having many imperfectly competitive markets, the level of efficiency is much higher than in command economies. Most socialist nations are recognizing the power of incentives. As noted in the text, the Soviet Union is embarking on major market-based reforms that require the pursuit of self-interest in order to succeed.

Pop Quiz

1.   The economic plan Angola intends to implement is similar to those being implemented in other socialist countries. The plan calls for autonomy for managers and decentralization in decision making. It also involves returning land to farmers and businesses to entrepreneurs in order to encourage private sector production. Prices will be determined by the market, and wages will be tied to labor productivity. Angola has turned to market incentives not because of a radical ideological shift from Marxism, but because the war against Unita, the rebel army supported by the United States and South Africa, is expensive and requires an economy that can produce enough output to support the war effort. Angola is using capitalism to defend Marxism!

2.   A thriving black market exists in Luanda, Angola. Here almost any good, including imported goods, can be found and at prices well below the official prices in state stores. The state stores have limited variety and encounter shortages. The "official" prices are ridiculously high and bear no relationship to market forces. In fact, either dollars or kwanzas are used to purchase beer at state stores for $12 or 30,000 kwanzas. The beer is then taken to the black market and sold for $15 in kwanzas, which can be traded for other goods on the market. "Money is meaningless...Beer has meaning." Angolans cope with scarcity in state stores and a worthless currency by having an efficient black market that produces true market prices.

In Marxist Angola, Capitalism Thrives, Using Beer Standard

* * *

Black Market at City Dump Outdraws State's Stores, Where Cigarettes Cost $60

By Roger Thurow
Staff Reporter of THE WALL STREET JOURNAL

LUANDA, Angola—Capitalism literally has ended up on the scrap heap in this fervently Marxist country.

On the top of a hill overlooking this decaying port city, smack in the middle of a dump, a thriving black market coexists profitably with the garbage and flies. Vendors' prices are guided by the hand of Adam Smith rather than by state planners devoted to Karl Marx. The nearly worthless local currency is pegged to the price of beer. Anyone with the time to browse through this vast outdoor bazaar will find everything the socialist stores on the streets below are supposed to have, but don't.

The vendors first set up their stalls at the dump because it was a convenient open space. Now, garbage is taken only to the fringes of the market. Everyone, it seems, shops here: peasant farmers, factory workers, bureaucrats, soldiers, bankers, diplomats. Even state economists come looking for inspiration and ideas, as well as turnips and onions.

Destroyed by War

"We're studying this market, which is a very efficient market," says Victor Nunes, a Finance Ministry official responsible for overseeing Angola's ambitious economic adjustment program. "We have much to learn from it."

As Angola tries desperately to resuscitate its gasping socialist economy, it is taking a crash course in capitalism. A new economic plan, not coincidentally, is being launched at the same time Luanda is pushing for membership in the International Monetary Fund. The plan is similar to those being tinkered with in other rundown socialist countries: decentralizing economic decision-making, giving more autonomy to managers of businesses, encouraging the private sector, returning land to farmers and shops to entrepreneurs, harnessing prices to market forces and salaries to productivity, promoting foreign investment.

The catalyst for Angola's economic restructuring is the 13-year war against the rebel army known as Unita, which is supported by South Africa and the U.S. The war has devastated the economy, potentially one of the richest in Africa. More

mines than maize is planted in the countryside, much of which is controlled by the guerrillas. The industries of the big cities have ground to a halt from lack of material and spare parts. Skilled managers, always scarce here, are drafted as soldiers.

"We have come up with a slogan," says Dumilde das Chagas Simoes Rangel, Angola's trade minister. "Develop the economy to fight the war; fight the war to defend the economy."

Thus, if capitalism is what it takes to defend Marxism in Angola, so be it. "It is possible," says Mr. Nunes, "to construct socialism with rational economic means."

Like the free market. In the past, the state tried mightily to crush the illegal black markets, which account for the bulk of the country's economic activity. Today, however, the police on duty at the black markets are responsible for crowd control, not crowd dispersement. The state has decided to fight capitalism with capitalism, rather than with bulldozers and truncheons.

"We have to combat the parallel market with economic mechanisms," says Mr. Nunes, favoring the word "parallel" over "black."

At the moment, the black market is winning easily. Because of the deregulated prices and the more realistic exchange rate, many imported goods go directly from the port of Luanda to the unofficial markets, bypassing the state stores that stand forlorn and empty.

Empty Shelves

In downtown Luanda, a drugstore crumbling under a burned-out neon sign offers only a couple of packages of sinus pills and some dental floss. Its glass cabinets are empty, except for one that displays color posters of stomach ulcers. In contrast, the black market has a long row of vendors offering everything from antacids and aspirin to cough medicine and laxatives.

Also available on the black market: fruit, vegetables and fish; bubble gum, underwear and gin. Soap comes from Brazil, skin lightener from England, antihistamines from Switzerland, spaghetti from Bulgaria and soda pop from West Germany (though there is little from the U.S., which doesn't have diplomatic relations with Angola).

These are the things people want, not the bulky paraffin cookers or the industrial-type waffle irons ordered by the central planners and made here or in Russia. Even the name of the market reflects consumer choice: Roque Santeiro, the title of a popular Brazilian soap opera that is broadcast regularly in this former Portuguese colony.

'Money Is Meaningless'

Throughout Luanda, dollars and beer are the currencies of choice, favored over the local currency, the kwanza.

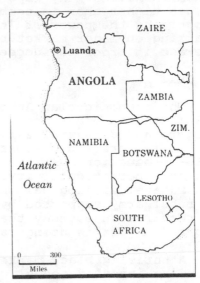

If anybody paid attention to the official rate of 30 kwanza to the dollar (nobody does), he would have to pay more than $60 for a packet of Marlboros or a can of orange pop. A heavy metal ashtray in the shape of a bug—its wings open up to collect the ashes—would cost more than $150 at a state store.

At the black market rate of 2,000 kwanza per dollar, the cigarettes and pop cost less than $1 each, and the ashtray is a steal at less than $3.

"Money is meaningless," says a budding economist who is wiling away Luanda's midnight-to-5 a.m. curfew by attending an all-night party. "Beer has meaning."

Imported Beer

He explains the two ways to get on the beer standard. If you have dollars, you simply head to one of the government-run hard-currency shops and buy a case of imported beer—Heineken, Beck's, Stella Artois—for $12. (Dollars aren't hard to get in Angola, at least for those in the middle class, who often travel abroad.)

But those who have only kwanza can get in on the deal, too. Typically, workers draw, as part of their salaries, coupons that can be redeemed at grocery stores run by their employers. These stores also have plenty of imported beer.

Having acquired a case of beer, you head to the neighborhood black market and cash in the 24 cans for 30,000 kwanza. (Recently, Stella Artois has been devalued to 15,000 kwanza because of unsubstantiated rumors here that it causes impotence.) This is worth $15 at the black-market rate and $1,000 at the official rate. Suddenly, you are rich, and you can load up on vegetables, fish, soap and clothes or even a plane ticket to Lisbon. The latter costs roughly two cases of beer.

Rich Food and Chic Clothes

The black marketeer, in turn, sells the

396

individual cans of beer for a nice profit: at 2,000 kwanza a can, he will collect 48,000 kwanza for a case. Everybody's happy.

"It works quite nicely," says the student economist at the all-night party. Because he hopes to work one day for the Bank of Angola, he agrees to speak on the condition he won't be identified. "You can get anything you want in Angola."

The party, attended by Luanda's young jet set, is proof of that. A feast unimaginable to all but a few Angolans is spread over several tables: lobster, prawns, beef, pork, chicken, cakes, pies and pastries. The bar is stocked with liquor from around the world, and the women are dressed in outfits from Lisbon, Paris and Rome.

The student giggles, somewhat embarrassed by these riches. "On the surface, Luanda looks miserable," he says. "But things aren't always as they seem."